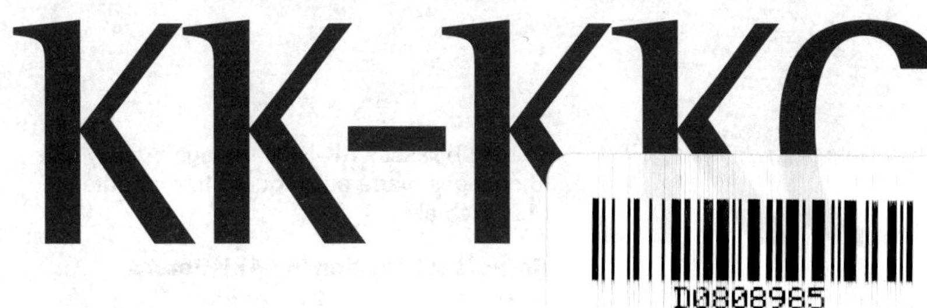

Law of Germany

Library of Congress Classification
2008

Prepared by the Cataloging Policy and Support Office
Library Services

LIBRARY OF CONGRESS
Cataloging Distribution Service
Washington, D.C.

This edition cumulates all additions and changes to subclasses KK-KKC through Weekly List 2008/03, dated January 16, 2008. Additions and changes made subsequent to that date are published in weekly lists posted on the World Wide Web at

<http://www.loc.gov/aba/cataloging/classification/weeklylists/>

and are also available in *Classification Web*, the online Web-based edition of the Library of Congress Classification.

Library of Congress Cataloging-in-Publication Data

Library of Congress.
Library of Congress classification. KK-KKC. Law of Germany / prepared by the Cataloging Policy and Support Office, Library Services. — 2008 ed.
p. cm.
"This edition cumulates all additions and changes to subclasses KK-KKC through Weekly list 2008/03, dated January 16, 2008. Additions and changes made subsequent to that date are published in weekly lists posted on the World Wide Web at <http://www.loc.gov/aba/cataloging/classification/weeklylists/> and are also available in *Classification Web*, the online Web-based edition of the Library of Congress classification." — T.p. verso.
Includes index.
ISBN-13: 978-0-8444-1196-5
ISBN-10: 0-8444-1196-5
1. Classification, Library of Congress. 2. Classification—Books—Law. 3. Classification—Books—Germany. 4. Law—Germany—Classification. I. Library of Congress. Cataloging Policy and Support Office. II. Title. III. Title: Law of Germany.
Z696.U5K7 2008 025.4'634943—dc22 2008001394

For sale by the Library of Congress Cataloging Distribution Service,
101 Independence Avenue, S.E., Washington, DC 20541-4912.
Product catalog available on the Web at **www.loc.gov/cds**.

PREFACE

The first edition of subclasses KK-KKC, *Law of Germany*, was published in 1982. A 2000 edition cumulated all additions and changes that had been made to the schedule between 1982 and 2000. This 2008 edition cumulates additions and changes made since the publication of the 2000 edition.

Classification numbers or spans of numbers that appear in parentheses are formerly valid numbers that are now obsolete. Numbers or spans that appear in angle brackets are optional numbers that have never been used at the Library of Congress but are provided for other libraries that wish to use them. In most cases, a parenthesized or angle-bracketed number is accompanied by a "see" reference directing the user to the actual number that the Library of Congress currently uses, or a note explaining Library of Congress practice.

Access to the online version of the full Library of Congress Classification is available on the World Wide Web by subscription to *Classification Web*. Details about ordering and pricing may be obtained from the Cataloging Distribution Service at:

<http://www.loc.gov/cds/>

New or revised numbers and captions are added to the L.C. Classification schedules as a result of development proposals made by the cataloging staff of the Library of Congress and cooperating institutions. Upon approval of these proposals by the weekly editorial meeting of the Cataloging Policy and Support Office, new classification records are created or existing records are revised in the master classification database. Weekly lists of newly approved or revised classification numbers and captions are posted on the World Wide Web at:

<http://www.loc.gov/aba/cataloging/classification/weeklylists/>

Paul Weiss and Jolande Goldberg, senior cataloging policy specialists in the Cataloging Policy and Support Office, are responsible for coordinating the overall intellectual and editorial content of subclasses KK-KKC. Kent Griffiths, assistant editor of classification schedules, is responsible for creating new classification records, maintaining the master database, and creating index terms for the captions.

This printed edition of KK-KKC must be used in conjunction with the separately published K Tables: Form Division Tables for Law, available for purchase from the Cataloging Distribution Service. This classification schedule includes references to form division tables within the range K1 to K24, which are found only in that publication.

Barbara B. Tillett, Chief
Cataloging Policy and Support Office

January 2008

KK2-9799.3	Law of Germany
KK2-4	Bibliography
KK7-12	Official gazettes
KK(16-23)	Legislative documents
KK27-38	Legislation
KK40-52	Court decisions and related material
KK56	Law dictionaries. Terms and phrases
KK61-63	Judicial statistics
KK64-64.7	Directories
KK65-75	Trials
KK76-83	Legal research. Legal bibliography
KK89-118	Legal education
KK122-124	Rechtsanwaltskammern (Bar associations)
KK139-143	Collected works
KK147	General works. Treatises
KK156	Civics
KK158	Addresses, essays, lectures
KK160	Manuals and other works for particular groups of users
KK164	Works on diverse aspects of a particular subject and falling within several branches of the law
KK170-862	History of law
KK175-175.8	Auxiliary sciences
KK183-185	Biography
KK195-286	Sources
KK290-378	Holy Roman Empire and its constitution
KK292-309	The estates of the realm
KK315-324	Feudal law
KK326-(337.6)	Rural (peasant) land tenure and peasantry
KK339-348	Crown and king
KK350-350.5	The court. Ministries
KK352-355	Diet. Generalis conventus
KK356-360	Military organization
KK362-373	Finance
KK375-378	Public safety, order, and welfare
KK379-388	Secular ecclesiastical law
KK390-585	Private law
KK595-743	Judiciary. Court organization and procedure
KK745-862	Criminal law and procedure
KK883-940	Philosophy, jurisprudence, and theory of German law
KK942	Law reform. Criticism
KK945	Concepts applying to several branches of the law
KK949-950	Private law
KK958-968	Private international law. Conflict of laws

OUTLINE

OUTLINE

OUTLINE

Law of Germany
Class here German statutory law, beginning with the major codifications of the late 19th century (ca. 1867, North German Confederation) and continuing as the law of the German Federal Republic
Including West Germany to 1991
For the law of the German Democratic Republic (East Germany), see KKA
For the law of a particular state, see KKB+
For the law of Germany prior to 1867 see KK170+
Bibliography
For bibliography of special topics, see the topic, e.g. KK170 , History of law
For manuals on legal bibliography, legal research, and the use of law books see KK76+
2 Bibliography of bibliography
3 General bibliography
3.5 Library catalogs. Union lists
3.6 Sales catalogs. Want lists
3.7 Indexes to periodical literature, society publications, collections
For indexes to particular publications, see the publication
4 Special classes or groups or writers, A-Z
4.J48 Jews
<6> Periodicals
For periodicals consisting predominantly of legal articles, regardless of subject matter and jurisdiction, see K1+
For periodicals consisting primarily of informative material (newsletters, bulletins, etc.) relating to a particular subject, see subject and form division for periodicals
For law reports, official bulletins or circulars, and official gazettes intended chiefly for the publication of laws and regulations, see appropriate entries in the text or form division tables
6.5 Monographic series
Official gazettes
State or city gazettes
see the issuing state or city
Departmental gazettes
see the issuing department or agency
7 Indexes (General)
8 Reichsgesetzblatt (1871-1945)
Including the earlier Bundesgesetzblatt of the North German Confederation (1867-1870)
8.5 Indexes
Military government gazettes (Allied occupation of Germany, 1945-1955)
9 Military Government Gazette

Official gazettes

Military government gazettes (Allied occupation of Germany, 1945-1955) -- Continued

9.2 Control Council Gazette

9.3 Gazette of the Allied High Commission for Germany

9.4 British Zone Gazette

9.5 French Zone Journal officiel du Commendement en Chef Francais en Allemagne

9.52 Russian Zone Zentralverordnungsblatt

United States Zone

9.6 Western Military District Gazette

9.7 Eastern Military District Gazette

9.73.A-Z Military government gazettes of individual states. By state, A-Z

9.73.W87 Württemberg-Baden

Vereinigtes Wirtschaftsgebiet

9.8 Bundesanzeiger und Offentlicher Anzeiger

Including the earlier Offentlicher Anzieger and Deutscher Reichsanzeiger

9.83 Gesetzblatt der Verwaltung des Vereinigten Wirtschaftsgebietes

9.9 Drucksachen of the Wirtschaftsrat

10 Bundesgesetzblatt (West Germany, 1949-)

Including parts I, II, and III

10.5 Indexes

12.A-Z Other, A-Z

<16-23> Legislative documents

see J351+

<16-17> North German Confederation and Empire (1867-1918)

<16> Bundesrat

<17> Reichstag

<18-19> Weimar Republic and Third Reich (1919-1945)

<18> Reichsrat

<19> Reichstag

Germany under Allied Occupation (1945-1955)

German Federal Republic (1949-)

<20> Bundesrat

<21-23> Bundestag

25 Other materials relating to legislative history

Legislation

Class here legislation beginning ca. 1867, and earlier legislation if included in collections or compilations extending beyond 1867

For statutes, statutory orders, regulations, etc., on a particular subject, see the subject

For legislation prior to 1867 see KK205+

Legislation -- Continued
Indexes and tables
Including indexes to statutes of several states
For indexes limited to one state, see the state
General
27 Serials
27.3 Monographs. By date of publication
27.5 Chronological indexes
28 Indexes to publisher editions (unannotated and annotated)
e.g. C.H. Beck'sche Ausgaben
28.5 Indexes of translations
29 Abridgements and digests
Statutes
Including statutory orders and regulations
Early and/or discontinued collections and compilations
Including official and private editions
30 Serials. By date of first publication
Monographs. By initial date of period covered
31 Unannotated. By compiler
32 Annotated. By author of annotations
33 Selections. By editor or compiler
Current and/or continuing collections and compilations
Including official and private editions
34 Comprehensive. By editor or compiler
35 Annotated. By author of annotations
35.5 Selective. By editor or compiler
Codifications and related material
Class here collections of codes and related material
For individual codes, see the subject
36 General
37 Legislative documents
38 Enactments
Class here collections of enactments of several states
For enactments of an individual state, see the state
For enactment of a particular code, see the code
Treaties
Treaties on international public law
see KZ
Treaties on uniform law not limited to a region
see subclass K
Treaties on uniform law of the European region
see KJC and KJE
Concordats see KK5520+

Court decisions and related material
Including authorized and private editions
Class here decisions beginning ca. 1867, and earlier decisions if included in collections or compilations extending beyond 1867 (e.g. Seufert's Archiv)
For decisions on a particular subject, see the subject
40 Several courts
Class here works on federal courts, federal and state courts, or courts of several jurisdictions
For courts (several or individual) of an individual jurisdiction, see the state or municipality
Particular courts
Subarrange each by Table KK-KKC5 , as indicated
Federal courts. Oberste Gerichte des Reiches und des Bundes
Staatsgerichtshof see KK4883+
Bundesverfassungsgericht see KK5461+
43 Reichsgericht (RG) (Table KK-KKC5)
44 Bundesgericht (BGH) (Table KK-KKC5)
Bundesverwaltungsgericht see KK5663+
Bundesarbeitsgericht see KK3223
Bundessozialgericht see KK3613
Bundesfinanzhof see KK7441
Regional courts
Courts in Germany under Allied Occupation (1945-1955)
45 Several (Table KK-KKC5)
British Zone
Supreme Restitution Court see KK7651
46 British Control Commission Court of Appeals (Table KK-KKC5)
47 Oberster Gerichtshof (Table KK-KKC5)
French Zone
Cour Superieure pour les Restitutions see KK7652
49 Russian Zone (Table KK-KKC5)
United States Zone
U.S. Courts of the Allied High Commission
50 Several (Table KK-KKC5)
51 U.S. Court of Appeals of the Allied High Commission (Table KK-KKC5)
U.S. Court of Restitution Appeals see KK7654
Supreme Restitution Court for Berlin see KK7655
Vereinigtes Wirtschaftsgebiet (Bizonal)
52 Deutsches Obergericht (Table KK-KKC5)
Ecclesiastical courts
see KBU
Administrative decisions on a particular subject
see the subject

54 Encyclopedias
56 Law dictionaries. Terms and phrases
For bilingual and multilingual dictionaries, see K52+
For law dictionaries on a particular subject, see the subject
58 Legal maxims. Quotations
(59) Form books
see KK147
For form books on a particular subject, see the subject
Judicial statistics
61 General works
62 Criminal statistics
63.A-Z Other, A-Z
Directories
64 National and regional
64.3.A-Z By state, A-Z
64.5.A-Z Local. By administrative district or city, A-Z
64.7.A-Z By specialization, A-Z
Attorneys see KK3770+
Trials
Class here trials beginning ca. 1867
For earlier trials see KK270+
Criminal trials and judicial investigations
For military trials see KK7920.A+
Collections. Compilations
65 General
67.A-Z Particular offenses, A-Z
67.A78 Arson
67.D87 Duress
67.F73 Fraud
67.P64 Political crimes
67.S48 Sex crimes
War crimes see KK73+
Individual trials
Including records, briefs, commentaries, and stories on a particular trial
69.A-Z By defendant, A-Z
72.A-Z By best known (popular) name, A-Z
72.C65 Contergan (Thalidomide)
72.K65 Kölner Gewerkschaft
72.K66 Köpenick
72.R44 Reichstagsbrand
72.S34 Scheinwerfer
War crime trials
Trials of German criminals by German courts
73 Collections. Compilations

Trials
Criminal trials and judicial investigations
War crime trials
Trials of German criminals by German courts -- Continued
73.5.A-Z Individual trials. By first named defendant or best known (popular) name, A-Z
Including records, briefs, commentaries, and stories on a particular trial
73.5.A98 Auschwitz (Concentration camp)
Bergen-Belsen (Concentration camp) see KZ1179.B45
73.5.D32 Dachau (Concentration camp)
73.5.H44 Heilman (Concentration camp)
73.5.H56 Hinzert (Concentration camp)
73.5.M34 Majdanek (Concentration camp)
73.5.S32 Sachsenhausen (Concentration camp)
Other trials
74 Collections. Compilations
75.A-Z Particular trials. By plaintiff, defendant, or best known (popular) name, A-Z
Including records, briefs, commentaries, and stories on a particular trial
Legal research. Legal bibliography
Including methods of bibliographic research and how to find the law
76 General (Table K11)
Electronic data processing. Information retrieval systems. Datenverarbeitung
Including JURIS and other related systems
79 General (Table K11)
82.A-Z By subject, A-Z
82.A35 Administrative law
82.C59 Civil law
82.C65 Constitutional law
82.C68 Court organization and procedure
82.C74 Criminal law
82.J83 Judicial statistics
82.S62 Social legislation. Social security
Social security see KK82.S62
82.2 Systems of citation. Legal abbreviations
83 Surveys of legal research. Überblicke über den Forschungsstand
84 Legal composition (Aufbautechnik)
Legal education
89 General (Table K11)
Study and teaching

Legal education
Study and teaching -- Continued
General works see KK89
Teaching methods
95 General works
97 Case method (Klausurentechnik)
Cf. KK84 Legal composition
100 Clinical method (Repetitorium)
For particular subjects, see the subject
102 Students' guides. Führer. Studienschema. Anleitung
For introductory surveys of the law see KK149
104 Teachers' manuals. Vorlesungen
106 Pre-law school education. Admission to law school
107 Law teachers
108 Law students
Law schools
Statutes, rules, and regulations
Class here collections only
For particular law schools see KK118.A+
111 General
Seminarordnungen see KK118.A+
Degrees
Including Dr. juris utriusque and Dr. honoris causa
112 General
114 Dr. juris utriusque
115 Dr. honoris causa
Administration
116 General works
Particular law schools see KK118.A+
118.A-Z Particular law schools. By place, A-Z
Including constitutions, statutes, regulations, general works (history), etc.
Post-law school education see KK3706+
The legal profession see KK3704+
Rechtsanwaltskammern (Bar associations)
Including courts of honor and disbarment
122 General (Table K11)
123 Bundesrechtsanwaltskammer
124 Rechtsanwaltskammern. By district (Oberlandesgerichtsbezirk), A-Z
132.A-Z Law societies and associations. By name, A-Z
Including the journals, proceedings, annual reports, etc. of such societies
132.D48 Deutsche Rechtsfront
132.D484 Deutscher Anwaltsverein
132.D487 Deutscher Notarsverein
132.N17 NS-Rechtswahrerbund

Law societies and associations. By name, A-Z -- Continued

132.R48 Republikanischer Anwaltsverein

132.U58 Untersuchungsausschuss Freiheitlicher Juristen

135.A-Z Congresses. Seminars. By name, A-Z

135.D48 Deutscher Juristentag

135.D483 Deutscher Notarstag

135.K65 Konstanzer Juristentag

135.T34 Tagung Deutscher Juristen

137.A-Z Academies. Institutes. By name, A-Z

137.A32 Akademie für Deutsches Recht

137.D48 Deutsch-Österreichische Arbeitsgemeinschaft

137.H38 Haus des Deutschen Rechts

139 Collected works (nonserial)

Including collections of several and individual authors

143 Individual authors

Including collected opinions

147 General works. Treatises

149 Compends, outlines, etc.

152 Examination aids

154 Popular works

156 Civics

158 Addresses, essays, lectures

158.5 Indexes to Festschriften

160.A-Z Manuals and other works for particular groups of users. By user, A-Z

Accountants see KK160.F56

160.A36 Administration officials and employees

160.A72 Architects

Art collectors see KK160.A79

160.A78 Artisans

160.A79 Artists and art collectors

160.B66 Bookdealers. Publishers

160.B85 Business consultants

160.B87 Businesspeople

160.C45 Chemists

160.F37 Farmers

160.F56 Finance advisors. Accountants. Tax consultants

160.H43 Health insurance officials and employees

160.I58 Internal revenue officials and employees

160.L47 Lesbians

160.M43 Medical professionals

160.M87 Musicians

160.N68 Notaries

160.P48 Pet owners

160.P75 Promoters

Publishers see KK160.B66

160.S78 Students (other than law students) and teachers

Manuals and other works for particular groups of users. By user, A-Z
Tax consultants see KK160.F56
Teachers see KK160.S78
Vocational and trade school teachers and students see KK160.S78
Semantics and language see KK907+
Legal symbolism see KK175.6+
Proverbs see KK177
Anecdotes, facetiae, satire, and humor see K184.4
Law and lawyers in literature
see PB+
Concept of law see KK185.A+
Dramatization of trials see KK285
Relation of law to other topics see K486+
164.A-Z Works on diverse aspects of a particular subject and falling within several branches of the law. By subject, A-Z
164.C66 Computers
164.D63 Dogs
164.H67 Horses
164.S66 Sponsorship
164.T42 Technology
(164.W65) Women
see KK1018.5
History of law. Rechts- und Verfassungsgeschichte
Class here general works on legal and constitutional history
For constitutional history beginning with 1806 see KK4455+
170 Bibliography
172 Encyclopedias
Methodology see KK195+
Auxiliary sciences. Hilfswissenschaften
175 General works
175.2 Genealogy
175.3 Paleography. Juristische Handschriftenkunde
175.5 Linguistics. Semantics. Rechtsaltertümer. Rechtsspracheforschung
Including Gaunersprache, etc.
Archaeology. Folklife. Symbolism. Rechtsarchäologie. Rechtliche Volkskunde. Rechtssymbolik
175.6 General works
175.62.A-Z By region, A-Z
175.62.B39 Bavaria
(175.7) Inscriptions. Inschriftenkunde
see KK195
175.8 Heraldry. Seals. Flags. Insignia. Armory
177 Proverbs. Rechtssprichwörter

History of law. Rechts- und Verfassungsgeschichte -- Continued

Clauses and formulae see KK275+

Law and literature

see PB-PH

(179) General works

(181) Trials in literature

Dramatization of trials see KK285

Biography

183 Collective

185.A-Z Individual, A-Z

Subarrange each by Table KK-KKC7

190 General (Table K11)

By period

Early period. Germanic tribes see KJ160+

Frankish period, ca. 500-ca. 919 see KJ160+

Period from ca. 919 to ca. 1867. Hochmittelalter, Spätmittelalter und Neuzeit

Sources. Rechtsquellen

Class here sources of the Gemeine Recht, i.e. the common law of the empire or its regions (Rechtskreise)

For the law of a particular territory or town, see the appropriate territory or town

195 Studies on sources

Including history of sources (Quellengeschichte) and methodology (Rechtsquellenforschung)

197 Collections. Compilations

Customals. Rechtsbücher. Spiegel. Rechtsaufzeichnungen. Weistümer

Class here general collections as well as laws either of general importance for the development of law throughout the Middle Ages (e.g. Magdeburg law) or governing large regions

Class other particular laws and adaptations with the jurisdiction, municipality, manorial estate, or dynasty

200 General works

Collections. Compilations

203 General

204.A-Z By region, A-Z

204.A48 Alsace

204.E33 Eifel

204.N67 North German region

204.U66 Upper Rhine region

Individual sources

205 Sachsenspiegel (1220-1235)

Texts. Unannotated editions

History of law. Rechts- und Verfassungsgeschichte
By period
Period from ca. 919 to ca. 1867. Hochmittelalter, Spätmittelalter und Neuzeit
Sources. Rechtsquellen
Customals. Rechtsbücher. Spiegel. Rechtsaufzeichnungen. Weistümer
Individual sources
Sachsenspiegel (1220-1235)
Texts. Unannotated editions -- Continued

205.2 Entire work. By date
Including Landrecht and Lehnrecht
205.22.A-Z Individual parts or sections. By title, A-Z
205.22.L35 Landrecht
205.22.L44 Lehnrecht
205.22.P72 Praefatio, prologus
205.22.V48 Vetus auctor de beneficiis
205.3.A-Z Particular manuscript editions. By title or location, A-Z
205.3.B47 Berliner Ms.
205.3.B73 Bremer Ms.
205.3.G66 Görlitzer Ms.
205.3.H37 Harffer Ms.
205.3.L44 Leipziger Ms.
205.3.Q43 Quedlinburger Ms.
Iconography. Hilderhandschriften
205.4 General
205.45.A-Z Particular manuscript editions. By title or location, A-Z
205.45.D73 Dresdener Bilderhandschrift (ca. 1350)
205.45.H44 Heidelberger Sachsenspiegel-Bilderhandschrift (ca. 1300-1315)
205.45.O43 Oldenburger Codex picturatus (1336)
205.45.W65 Wolfenbüttler Handschrift (ca. 1350-1375)
Glosses. Commentaries. Annotated editions
By annotator, editor, or commentator
205.5.A-Z Entire work
Including Landrecht and Lehnrecht
205.5.B62 Bocksdorf, Dietrich von. (Bocksdorf'sche Rezensionen. 15th cent.)
205.5.B625 Bocksdorf, Tammo von (first half 15th cent.)
205.5.B72 Brand von Tzerstede (1442)
205.5.S73 Stendal gloss (Altmärkische Glosse. 2nd half 14th cent.)
205.5.W87 Wurm, Nicolaus (Blume des Sachsenspiegels. ca. 1386)
Including Blume von Magdeburg

History of law. Rechts- und Verfassungsgeschichte
By period
Period from ca. 919 to ca. 1867. Hochmittelalter, Spätmittelalter und Neuzeit
Sources. Rechtsquellen
Customals. Rechtsbücher. Spiegel. Rechtsaufzeichnungen. Weistümer
Individual sources
Sachsenspiegel (1220-1235)
Glosses. Commentaries. Annotated editions -- Continued

205.52.A-Z Individual parts
205.52.A56 Anonymous gloss of Lehnrecht (before 1386)
205.52.B62 Bocksdorf, Dietrich von (Landrecht and gloss. 1484)
205.52.B82 Buch, Johann von (1325)
205.52.P48 Petrus de Posena (Petrinische Glosse of Landrecht)
205.55 Individual sections
205.6 Translations
205.7 Treatises. Textual criticism. Controversies
205.7.A78 Articuli reprobati in Bulla Salvator generis humani (1374)
205.7.K53 Klenkok, Johannes (Decadicon. 1372)
205.8.A-Z Special topics, A-Z
205.8.E35 Eike von Repgow
205.8.E88 Estates of the realm
205.8.J49 Jews in the Sachsenspiegel
208-208.8 Schwabenspiegel (1274-1275) (Table K20c modified)
Text. Unannotated editions
208.22.A-Z Individual parts or sections. By title, A-Z
208.22.L35 Landrecht
208.3.A-Z Particular manuscript editions. By title or location, A-Z
Including editions of entire work as well as parts or sections
208.3.T35 Tambacher Ms.
208.8.A-Z Special topics, A-Z
208.8.B47 Berthold von Regensburg
208.8.C74 Criminal law
210-210.8 Deutschenspiegel (1235-1275) (Table K20c modified)
Text. Unannotated editions

History of law. Rechts- und Verfassungsgeschichte
By period
Period from ca. 919 to ca. 1867. Hochmittelalter, Spätmittelalter und Neuzeit
Sources. Rechtsquellen
Customals. Rechtsbücher. Spiegel. Rechtsaufzeichnungen. Weistümer
Individual sources
Deutschenspiegel (1235-1275)
Text. Unannotated editions -- Continued

210.3.A-Z Particular manuscript editions. By title or location, A-Z
Including editions of entire work as well as parts or sections
210.3.I55 Innsbrucker Handschrift
212-212.8 Kleines Kaiserrecht (Kaiser Karls Recht. Frankenspiegel. 1328-1338) (Table K20c modified)
Text. Unannotated editions
212.3.A-Z Particular manuscript editions. By title or location, A-Z
Including editions of entire work as well as parts or sections
212.3.M35 Manuscript of 1372
214-214.8 Rudolfsbuch (Friesian. Early 13th century) (Table K20c)
216-216.8 Freisinger Rechtsbuch (Ruuprecht von Freising. ca. 1328) (Table K20c modified)
Text. Unannotated editions
216.22.A-Z Individual parts or sections. By title, A-Z
216.22.L35 Landrecht
216.22.S82 Stadtrecht
216.3.A-Z Particular manuscript editions. By title or location, A-Z
Including editions of entire work as well as parts or sections
216.3.M83 Münchner Ms.
216.8.A-Z Special topics, A-Z
216.8.W37 Warranty
218-218.8 Breslauer Landrecht (1356) (Table K20c)
219-219.8 Landrecht von Burg (Table K20c)
220-220.8 Mühlhäuser Rechtsbuch (early 13th century) (Table K20c modified)
220.8.A-Z Special topics, A-Z
220.8.M37 Marriage law
222-222.8 Eisenacher Rechtsbuch (Table K20c)
224-224.8 Zwickauer Rechtsbuch (Table K20c)

History of law. Rechts- und Verfassungsgeschichte
By period
Period from ca. 919 to ca. 1867. Hochmittelalter, Spätmittelalter und Neuzeit
Sources. Rechtsquellen
Customals. Rechtsbücher. Spiegel. Rechtsaufzeichnungen. Weistümer
Individual sources -- Continued

226-226.8 Görlitzer Rechtsbuch (14th century) (Table K20c)

228-228.8 Meissner Rechtsbuch (Rechtsbuch nach Distinctionen. 14th century) (Table K20c)

229-229.8 Leobschützer Rechtsbuch (1275-1421) (Table K20c)

230-230.8 Freiberger Stadtrechtsbuch (1296-1307) (Table K20c)

232-232.8 Goslarische Statuten (Table K20c)

Friesian law

see KJ552+ ; KKM

Magdeburg law

237 General works

238 Collections. Compilations

Individual sources

239-239.8 Statutes. Privileges (1188) (Table K20c)

240-240.8 Rechtsbuch von der Gerichtsverfassung (mid 13th century) (Table K20c)

241-241.8 Magdeburger Schöffenrecht (Table K20c modified)

Text. Unannotated editions

241.3.A-Z Particular manuscript editions. By title or location, A-Z

Including editions of entire work as well as parts or sections

241.3.B73 Breslauer codex

241.3.N38 Naumburger codex

241.3.U33 Uffenbach Ms.

242-242.8 Sächsisches Weichbild (14th century) (Table K20c modified)

Including Magdeburgisch Weichbild

Text. Unannotated editions

242.3.A-Z Particular manuscript editions. By title or location, A-Z

Including editions of entire work as well as parts or sections

242.3.B47 Berliner Ms.

242.3.C63 Codex Palatinus 461

243-243.8 Vulgata des sächsischen Weichbildes (Table K20c modified)

History of law. Rechts- und Verfassungsgeschichte
By period
Period from ca. 919 to ca. 1867. Hochmittelalter, Spätmittelalter und Neuzeit
Sources. Rechtsquellen
Customals. Rechtsbücher. Spiegel. Rechtsaufzeichnungen. Weistümer
Magdeburg law
Individual sources
Vulgata des sächsischen Weichbildes -- Continued
Glosses. Commentaries. Annotated editions

243.5.A-Z Entire work
243.5.W87 Wurm, Nicolaus
Blume von Magdeburg see KK205.5.W87
244 Magdeburger Fragen
Magdeburgisch Weichbild see KK243+
Dooms. Rechtsmitteilungen.
Oberhofentscheidungen
Class here decisions and precedents issued by the Magdeburg Schöffenstuhl for other jurisdictions (daughter cities), or issued by the Schöffenstuhl of a daughter city
245 Several jurisdictions
245.3.A-Z Particular jurisdictions, A-Z
245.3.B72 Bradenburg
245.3.B73 Breslau (1261 and 1295)
245.3.G63 Görlitz (1304)
245.3.G65 Goldberg (1201-1238)
245.3.H35 Halle (1364)
245.3.K72 Krakau (Krakow)
245.3.K85 Kulm (1338)
245.3.L38 Lausitz
245.3.L44 Leipzig
245.3.N48 Neumarkt
245.3.S34 Schweidnitz (1336)
245.3.S73 Stendal
Lubeck law. Lübisches Recht
246 General works
Dooms. Rechtsmitteilungen.
Oberhofentscheidungen
Class here decisions and precedents of the Oberhof for other jurisdictions
246.2 Several jurisdictions
246.4 Kulmer Recht

History of law. Rechts- und Verfassungsgeschichte
By period
Period from ca. 919 to ca. 1867. Hochmittelalter, Spätmittelalter und Neuzeit
Sources. Rechtsquellen
Customals. Rechtsbücher. Spiegel. Rechtsaufzeichnungen. Weistümer -- Continued
Municipal law, statutes, etc.
For law of a particular municipality or locality, see the municipality or locality
For collections and compilations see KK203+

248 General works
Spread of municipal laws to other regions
248.2 Magdeburg law and other municipal law in Eastern Europe
Weisthümer
249 General works
Collections. Compilations
249.5 General
249.7.A-Z By region, A-Z
249.7.A48 Alsace
249.7.B33 Baden
249.7.P35 Palatinate
249.7.R44 Rhine Valley
249.7.S22 Saar Valley
Imperial laws and legislation. Reichsabschiede
Including constitutional laws (Reichsgrundgesetze, leges fundamentales)
250 Collections. Compilations
253 Individual. By date
253 1103 Mainz (Heinrich IV)
253 1152 Regensburg (Friedrich I. Landfrieden)
253 1158 Roncaglia (Friedrich I)
253 1186 Nuremburg (Friedrich I. Constituto contra incendiarios)
253 1224 Würzburg (Heinrich VII. Treuga Henrici)
253 1235 Mainz (Friedrich II. Constitutio Moguntina)
253 1238 Frankfurt (Ludwig of Bavaria. Licet iuris)
253 1356 Nuremberg (Karl IV. Bulla aurea)
253 1383 Nuremberg (Wenzeslaus)
253 1422 Nuremberg (Sigismund)
253 1427 Frankfurt (Sigismund)
253 1431 Nuremberg (Sigismund)
253 1442 Frankfurt (Friedrich III. Frankfurter Reformation or Kaiser Friedrichs Reformation)
<253 1495> Worms (Maximilian I. Ewiger Landfrieden)
see KK596.5

History of law. Rechts- und Verfassungsgeschichte
By period
Period from ca. 919 to ca. 1867. Hochmittelalter, Spätmittelalter und Neuzeit
Sources. Rechtsquellen
Imperial laws and legislation. Reichsabschiede
Individual. By date -- Continued

253 1512 Treves and Cologne (Maximilian I)
253 1532 Ratisbon (Karl V)
253 1544 Speyer (Karl V)
253 1803 Ratisbon (Franz II. Reichsdeputationshauptschluss)

Imperial privileges
Including Jews, ecclesiastical rulers, etc.
255 Collections. Compilations
256 Individual privileges. By date
258 Imperial mandates
Treaties
Including texts, annotations (commentaries), and general works
259 General. By date
Special
260 Peace treaty of Westphalia (1648)
Concordats see KK5520+

Court decisions. Cases. Advisory opinions. Dooms. Digests. By editor or compiler, A-Z
262 Several courts
Particular courts
262.5 Curia regis (ca. 1150-1350)
263 Kammergericht. Kaiserlicher Reichshofrat (ca. 1415)
264.A-Z Reichskammergericht (1495-1806)
264.C52 Claproth, Justus
264.C72 Cramer, Johann Ulrich
264.G34 Gaill, Andreas
264.M95 Mynsinger, Joachimus
Landgericht. Kaiserliche Landgerichte. Oberhöfe. Schöffenstühle. Courts of appeal or last resort
265 Several courts
Individual courts
Brandenburg, Schöffenstuhl see KK245.3.B72
Hanseatic courts. Hanseatische Oberlandesgerichte see KK265+
265.3 Herzogtum Franken zu Würzburg
265.4 Ingelheimer Oberhof
Leipzig, Schöffenstuhl see KK245.3.L44

History of law. Rechts- und Verfassungsgeschichte
By period
Period from ca. 919 to ca. 1867. Hochmittelalter, Spätmittelalter und Neuzeit
Sources. Rechtsquellen
Court decisions. Cases. Advisory opinions. Dooms. Digests
Particular courts
Landgericht. Kaiserliche Landgerichte. Oberhöfe. Schöffenstühle. Courts of appeal or last resort
Individual courts -- Continued

265.5 Leutkircher Heide, Landgericht in Ober- und Niederschwaben

Magdeburg, Schöffenstuhl see KK245+

Law faculties. Juristenfakultäten

266 Several faculties

267.A-Z Individual faculties. By place, A-Z

267.E73 Erfurt

267.E75 Erlangen

267.H35 Halle

267.H44 Heidelberg

267.I54 Ingolstadt

267.J45 Jena

267.L44 Leipzig

267.M37 Marburg

267.R78 Rostock

269 Consilia juris. Advisory opinions of lawyers

Weistumer see KK249+

Trials

Criminal trials and judicial investigations

For dramatization of trials see KK285

Collections. Compilations

270 General

270.5.A-Z Particular offenses, A-Z

270.5.I54 Infanticide

Insult see KK270.5.S56

270.5.S56 Slander. Insult

270.5.W58 Witchcraft

270.7.A-Z Individual trials. By defendant or best known name, A-Z

Including records, briefs, commentaries, and stories on a particular trial

Civil trials

272 Collections. Compilations

272.5.A-Z Individual trials. By plaintiff, A-Z

Contemporary legal literature

History of law. Rechts- und Verfassungsgeschichte
By period
Period from ca. 919 to ca. 1867. Hochmittelalter, Spätmittelalter und Neuzeit
Sources. Rechtsquellen
Contemporary legal literature -- Continued

274 Compends. Digests. Indexes
Including abecedaria, claves, slotel, repertoria, remissoria, registra, promptuaria, regesta, etc.
e.g.
274.B47 Berthold von Freiburg. fl. 1304 (Rechtssumme)
274.B62 Bocksdorf, Dietrich von (Remissorium. Mid 15th cent.)
274.B625 Bocksdorf, Tammo von (Abecedarium des sächsischen Landrechts. 1426)
274.K36 Kappler, Friedrich (Promptuarium. 1837)
274.R45 Remissorium oder Register über den Sachsenspiegel (1583)
274.R46 Repertorium (Remissorium. 1484-1490)
274.S34 Schlüssel des sächsischen Landrechts

Formularies
Including dictamen, summa dictaminis, usus sive, practica dictaminis, rhetorica, ars notarii, etc.
275 General
e.g.
275.K62 Koch, Christian Friedrich (1862)
275.N49 New formular teutsch (1545)
275.R62 Rockinger, Ludwig von (Formularbücher. 1855)
275.S34 Schott, August Ludwig (Schreibart. 1800)
Particular clauses and formulae
275.5 Contractual penalties
275.7 Renuntiationes
275.8.A-Z By wording or phrasing, A-Z
e.g.
275.8.A53 Ane geverde. Ane argliste unde geverde

276 Handbooks
Including handbooks for lawyers, public officers, and private persons, court (trial) practice, pleading, etc.
e.g.
276.B87 Burgermeister, Johann Stephen
276.G62 Gobler, Justinus
276.H65 Hommel, Karl Ferdinand (Teutscher Flavius)
276.J63 Jodocus of Erfurt (Vocabularis iuris utriusque 1452)
276.K56 Knorren, Carl Gottlieb
276.L55 Lingenthal, Zacharia von
276.O53 Oldendorpp. Johann (Ratsmannenspiegel. 1530)
276.P47 Perneder, Andreas

History of law. Rechts- und Verfassungsgeschichte
By period
Period from ca. 919 to ca. 1867. Hochmittelalter, Spätmittelalter und Neuzeit
Sources. Rechtsquellen
Contemporary legal literature
Handbooks -- Continued

276.P83 Pütter, Johan Stephan
276.S77 Strube, David Georg
278 Encyclopedic works
e.g.
278.N48 Nettelbladt, Daniel (Anleitung. 1784)
Collected works
280.A-Z Several authors. By editor or compiler
e.g.
280.H34 Hagemann, Theodor
281.A-Z Individual authors
e.g.
281.B63 Böhmer, Georg Ludwig
281.E88 Estor, Johann Georg
281.P83 Pufendorf, Wilhelm von
282 General works
284 Examination aids
285 Popular works
Including dramatization of trials, Satansprozess, etc.
e.g.
285.A97 Ayrer, Jacob (Historischer Prozeussus juris. Before 1605)
Brant, Sebastian see KK285.K52
285.F38 Fastnachtsspiele (15th century)
Keller, Adalbert von see KK285.F38
285.K52 Klagspiegel (15th century)
285.T45 Tengler, Ulrich (Laienspiegel. 1509)
286 Addresses, essays, lectures
Holy Roman Empire and its constitution. Deutsches Reich (Heiliges Römisches Reich Deutscher Nation) und seine Verfassung
For works on all aspects of public law see KK4413+
For constitutional history after 1806 see KK4460+
290 General (Table K22)
Law collections. Compilations (Grundrechtssammlungen) see KK250
291.A-Z Concepts and principles, A-Z
291.E46 Empire. Reichsgedanke
The estates of the realm. Reichsständewesen
Including Heerschildordnung (Ständische Gliederung)
292 General works

History of law. Rechts- und Verfassungsgeschichte
By period
Period from ca. 919 to ca. 1867. Hochmittelalter, Spätmittelalter und Neuzeit
Holy Roman Empire and its constitution. Deutsches Reich (Heiliges Römisches Reich Deutscher Nation) und seine Verfassung
The estates of the realm. Reichsständewesen -- Continued
Particular estates. Die Stände

293 The King. Erster Heerschild
Ministeriales. Nobility. Dynasties
294 General (Table K22)
(Reichs) Fürsten. Grafen. Regierende Häuser
295 General works
Dynastic rules. Hausgesetz, etc.
295.5 Collections. Compilations
295.6.A-Z Individual. By dynasty, A-Z
295.6.C76 Croy
295.6.H64 Hohenzollern
295.6.S34 Schleswig-Holstein
296 Freie Herren
Including Semperfreie, Mittelbarfreie, Schöffenbarfreie
Knights. Ritterstand
Including Unfreie Ritter and Dienstmannen
297 General (Table K22)
Individual laws
297.A4A-.A4Z Annotated editions. Glosses. Commentaries. By author of annotations or commentary, A-Z
e.g.
297.A4R68 Rothe, Johann (Ritterspiegel. Early 15th century)
Ritterbürtigkeit see KK301.E62
Feudal capacity see KK319+
299 Admission to tournaments. Turnierfähigkeit
300 Admission to orders and foundations. Stiftsfähigkeit
301.A-Z Special topics, A-Z
301.B57 Birth rights
301.E62 Equality of birth. Ebenbürtigkeit
Erstgeburtsrecht see KK301.B57
301.J87 Juristic personality of dynasty. Rechtspersönlichkeit des Hauses oder standesherrlichen Familie
Officials of the empire see KK350+

History of law. Rechts- und Verfassungsgeschichte
By period
Period from ca. 919 to ca. 1867. Hochmittelalter, Spätmittelalter und Neuzeit
Holy Roman Empire and its constitution. Deutsches Reich (Heiliges Römisches Reich Deutscher Nation) und seine Verfassung
The estates of the realm. Reichsständewesen
Particular estates. Die Stände
Ministeriales. Nobility. Dynasties
Special topics, A-Z -- Continued

301.P73 Prerogatives. Sonderrechte
301.S92 Succession. Inheritance
302 Gemeinfreie. Commons. Freemen
Including peasants and city dwellers (Bürger)
303 Censuales. Zinsleute. Grund- und Schutzhörige
304 Serfs. Slaves. Leibeigene. Hörige
Including peasants and city dwellers (Bürger)
Jews
305 General (Table K22)
Judenregal see KK373.J83
Peregrini. Aliens and strangers. Fremdenrecht
306 General (Table K22)
Gabella hereditaria see KK373.S47
Gabella emigrationis see KK373.S47
309.A-Z Special topics, A-Z
Birth rights see KK301.B57
309.E24 Echtlosigkeit. Illegitimacy
Inheritance see KK301.S92
Marriage impediments see KK414.5
309.O88 Outlawry
Empire and estates. Reich und Reichstände
Including Reichsstädte
310 General works
310.5 Reform. Reichsreform
Dynastic rules see KK295.5+
311 Territories, Landstände, and Landschaft
Reichskreise see KK376+
Territorial confederations. Bündnisse und Einigungen der Stände
312 Hanseatic League
312.2 Schwäbischer Bund
Empire and church see KK379+
Territory of the realm. Reichsgebiet. Ausdehnung des Reiches
313 General works
313.2 Sicily

History of law. Rechts- und Verfassungsgeschichte
By period
Period from ca. 919 to ca. 1867. Hochmittelalter, Spätmittelalter und Neuzeit
Holy Roman Empire and its constitution. Deutsches Reich (Heiliges Römisches Reich Deutscher Nation) und seine Verfassung
Territory of the realm. Reichsgebiet. Ausdehnung des Reiches -- Continued
Mediatisierung und Säkularisierung

314 General works
314.2 Reichsdeputationshauptschluss
314.3.A-Z Individual estates. By name, A-Z
314.5 Foreign relations

Feudal law. Lehnrecht
General
Statutes. Regulations. Privileges. Custumals. Treaties, etc.
315.A2 Collections. Selections
Individual laws
315.A3A-.A3Z Texts. Unannotated editions. By title or editor, A-Z
e.g.
Libri feudorum see KJC4434.5
315.A3R42 Rechte Weise des Lehnrechts (15th century)
315.A3R52 Richtsteig Lehnrecht (late 14th century)
315.A4 Annotated editions. Glosses
315.A55 Court decisions. Dooms. Advisory opinions
315.A7-.Z79 General works. Treatises
Feudal institutes
316 Feudal lord and vassal. Lehnsherr und Vasall
Fief. Lehen
317 General (Table K22)
318.A-Z Special topics, A-Z
318.A59 Anwartschaft. Unbenanntes Gedinge
318.C65 Commendation. Homage
318.C655 Contract
318.D43 Deed of feoffment. Counterdeed. Lehnbrief und Lehnrevers
318.E53 Enfeoffment of several vassals in collective hands. Gesamtbelehnung
For Ganerbschaft see KK459.5
Expectancies see KK318.A59
318.F45 Feoffments in reversion. Eventualbelehnung
318.F48 Feudal seisin (Vassal). Lehngewere
318.P75 Proprietary seisin (Lord). Eigengewehre
318.S24 Sala. Investiture

History of law. Rechts- und Verfassungsgeschichte
By period
Period from ca. 919 to ca. 1867. Hochmittelalter, Spätmittelalter und Neuzeit
Holy Roman Empire and its constitution. Deutsches Reich (Heiliges Römisches Reich Deutscher Nation) und seine Verfassung
Feudal law. Lehnrecht
Feudal institutes
Fief. Lehen
Special topics, A-Z -- Continued

318.S82 Subfeuds
318.S95 Symbolic investiture
Feudal capacity. Lehnsfähigkeit
319 General works
Estates of the realm (Heerschildordnung) see KK292+
320 Rights of eschat. Compulsory refeoffment. Heimfallrecht und Leihezwang
Felony. Untreue. Felonie
Including procedure
321 General works
321.5.A-Z Special topics, A-Z
321.5.A Heinrich der Löwe. Trial
322 Feudal succession
Including change in person or lord or vassal
323 Feudal liability. Debts
324.A-Z Particular objects of feudal tenure other than land, A-Z
324.C36 Capital. Money
324.F48 Feudal office. Amtslehn
Money see KK324.C36
324.M69 Movables
Rural (peasant) land tenure and peasantry
326 General (Table K22)
327 Peasantry. Bauernstand (Table K22)
328 Mark communities. Village communities. Markgenossenschaften. Dorfschaften (Table K22)
Including Commons (Allmende)
Precarious tenures and benefices (older form) see KK387
329 Free tenures. Freies Eigen
Manorial estates. Lordships. Seigniories. Gutsherrschaft. Gutsverband
330 General (Table K22)

History of law. Rechts- und Verfassungsgeschichte
By period
Period from ca. 919 to ca. 1867. Hochmittelalter, Spätmittelalter und Neuzeit
Holy Roman Empire and its constitution. Deutsches Reich (Heiliges Römisches Reich Deutscher Nation) und seine Verfassung
Rural (peasant) land tenure and peasantry
Manorial estates. Lordships. Seigniories. Gutsherrschaft. Gutsverband -- Continued

331 Virgate and manorial villeins. Hufe and Hufebauern. Hintersassen
332 Manorial serfdom. Hofhörigkeit. Leibeigenschaft (Table K22)
334 Lord's demesne. Fronhof. Meierhof
334.5 Bailiff (Maior). Meier (Table K22)
335.A-Z Special topics, A-Z
Charges, rents, etc. see KK465+
335.I88 Ius primae noctis
Leasehold for years and inheritance
336 General works
336.5.A-Z Special topics, A-Z
Charges, rents, etc. see KK465+
336.5.E46 Emphyteusis. Erbpacht und Erbpachtgüter
336.5.E88 Estates subject to heritable rents. Erbzinsgüter
336.5.E885 Estates subject to rent charges. Rentengüter
336.5.F43 Free-farms. Meiergüter
336.5.I58 Interim farm and interim management
336.5.L42 Leasehold seisin. Leihegewere (Tenant)
336.5.P76 Proprietary seisin. Eigengewere (Feudal lord)
Succession to rural holdings
Including inheritance, sale, lease, etc.
337 General (Table K22)
337.5 Preemption rights. Näherrecht. Zugrecht. Retractive purchase. Rückkauf
(337.6) Entail
see KK6613+
Urban leaseholds see KK525
Crown and king. Das Königtum
339 General (Table K22)
339.5 Title
340 Insignia regni. Reichskleinodien
341 Rights and prerogatives. Vorrechte
Succession and designation. Thronfolge. Geblütsrecht
342 General (Table K22)
Individual laws

History of law. Rechts- und Verfassungsgeschichte
By period
Period from ca. 919 to ca. 1867. Hochmittelalter, Spätmittelalter und Neuzeit
Holy Roman Empire and its constitution. Deutsches Reich (Heiliges Römisches Reich Deutscher Nation) und seine Verfassung
Crown and king. Das Königtum
Succession and designation. Thronfolge. Geblütsrecht
General
Individual laws -- Continued
Licet iuris 1338 see KK253
Bulla aurea 1356 see KK253
Election. Wahl. Kur
343 General (Table K22)
Electors and electoral colleagues. Kurfürsten
343.5 General works
343.52 Archministries. Erzämter
343.7 Coronation, anointing, and enthronement. Krönung. Salbung. Erhebung
343.72 Deposition. Absetzung
345 Vicars of the empire. Reichsvikariat
Crown goods and dynastic estates see KK364+
Imperium (Bannum). Herrscher- und Regierungsgewalt. Königsbann
346 General works
Judicial power see KK597
348 Palatinum. Pfalz. Königspfalz
The court. Ministries. Officials of the empire. Königshof. Hofämter. Reichsämter
350 General works
350.5.A-Z Particular ministries, A-Z
350.5.A72 Archicancellarius (Erzbischof von Mainz). Erzkanzler
Camera imperialis see KK362.3
350.5.C35 Cancellarius. Notarius. Hofkanzler. Reichskanzler
350.5.C36 Capella. Hofkapelle. Organisation
350.5.C42 Chancellery. Hofkanzlei. Reichskanzlei
350.5.C65 Consiliarii. Hofrat. Reichshofrat
350.5.M37 Marschal
350.5.P76 Protonotarius. Vizekanzler
Diet. Generalis conventus. Generale parlamentum. Hoftag. Reichstag
352 General (Table K22)
352.5 Electoral college. Kurfürstenkollegium

History of law. Rechts- und Verfassungsgeschichte
By period
Period from ca. 919 to ca. 1867. Hochmittelalter, Spätmittelalter und Neuzeit
Holy Roman Empire and its constitution. Deutsches Reich (Heiliges Römisches Reich Deutscher Nation) und seine Verfassung
Diet. Generalis conventus. Generale parlamentum. Hoftag. Reichstag -- Continued

353 Estates of the realm. Reichstände
Including Fürsten and Reichsstädte
353.5 Corpora evangelicorum and catholicorum
354 Deputations. Reichsdeputationen
355.A-Z Individual diets. By place or ruler, A-Z
Class here general works on a particular diet
For legislative acts see KK253
355.N87 Nuremberg (1524)
355.R44 Regensburg (1640)
Reichsregiment see KK376
The judiciary see KK595+
Military organization. Militär- und Kriegswesen
356 General (Table K22)
Reform. Reichsheeresreform. Söldnerheer
357 General (Table K22 modified)
Statutes. Regulations. Privileges. Custumals. Treaties, etc.
357.A4 Individual laws
Including unannotated and annotated editions (Glosses)
357.A4R44 Reichsheeresordnung (1422)
357.A4R442 Reichsheeresordnung (1427)
357.A4R443 Reichsheeresordnung (1431)
358 Aufgebot. Kontingente
359 Compulsory military service. Heerfahrt. Heeresfolge
360 Fortifications. Burgwerk. Befestigungen
Finance. Fiskalat
362 General (Table K22)
362.3 Camera. Königliche Kammer. Finanzverwaltung
362.5 Local administration. Vögte. Schultheissen. Reichskommissare
Crown goods and dynastic house goods. Reichsgüter und Hausgüter
364 General (Table K22)
Rights of exchat see KK320
Property of the church. Reichskirchengut
Cf. KK386+ Secular ecclesiastical law
365 General works

History of law. Rechts- und Verfassungsgeschichte
By period
Period from ca. 919 to ca. 1867. Hochmittelalter, Spätmittelalter und Neuzeit
Holy Roman Empire and its constitution. Deutsches Reich (Heiliges Römisches Reich Deutscher Nation) und seine Verfassung
Finance. Fiskalat
Property of the church. Reichskirchengut -- Continued
Sevitium regis see KK373.S47
Mint regulations. Coinage. Münzwesen
366 General (Table K22)
Regality see KK373.M543
367 Expenditures. Ausgaben
Debts. Schuldenwesen des Reichs und der Reichsstände
368 General (Table K22)
368.5 Pledges. Reichspfandschaften
Taxes. Reichssteuern
Including Bede, petitiones, precariae, collectae, stiura, Schoss, etc.
369 General (Table K22)
369.5 Registration. Bederegister
Real property tax. Landbede
370 General (Table K22)
370.5.A-Z Registration. Landbederegister. By place, A-Z
370.5.M42 Mecklenburg
370.5.T92 Tübingen
371 Extraordinary and ad hoc taxes. Taxes pro conservatione imperii
Regalia. Customs. Royal prerogatives, etc.
372 General (Table K22)
Individual laws
372.A3A-.A3Z Texts. Unannotated editions. By title or editor, A-Z
372.A3C65 Constitutio de regalibus (1158)
373.A-Z Special topics, A-Z
Bridges see KK373.W38
Budengeld see KK373.M37
Conductus in flumine see KK373.W38
373.C65 Confiscation of (Feudal) estates. Vermögenseinziehung
373.C88 Customs. Duties. Zollgerechtigkeit
373.D35 Dikes. Deichrecht
373.E82 Eschat. Heimfall von Reichsgütern (Lehnsgütern)
373.F58 Fishery. Fischereirecht

History of law. Rechts- und Verfassungsgeschichte
By period
Period from ca. 919 to ca. 1867. Hochmittelalter, Spätmittelalter und Neuzeit
Holy Roman Empire and its constitution. Deutsches Reich (Heiliges Römisches Reich Deutscher Nation) und seine Verfassung
Finance. Fiskalat
Regalia. Customs. Royal prerogatives, etc.
Special topics, A-Z -- Continued

373.F67 Forestry. Games laws. Forstrecht. Jagdrecht
Free mining (Privilege) see KK554
Free or franchised mountain see KK554
Gabella emigrationis (Abzugsteuer) see KK373.S47
Gabella hereditaria (Abschossrecht) see KK373.S47
373.I98 Ius albanagii
373.I983 Ius conductus, ducatus. Geleitsregal. Geleitschutz
Ius primarium precum see KK373.S47
373.J83 Judenschatz. Judenregal
373.J833 Judicial (Court) costs. Gerichsgefälle
Kings' highways see KK373.V52
373.L35 Land regalia. Unclaimed (Derelict) land Bodenregal. Recht auf herrenloses Land
373.M37 Markets. Marktgerechtigkeit. Marktzölle
373.M54 Mills. Mühlenregal
373.M543 Mint regality. Münzregal
373.N38 Naturalia. Naturalleistungen an den Hof
Ports see KK373.W38
Regalia metallorum et salinarum (mines and salterns) see KK554
Rivers see KK373.W38
373.S25 Salvage. Strandrecht. Strandregal
373.S47 Servitia, subsidia regis (of the church) Renten aus dem Reichskirchengut
373.T58 Tithe. Zehnte
373.T73 Treasure troves. Schatzfund
373.T74 Tributes. Jahrgeschenke. Investiturgeschenke. Ehrungen
373.V52 Viae publicae. Land-, Königs- und Heerstrassen. Wegebann
373.W38 Water rights. Water transportation. Wasserrecht. Wasserstrassenrecht
Including tow paths (Leinpfade)

Public safety, order, and welfare. Reichspolizei

History of law. Rechts- und Verfassungsgeschichte
By period
Period from ca. 919 to ca. 1867. Hochmittelalter, Spätmittelalter und Neuzeit
Holy Roman Empire and its constitution. Deutsches Reich (Heiliges Römisches Reich Deutscher Nation) und seine Verfassung
Public safety, order, and welfare. Reichspolizei -- Continued

375 General (Table K22)
Individual sources
375.A3A-.A3Z Texts. Unannotated editions. By title or editor, A-Z
375.A3R44 Reichspolizeiordnung (1530, 1548, 1577)
375.5.A-Z Special topics, A-Z
375.5.A78 Artisans
Cf. KK578+ Guilds
Coinage see KK366+
375.5.D78 Drug laws
Hospitals see KK375.5.M43
375.5.L35 Landfrieden
375.5.M43 Medical laws
375.5.P38 Paupers. Armenrecht
Physicians see KK375.5.M43
375.5.P68 Postal service
Quacks see KK375.5.M43
375.5.S95 Sumptuary laws. Luxusordnungen

Administrative districts of the realm. Reichskreise. Reichsregiment
376 General (Table K22)
376.A2A-.A2Z Law collections and compilations. By editor, compiler or title, A-Z
376.A2K73 Kreisabschiede
376.A2R44 Reichskreisordnungen
376.A2R445 Reichsregimentordnungen
377 Organs of district government
Including Kreistag, Kreishauptmann, etc.
378.A-Z Individual Reichskreise, A-Z
378.B39 Bayerischer Kreis
378.B87 Burgundischer Kreis
378.F72 Fränkischer Kreis
378.K87 Kurrheinischer Kreis
378.N53 Niedersächsischer Kreis
378.O23 Oberrheinischer Kreis
378.O24 Obersächsischer Kreis
378.O77 Osterreichischer Kreis
378.S34 Schwäbischer Kreis

History of law. Rechts- und Verfassungsgeschichte
By period
Period from ca. 919 to ca. 1867. Hochmittelalter, Spätmittelalter und Neuzeit
Holy Roman Empire and its constitution. Deutsches Reich (Heiliges Römisches Reich Deutscher Nation) und seine Verfassung
Public safety, order, and welfare. Reichspolizei
Administrative districts of the realm. Reichskreise. Reichsregiment
Individual Reichskreise, A-Z -- Continued
378.W48 Westfälischer Kreis
Secular ecclesiastical law. Kirchenrecht
Class here historical works on the relationship of church and state
For historical works on the internal law and government of a church, see KBR and KBU
Sources
Including treaties (Kirchenverträge) between church and state, i.e. concordats (Catholic Church) and contracts (Protestant Church)
For treaties relating to a particular region and/or state, see the region or state
For treaties on a particular subject, see the subject
379 Collections. Compilations
380 Individual concordats. By date
380 1122 Worms
380 1418 Constance
380 1447 Fürstenkonkordat
380 1448 Vienna
381 General works
Systems of church and state relationships
381.5 General works
Eigenkirche
382 General works
Germanic period see KJ724+
Carlovingian state church
see KJ726 and KBR
383 Investiture struggle. Investiturstreit. Zweischwerterlehre (Table K22)
State churches and rulers. Landesherrliches Kirchenregiment
384 Royal supremacy. Summepiscopat
384.2 Reformation and jus reformandi. Religionsbann
384.3 Patronage. Patronatsrecht
384.4 Jurisdiction, autonomy, and government
Protestant church. Lutheran church

History of law. Rechts- und Verfassungsgeschichte
By period
Period from ca. 919 to ca. 1867. Hochmittelalter, Spätmittelalter und Neuzeit
Secular ecclesiastical law. Kirchenrecht
Systems of church and state relationships
State churches and rulers. Landesherrliches Kirchenregiment
Protestant church. Lutheran church -- Continued
384.6 General works
384.62 Jus episcopale. Ius in sacra
Church orders and local legislation see KBU
Autonomy and legislature see KK384.4
384.7.A-Z By state, A-Z
Catholic Church
384.8 General works
Royal supremacy see KK384
384.9.A-Z By state, A-Z
384.9.B39 Bavaria
384.95.A-Z Special topics, A-Z
384.95.E43 Election, coronation, and anointment of kings
Church finance and estate
Cf. KK365+ Imperial finance
386 General works
Church property. Kirchengut
386.5 General works
Catholic Church
General works see KK386.5
386.6.A-Z By region or state, A-Z
386.6.E33 Eifel
Protestant Church
General works see KK386.5
386.8.A-Z By region or state, A-Z
386.8.W88 Württemberg
387 Feudal fiefs. Precariae. Benefices
388 Tithes. Regalia. Revenue
Ius primarium precum of the crown. Servitia regis see KK373.S47
Secularization (Einziehung geistlicher Güter) see KK314+
Private law. Privatrecht
390 General (Table K22)
Pandektistik see KK949
Civil law. Zivilrecht
394 General (Table K22)
Persons

History of law. Rechts- und Verfassungsgeschichte
By period
Period from ca. 919 to ca. 1867. Hochmittelalter, Spätmittelalter und Neuzeit
Private law. Privatrecht
Civil law. Zivilrecht
Persons -- Continued
396 General works
396.5 Personality and capacity. Rechtsfähigkeit und Geschäftsfähigkeit
397 Juristic persons
Associations. Communities. Cooperatives. Genossenschaftsrecht
399 General works
400 The sib. Sippe
Mark communities see KK328
Village communities see KK328
404 Craft guilds. Zünfte
405 Associations. Vereine
Legal transactions. Rechtsgeschäfte
408 General works
Declaration of intention. Willenserklärung
409 General works
410 Error. Irrtum
Domestic relations. Familienrecht
412 General works
Marriage law. Eherecht
413 General works
414 Betrothal. Verlöbnis
414.5 Marriage impediments. Ehehindernisse
Including serfdom, difference of social class, etc.
Marriage bond. Persönliches Eherecht
415 General works
416 Household. Domicile. Häusliche Gemeinschaft
416.5 Legal status of women
Mutual support see KK1137
Matrimonial actions. Dissolution of marriage
417 General works
418 Divorce
418.3 Claims resulting from divorce, etc.
Matrimonial property and regime. Ehegüterrecht und Güterstände
419 General works
420 Community of property. Gütergemeinschaft
422 Morgengabe. Dos
Including Verfangenschaft

History of law. Rechts- und Verfassungsgeschichte
By period
Period from ca. 919 to ca. 1867. Hochmittelalter, Spätmittelalter und Neuzeit
Private law. Privatrecht
Civil law. Zivilrecht
Domestic relations. Familienrecht -- Continued
Marriage, church, and state
see KBR and KBU
Consanguinity and affinity. Verwandtschaft. Schwagerschaft
426 General works
Consanguinity
426.5 General works
427 Schwertmagen
Parent and child. Elternrecht
428 General works
428.5 Support. Dowry. Advancement. Unterhalt und Ausstattung
429 Adoption
429.5 Illegitimate children
431 Guardian and ward. Vormundschaft
Property. Law of things. Sachenrecht
433 General (Table K22)
Possession. Seisin. Gewere. Besitz
434 General (Table K22)
435 Possession by virtue of agency. Besitzdienerschaft
435.5 Acquisition and transfer of possession. Erwerb und Verlust
Violation of possession. Besitzstörungen. Besitzschutz
436 General (Table K22)
437 Possessory actions. Besitzschutzklagen
Ownership. Eigentum
438 General (Table K22)
Acquisition and loss of ownership. Erwerb und Verlust
439 General (Table K22)
440 Occupancy. Aneignung. Inbesitznahme
441 Lost property. Fund
442 Treasure troves. Schatzfund
443 Accessions
444 Prescription. Ersitzung
445 Succession. Erbgang

History of law. Rechts- und Verfassungsgeschichte
By period
Period from ca. 919 to ca. 1867. Hochmittelalter, Spätmittelalter und Neuzeit
Private law. Privatrecht
Civil law. Zivilrecht
Property. Law of things. Sachenrecht
Ownership. Eigentum
Acquisition and loss of ownership. Erwerb und Verlust -- Continued

447 Contractual acquisition
Including acquisition bona fide (Erwerb kraft guten Glaubens)

Loss of ownership. Verlust

449 General works

449.5 Abandonment. Dereliktion

Co-ownership. Miteigentum

450 General (Table K22)

450.5 Gesamthand

Claims and actions resulting from ownership. Ansprüche aus dem Eigentum

451 General (Table K22)

451.3 Rei vindicatio

451.5 Actio negatoria

Real property. Liegenschaftsrecht

452 General (Table K22)

Land registers and rent registers see KK482

Restraints on real property

453 General works

Restraint on alienation of agricultural land see KK6595+

Entail see KK6613+

Entailed estates of the greater nobility. Fideicommissum. Familiengüterrecht. Stammgüterrecht

454 General (Table K22)

454.3 Inheritance and succession

454.5 Courts and procedure

454.7.A-Z By state, A-Z

454.7.B39 Bavaria

Ownership of real property

General see KK438+

455 Acquisition and loss of ownership

Co-ownership see KK450+

Rights incident to ownership of land

457 General works

457.2 Air and space above ground

History of law. Rechts- und Verfassungsgeschichte
By period
Period from ca. 919 to ca. 1867. Hochmittelalter, Spätmittelalter und Neuzeit
Private law. Privatrecht
Civil law. Zivilrecht
Property. Law of things. Sachenrecht
Real property. Liegenschaftsrecht
Rights incident to ownership of land -- Continued
457.3 Riparian rights. Water rights
457.5 Game and fishing rights
Law of adjoining landowners
458 General (Table K22)
459.A-Z Special topics, A-Z
459.A59 Anwenderecht. Kehr- oder Tretrecht. Pflugrecht
459.B68 Boundaries. Building across boundaries. Party walls
459.E39 Eaves-drip. Trauf
459.H35 Hammerschlag- und Leiterrecht
Leiterrecht see KK459.H35
459.L54 Light and window. Licht- und Fensterrecht
459.N84 Nuisances. Nachbarliche Einwirkungen
459.O83 Overhang. Overfall. Überhang. Überfall
Pflugrecht see KK459.A59
459.W39 Way by necessity. Notwegrecht
Particular kinds of real property
Rentengüter see KK336.5.E885
459.5 Ganerbenburgen
460 Ships. Schiffe. Schiffsbauwerke
461 Superficies. Erbbaurecht
Rights to use and profits of another's land
461.5 General works
Fief see KK317+
Rural (peasant) land tenure see KK326+
Precarious tenures see KK387
Emphyteusis. Erbpachtrecht
462 General works
463 Büdnerrecht. Häuslerrecht
Servitudes. Easements
464 General works
Real servitudes. Grunddienstbarkeiten
465 General (Table K22)
465.5 Right-of-way
Personal servitudes. Persönliche Dienstbarkeiten
465.7 General works

History of law. Rechts- und Verfassungsgeschichte
By period
Period from ca. 919 to ca. 1867. Hochmittelalter, Spätmittelalter und Neuzeit
Private law. Privatrecht
Civil law. Zivilrecht
Property. Law of things. Sachenrecht
Real property. Liegenschaftsrecht
Rights to use and profits of another's land
Servitudes. Easements
Personal servitudes. Persönliche Dienstbarkeiten -- Continued
Limited personal servitudes. Beschränkte persönliche Dienstbarkeit
465.9 Right of habitation. Wohnrecht
Reallast
466 General works
466.3 Hand- und Spanndienste. Frohndienste
466.5 Tithe. Zehnte. Rentenreallast
466.7 Conveyance and life annuities. Altenteil. Leibzucht
467 Usufruct
468 Right of pre-emption. Vorkaufsrecht
Hypothecation. Grundpfandrechte
470 General (Table K22)
472 Hypotheca. Mortgage. Hypothek
474 Land charge. Grundschuld
Pledges. Pfandrecht an beweglichen Sachen und Rechten
476 General (Table K22)
Contractual pledges. Vertragspfandrechte
477 General works
Pledges of personal property. Fahrnispfand
478 General (Table K22)
478.5 Fasutpfand
479 Pledges of rights. Pfandrecht an Rechten
480.A-Z Other pledges, A-Z
Land registers. Grundbuchwesen. Schreinsbücher
482 General (Table K22)
483 Rent registers. Zinsregister
Inheritance and succession. Erbrecht
485 General (Table K22)
Intestate and testamentory succession. Gesetzliche und gewillkürte Erbfolge
486 General works
Estate. Inheritance. Nachlass
488 General works

History of law. Rechts- und Verfassungsgeschichte
By period
Period from ca. 919 to ca. 1867. Hochmittelalter, Spätmittelalter und Neuzeit
Private law. Privatrecht
Civil law. Zivilrecht
Inheritance and succession. Erbrecht
Intestate and testamentory succession. Gesetzliche und gewillkürte Erbfolge
Estate. Inheritance. Nachlass -- Continued
Fideicommissum see KK454
Entail see KK6613+
Feudal land holdings see KK320
490 Gerade. Heergewäte. Besthaupt. Dos
Ganerbschaft see KK459.5
Heirs. Legal status
492 General works
493 Joint heirs. Co-heirs. Miterben
494 Acceptance and disclaimer. Annahme und Ausschlagung
Wills. Testaments
495 General works
495.5 Legacy
Contract of inheritance. Erbvertrag
495.7 General works
496 Statutory portion. Pflichtteil
Obligations. Schuldrecht
497 General works
Debtor and creditor see KK1502+
498 Transfer and assumption of obligation
Extinction of obligation
499 General works
Performance
500 General works
501 Enforcement. Imprisonment for debts. Einlager
502 Liens. Zurückbehaltungsrechte
502.5 Revocation. Cancellation
503 Novation
504 Confusion of rights
505 Remission of debts. Schulderlass
Non-performance
506 General works
506.3 Culpa
507 Default. Verzug
Damages
509 General works
510 Causa

History of law. Rechts- und Verfassungsgeschichte
By period
Period from ca. 919 to ca. 1867. Hochmittelalter, Spätmittelalter und Neuzeit
Private law. Privatrecht
Civil law. Zivilrecht
Obligations. Schuldrecht -- Continued
Contracts

511 General works
511.5 Good faith. Treu und Glaube
Formation of contract
512 General works
Clauses
513 Contractual penalties
514 Stipulation
Sale. Kaufrecht
517 General works
518 Default. Mora accepiendi
Warranty
519 General works
520 Defects of goods
Conditional sale see KK1713+
521 Retractive purchase. Re-purchase
522 Preemption rights
523 Exchange. Barter. Tausch
524 Donations. Schenkung
525 Landlord and tenant. Mietrecht
525.5 Loan for use. Commodation. Leihe
Contract of service and labor. Master and servant
526 General works
526.5 Dienst und Arbeitsvertragsrecht
527 Contract for work and labor. Werkvertrag
528 Reward. Award. Auslobung
529 Brokerage. Mäklervertrag
530 Deposit. Verwahrung
Power of attorney. Agency. Mandat. Vertretung. Vollmacht. Auftrag
531 General works
532 Negotiorum gestio
533 Community by undivided shares. Gemeinschaft
534 Aleatory contracts. Natural obligations
535 Suretyship. Bürgschaft
537 Bearer negotiable instruments. Schuldverschreibung auf den Inhaber
Unjust enrichment see KK1907+
Delicts. Torts. Unerlaubte Handlungen
542 General works

History of law. Rechts- und Verfassungsgeschichte
By period
Period from ca. 919 to ca. 1867. Hochmittelalter, Spätmittelalter und Neuzeit
Private law. Privatrecht
Civil law. Zivilrecht
Obligations. Schuldrecht
Delicts. Torts. Unerlaubte Handlungen -- Continued
543 Protected rights. Geschützte Rechtsgüter
545 Strict liability. Gefährdungshaftung
Industry, trade, and commerce. Handel, Wirtschaft und Gewerbe
550 General works
Primary production. Extractive industries
Agricultural laws see KK6601+
Mining. Quarrying
553 General (Table K22)
554 Regalia metallorum et salinarum. Bergbannrecht. Berg- und Salzregal
555 Mining co-operatives. Gewerkschaften und Gwerken
Forestry, game laws, and hunting see KK373.F67
Fishery see KK373.F58
Wine making see KK6671+
Apiculture and beekeeping see KK6674
Horticulture see KK6675
Commerce. Commercial law
560 General (Table K22)
562 The merchant
563 Commercial register
565 Consignment. Commission merchant
566 Warehousing. Lagergeschäft
Freight forwarders. Carriers. Speditions- und Frachtrecht
567 General works
Particular carriers
569 Horse wagon. Horses
Maritime law see KK2256+
Companies. Partnerships. Corporations
574 General works
Co-operative societies. Wirtschafts- und Erwerbsgenossenschaften
575 General works
Mining co-operatives see KK555
576 Colonial companies. Kolonialgesellschaften
Guilds. Zünfte

History of law. Rechts- und Verfassungsgeschichte
By period
Period from ca. 919 to ca. 1867. Hochmittelalter, Spätmittelalter und Neuzeit
Private law. Privatrecht
Industry, trade, and commerce. Handel, Wirtschaft und Gewerbe
Commerce. Commercial law
Companies. Partnerships. Corporations
Guilds. Zünfte -- Continued

578 General
579.A-Z Parituclar crafts, A-Z
579.G64 Goldwork. Silverwork
Including regulation of fineness and hallmarks
Silverwork see KK579.G64
Labor unions see KK3123+
Bills of exchange see KK2162+
Banking see KK2188
Occupations and trades
Artisans. Handwerksrecht
584 General works
585.A-Z Particular crafts, A-Z
Guilds see KK578+
Press and publishing see KK7005+
Judiciary. Court organization and procedure
Class procedural law pertaining to a particular court with the court
595 General works
Jurisdiction. Jus evocandi. Imperium. Gerichtsgewalt. Gerichtshalterschaft
596 General works
596.5 Reform. King's peace (1495)
597 Bannum. Königsbann und Bannleihe. Gerichtsbann
Cf. KK618.5+ Landgerichte
598 Dingum unter Königsbann
Dingen bei seinen eigenen Hulden see KK639
599 Zwing und Bann
600 Sale, rent, or loan of jurisdiction. Patrimonial (manorial) jurisdiction
601 Contracts concerning jurisdiction. Jurisdictionsverträge
Privilegia de non appellando see KK255+
Particular courts
Including procedures
Imperial courts. Reichsgerichte. Königliche (kaiserliche) Gerichte
602 General (Table K22)

History of law. Rechts- und Verfassungsgeschichte
By period
Period from ca. 919 to ca. 1867. Hochmittelalter, Spätmittelalter und Neuzeit
Judiciary. Court organization and procedure
Particular courts
Imperial courts. Reichsgerichte. Königliche (kaiserliche) Gerichte -- Continued
Curia regis. Reichshofgericht. Königliches Hofgericht (ca. 1150-1350)

603 General
Statutes. Regulations. Privileges. Custumals. Treaties, etc.
603.A2 Collections. Selections
Individual laws
Including unannotated and annotated editions (Glosses)
603.A3A-.A3Z Texts. Unannotated editions. By title or editor, A-Z
603.A3P74 Privilegia de non appellando
603.A3P744 Privilegia de non evocando
603.A4 Annotated editions. Glosses
Decisions see KK262.5
603.A7-.Z79 General works. Treatises
606.A-Z Individual courts. By name of place, A-Z
606.R68 Rottweil
Kaiserlicher Reichshofrat. Kammergericht. Imperial council (ca. 1415)
608 General (Table K22)
Decisions see KK263
610.A-Z Special topics, A-Z
610.I53 In forma pauperis
Reichskammergericht (1495-1806). Camera imperialis
612 General
Statutes. Regulations. Privileges. Custumals. Treaties, etc.
612.A2 Collections. Selections
Individual laws
Including unannotated and annotated editions (Glosses)
612.A3A-.A3Z Texts. Unannotated editions. By title or editor, A-Z
612.A3K35 Kammergerichtsordnung 1613

History of law. Rechts- und Verfassungsgeschichte
By period
Period from ca. 919 to ca. 1867. Hochmittelalter, Spätmittelalter und Neuzeit
Judiciary. Court organization and procedure
Particular courts
Imperial courts. Reichsgerichte. Königliche (kaiserliche) Gerichte
Reichskammergericht (1495-1806). Camera imperialis
General
Statutes. Regulations. Privileges. Custumals. Treaties, etc.
Individual laws -- Continued
612.A4A-.A4Z Annotated editions. Glosses. Commentaries. By author, editor, or title, A-Z
e.g.
612.A4M48 Meurer, Noe (1584)
612.A4Z94 Zwierlein, Johann Jacob (1744)
Decisions see KK264.A+
612.A7-.Z79 General works. Treatises
614.A-Z Special topics, A-Z
614.A66 Appellate procedures
Auxiliary personnel see KK614.J83
614.J83 Judges. Auxiliary personnel
Kaiserliche Landgerichte see KK635+
Landfriedensgerichte. Conventus fidelium principum de pace facienda et sedenda latronum tyrannide et raptorum compensanda seditione
615 General (Table K22)
616.A-Z Regional divisions, A-Z
616.A48 Alsace
616.R44 Rhine, Lower
616.S39 Saxony
616.T48 Thuringia
616.W48 Westphalia
Landgerichte. Grafengerichte
Class here works on courts of the empire and courts of other princes or rulers
For courts (several or individual) of an individual jurisdiction, see the jurisdiction
618 General (Table K22)
Jurisdiction. Gerichsbezirk. Grafschaft
618.5 General works
619 Subdivisions. Districts
Including Go, Zent, Pflege, and Bann

History of law. Rechts- und Verfassungsgeschichte
By period
Period from ca. 919 to ca. 1867. Hochmittelalter, Spätmittelalter und Neuzeit
Judiciary. Court organization and procedure
Particular courts
Landgerichte. Grafengerichte -- Continued

620 Dinstühle. Dingstätten. Schrannen
620.5 Ding. Thing
Including Echtes Ding, Notding, and Gebotenes Ding
621 Dingpflicht. Dinggenosse
622 Schöffen. Jurors (Table K22)
For works on a particular court, see the court
Höhere Landgerichte. Iudicia majora
Including Grafengerichte, Fürstliche Hofgerichte, Kanzleien, and Kammergerichte
623 General
Statutes. Regulations. Privileges. Custumals. Treaties, etc.
623.A2 Collections. Selections
Individual laws
Including unannotated and annotated editions (Glosses)
623.A3A-.A3Z Texts. Unannotated editions. By title or editor, A-Z
623.A3P74 Privilegia de non appellando, non evocando
623.A4 Annotated editions. Glosses
Decisions see KK265+
623.A7-.Z79 General works. Treatises
Niedere Landgerichte. Iudicia minora. Niedergerichte
626 General (Table K22)
628 Judges
Including Zentgraf (Centurio), Hunne, Schultheiss, Gograf (Tribunus), Heimbürge, Bauermeister
629 Urteiler. Schöffen. Vorsprechen
Kirchspiel-, Dorf-, Zenderei-, Hofmarkgerichte
Judges see KK628
Kaiserliche (Imperial) Landgerichte
635 General (Table K22)
637.A-Z Individual courts. By name or place, A-Z
637.B67 Bornheimer Berg
637.H47 Herzogtum Franken zu Würzburg
637.H57 Hirschberg
637.I54 Ingelheim
637.K34 Kaichen

History of law. Rechts- und Verfassungsgeschichte
By period
Period from ca. 919 to ca. 1867. Hochmittelalter, Spätmittelalter und Neuzeit
Judiciary. Court organization and procedure
Particular courts
Landgerichte. Grafengerichte
Kaiserliche (Imperial) Landgerichte
Individual courts. By name or place, A-Z -- Continued

637.L48 Leutkircher Haide
637.N88 Nürnberg (Onolzbach, Ansbach)
637.P88 Pürss
639 Markgerichte
Kirchspiel-, Dorf-, Zenderei-, Hofmarkgerichte see KK631+
Reichsvogteien. Kirchenvogteien. Landvogteien.
642 General (Table K22)
644.A-Z Individual courts. By name or place, A-Z
644.G68 Goslar
Kirchenvogteien. Hohe and niedere Vogteien. Landvogteien
647 General (Table K22)
649 Immunity. Exemption
650 Vogt. Stiftsvogt. Kirchenvogt
651.A-Z Special topics, A-Z
651.K56 Klostervogtei
651.P76 Propstei
654 Fehmic courts. Frei- oder Femgerichte
Ecclesiastical courts
654.5 General works
655 Sendgerichte
656 Consistorium
658 Feudal and servitary courts. Lehnsgerichte (Table K22)
Constitutional tribunals and courts see KK4697
660 Hanseatic courts. Hanseatische Oberlandesgerichte (Table K22)
Law faculties and courts of jurors. Juristenfakultäten, Schöffenstühle und Oberhöfe
661 General (Table K22 modified)
Decisions
see KK245+ ; KK266+
662 Several faculties and/or courts
663.A-Z Individual faculties. By name of place, A-Z
663.E75 Erlangen
663.G66 Göttingen

History of law. Rechts- und Verfassungsgeschichte
By period
Period from ca. 919 to ca. 1867. Hochmittelalter, Spätmittelalter und Neuzeit
Judiciary. Court organization and procedure
Particular courts
Law faculties and courts of jurors. Juristenfakultäten, Schöffenstühle und Oberhöfe
Individual faculties. By name of place, A-Z -- Continued

663.H44 Heidelberg
663.H45 Helmstedt
663.L44 Leipzig
663.M34 Mainz
663.M37 Marburg
664.A-Z Individual courts of jurors. By name or place, A-Z
664.B72 Brandenburg
664.C62 Coburg
664.F72 Frankfurt
664.L44 Leipzig
664.L83 Lübeck
664.M34 Magdeburg

Patrimonial (manorial) courts. Grundherrliche Hofgerichte
Including Bau- und Hubding, Urbargerichte, Hofsprachen

666 General (Table K22)
667 Dingpflicht
668 Judges
Including Seigneur, lord of the manor, and Villicus (Meier)
669 Urteiler
Including Hofgenossen and Schöffen

Märkerdinge. Dorfgemeindegerichte
670 General (Table K22)
671 Dingpflicht. Markgenossen
672 Judge. Oberster Märker
673 Urteiler
Including Hofgenossen und Markschöffen
675 Heimgereide. Bauernsprachen. Dorfgemeindegerichte
676.A-Z Individual courts. By name or place, A-Z
676.O43 Oldershausen
Westerhof see KK676.O43

Austrage. Austrägalgerichte see KK728

Judicial officers other than judges
678 General works

History of law. Rechts- und Verfassungsgeschichte
By period
Period from ca. 919 to ca. 1867. Hochmittelalter, Spätmittelalter und Neuzeit
Judiciary. Court organization and procedure
Particular courts
Judicial officers other than judges -- Continued
Public prosecutors see KK3728+
680 Notaries
Attorneys see KK3770+
Procedure. Prozessgang
Including civil procedure and criminal procedure before the reception (ca. 1495)
For procedures before a particular court, see the court, e.g., KK612, Kameralprozess
685 General (Table K22 modified)
Regulations. Privileges. Custumals. Treaties, etc.
Individual laws
Including unannotated and annotated editions (Glosses)
685.A3 Unannotated texts. By date
685.A4 Annotated editions. Glosses. Commentaries. By author, editor, or title
685.A4B82 Buch, Johann von (Richtsteig landrechts, ca. 1335)
Wurm, Nicolaus (Blume des Sachsenspiegels) see KK205.5.W87
Wurm, Nicolaus (Blume von Magdeburg) see KK205.5.W87
Parties to action
686 General works
686.2 Accused
686.4 Victim
687 Judge
687.2 Urteiler
688 Fürspreche
689 Aliens. Peregrini. Gäste
Actions and defenses
690 General works
691 Formalities. Verborum insidia. Formstrenge (Gefahr)
692 Exceptions. Einreden. Einwendungen
Particular actions
693 Action for payment due. Klage um Schuld
Action involving personal property (mobilia). Klage um Gut
694 General works

History of law. Rechts- und Verfassungsgeschichte
By period
Period from ca. 919 to ca. 1867. Hochmittelalter, Spätmittelalter und Neuzeit
Judiciary. Court organization and procedure
Procedure. Prozessgang
Actions and defenses
Particular actions
Action involving personal property (mobilia). Klage um Gut -- Continued
695 Anefang. Spurfolge
Action involving real property (immobilia), feudum, or inheritance
696 General works
697 Gewere
698 Fist law. Faustrecht
Peinliche Klage see KK790+
Kampfklage see KK835
Evidence. Burden of proof
700 General works
702 Gerüfte
Oath. Witnesses
704 General works
705 Eideshelfer. Schreimannen
707 Duellum. Gerichtlicher Zweikampf
Including Kampfvormund, Lohnkämpfer, etc.
Particular proceedings
710 Summary procedures. Summarischer Prozess
712 Contumacy. Ungehorsamsverfahren
714 Judicial decisions. Judgments
Remedies
716 General works
717 Urteilsschelte
718 Appellate procedure
720 Res judicata
721 Vollbort
Civil procedure. Gemeiner Zivilprozess
722 General (Table K22)
724 Litis contestatio
Special procedures
Summary procedures see KK710
726 Distribution. Teilungssachen
Procedures concerning documents and bills of exchange see KK3987
728 Arbitration. Austräge
Including Hanseatic League
Non-contentious jurisdiction see KK4044+

History of law. Rechts- und Verfassungsgeschichte
By period
Period from ca. 919 to ca. 1867. Hochmittelalter, Spätmittelalter und Neuzeit
Judiciary. Court organization and procedure
Procedure. Prozessgang -- Continued
Insolvency
729 General works
730 Bankruptcy
Execution. Zwangsvollstreckung
732 General (Table K22)
734 Budellus. Praeco. Büttel
735 Arrest. Seizure. Fronung. Anleite
737 Attachment and garnishment
739 Imprisonment. Einlager
740 Forced labor. Zwangsarbeit. Arbeitshaus
742 Objections of third parties claiming ownership and seeking release. Drittwiderspruchsklage
743 Costs
Criminal law and procedure
Sources
745 Collections. Compilations
Individual sources
747-747.8 Bambergensis constitutio criminalis (1507) (Table K20c)
749-749.8 Carolina constitutio criminalis (1532) (Table K20c)
752-752.8 Radolfszeller Halsgerichts-Ordnung (1506) (Table K20c)
Reichspolizeiordnungen (1530, 1548, 1577) see KK375.A3R44
754 General works
756.A-Z Special topics, A-Z
Accomplices see KK756.P74
756.C64 Criminal intent. Vorsatz
756.C643 Criminal liability. Guilt. Schuld
756.C646 Criminal offense
Guilt see KK756.C643
756.I456 Illegality
756.J88 Justification. Rechtfertigungsgrunde
Negligence and wantonness see KK8126+
756.P74 Principles and accessories. Accomplices. Täter. Anstifter. Gehilfe
Self-defense see KK8090+
Punishment
758 Theory and philosophy of punishment
759 General works
760.A-Z Particular penalties. Strafen, A-Z

History of law. Rechts- und Verfassungsgeschichte
By period
Period from ca. 919 to ca. 1867. Hochmittelalter, Spätmittelalter und Neuzeit
Criminal law and procedure
Punishment
Particular penalties, A-Z -- Continued
Banishment see KK760.E86
760.B73 Breaking on the wheel. Rädern
760.C37 Carrying of a millstone around the neck. Steintragen
Civil death see KK760.L68
760.D42 Death by fire. Feuertod
760.D423 Decapitation. Köpfen
760.D48 Destruction of buildings. Wüstung
Disenfranchisement see KK760.L68
760.D72 Drawing and quartering. Schleifen und Vierteilen
760.E86 Expulsion. Banishment. Vertreibung. Verbannung
760.F55 Fines
760.F67 Fortress. Festungshaft. Einschliessung
760.H35 Hanging. Hängen
Imprisonment see KK862
Infamy see KK760.L68
760.L68 Loss of civil rights. Aberkennung bürgerlicher Ehrenrechte
760.S72 Standing at the pillory. Am Schamdpfahl stehen
760.S76 Stoning. Steinigung
760.V47 Verstrickung
760.W47 Wergild
760.W54 Whipping. Staupen. Staupenschlag
760.W67 Workhouse. Arbeitshaus
765 Measures of rehabilitation and safety
772 Outlawry. Rechtlosigkeit
775 Punishment reflecting the kind of crime committed. Talion Spiegelnde Strafen
e.g. cutting off the hand of a thief
Sentencing. Determining punishment
778 General works
Fixed and indeterminate sentences see KK8308
Recidivism see KK8312
782 Pardon and amnesty. Clemency. Gnadenrecht
785.A-DD785.Z Individual offenses, A-Z
Aberglaube see KK785.W58
785.A25 Abortion
Adultery see KK785.I52
Annoyance to the public see KK8944
785.A87 Assault and battery

History of law. Rechts- und Verfassungsgeschichte
By period
Period from ca. 919 to ca. 1867. Hochmittelalter, Spätmittelalter und Neuzeit
Criminal law and procedure
Individual offenses, A-Z -- Continued

	Bigamy see KK785.I52
785.B52	Blasphemy
785.B73	Breach of trust
785.C65	Constraint
785.C74	Crimen laesae maiestatis. Majestätsbeleidigung
	Crimes involving documents see KK8818+
	Defamation see KK785.L52
785.D83	Duelling
	Embezzlement see KK785.T43
	Extortion see KK785.F72
785.F35	False testimony
785.F357	Falsum
785.F67	Forgery
785.F72	Fraud. Extortion
785.G35	Game and fish poaching
785.H54	High treason
785.I52	Incest. Adultery. Bigamy
785.I53	Infanticide
785.I58	Intoxicant misuse
785.L52	Libel. Slander. Defamation
785.M35	Manslaughter
785.M87	Murder
785.P37	Parricide
785.P47	Perjury
	Poaching see KK785.G35
785.P64	Poisoning
785.R42	Receiving stolen goods
785.R62	Robbery and rapacious theft
	Seduction see KK785.S49
785.S49	Sex crimes
	Slander see KK785.L52
785.S94	Suicide
	Superstition see KK785.W58
785.T43	Theft and embezzlement
785.T47	Threats
	Treason see KK785.C74
785.W58	Witchcraft. Hexerei
	Zauberei see KK785.W58

Criminal procedure

Class here works on criminal procedure after the reception (ca. 1495)

History of law. Rechts- und Verfassungsgeschichte
By period
Period from ca. 919 to ca. 1867. Hochmittelalter, Spätmittelalter und Neuzeit
Criminal law and procedure
Criminal procedure -- Continued
790 General (Table K22)
792 Accusation. Akkusationsprozess
795 Inquisition. Inquisitionsprozess
Parties to action
Accused. Person charged. Defendant
797 General works
Legal status. Estates
800 General works
802 Jews
804 Serfs. Slaves
Pretrial procedures
Investigations. Examinations. Preparation of defense
806 General works
Torture see KK829
808 Summonses. Subpoenas
Compulsory measures against the accused
810 Search and seizure. Arrest and pretrial detention
812 Right of asylum. Freistätten. Freihöfe
815 Extradition
Trial
817 General works
Evidence. Burden of proof
819 General (Table K22)
821 Confession. Self-incrimination. Urgicht
Oath. Witnesses
823 General works
825 Schreimannen. Eideshelfer
827 Circumstantial evidence. Augenschein
829 Torture
Ordeal. Gottesurteil
833 General works
835 Duellum. Wager of battle. Gerichtlicher Zweikampf
840.A-Z Particular proceedings, A-Z
840.A53 Anefangklage. Zug auf den Gewären
840.D35 Dangerous people. Landschädliche Leute
840.D42 Dead man, Procedure against. Klage gegen den toten Mann. Verklarung
840.J87 Juries and jurors. Assizes
Summary proceedings see KK710

History of law. Rechts- und Verfassungsgeschichte
By period
Period from ca. 919 to ca. 1867. Hochmittelalter, Spätmittelalter und Neuzeit
Criminal law and procedure
Criminal procedure
Trial -- Continued
843 Sentence. Judgment. Res judicata
845 Remedies. Appellate procedures
Special procedures
850 Procedures in witch trials (Table K22 modified)
Statutes. Regulations. Privileges. Custumals. Treaties, etc.
Individual laws
Including unannotated and annotated editions (Glosses)
850.A3A-.A3Z Texts. Unannotated editions. By title or editor, A-Z
850.A3H49 Hexenhammer (Friedrich Spee, 1591-1635)
850.A3K45 Kelheimer Hexenhammer
850.A4 Annotated editions. Glosses
Execution of sentence. Strafvollstreckung
855 General (Table K22)
Capital punishment
858 General works
Particular kinds of capital punishment see KK760.A+
860 Last meal. Henkersmahlzeit
862 Imprisonment. Zuchthaus- und Gefängniswesen (Table K22)
Philosophy, jurisprudence, and theory of German law
Class here works on doctrines peculiar to German legal institutions
For works by German authors on the philosophy of law in general, see K237+
For works on the philosophy of a particular branch of law (e.g. constitutional law or criminal law), see the branch
883 General (Table K11)
The concept of law
Including the definition of law
885 General works
886 The object of law. Law and justice. Gerechtigkeit
Ethics. Morality of law. Sittengesetz
887 General works
887.5 Public policy. Verkehrssitte

Philosophy, jurisprudence, and theory of German law
The concept of law
Ethics. Morality of law. Sittengesetz
887.7 Chicanery. Abuse of rights. Unzulässige Rechtsausübung
888 Equity. Fairness. Billigkeit
889 Esthetics
890 Law and the state. Legal order. Respect for law
891 Rights and duties. Sanctions
892 Effectiveness and validity of law. Rechtsgeltung und Rechtsbegründung
893 Certainty of law. Rechtssicherheit
Cf. KK3833 Civil procedure
Cf. KK9488 Criminal procedure
893.5.A-Z Other topics, A-Z
893.5.F73 Free will and determinism
893.5.N38 Natur der Sache
Legal science. Rechtswissenschaft
896 General works
Sources of law. Rechtsquellenlehre
897 General works
899 Custom and observance. Gewohnheitsrecht
900 Legislation
Judge-made law (Richterrecht) see KK904
Volksgeist see KK911+
Volksrecht see KK911+
Rule of law see KK4426+
Law reform. Criticism see KK942
Methodology. Juristische Methode
903 General works
904 Legal hermeneutics. Interpretation and construction. Technik der Rechtsfindung und Rechtsfortbildung. Tatsachenforschung
Including lacunae in law and judge-made law
Semantics
Cf. KK175.5 Legal history
907 General works
Abbreviations see KK82.2
Schools of legal theory
911 General works
912 Usus modernus
913 Humanism
914 Natural law
915 Philosophical idealism. Metaphysical school. Kanteanism
Historical jurisprudence
917 General works
Primitive law, ethnological jurisprudence see K190+

Philosophy, jurisprudence, and theory of German law
Schools of legal theory
Historical jurisprudence -- Continued
Racial theory of law see KK927+
Biological interpretation. Legal evolution see K328
Positivism
918 General works
919 Analytical jurisprudence. Bergriffsjurisprudenz
920 The pure theory of law. Reine Rechtslehre
921 Utilitarianism
Cf. KK930+ Sociological jurisprudence
Cf. KK938 Jurisprudence of interest
922 Psychological theory of law. Psychoanalytic jurisprudence
Cf. KK932 Social psychology of law
923 Existentialist legal theory
924 Phenomenology of law
Modern political theory of law
925 General works
926 Socialist. Communist
Nazi. Fascist
927 General works
928 Judaism. Jewish question
Sociological jurisprudence. Rechtssoziologie
930 General (Table K11)
931 Law and public policy
932 Social psychology of law
933 Social pathology
935 Neo-Kantianism
936 Free-law movement. Freirechtslehre
938 Jurisprudence of interest. Interessenjurisprudenz
940 Pluralism in law
941 Influence of other legal systems on German law (Reception)
942 Law reform and policies. Criticism. rechtserneuerung und Rechtspolitik. Polemik (Table K11)
Including reform of administration of justice in general (Justizreform)
For reform of criminal justice administration see KK7967
945.A-Z Concepts applying to several branches of the law, A-Z
Abuse of rights see KK887.7
Bona fides see KK945.G66
Chicanery see KK887.7
945.C65 Concurrent legislation. Gesetzeskonkurrenz
Deadlines see KK945.T55
945.D65 Dolus. Vorsatz
945.E65 Equality. Gleichheit
Equity see KK888
945.F52 Fictions

Concepts applying to several branches of the law, A-Z -- Continued

945.F67 Forfeiture. Verwirkung

945.F73 Freedom of conscience. Gewissensfreiheit

945.G66 Good faith. Reliance. Treu und Glaube

Legal advertising see KK945.N68

945.L44 Legal documents. Urkunden

945.L52 Liability

945.N44 Negligence. Fahrlässigkeit

945.N68 Notice. Legal advertising

945.O28 Oath

Ownership see KK945.P68

945.P68 Possession. Ownership. Besitz und Eigentum

945.P73 Presumption. Rechts(Gesetzes-)vermutung

945.P74 Privacy, Right of. Privatsphäre

945.P76 Property. Property damage

945.P92 Publicity. Publizitätsprinzip. Rechtsschein

Reliance see KK945.G66

945.S45 Self-incrimination. Selbstbelastungspflicht

Surrogat see KK1553

945.T55 Time periods. Deadlines. Fristen. Termine

945.V58 Vis major. Höhere Gewalt

Private law. Privatrecht

949 History

Class here works on recent history and development of private law (Pandektenwissenschaft) beginning ca. 1850

For all other works on the law prior to 1850 see KK390+

950 General (Table K11)

Private international law. Conflict of laws. Internationales Privatrecht

For works on conflict rules of branches other than private law (e.g. tax law, criminal law, etc.), see the subject

For conflict of laws between the United States and Germany see KF416.A+

For legislative documents see KK984+

958 Criticism. Reform

960 General (Table K11)

960.5 Constitutional aspects

961 Public order. Public policy

961.5 Classification. Qualification

961.7 Jurisdiction

963 Renvoi. Rückverweisung

Points of contact

964 Domicile

966 Interlocal (interstate) and interzonal law. Interlokales und interzonales Recht

968.A-Z Particular branches and subjects of the law, A-Z

Private international law. Conflict of laws. Internationales Privatrecht (IPR)

Particular branches and subjects of the law, A-Z

Administrative acts see KK5629
Adoption see KK968.F35
Arbitration see KK968.P76
Author and publisher see KK968.P92
Bankruptcy see KK968.P76
Capacity see KK968.P47
Cartels see KK968.C67
968.C48 Cessio legis. Gesetzlicher Forderungsübergang
968.C65 Commercial agents
968.C655 Commercial papers and negotiable instruments
968.C657 Commercial sales
968.C658 Contracts. Obligations. Debtor and creditor
968.C66 Copyright
968.C67 Corporations. Industrial trusts. Cartels
For procedure in anti-trust cases see KK6522
Criminal law see KK8042+
Debtor and creditor see KK968.C658
Divorce see KK968.M375
968.E92 Evasion
Execution see KK968.P76
968.F35 Family. Parent and child. Adoption
Foreign exchange. Divisenrecht see KK7097
Foreign judgments see KK3800
968.G83 Guardian and ward
Illegality see KK968.T67
Incapacity see KK968.P47
Industrial trusts see KK968.C67
968.I54 Inheritance and succession. Decedents' estates
968.I58 Insurance
968.I583 Intellectual and industrial property
Judicial assistance (Civil procedure) see KK3797
Judicial assistance (Criminal procedure) see KK9432+
Justification see KK968.T67
Labor law see KK2869.7
968.L45 Limitation of action
968.L62 Loans
968.M37 Maritime (commercial) law
968.M375 Marriage. Matrimonial actions. Matrimonial property
Negotiable instruments see KK968.C655
Obligations see KK968.C658
Parent and child see KK968.F35
968.P47 Persons. Capacity. Incapacity
968.P76 Procedure. Arbitral awards. Execution and bankruptcy
968.P78 Property

Private international law. Conflict of laws. Internationales Privatrecht
Particular branches and subjects of the law, A-Z -- Continued
968.P92 Publishing contract. Author and publisher. Verlagsvertragsrecht
968.R4 Real property
968.R43 Refugees. Statelessness
Social insurance see KK3305
Statelessness see KK968.R43
Taxation see KK7100.2+
968.T67 Torts. Illegality. Justification
968.T72 Trademarks
968.T725 Transfer
968.T78 Trusts and trustees
968.U53 Unfair competition
968.U534 Unjust enrichment
968.V45 Vendor and purchaser
Ward and guardian see KK968.G83
970 Intertemporal law. Retroactive law. Übergangsrecht. Rückwirkendes Recht
Including conflict of laws
Civil law. Bürgerliches Recht
981 Bibliography
982 Periodicals
982.5 Monographic series
Federal legislation
Statutes. Zivilrechtsgesetze
984 Collections. Compilations
Particular acts
Codes. Gesetzbücher
985.5<date> Individual codes
Arrange chronologically by appending the date of original enactment or revision of code to the number KK985.5 and deleting any trailing zeros
985.51896 Code of 1896/1900
985.51896.A12A-.A12Z Indexes
Legislative papers and related works
Bills
Including records or proceedings and minutes of evidence
985.51896.A14 Texts. By date
Including individual readings (first, second, and third)
985.51896.A16A-.A16Z Indexes

Civil law. Bürgerliches Recht
Federal legislation
Statutes. Zivilrechtsgesetze
Particular acts
Codes. Gesetzbücher
Individual codes
Code of 1896/1900
Legislative papers and related works -- Continued

985.51896.A32 Documents of code commissions and revision commissions. Official reports and memoranda. By date
Including legislative proposals (official drafts) of the executive branch and commentaries on official drafts

Criticism and comment. Private drafts see KK985.51896.A6A+

985.51896.A52 Text of the code. Unannotated and annotated editions. By date of publication
Including official editions (with or without annotation) and works containing the Introductory Act and complementary legislation along with the text of the code, and including short commentaries
For individual complementary laws, see the subject
For collected complementary legislation see KK984
For the Introductory Act see KK986.51896

985.51896.A6A-.A6Z Commentaries on the code. Annotated editions
Including short commentaries and commentaries incorporating court decisions (e.g., Reichsgerichträte-Kommentar, Warneyer, etc.)
For commentaries on a part of the code, see the subject, e.g. KK1100+, Family law

985.51896.A7A-.A7Z General works

985.51896.A8 Amendatory laws. By date of enactment
For amendatory laws pertaining to a particular subject, see the subject, e.g. KK1134+, Equality

986.51896 The Introductory Act to the Civil Code (BGB). Einführungsgesetz zum BGB (EG BGB)
Including Art. 7-31, Conflict of laws. Internationales Privatrecht (IPR)

Legislative documents and related works

986.51896.A15 Bills. By date
Including individual readings (first, second, and third)

Civil law. Bürgerliches Recht
Federal legislation
Statutes. Zivilrechtsgesetze
Particular acts
The Introductory Act to the Civil Code (BGB). Einführungsgesetz zum BGB (EG BGB)
Legislative documents and related works -- Continued

986.51896.A18 Official reports and memoranda. By date
Including legislative proposals (official drafts) of the executive branch, and separate drafts of Art. 7-31 (IPR)

986.51896.A4 Unannotated and annotated editions. By date
Including official editions (with or without annotation) and separate editions of Art. 7-31 (IPR)

986.51896.A6A-.A6Z General works. Commentaries

Comparative state legislation
Including works comparing federal legislation with legislation of two or more states, and comparison of legislation by period
For comparison of federal legislation with legislation of an individual state, see the state

988 Texts. Unannotated and annotated editions. By date of publication
Including enactment statutes of individual states (Ausführungsgesetze)

988.2 Annotated editions. Commentaries

988.6 General works

989 Court decisions

991 Collections of summaries of cases decided by courts or regulatory agencies

992 Encyclopedias. Dictionaries. Words and phrases

992.2 Form books

Yearbooks see KK982

993.5 Surveys of legal research. Forschungsstand. Fortschrittsberichte

993.6 History
Class here works on recent history and development of civil law beginning ca. 1850
For works on the law prior to 1850 see KK394+

993.8 War and emergency legislation

993.9 Criticism. Reform. Rechtserneuerung. Polemik
For works pertaining exclusively to the codes see KK985.49+

994 Congresses. Conferences

995 Collected works (nonserial)

Civil law. Bürgerliches Recht -- Continued

997 General works. Treatises

Including compends, outlines, examination aids, popular works, form books, addresses, essays, lectures, and including single essays, collected essays of several authors, Festschriften, Vorlesungen, etc.

1000.A-Z Works for particular groups of users, A-Z

1000.A36 Aged. Older people. Retired persons

Older people see KK1000.A36

Retired persons see KK1000.A36

1000.T3 Tax consultants

Concepts and principles. Allgemeiner Teil

1001-1010 General (Table K9c)

Ethics (Morality of law). Public policy see KK887+

Chicanery and abuse of rights see KK887.7

Equity see KK888

Presumption see KK945.P73

Publicity see KK945.P92

Vis major see KK945.V58

Persons

1011 General (Table K11)

Natural persons

Personality. Rechtsfähigkeit

1012 General works

Birth

1013 General works

1013.3 Unborn children. Nasciturus

Death

1013.5 General works

1014 Missing persons. Presumption of death. Verschollenheit. Todesvermutung

1015 Declaration and certification of death. Definition of death. Todeserklärung und Totenschein

Civil register see KK4087+

Civil death see KK8270

Capacity and incapacity. Geschäfts- und Deliktsfähigkeit. Geschäftsungfähigkeit

Including liability

For civil disability see KK8270

1016 General (Table K11)

Minors. Unmündige

1016.5 General (Table K11)

1017 Majority. Declaration of majority. Volljährigkeit

Limited capacity. Beschränkte Geschäftsfähigkeit und Deliktsfähigkeit

1018 General works

1018.2.A-Z Special topics, A-Z

Civil law. Bürgerliches Recht
Concepts and principles. Allgemeiner Teil
Persons
Natural persons
Capacity and incapacity. Geschäfts- und Deliktsfähigkeit. Geschäftsungfähigkeit
Minors. Unmündige
Limited capacity. Beschränkte Geschäftsfähigkeit und Deliktsfähigkeit
Special topics, A-Z -- Continued

1018.2.D44 Delicts
1018.2.L32 Labor contract. Arbeitsmündigkeit
1018.2.M37 Marriage. Ehemündigkeit
1018.5 Women
Class here works on legal status in both private and public law
1019 Insane persons. People with mental disabilities. Geisteskranke und Geistesschwache (Table K11)
For institutional care of the mentally ill see KK6226
Unborn children. Nasciturus see KK1013.3
1019.3 Prodigals
Interdiction (Entmündigung) see KK1244+
1019.5 Domicile. Wohnsitz
1019.7 Citizenship. Staatsbürgerschaft
For aliens see KK6050+
Personality rights. Persönlichkeitsrechte
1020 General works
1022 Allgemeines Persönlichkeitsrecht
1022.5 Life. Body. Health
Freedom see KK1955
Name
1023 General (Table K11)
1024 Change of name. Namensänderrung (Table K11)
1024.5 Title of nobility. Adelsprädikat
Including coat of arms
Dignity, honor, and reputation see KK1962+
Privacy see KK1965+
Intellectual property see KK2712.P47
Protection of personality rights see KK1923+
Juristic persons of private law. Juristische Personen des Privatrechts
For business corporations see KK2448+
For juristic persons of public law see KK5807+
1026 General (Table K11)
1027 Personality. Rechtsfähigkeit (Table K11)
1028 Capacity. Ultra vires. Geschäftsfähigkeit

Civil law. Bürgerliches Recht
Concepts and principles. Allgemeiner Teil
Persons
Juristic persons of private law. Juristische Personen des Privatrechts -- Continued

1028.5 Personality rights
For protection of personality rights see KK1923+
1029 Liability
Associations. Vereinsrecht
1031 General (Table K11)
Eingetragener rechtsfähiger Verein. Incorporated society
Including profit and nonprofit corporations
1032 General (Table K11)
1032.3 Constitution. Dissolution
1032.5 Registration
1033 Directors. Executive boards
1034 Membership
1035 Liability
Including tort and criminal liability of officers (Organhaftung)
1035.5.A-Z Other, A-Z
1035.5.C65 Consolidation and merger. Verschmelzung
Disciplinary measures see KK1035.5.P45
1035.5.P45 Penalties. Disciplinary measures
Nichteingetragener Verein. Unincorporated society
1036 General (Table K11)
1036.5 Liability
Including tort and criminal liability of officers (Organhaftung)
Foundations. Charitable trusts and uses. Endowments. Stiftungsrecht
Including selbständige und unselbständige Stiftungen
1037 General (Table K11)
1038.A-Z Individual foundations. By name, A-Z
1038.C37 Carl-Zeiss-Stiftung
1038.V65 Volkswagenwerk, Stiftung
1039.A-Z Particular kinds of foundations, A-Z
1039.F35 Family foundations
1039.R44 Religious foundations. Kirchliche Stiftungen
Fiscus see KK5853.5
Things. Sachen
1041 General (Table K11)
1042.A-Z Classes of things, A-Z
1042.A66 Appurtenances. Zubehör
Civil fruits see KK1042.F68
1042.C65 Consumer goods. Verbrauchbare Sachen

Civil law. Bürgerliches Recht
Concepts and principles. Allgemeiner Teil
Things. Sachen
Classes of things, A-Z -- Continued
Corpse see KK1042.R48
1042.E52 Encumbrances. Lasten
1042.E58 Entities. Sachgesamtheiten
1042.E92 Exchangeable things. Vertretbare Sachen
1042.F59 Fixtures. Inventar
Including domestic, agricultural, and trade fixtures
1042.F68 Fruits. Früchte und Nutzungen
Government property see KK1042.R48
1042.I53 Individual things. Einzelsachen
1042.I535 Indivisible things. Unteilbare Sachen
Money see KK1042.E92
Natural fruits see KK1042.F68
Nutzungen see KK1042.F68
1042.P37 Parts (constituent and essential). Bestandteile und wesentliche Bestandteile
1042.R48 Res extra commercium
Res publicae. Res communes omnium see KK1042.R48
Res sacrae see KK1042.R48
Securities see KK1042.E92
Rights. Rechte. Künftige Rechte
1044 General works
1044.5 Gestaltungsrechte
1045 Immaterial rights. Immaterialgüterrecht
Legal documents see KK945.L44
Legal transactions. Rechtsgeschäfte
1047 General (Table K11)
1047.5 Legal status. Rechtsstellungen
1048 Juristic acts. Rechtmässige Handlungen
Including transactions, quasi-transactions (rechtsgeschaftsahnliche Handlungen), acts, and events (Tathandlungen, Realakte)
De facto contracts (Faktische Verträge) see KK1664
For contracts see KK1640+
1049 Illegal and unlawful acts. Rechtswidrige Handlungen
For delicts and torts see KK1922+
1050 Unilateral acts. Einseitige Rechtsgeschäfte
1051 Inter vivos and mortis causa. Transactions
1051.5 Gratuitous and onerous transactions. Entgeltliche und unentgeltliche Zuwendungen
1052 Nondelegatable transactions. Hochstpersönliche Rechtsgeschäfte
1053 Power to dispose. Verfügungsgewalt

Civil law. Bürgerliches Recht
Concepts and principles. Allgemeiner Teil
Legal transactions. Rechtsgeschäfte -- Continued
Declaration of intention. Willenserklärung
1054 General (Table K11)
1055 Reliance theory. Will theory
1055.5 Private autonomy
1056 Interpretation
1057 Mental reservation. Simulation. Mangelnde Ernstlichkeit. Vorbehalt. Scheingeschäft
1057.5 Silence
Error see KK1063.5
1060 Fraud. Duress. Arglist. Tauschung. Drohung
Cf. KK8690+ Criminal law
1061 Form requirements. Notice. Time of effectiveness
Void and voidable transactions. Nichtige und anfechtbare Rechtsgeschäfte
Including void and voidable contracts
1063 General works
1063.5 Error. Irrtum (Table K11)
Immoral transactions. Unconscionable transactions. Sittenwidrige Rechtsgeschäfte
Including mortis causa
1064 General works
1065.A-Z Special topics, A-Z
1065.R47 Requirement contracts and other contracts limiting contractual freedom. Knebelverträge
1065.U88 Usury. Wucher
1066 Part nullity. Teilnichtigkeit
Umdeutung nichtiger Rechtsgeschäfte see KK1056
1068 Restraints of alienation. Veräusserungsverbote
Including statutory, official, and contractual restraints
1069 Consent. Zustimmung
Agency. Stellvertretung
Including statutory agency (gesetzliche Stellvertretung)
1070 General (Table K11)
Authorized representation. Vertreter mit Vertretungsmacht
1071 General works
1071.3 To whom it may concern. Für wen es angeht
1071.5 Receiving or delivering of declaration. Erklärungsstellvertreter
1072 Unauthorized representation. Falsus procurator. Vertreter ohne Vertretungsmacht
1073 Subsequent authorization
1074 Agent for both contracting parties. Selbstkontrahieren
1075 Indirect agency. Mittelbare Stellvertretung

Civil law. Bürgerliches Recht
Concepts and principles. Allgemeiner Teil
Legal transactions. Rechtsgeschäfte
Agency. Stellvertretung -- Continued

1076 Liability
Including both agent and falsus procurator

Power of attorney. Vollmacht
Including Anscheinsvollmacht und Duldungsvollmacht

1078 General (Table K11)
1078.2 General discretionary power of attorney. Generalvollmacht
1078.3 Delegation
1078.4 Power of attorney given in case of death
1079 Form requirements. Forms
1080 Expiration and termination. Cancellation

Mandate. Auftrag

1081 General (Table K11)
1082 Liability

Negotiorum gestio. Geschäftsbesorgung

1083 General (Table K11)
1084.A-Z Special topics, A-Z
1084.A73 Architects
1084.A88 Attorneys
1084.H68 House management. Hausverwaltung
1085 Liability for counseling. Haftung für Auskunft, Rat, Empfehlung, etc.

Negotiorum gestio without mandate. Geschäftsführung ohne Auftrag

1086 General (Table K11)
1087.A-Z Special topics, A-Z
1088 Secured transactions. Security. Sicherheitsleistung
Class here general works
For particular secured transactions, see the transaction, e.g., KK1360+ Hypothecation; KK1382+ Pledges; KK1886 Suretyship; etc.

Fiduciary transactions. Trust and trustee. Treuhand

1089 General (Table K11)
1090 Liability

Charitable trusts see KK1037+

Contracts see KK1640+

Conditions. Bedingungen

1090.5 General (Table K11)
1091 Suspensive conditions. Aufschiebende Bedingungen
1091.5 Resolutory conditions. Auflösende Bedingungen
1092 Retroactivity. Rückwirkung

Time periods see KK945.T55

Limitation of actions. Verjährung

Civil law. Bürgerliches Recht
Concepts and principles. Allgemeiner Teil
Limitation of actions. Verjährung -- Continued
1093 General (Table K11)
1094 Delay. Hemmuing und Unterbrechung
1095.A-Z Special topics, A-Z
1095.D55 Dilatory and peremptory pleas. Einwendungen
Exercise of rights. Protection of rights
1096 General works
1097 Self-defense. Notwehr
Cf. KK8090+ Criminal law
1098 Necessity. Notstand
1099 Assistance in emergencies. Aufopferung. Nothilfe
Domestic relations. Family law. Familienrecht
For the federal department for family and children see KK3560
1100 History
Class here works on recent history and development of the law beginning ca. 1850
For works on the law prior to 1850 see KK412+
1100.5 Criticism. Reform
1101-1110 General (Table K9c)
1112 Constitutional guaranties
Marriage. Eherecht
1118 History
Class here works on recent history and development of the law beginning ca. 1850.
For works on the law prior to 1850 see KK413+
1120 Criticism. Reform
1121 General (Table K11)
Constitutional guaranties see KK1112
1122 Betrothal. Verlöbnis (Table K11)
Marriage impediments. Ehehindernisse
1123 General works
1124.A-Z Individual impediments, A-Z
1124.A36 Adoption
1124.A38 Adultery
1124.A43 Affinity. Schwägerschaft
Bigamy see KK1124.E94
1124.C65 Consanguinity. Blutsverwandtschaft
1124.E84 Eugenics
1124.E94 Existing marriage bond. Bigamy
Jewish question see KK1124.R32
Miscegenation see KK1124.R32
1124.R32 Race. Miscegenation. Jewish question
1124.W34 Waiting period for widow. Wartestand
1125 Premarital examinations. Marriage banns. Aufgebot

Civil law. Bürgerliches Recht
Domestic relations. Family law. Familienrecht
Marriage. Eherecht -- Continued
Performance of marriage
1126 Civil marriage. Standesamtliche Eheschliessung
Registration see KK4105
Marital (religious) rites (Kirchliche Eheschliessung) see KBR and KBU
Marriage bond. Persönliches Eherecht
1128 General works
1129 Conjugal community. Eheliche Lebensgemeinschaft
1130 Domicile. Household. Häusliche Gemeinschaft (Table K11)
1131 Family name
Legal status of married women. Stellung der Frau in Ehe Familie
1132 General (Table K11)
1133 Minors. Unmündige
Equal rights. Emancipation and decision-making. Gleichberechtigung
Cf. KK5142+ Constitutional law
1134 General (Table K11)
1135 Work and occupations of marital partners
1136 Management of household and transactions. Schlüsselgewalt
1137 Mutual support (Table K22)
1138 Liability
Defective or dissolved marriage
1139 General works
1140 Non-marriage. Nichtehe
1141 Marriage void ab initio. Annulment ex tunc. Nichtige Ehe
1142 Voidable marriage. Annulment ex nunc. Aufhebbare Ehe
Including mistake, misrepresentation, threats (duress), false presumption and declaration of death, etc.
1143 Improper form of ceremony
Divorce. Scheidung
1146 General (Table K11)
1147.A-Z Individual grounds for divorce, A-Z
1147.A38 Adultery
1147.D58 Disruption of conjugal relations. Ehewidriges Verhalten
1147.F45 Felony
Mental illness see KK1147.S52
1147.M88 Mutual agreement
1147.S52 Sickness. Mental illness

Civil law. Bürgerliches Recht
Domestic relations. Family law. Familienrecht
Marriage. Eherecht
Defective or dissolved marriage
Divorce. Scheidung -- Continued

1148 Reconciliation (Condonation). Verzeihung
Procedure. Divorce suits
1150 General (Table K11)
1151.A-Z Special topics, A-Z
1151.D35 Damages
1151.F38 Fault. Verschuldensprinzip
1151.N49 New trial
1151.R48 Res judicata
Effects of divorce
1152 General works
1152.2 Name of divorced wife. Forfeiture of marital (husband's) family name
1152.3 Alimony. Disclaimer (Table K11)
1154 Separation
1155 Settlement of claims from defective or dissolved marriages (Table K11)
Cf. KK4122 Distribution of household after divorce
1159 Quasi-matrimonial relationships. Concubinage. Wilde Ehe (Table K11)
Matrimonial property and regime. Ehegüterrecht und Güterstände
1162 General (Table K11)
Statutory regimes. Gesetzliche Güterstände
1163 General works
1164 Replacement by antenuptial agreement and transactions mortis causa
1165 Contractual regimes. Antenuptial agreement. Freedom of contract. Ehevertrag
Management and usufruct by husband. Ehemännliche Verwaltung und Nutzniessung
1167 General (Table K11)
1168.A-Z Special topics, A-Z
1168.B35 Bankruptcy of husband
1168.B88 Business enterprise of wife
1168.L59 Inventory of estate by wife
1168.M67 Mortgage of wife
1169 Separation of property. Gütertrennung
Community of property. Gütergemeinschaft
1170 General (Table K11)
1173 Continued community of property. Fortgesetzte Gütergemeinschaft

Civil law. Bürgerliches Recht
Domestic relations. Family law. Familienrecht
Matrimonial property and regime. Ehegüterrecht und Güterstände
Community of property. Gütergemeinschaft -- Continued
1174 Community of income and property. Errungenschaftsgemeinschaft
1175 Community of movable property. Fahrnisgemeinschaft
Zugewinngemeinschaft
1176 General (Table K11)
1177 Restraint of power of disposition. Verfügungsbeschränkung
Matrimonial property register see KK4117
1180.A-Z Special topics, A-Z
Bankruptcy see KK1180.E93
1180.C42 Change of marital regime during marriage
Creditor see KK1180.D42
1180.D42 Debtor and creditor
1180.E93 Executions. Bankruptcy
1180.R46 Restraints on alienation
Marriage, church, and state. Religiöses Eherecht
1182 General works
Catholic (Canon) marriage law see KBR ; KBU
Protestant marriage law see KBX
Jewish marriage law see KBM
Mixed marriages
Catholic-Protestant see KBR ; KBU
Jewish-Christian see KBM ; KBR ; KBU
1183 Secular (civil) marriage law and ecclesiastical law
Consanguinity and affinity. Verwandtschaft und Schwägerschaft
1185 General (Table K11)
1186 Support (Table K11)
1187 Family
Parent and child. Elternrecht
1189 General (Table K11)
1190 Constitutional guaranties
Child welfare see KK3556+
Paternity see KK1226+

Civil law. Bürgerliches Recht
Domestic relations. Family law. Familienrecht
Consanguinity and affinity. Verwandtschaft und Schwägerschaft
Parent and child. Elternrecht -- Continued
Legitimate children. Eheliche Kinder
Including children from defective marriages, divorced marriages, legitimized children from subsequent marriages, etc.

1192 General (Table K11)
1193 Human rights of the child
1194 Citizenship of children
1195 Legal status of children during and after divorce
1196 Legal status of children from void marriages
1197 Legitimation of children by subsequent marriages
1198 Legitimation of children by declaration of legitimacy. Ehelichkeitserklärung
1199 Avoidance of legitimacy of children. Ehelichkeitsanfechtung
Parental power. Elterliche Gewalt
1200 General (Table K11)
1201 Equal rights of parents. Mutual agreements
1202 Religion. Choice of denomination
1202.5 Visitation rights
Custody. Personensorge
1203 General works
1204 Agency
1205 Misuse. Negligence. Abuse
Education see KK6266+
Custodial education see KK3573+
1206 Property management. Verwaltung und Nutzniessung
1207 Support. Dowry
Parental power of mother
1208 General (Table K11)
Illegitimate children see KK1224
Guardianship court see KK4130+
1210 Stepchildren. Stiefkinder
Adoption. Annahme an Kindes Statt
1212 General (Table K11)
1213 Consent of natural parents
For procedure see KK4126
1214.A-Z Special topics, A-Z
1214.A36 Adoption of adults
Inter-country adoption of children see KK968.F35
Illegitimate children. Uneheliche Kinder
1216 General (Table K11)

Civil Law. Bürgerliches Recht
Domestic relations. Family law. Familienrecht
Consanguinity and affinity. Verwandtschaft und Schwägerschaft
Parent and child. Elternrecht
Illegitimate children. Uneheliche Kinder
Human rights of the child see KK1193
Citizenship of children see KK1194
1219 Legal status
1220 Right of name
1222 Support
1223 Inheritance and succession
Parental power of mother
1224 Custody. Agency
Affiliation. Paternity. Vaterschaft
Illegitimate children
1226 General works
1227 Procedure in paternity suits. Vaterschaftsklagen
1228 Support
Artificial insemination
Cf. KK6229.A78 Public health
Cf. KK8422 Criminal law
1229 General works
1230 Constitutional aspects
Guardian and ward. Vormundschaftsrecht
1232 General (Table K11)
1233 Care for ward. Agency
1234 Property management
Guardianship courts see KK4130+
Government guardianship see KK3571
Guardianship over minors
1236 General (Table K11)
1237 Education
Including religious education
1239 Property management. Legal investment
Guardianship over adults
1242 General (Table K11)
Interdiction. Entmündigung
1244 General (Table K11)
1245.A-Z Special topics, A-Z
1245.A42 Alcoholics
1245.M45 Mentally ill
1245.P76 Prodigals
Curatorship. Pflegschaft
1247 General (Table K11)
1248 Curatorship for helpless (frail) adults. Gebrechlichkeitspfleger

Civil law. Bürgerliches Recht -- Continued
Property. Law of things. Sachenrecht
1250 History
Class here works on recent history and development of the law beginning ca. 1850
For works on the law prior to 1850 see KK433+
1251-1260 General (Table K9c)
Right of property. Constitutional guaranty
1261 General works
1261.5 Social obligation. Sozialpflichtigkeit
General principles
Things see KK1041+
1262 Abstraktionsprinzip. Dinglichkeit
Possession. Besitz
1263 General (Table K11)
Types of possession
1264 General works
1264.2 Actual (immediate) possession. Unmittelbarer Besitz
1264.3 Possession by virtue of agency. Besitzdienerschaft
1264.4 Joint possession. Mitbesitz
1264.6 Possession of owner. Eigenbesitz
1264.7 Derivative possession. Fremdbesitz
1264.8 Possession of rights. Rechtsbesitz
Acquisition and transfer of possession
1265 General (Table K11)
1266 Intent to possess. Besitzwille
1267 Brevi manu traditio. Übergabe kurzer Hand
1267.5 Constitutum possessorium. Besitzmittlungsverhältnis
1268 Assignment of chose in possession. Abtretung de Herausgabeanspruches
Violation of possession. Besitzstörung
1269 General (Table K11)
1270 Dispossession. Besitzenzug
1272 Possessory actions. Besitzschutzklagen
Ownership. Eigentum
1275 General (Table K11)
Right of ownership see KK1261+
Acquisition and loss of ownership
1276 General (Table K11)
Occupancy. Aneignung
1277 General (Table K11)
Abandoned and derelict things. Herrenlose Sachen
Game see KK6681+
Fish see KK6695+
Bees see KK6674
1278 Wrecks
1279 Lost property. Fund

Civil law. Bürgerliches Recht
Property. Law of things. Sachenrecht
Ownership. Eigentum
Acquisition and loss of ownership -- Continued
1280 Treasure troves. Schatzfund
Accessions
1281 General works
1282 Annexation (incorporatio). Verbindung
Including incorporation in inventory (Einverleibung)
1283 Confusion (confusio, commixtio). Vermischung
1284 Specification. Verarbeitung
1285 Acquisition of fruits and parts of things
1286 Prescription. Ersitzung
1287 Succession. Erbgang
Contractual acquisition
Dingliche Einigung
1289 General works
Conditions. Bedingte Einigung
1290 General works
1291 Retention of ownership. Eigentumsvorbehalt
Cf. KK1714 Sale
Fiduciary transfer of ownership see KK1397+
1292 Expectancies. Anwartschaftsrecht
Tradition. Übergabe
1294 General works
1295 Constitutum possessorium. Besitzkonstitut
1296 Assignment of chose in possession. Abtretung des Herausgabeanspruches
1297 Acquisition bona fide. Gutglaubensschutz
1298 Acquisition by agent
Acquisition of a business enterprise see KK2085
1300 Judicial sale
Loss of ownership
1302 Abandonment. Dereliction
Expropriation see KK5769+
Co-ownership. Miteigentum
Including Bruchteilseigentum and Gesamthandseigentum
1304 General (Table K11)
1305 Housing cooperatives
Condominium and horizontal property see KK1340
Claims and actions resulting from ownership. Ansprüche aus dem Eigentum
1306 General works
1307 Rei vindicatio. Herausgabeanspruch

Civil law. Bürgerliches Recht
Property. Law of things. Sachenrecht
Ownership. Eigentum
Claims and actions resulting from ownership. Ansprüche aus dem Eigentum -- Continued
1308 Actio negatoria. Nuisances. Abwehrklage
For particular nuisances see KK1338.A+
For ecological aspects of regional planning, e.g. Immissionsschutz see KK6138
Liability of possessor. Haftung des Besitzers
Including bona fide and mala fide possessor
1310 General works
1311 Damages
Rights and defenses of possessor
Including bona fide and mala fide possessor
1311.5 General works
1312 Payment for improvements. Verwendungsersatz
1313 Removal of fixtures
Real property. Liegenschaftsrecht
1315 General (Table K11)
Land registration law see KK1410+
Public and private restraint on real property
1318 General works
Sozialbindung des Eigentums see KK1261.5
Eminent domain see KK5769+
Land reform and land policy legislation see KK6130+
Zoning laws see KK6145
Homestead law. Soziales Siedlungsrecht. Heimstättenrecht
Including agricultural colonies, workinging class dwellings, pensioners' low cost housing, etc. (Landwirtschaftliche Siedlung, Kleinsiedlungswesen, Beamaten- und Rentnerheimstätten)
1321 General (Table K11)
1322 Preemption rights
Entail see KK6613+
Entailed estates of the greater nobility. Fideicommissum see KK454+
Workers' gardens see KK6627
Ownership
1323 General works
Acquisition and loss of ownership
Occupancy see KK1277+
Prescription see KK1413
Succession see KK1287
Contractual acquisition
Dingliche Einigung. Auflassung

Civil law. Bürgerliches Recht
Property. Law of things. Sachenrecht
Real property. Liegenschaftsrecht
Ownership
Acquisition and loss of ownership
Contractual acquisition
Dingliche Einigung. Auflassung -- Continued

1324 General works

Conditions. Bedingte Einigung

1325 General works

1327 Expectancies. Anwartschaftsrecht

Cf. KK1398 Pledges

Registration see KK1410+

Form requirements see KK1427

Judicial sale see KK1425

Loss of ownership

Abandonment see KK1302

1329 Judicial decree. Aufgebotsverfahren

1330 Expropriation

For procedure see KK5778

Co-ownership see KK1304+

Rights incident to ownership of land

1331 General works

1332 Air and space above ground. Aeronautics

1333 Underground. Minerals, metals, and other resources

Cf. KK6706.2+ Mining law

1334 Riparian rights. Water rights. Underground water

Cf. KK6096 Public property

1335 Animals and fish. Game and fishing rights

Cf. KK6681+ Game laws

Cf. KK6695+ Fishery laws

Law of adjoining landowners. Nachbarrecht

1337 General (Table K11)

1338.A-Z Special topics, A-Z

1338.A59 Anwenderecht. Kehr- oder Tretrecht

1338.B68 Boundaries. Building across boundaries. Party walls

1338.E29 Eaves-drip. Trauf

Hammerschlag- und Leiterrecht see KK459.H35

1338.L54 Light or window rights. Licht- und Fensterrecht

Mining rights see KK6710

1338.N84 Nuisances. Nachbarliche Einwirkungen

Including fumes, heat, noise, smoke, and odor

1338.O83 Overhang. Overfall. Überhang. Überfall

Including fumes, heat, noise, smoke, and odor

Party walls see KK1338.B68

Pflugrecht see KK1338.A59

Civil law. Bürgerliches Recht
Property. Law of things. Sachenrecht
Real property. Liegenschaftsrecht
Ownership
Rights incident to ownership of land
Law of adjoining landowners. Nachbarrecht
Special topics, A-Z
1338.P82 Public enterprises
1338.T39 Taverns
1338.W38 Water laws
1338.W39 Way by necessity. Notwegrecht
Types of real property
1340 Condominium. Horizontal property. Wohnungseigentum. Stockwerkseigentum (Table K11)
Rentenguter see KK336.5.E885
Ships. Schiffe. Schiffsbauwerke
1342 General (Table K11)
Ship registers see KK2282
Ship mortgages see KK2275
Maritime liens see KK2276
Superficies. Erbbaurecht
1344 General (Table K11)
1345.A-Z Special topics, A-Z
1345.R45 Rent. Erbbauzins
1345.R49 Reversion. Heimfall
Rights as to the use and profits of another's land
1346 General (Table K11)
Fief see KK317+
Superficies see KK1344+
1347 Emphyteusis. Erbpachtrecht (Table K11)
Servitudes. Dienstbarkeiten
1348 General (Table K11)
Real servitudes. Grunddienstbarkeiten
1349 General works
1350.A-Z Special types, A-Z
1350.O85 Owners real servitudes. Eigentümergrunddienstbarkeit
1350.R48 Restraint of trade
1350.R54 Right of way
For Notwegrecht see KK1338.W39
Personal servitudes. Persönliche Dienstbarkeiten
1351 General works
Limited personal servitudes. Beschränkt persönliche Dienstbarkeit
1352 Right of habitation. Wohnrecht
Reallast

Civil law. Bürgerliches Recht
Property. Law of things. Sachenrecht
Real property. Liegenschaftsrecht
Rights as to the use and profits of another's land
Servitudes. Dienstbarkeiten
Personal servitudes. Persönliche Dienstbarkeiten
Reallast -- Continued

1353 General works
Altenteil see KK6615.C65
Usufruct. Niessbrauch
1355 General (Table K11)
1356.A-Z Particular, A-Z
1356.C65 Commercial enterprise
1356.E88 Estate and inheritance
Inheritance see KK1356.E88
1356.R54 Rights
1356.T44 Things
1357 Right of pre-emption. Vorkaufsrecht (Table K11)
Hypothecation. Grundpfandrechte
1360 General (Table K11)
Mortgage. Hypotheca
1362 General (Table K11)
Types of mortgages
1363 Buchhypothek
1364 Briefhypothek
1364.5 Owners' mortgage. Eigentümerhypothek
Verkehrshypothek
1365 General works
1366 Tilgungshypothek. Amortisationshypothek
Sicherungshypothek
1367 General works
1368 Blanket mortgage with a stated maximum. Höchstbetragshypothek
1369 Zwangs- und Arresthypothek
Ship mortgages see KK2275
Aircraft mortgage see KK1395
1370 Mortgage for claims from negotiable instruments. Wertpapierhypothek
1372 Gesamthypothek
Erbhofhypothek see KK6613+
1373.A-Z Special topics, A-Z
1373.A32 Accessority
1373.A66 Appurtenances
1373.C65 Condominium
1373.C73 Creation
1373.C87 Currency reforms
1373.D55 Dilatory and peremptory pleas. Einwendungen

Civil law. Bürgerliches Recht
Property. Law of things. Sachenrecht
Hypothecation. Grundpfandrechte
Mortgage. Hypotheca
Special topics, A-Z -- Continued

1373.D83 Due date of payment
1373.G66 Good faith
1373.I58 Interest
Mortgage on destroyed property see KK1373.R84
1373.P74 Priority. Rang
Registration see KK1419+
1373.R84 Ruins. Mortgage on destroyed property. Ruinenhypothek

Land charge. Grundschuld
1375 General (Table K11)
Types of land charges
1376 Owners' land charge. Eigentümergrundschuld
1377 Sicherungsgrundschuld
1378.A-Z Special topics, A-Z
1378.B94 Building loans
1380 Rent charge. Rentenschuld

Pledges. Pfandrechte an beweglichen Sachen und Rechten
1382 General (Table K11)
Contractual pledges
Pledges of personal property. Fahrnispfand
1384 General (Table K11)
1385 Possessory pledge. Faustpfand. Besitzpfand (Table K11)
1386 Nonpossessory pledge. Besitzloses Pfandrecht
1387.A-Z Special topics, A-Z
1387.A32 Accessority
1387.B34 Bailment. Verwahrung
1387.E35 Einigung
Pawnbrokers see KK6815.P39
1387.P74 Priority. Rang
1387.P76 Protection of the right
1387.P82 Publicity
1387.T72 Tradition
Pledges of rights. Pfandrecht an Rechten
1389 General (Table K11)
1390.A-Z Special topics, A-Z
Bonds see KK1390.S42
1390.C46 Choses in action. Forderungen
1390.E86 Expectancies. Anwartschaftsrechte
1390.J64 Joint tenancy. Co-ownership. Gesamthand
1390.S42 Securities. Bonds. Stocks

Civil law. Bürgerliches Recht
Property. Law of things. Sachenrecht
Pledges. Pfandrechte an beweglichen Sachen und Rechten
Contractual pledges
Pledges of rights. Pfandrecht an Rechten
Special topics, A-Z -- Continued
Stocks see KK1390.S42
1392 Lien or statutory pledge. Gesetzliches Pfandrecht
Pfändungspfandrecht see KK4211
Registerpfandrechte
1393 General (Table K11)
1394 Cable. Kabelpfandrecht
Security for agricultural credits see KK6640
1395 Aircraft mortgage
Ship mortgages see KK2275
Transfer of ownership as security. Sicherungsübereignung
1397 General works
1398 Expectancies. Anwartschaftsrecht
1400.A-Z Special topics, A-Z
1400.A88 Assignment of choses in action. Forderungsabtretung
Bankruptcy see KK1400.E83
1400.E83 Execution and bankruptcy
1400.I45 Immoral transactions
1400.P47 Personal property
1400.S52 Shares and shareholders' rights
Criminal law see KK9212
Land register and registration. Grundbuchrecht
1410 General (Table K11)
1411 Principles
Including Eintragungsprinzip, Konsensprinzip, Rangprinzip, and Publizitätsprinzip
Publicity. Offentlicher Glaube des Grundbuches
1412 General works
1413 Prescription by registration. Buchersitzung
Divisions of the land register. Grundbuchabteilungen
1415 General works
1416 Regional division
1417 Realfolium and personalfolium
Courts and procedure. Formelles Grundbuchrecht
Including judges (Grundbuchrichter)
1419 General (Table K11)
1420 Application
1422 Principle of legality
Entry. Eintrag

Civil law. Bürgerliches Recht
Property. Law of things. Sachenrecht
Land register and registration. Grundbuchrecht
Courts and procedure. formelles Grundbuchrecht
Entry. Eintrag -- Continued
1423 General works
1424 Consent. Bewilligung
1425 Entry ex officio
Including injunctions (Einstweilige Verfügungen), bankruptcy, judicial sale (Versteigerung), Sicherungshypotheken, etc.
1426 Registration of future rights to secure priority or right. Vormerkung
1427 Form requirements
1428.A-Z Special topics, A-Z
1428.A28 Abschreibung und Zuschreibung
1428.P37 Partition. Landaufteilung
Parzellierung see KK1428.P37
Zuschreibung see KK1428.A28
Remedies
1430 General works
1431 Correction (rectification) ex officio
1432 Entry of objection. Widerspruch
Effect of registration. Materielles Grundbuchrecht
1433 General works
Creation of rights in land
1434 General works
Ownership in land
1435 General works
Dingliche Einigung see KK1324+
Conditions and expectancies see KK1325+
1436.A-Z Other, A-Z
1436.C42 Change or extinction of rights
1436.P74 Priority of rights. Rangverhältnisse
1437 Cadastral surveys. Cadaster. Vermessungswesen. Kataster
Class here general works on surveying and surveying agencies
For an individual surveying agency of the state or locality (Landesvermessungsamt. Vermessungsamt), see the state or locality
Inheritance. Succession upon death. Erbrecht
1440 History
Class here works on recent history and development of the law beginning ca. 1850
For works on the law prior to 1850 see KK485+
1441-1450 General (Table K9c)

Civil law. Bürgerliches Recht
Inheritance. Succession upon death. Erbrecht -- Continued
1451 Right of inheritance. Constitutional guaranty
1452 Testamentary succession. Gewillkürte Erbfolge
1454 Intestate succession. Gesetzliche Erbfolge
Inheritance. Estate. Nachlass
1455 General works
1456 Particular estates or parts
Entail see KK6613+
Fideicommissum see KK454+
Heirs
1457 General works
1458 Acceptance and disclaimer of inheritance. Annahme und Ausschlagung (Table K11)
Joint heirs. Co-heirs. Miterben
1459 General (Table K11)
1460 Community of heirs. Miterbengemeinschaft
Distributive share in estate. Miterbenanteil
1462 Transfer. Attachment and garnishment
1463 Hotchpot liability. Ausgleichspflicht
Limited and reversionary heir see KK1472
Liability
1464 General works
1465 Debts of estate. Nachlassverbindlichkeiten
1466 Possessor of an inheritance. Erbschaftsbesitzer
Wills. Testaments
1467 General (Table K11)
1468 Freedom of testation. Testierfreiheit
1469.A-Z Types of wills, A-Z
1469.B88 Businessmen's testament. Unternehmertestament
1469.H65 Holographic will. Private will
1469.J64 Joint will. Gemeinsames Testament
1469.M88 Mutual will. Gegenseitiges Testament
1469.N68 Notarized will. Will declared before judge. Offentliches Testament
Nuncupative will see KK1469.P74
Private will see KK1469.H65
1469.P74 Privileged wills
Including wills of sailors, military personnel, etc.
Appointment of heir. Erbeinsetzung
1471 General works
1472 Limited and reversionary heir. Vorerbe und Nacherbe
1472.5 Form requirements
1473 Void and voidable wills. Immoral conditions
Including error
1475 Opening of the testament

Civil law. Bürgerliches Recht
Inheritance. Succession upon death. Erbrecht
Wills. Testaments
Appointment of heir. Erbeinsetzung -- Continued
1476 Legacy. Testamentary burden. Distribution of estate. Vermächtnis. Auflagen. Teilungsanordnung
1477 Revocation. Widerruf
1478 Executors and administrators
Including Testamentvollstrecker, Nachlassverwalter, Nachlasspfleger, etc.
Contract of inheritance. Erbvertrag
1480 General (Table K11)
1481 Statutory portion. Pflichtteil (Table K11)
1482 Renunciation of inheritance. Erbverzicht
1483 Unworthiness of heirs. Disinheritance. Erbunwurdigkeit. Enterbung
1485 Purchase of inheritance. Erbschaftskauf
1486 Certificate of inheritance. Proof of heirship. Erbschein
1487 Gift causa mortis. Zuwendungen unter Lebenden auf den Todesfall
1488 Fiscus as heir
Inheritance tax see KK7360
Obligations. Schuldrecht
1490 History
Class here works on recent history and development of the law beginning ca. 1850
For works on the law prior to 1850 see KK497+
1491-1500 General (Table K9c)
Debtor and creditor. Chose in action and obligation. Schuldverhaltnis
1502 General (Table K11)
1503 Schuld und Haftung. Debitum (duty to perform) and obligatio (liability to enforcement)
Including history
Plurality of debtors and creditors. Joint obligations. Mehrheit von Gläubigern und Schuldnern
1505 General (Table K11)
Divisibility of obligation see KK1527
Correality and solidarity. Gesamtschuldverhältnis
1508 General (Table K11)
1510 Solidary obligation. Joint and several obligation. Gesamtschuld (echte und unechte)
Community by undivided shares see KK1876+
1512 Gesamthandschuldverhältnis (Table K11)
1514 Community of creditors. Gläubigergemeinschaft
1516 Community of debtors. Schuldnergemeinschaft
1518 Multiplicity of obligations. Schuldenhäufung

Civil law. Bürgerliches Recht
Obligations. Schuldrecht -- Continued
Types of obligations
1520 Civil and natural obligations
Cf. KK1880+ Aleatory contracts
Obligation to give
1521 General works
Obligation in kind. Gattungsschulden
1522 General works
Money obligations see KK1556+
1524 Obligation to do or to refrain from doing. Verpflichtung zu Handlung oder Unterlassung
1525 Alternative and optional obligations. Wahlschuld
1526 Obligation without liability. Nichtvertretbare Schulden
1527 Divisible and indivisible obligations. Teilbare und unteilbare Schulden
1528 Principle and accessory obligations
Conditional obligation see KK1090.5+
Transfer and assumption of obligations
1529 General works
1530 Assignment of chose in action. Forderungsabtretung
Including future claims
1532 Collection. Inkassomandat. Einziehungsermächtigung
Assumption of debts. Schuldübernahme
1534 General works
1535 Hypothekenübernahme
1536 Vermögensübernahme
Extinction of obligation. Erlöschen des Schuldverhältnisses
1540 General (Table K11)
Performance. Payment. Erfüllung. Zahlung
1542 General (Table K11)
1543 Observance. Verkehrssitte
1543.2 Due date of payment. Fälligkeit
1544 Place of performance. Erfüllungsort
Time of performance. Erfüllungszeit
1545 General works
1546 Futures. Fixgeschäft
Default see KK1603+
1547 Part performance. Teilleistung
1548 Performance through third party
1549 Special modes of performance
e.g. Zug um Zug
1550 Leistung erfüllungsstatt and erfüllungshalber
1552 Consignation. Hinterlegung
Including emergency sale of perishables (Selbsthilfeverkauf)

Civil law. Bürgerliches Recht
Obligations. Schuldrecht
Extinction of obligation. Erlöschen des Schuldverhältnisses
Performance. Payment. Erfüllung. Zahlung -- Continued

1553 Substituted performance. Surrogat
Special rules as to payment of money debts
1556 General (Table K11)
1557 Gold clause. Valuta clause. Foreign currency debts
Cf. KK7095+ Foreign exchange control
1558 Escalator clause. Anpassungsklausel. Gleitklausel
1559 Revalorization of debts. Währungsreform
Cf. KK7094 Public finance
1560 Interest rate. Zinssatz
For usury see KK8732+
1561 Noncash payments. Bargeldlose Zahlung
1562 Receipt. Acknowledgement. Quittung
1563 Compensation for maintenance and improvement. Aufwendungsersatz
1564 Exoneration. Befreiungsanspruch
1564.5 Enforcement. Schuldhaft
Defective performance see KK1580+
1565 Liens. Zurückbehaltungsrecht
For liens of landlord see KK1766
For commercial liens see KK2147+
1566 Compensation. Set-off. Aufrechnung
1567 Confusion of rights. Vereinigung von Forderung und Schuld
Tender of payment and consignation see KK1552
1569 Novation. Abänderungsvertrag und Schuldumschaffung
1570 Remission of debt. Schulderlass
Rescission. Rücktritt
Including reservation of rescission, contractual rescission, and statutory recission
1572 General works
Rebus sic stantibus clause see KK1654
1574 Withdrawal. Cancellation. Widerruf. Küundigung
1575 Contractual discharge. Aufhebungsvertrag
1576 Expiration and termination. Zeitablauf
1577 Achievement of purpose. Zweckerreichung
1578 Resolution. Occurrence of resolutory condition. Auflösung
Exoneration see KK1564
Nonperformance. Leistungsstörungen
1580 General (Table K11)
Culpa. Verschuldenslehre

Civil law. Bürgerliches Recht
Obligations. Schuldrecht
Nonperformance. Leistungsstörungen
Culpa. Verschuldenslehre -- Continued
1582 General (Table K11)
1583 Dolus. Vorsatz
Negligence. Gross negligence. Fahrlässigkeit und grobe Fahrlässigkeit
1584 General works
1585 Diligentia quam suis rebus
1586 Haftung für Erfüllungsgehilfen
1588 Culpa in contrahendo (Table K11)
Breach of contract. Positive Forderungsverletzung
1592 General (Table K11)
1593 Synallagmatic contracts
1595 Dauerschuldverhältnisse
Impossibility of performance. Unmöglichkeit der Leistung
1597 General (Table K11)
1598 Distinction between inability to perform (Unvermögen) and default
Including debtor and creditor
1599 Original impossibility. Anfängliche Unmöglichkeit
1600 Supervening impossibility. Nachträgliche Unmöglichkeit
Default. Verzug
1603 General (Table K11)
Distinction between impossibility of performance and default see KK1598
Damages. Schadensersatzrecht
1610 General (Table K11)
1611 Liability
Class here general works, including works comparing various sources of liability
For contractual liability see KK1580+
For tort liability see KK1941+
For strict liability see KK1949+
Causation
1612 General (Table K11)
1613 Conditio-sine-qua-non theory. Bedingungslehre (Äquivalenzlehre)
1614 Adequate causation. Adäquater Zusammenhang
1615 Remote and proximate cause. Mittelbare und überholende Kausalität
1619 Positives Interesse
1620 Negatives Interesse
1622 Specific restitution. Naturalherstellung
1623 Folgenbeseitigung

Civil law. Bürgerliches Recht
Obligations. Schuldrecht
Damages. Schadensersatzrecht -- Continued

1624 Lost profits. Entgangener Gewinn
1625 Cash payments
Damages for pain and suffering. Schmerzensgeld
1627 General (Table K11)
1628.A-Z Specific damages, A-Z
1628.N48 Neuroses
Substituted performance see KK1553
Adjustment of claims. Schadensberechnung
1630 General works
1632 Contributory and comparative negligence. Eigenes Verschulden und Mitverursachung
1634 Balance. Vorteils- und Schadensausgleich
1635 Damages as counterplea
1636.A-Z Special topics, A-Z
Compensation to or indemnification of victims of crimes see KK5792.V52
1636.S82 Subrogation. Anspruchsabtretung
1636.T54 Third parties. Schadensliquidation im Drittinteresse

Contracts. Vertragsrecht
1640 General (Table K11)
Types of contracts
1642 Unilateral contract
1643 Bilateral (synallagmatic) contract
1644 Incomplete bilateral contract
1646 Consensual contract and real contract
1647 Kausaler und abstrakter Vertrag
1648 Onerous and gratuitous contracts. Entgeltlicher und unentgeltlicher Vertrag
1649 Pactum de contrahendo. Preliminary contracts. Vorvertrag
Atypical or mixed contracts
1650 General works
Contract concerning delivery of beer see KK1830
Contract concerning service stations see KK1832
Computer service and maintenance contract see KK1855.C65
Contract by implied consent see KK1664
Standardized terms of contract see KK1670
1653 Option
Good faith see KK945.G66
1654 Clausula rebus sic stantibus. Fehlen und Wegfall der Geschaftsgrundlage
1655 Liberty of contract. Vertragsfreiheit
For standardized terms of contract see KK1670

Civil law. Bürgerliches Recht
Obligations. Schuldrecht
Contracts. Vertragsrecht -- Continued

1657 Party autonomy
Cf. KK1055.5 Legal concepts and principles
1658 Fides. Vertragstreue
Formation of contract
Including preliminary contract (Vorvertrag)
1660 General (Table K11)
Offer and acceptance. Antrag und Annahme
1661 General works
1662 Contracts through correspondence, telephone, teletype, wire, etc.
1663 Unordered merchandise by mail. Zusendung unbestellter Waren
Cf. KK2811 Unfair competition
1664 Implied consent. De facto contract. Vertragsschluss durch sozialtypisches Verhalten
Clauses
1665 General (Table K11)
Clausula rebus sic stantibus see KK1654
1666 Taxation clause
Conditions see KK1090.5+
1667 Contractual penalties. Vertragsstrafen
Warranty see KK1698+
1668 Earnest. Draufgage
1669 Pactum de non petendo. Release. Convenant not to sue
1670 Standardized terms of contracts. Normierter Vertrag (Table K11)
Including Formularvertrag, Typenvertrag, Allgemeine Geschäftsbedingungen, Allgemeine Lieferbedingungen
1672 Stipulation (Table K11)
Formalities
1674 General (Table K11)
Formation by telephone, teletype, wire, etc. see KK1662
Parties to contract
1680 General works
Third parties
1682 Third party beneficiary. Vertrag zu Gunsten Dritter
1683 Limitation of liability of third party. Haftungsbeschränkung und Ausschluss zu Gunsten Dritter
1684 Schutzwirkung zu Gunsten Dritter
Void and voidable contracts see KK1063+

Civil law. Bürgerliches Recht
Obligations. Schuldrecht
Contracts. Vertragsrecht -- Continued
Breach of contract see KK1592+
Discharge of contract see KK1542+
1685 Effect of retroactive legislation on contract
1686 Effect of market orders and price controls on contracts
Individual contracts and obligations
Sale. Kauf
Cf. KK2096+ Commercial law
1690 General (Table K11)
1692 Risk. Gefahrtragung
1693 Impossibility. Unmöglichkeit
Including supervening impossibility
Default. Verzug
1694 General works
1695 Mora accipiendi. Annahmeverzug
1696 Malperformance. Schlechterfüllung
Warranty. Gewährleistung
1698 General (Table K11)
1699 Infirmity of title. Rechtsmängel
1700 Existence of right or chose in action
Defects of goods sold
1701 General (Table K11)
1703 Bettering. Nachbesserung
1704 Wandelung
1705 Minderung
1706 Damages. Compensation
1707 Rescission. Rücktritt
1708 Avoidance. Anfechtung
1710 Liability of manufacturer. Haftung von Warenherstellern und Warenvertrieb (Table K11)
Modes of sale
Conditional sale. Vorbehaltskauf
1713 General (Table K11)
1714 Retention of ownership and expectancies. Eigentumsvorbehalt und Anwartschaftsrechte
Cf. KK1291 Ownership
1715 Installment plans. Ratenzahlung
Including installment payments through commercial finance companies
1716 Warranty. Gewährleistung
1717 Execution
1719 Sale in kind (species). Gattungskauf
1721 Sale after approval. Kauf nach Probe
1722 Sale on approval. Kauf auf Probe
1724 Retractive purchase. Wiederkauf

Civil law. Bürgerliches Recht
Obligations. Schuldrecht
Individual contracts and obligations
Sale. Kauf
Modes of sale -- Continued

1725 Preemption. Vorkauf
1726 Self-service. Selbstbedienungskauf
Commodities (goods) for sale
Automobiles (new or used) see KK2105.A88
Cattle
1730 General works
1732 Conditional sale
1733 Warranty
1734.A-Z Other, A-Z
Bauherrenmodelle see KK1734.5.R43
1734.C65 Computers
1734.H67 Horses
1734.5.A-Z Atypical or mixed contracts, A-Z
1734.5.R43 Real estate development. Bauherrenmodelle
1735 Exchange. Barter. Tausch
For exchange of apartments see KK1791+
1737 Donations. Gifts. Schenkungen
For dispositions mortis causa see KK1487
1739 Aestimatum. Trödelvertrag
Consignment see KK2108+
Lease. Landlord and tenant. Mietrecht
1740 History
Class here works on recent history and development of the law beginning ca. 1850
For works on the law prior to 1850 see KK525
1741-1745.8 General (Table K10)
Formation of contract
1746 General works
Clauses and terms
1747 Standardized terms of contract. Deutscher Einheitsmietvertrag
1748 Heating
1749 Keeping of domestic animals
Parties to contract
1760 Landlord and tenant
1761 Subtenants
1762 Third parties
Rights and claims from lease contract
Including subtenant
1763 Rent. Mietzins
For rent control see KK1816
For rent subsidies see KK3448

Civil law. Bürgerliches Recht
Obligations. Schuldrecht
Individual contracts and obligations
Lease. Landlord and tenant. Mietrecht
Rights and claims from lease contract -- Continued

1764 Compensation for improvements by tenant. Verwendungsanspruch und Wegnahmeanspruch
1765 Delivery after termination of lease. Herausgabe der Mietsache
1766 Liens of landlord. Zurückbehaltungsrechte
Termination of lease. Beendigung des Mietverhaltnisses
1767 Sale does not effect lease. Kauf bricht nicht Miete
1769 Expiration. Zeitablauf
1770 Rescission. Rücktritt
Notice. Kündigung
1772 General works
1773 Social clause
Protection of the tenant. Mieterschutz. Kündigungsschutz
For Mieteinigungämter see KK1778+
1775 General (Table K11)
1776.A-Z Particular kinds of tenants, A-Z
1776.A37 Air raid victims. Fliegergeschädigte
Lease litigation and execution. Mietstreitrecht
Including procedure at regular civil courts and special tribunals (Mieteinigungsämter)
1778 General (Table K11)
1779 Remedies
1780 Deadlines for vacating. Räumungsfristen
Eviction. Forced vacating. Räumung
Including subtenant
1781 General works
1782 Protection against claims enforcement. Vollstreckungsschutz
Types of property
Real property. Grundstücksmiete
1784 General works
1785 Co-ownership and lease
1786 Lease of partition
Buildings. Rooms. Raummiete
1789 General works
1790 Commercial space. Geschäftsraummiete
Housing. Apartments. Wohnraummiete. Wohnungswirtschaft
Including exchange of apartments (Wohnungstausch)

Civil law. Bürgerliches Recht
Obligations. Schuldrecht
Individual contracts and obligations
Lease. Landlord and tenant. Mietrecht
Types of property
Buildings. Rooms. Raummiete
Housing. Apartments. Wohnraummiete.
Wohnungswirtschaft -- Continued

1791-1795.8 General (Table K10)

Emergency housing measures. Wohnungsnotrecht und Wohnraumzwangswirtschaft

1801-1805.8 General (Table K10)

Public subsidies for reconstruction

1806 General (Table K11)

1807 Special premiums for savings at building and loan associations. Prämienbegünstigung für Bausparer

1808 Tax exemptions and deductions for home building

Private subsidies

1809 General works

1810 Building subsidies from future tenant. Baukostenzuschüsse

Including lost (verlorene) and deductible (abwohnbare) subsidies

1811 Advance payment of annual rent. Mietvorauszahlung

1813 Rationing and distribution of housing. Wohnraumbewirtschaftung

For social housing see KK1822

1816 Rent control. Mietpreisbindung (Table K11)

Including subtenant (Untermieter)

1818 Lifting of controls and emergency measures. Abbau und Aufhebung der Wohnraumzwangswirtschaft

Social measures. Soziales Mietrecht

1821 General (Table K11)

1822 Publicly subsidized housing. Sozialwohnungen

Rent subsidies see KK3448

1824.A-Z Housing provided for particular groups, A-Z

Civil servants see KK5952

1824.E46 Employees and laborers. Werkdienstwohnungen. Werkmietwohnungen

1824.F37 Farmworkers

Laborers see KK1824.E46

Civil law. Bürgerliches Recht
Obligations. Schuldrecht
Individual contracts and obligations
Lease. Landlord and tenant. Mietrecht
Types of property
Buildings. Rooms. Raummiete
Housing. Apartments. Wohnraummiete. Wohnungswirtschaft
Social measures. Soziales Mietrecht
Housing provided for particular groups, A-Z -- Continued

1824.M55 Miners

1825 Commercial and industrial property
Including operating leasing, producer leasing (Herstellerleasing), etc.

Atypical or mixed contracts

1826 Investment leasing. Finanzierungsleasing
Including sale-and-lease-back, Industrieanlagenvertrag, etc.
Commercial and industrial leasing see KK1825
Farm and farm equipment leasing see KK6624+

1830 Perpetual delivery of beer and lease of space and equipment. Bierlieferungsvertrag

1832 Service stations. Tankstellenvertrag

Pacht (Ground lease)

1836 General (Table K11)

Types of property
Rural property see KK6624+
Fisheries see KK6696
Pharmacies see KK6198

1838 Restaurants. Cafeterias. Gaststättenpacht. Kantinenpacht

1840 Loan for use. Commodatum. Leihe

Personal loans. Mutuum. Darlehenvon Geld oder vertretbarer Sachen
Cf. KK2224+ Commercial law

1841 General (Table K11)

Interest rate see KK1560
Clauses see KK1556+
Securities

1841.5 General works

1841.6 Lombard. Vinkulationsgeschäft

1842 Bonds. Schuldschein

Contracts of service and labor. Master and servant. Dients- und Arbeitsvertragsrecht

1844 General (Table K11)

Civil law. Bürgerliches Recht
Obligations. Schuldrecht
Individual contracts and obligations
Contracts of service and labor. Master and servant.
Dients- und Arbeitsvertragsrecht -- Continued

1845 Difference between contract of service and contract for work and labor
Dienstbesorgungsvertrag see KK1081+
Independent work. Professions. Dienste höherer Art
1846 General works
1847.A-Z Particular professions and services, A-Z
Architect see KK1084.A73
Attorney see KK1084.A88
1847.E96 Executives
Management of house or estate see KK1084.H68
(1847.M85) Musicians
see KK6357+
1847.P49 Physician. Arzt
Dependent work. Abhängige Arbeit
1848 General works
1849 Servants. Gesinderecht (Table K11)
Employees. Labor contract see KK2870+
1852.A-Z Particular groups, A-Z
Apprentices see KK6832
Civil servants see KK5930+
Merchant mariners see KK2290+
Contract for work and labor. Werkvertrag
1854 General (Table K11)
1855.A-Z Particular contracts, A-Z
Building contracts. Bauverträge see KK6788
1855.C65 Computer contracts
Geschäftsbesorgung see KK1083+
1855.I53 Information retrieval
1855.M48 Metal work. Metallumarbeitung
1855.R46 Repairing
1855.R47 Research and development contracts
1855.T72 Transportation contracts
Including travel contracts and package tours (Pauschalreisen)
1857 Liability and warranty
Including damages, bettering, Wandelung, and Minderung
1858 Risk. Gefahrtragung
1859 Security. Liens
Brokerage see KK2110+
1862 Reward. Award. Auslobung
Mandat see KK1081+

Civil law. Bürgerliches Recht
Obligations. Schuldrecht
Individual contracts and obligations -- Continued
1864 Deposit. Verwahrung (Table K11)
Including depositum irregulare
Cf. KK2232 Banking
1866 Bailment and liens of innkeepers. Verwahrung und Zurückbehaltungsrechte der Gastwirte
Civil companies. Gesellschaft Bürgerlichen Rechts
For associations see KK1031+
For personal companies and stock companies see KK2435+
1868 General works
1869 Formation of contract
1870 De facto company. Faktische Gesellschaft
1872 Assets. Gesellschaftsvermögen
1873 Termination. Liquidation. Befristung. Auflösung
Community by undivided shares. Gemeinschaft
1876 General works
1877 Partition
1878 Life annuity. Leibrente (Table K11)
Cf. KK6615.C65 Agriculture
Aleatory contracts. Natural obligations
1880 General (Table K11)
1882 Gambling. Betting
1883 Lotteries
1884 Futures
Marriage brokers' fees see KK2112.M37
Suretyship. Bürgschaft
Including special forms such as Nachbürgschaft, Rückbürgschaft, Ausfallbürgschaft, Kredit- und Höchstbetragsbürgschaft, Zeitbürgschaft, Selbstschuldnerische Bürgschaft, Mitbürgschaft, etc.
1886 General (Table K11)
1887 Liability
1888 Accessority
1889 Guaranty contract. Garantievertrag
1890 Mandatum crediti. Kreditauftrag
Schuldmitübernahme see KK1534+
1892 Compromise. Vergleich (Table K11)
Promise of debt. Promissory note. Schuldversprechen
1894 General (Table K11)
1895 Causa
Acknowledgment of debt. Schuldanerkenntnis
1897 General (Table K11)
1898 Causa

Civil law. Bürgerliches Recht
Obligations. Schuldrecht
Individual contracts and obligations -- Continued
1905 Discovery (Disclosure). Vorlegung von Sachen. Rechnungslegung
For poor debtor's oath see KK4194
Unjust enrichment. Ungerechtfertigte Bereicherung. Kondiktionenrecht
1907 General (Table K11)
1908 Performance. Leistung
1909 Sine causa. Without cause. Rechtsgrundlosigkeit
1910 Transaction. Vermögensverschiebung
1911 Enrichment. Bereicherung
1912 Subrogation
1914 Restitution. Rückerstattung
1916 Unjust enrichment as counterplea. Einrede der ungerechtfertigten Bereicherung
Delicts. Torts. Unerlaubte Handlungen. Deliktsrecht
1922 General (Table K11)
Protected rights. Rechtsgüter
1922.5 General works
Personality rights. Persönlichkeitsrechte
1923 General works
1923.5 Constitutional aspects
Freedom see KK1955
Life, body, and health see KK1022.5
Name see KK1023+
Integrity see KK1962+
Privacy see KK1965+
1925 Privacy of communication
For secrets in general see KK1966
For trade and industrial secrets see KK2827.T72
For violation of confidential disclosure see KK8494
For letters see KK8496
1927 Property
1928 Business enterprise. Eingerichteter Gewerbebetrieb
Parties to action in torts
1930 General works
1932 Principal. Accessories
1933 Joint tortfeasors
Illegality. Widerrechtlichkeit
1935 General works
Justification grounds. Ausschluss der Widerrechtlichkeit. Rechtfertigungsgründe
1936 General works
1937 Standard of conduct. Sozialadäquates Verhalten
1938 Privilege. Wahrnehmung berechtigter Interesse

Civil law. Bürgerliches Recht
Obligations. Schuldrecht
Delicts. Torts. Unerlaubte Handlungen. Deliktsrecht
Illegality. Widerrechtlichkeit
Justification grounds. Ausschluss der Widerrechtlichkeit. Rechtfertigungsgründe -- Continued

1939 Self-defense. Self-help
1940 Consent of the injured party. Einwilligung

Liability. Haftung für Verschulden

1941 General works
1942 Dolus
1943 Negligence. Aggravated negligence. Foresight
1945 Liability for torts of others
Including Respondeat superior doctrine

Exclusion of liability. Haftungsausschluss

1946 Contractual agreement excluding liability
1947 Assumption of risk by injured. Handeln auf eigene Gefahr
1948 Tacit (implied) agreement. Stillschweigende Vereinbarung

Strict liability. Gefährdungshaftung
For strict liability related to particular dangers or risks, see the topic

1949 General (Table K11)
1950 Inherent danger. Betriebsgefahr
1951 Procedure. Haftpülichtprozess

Individual torts

1955 Violation of freedom. Beeinträchtigung der Freiheit (Table K11)

Physical injuries

1957 General (Table K11)
1958 Accidents (Table K11)
For particular types of accidents, see KK1982+, Sports accidents; KK2002, Traffic accidents; KK2026.S34, Playground accidents, etc.

(1959) Malpractice (Medical)
see KK6208+

1959.5 Wrongful life
1960 Death by wrongful act

Violation of integrity. Schädigung des Ansehens
Including honor, dignity, and reputation

1962 General (Table K11)
1963 Libel and slander

Violation of privacy. Verletzung der Intimsphäre

1965 General (Table K11)
1966 Secrets in general. Geheimnisbereich

Civil law. Bürgerliches Recht
Obligations. Schuldrecht
Delicts. Torts. Unerlaubte Handlungen. Deliktsrecht
Individual torts
Violation of privacy. Verletzung der Intimsphäre -- Continued

1967 Right in one's own picture. Recht am eigenen Bilde
1968 Public opinion polls. Meinungsforschung
1968.5 Personal data in information retrieval systems. Schutz personenbezogener Daten
Including public and private records, registers, statistics, etc.

Immoral transactions and acts. Sittenwidrige Handlungen
1969 General (Table K11)
Abuse of rights in general see KK887.7
1970 Exceptio doli. Allgemeine Arglisteinrede
1972 Deceit. Misrepresentation. Forgery. Betrug. Urkundenfälschung

Breach of contract. Interference with contractual relations see KK1592+
Enticement see KK2828.E58
Industrial espionage see KK2828.E86

Ultrahazardous activities and occupations
1976 General works
1977 Power lines
1978 Nuclear reactors. Nuclear damages

Sports. Sport fields or installations
1982 General (Table K11)
1984.A-Z Particular torts, A-Z
1984.M68 Mountaineering accidents
1984.S54 Skiing accidents

Liability for safe traffic conditions and accidents. Verkehrshaftpflicht
1987 General (Table K11)
1988 Railroads and streetcars. Eisenbahn und Strassenbahn
1994 Aviation. Flugverkehr (Table K11)
Automotive transportation and road traffic. Kraftverkehr
2000 General (Table K11)
2002 Liability for accidents of owner and/or driver
Cf. KK2414+ Liability insurance (Automobiles)

Liability for safe conditions of streets, highways, public places, etc. Verkehrssicherungspflicht
2008 General (Table K11)
2010 Traffic signs

Civil law. Bürgerliches Recht
Obligations. Schuldrecht
Delicts. Torts. Unerlaubte Handlungen. Deliktsrecht
Individual torts
Liability for safe conditions of streets, highways, public places, etc. Verkehrssicherungspflicht -- Continued
2012 Snow removal. Sanding of streets. Streupflicht
2014 Blackouts. Verdunklung
Violation of official duties. Amtspflichtverletzung. Beamtenhaftung
Cf. KK5786+ Government liability
2020 General (Table K11)
2022.A-Z Special topics, A-Z
2022.J83 Judges
2022.P68 Postal employees
2024 Liability for environmental damages (Table K11)
For environmental crimes see KK8879+
2026.A-Z Other liabilities, A-Z
2026.A54 Animals. Tierhalterhaftung
2026.B84 Buildings, Liability for
Including public buildings
2026.C65 Construction sites, Liability for
2026.N84 Nuisance
Playground accidents see KK2026.S34
Public buildings see KK2026.B84
2026.S34 School and playground accidents, Liability for. Schul- und Spielplatzunfälle
Commercial law. Handelsrecht
2038 History
Class here works on recent history and development of commercial law beginning ca. 1850
For works on the law prior to 1850 see KK560+
2039 Criticism. Reform. Rechtserneuerung. Polemik
2041-2057 General (Table K9a)
Commercial courts see KK3207
Kammer für Handelssachen see KK3678
Merchant and business enterprise. Handelsstand und Handelsgewerbe
2061 General (Table K11)
2062 The merchant. Kaufmann (Table K11)
Business names. Firma. Firmenrecht
Including Internet domain names
2063 General works
2064 Registration
2065 Liability
2066 Transfer and succession
2067 Goodwill

Commercial law. Handelsrecht
Merchant and business enterprise. Handelsstand und Handelsgewerbe -- Continued
Domicile. Sitz des Gewerbes
2068 General works
2069 Branches. Zweigniederlassung. Nebengewerbe
Auxiliary personnel. Kaufmännische Hilfspersonen
2070 General (Table K11)
2072 Competition. Konkurrenzverbot
Including trade secrets
Cf. KK2827.T72 Unfair competition
2073.A-Z Special personnel, A-Z
2073.A66 Apprentices. Handlungslehrlinge
2073.C53 Clerks. Handlungsgehilfen
Accounting. Handelsbücher
Including inventory (Bilanz. Rechnungslegung)
2074 General (Table K11)
2075 Electronic data processing
2076 Liquidation. Liquidationsbilanz
Tax accounting see KK7138+
Agency and prokura. Stellvertretung und Handlungsvollmacht
2078 General (Table K11)
Commercial agents. Handelsvertreter
2079 General (Table K11)
2080 Legal status, salaries, etc
2081 Liens
Commercial registers. Handelsregister
2083 General (Table K11)
Publicity see KK4085
2085 Sale of business enterprise as a whole. Veräusserung und Übertragung von Gewerbebetrieben
Commercial transactions. Handelsgeschäfte
2086 General (Table K11)
2087 Presumption of commercial nature
2088 Protection of good faith. Rechtsschein und Publizitätsprinzip
Including publicity
2089 Observance. Handelsbrauch
Formation of contract
2090 General works
2092 Invoice. Bestätigungsschreiben
2093 Liability. Sorgfalt und Haftung
2094 Formalities. Informality
Sale. Handelskauf
2096 General (Table K11)

Commercial law. Handelsrecht
Commercial transactions. Handelsgeschäfte
Sale. Handelskauf -- Continued
Examination of goods sold and prompt filing of claim. Untersuchungs- und Rügepflicht
2097 General works
2098 Emergency sale of perishables. Notverkauf
2099 Default of buyer
2100 Consignation. Hinterlegung
2101 Franchises. Franchisingvertrage
2102 Futures. Fixgeschätt
2103.A-Z Special modes of selling, A-Z
2103.S76 Stores
2103.T73 Traveling salesmen. Handlungsreisende
Vending machines see KK6808.V45
2105.A-Z Particular products or goods, A-Z
2105.A88 Automobiles (new or used)
Cattle see KK1730+
Used automobiles see KK2105.A88
Commercial agents see KK2079+
Consignment. Commission merchant. Kommissiongeschäft
2108 General (Table K11)
2109 Liability
Brokerage. Handelsmakler
2110 General (Table K11)
2112.A-Z Types of brokers, A-Z
2112.M37 Marriage brokers. Ehemakler
2112.R42 Real estate agents. Immobilienmakler
2114 Auctioneers. Versteigerer. Auctions (Table K11)
Warehousing. Lagergeschäft
2118 General (Table K11)
2119 Warehouse receipt. Lagerschein
Freight forwarders and carriers. Speditions- und Frachtrecht
Including carriage of passengers and goods
For regulatory (administrative) aspects see KK6897+
2121 General (Table K11)
2123 Liability
2124 Bill of lading. Ladeschein. Frachtbrief
2126 Liens. Zurückbehaltungsrecht. Pfandrecht des Spediteurs
2128 Insurance
2130 Delivery
Types of carriers
For regulatory (administrative) aspects see KK6868+
2132 Railroads (Table K11)

Commercial law. Handelsrecht
Commercial transactions. Handelsgeschäfte
Freight forwarders and carriers. Speditions- und Frachtrecht
Types of carriers
Railroads -- Continued
2135 Liability for freight claims (Table K11)
2136 Passenger carriers. Bus lines. Personbeförderung (Table K11)
2138 Trucklines. Güterkraftverkehr (Table K11)
Including Fernverkehr and Nahverkehr
2139 Liability for freight claims
Airlines. Airfreight. Luftfracht
2142 General (Table K11)
2143 Liability for freight claims
2144 Airline creditors. Aircraft mortgages
2145 Aircraft registration. Luftfahzeugrolle (Table K11)
Carriage by sea see KK2260+
Commercial instruments see KK2150+
Commercial liens. Kaufmännische Zurückbehaltungsrechte
2147 General works
Freight forwarder liens see KK2126
Negotiable instruments. Titles of credit. Wertpapiere
Including Rekta-, Order-, Inhaber-, Legitimations- und Traditionspapiere
2150 General (Table K11)
2151 Theory
Including Kreationstheorie, Vertragstheorie und Rechtscheintheorie
2155 Possession, ownership, and transfer
Including electronic data processing
2157 Liability
2159 Legitimation and identification
Bills of exchange. Wechsel
2162 General (Table K11)
2164 Negotiability. Verkehrsfähigkeit
2168.A-Z Special topics, A-Z
2168.A22 Acceptance. Annahme
2168.B22 Blanks
2168.C52 Clauses
Including Avis-, Deckungs-, Valutaklausel
2168.D43 Defenses, Real and personal. Einwendungen
2168.D58 Dishonor
2168.E34 Eigener Wechsel
2168.E53 Endorsement. Indossament
Including pledge and procura endorsement

Commercial law. Handelsrecht
Commercial transactions. Handelsgeschäfte
Negotiable instruments. Titles of credit. Wertpapiere
Bills of exchange. Wechsel
Special topics, A-Z -- Continued

2168.L52 Liability
Including drawer, acceptor, and endorser
2168.P39 Payment and return of instrument
2168.P76 Prolongation. Contango
2168.P765 Protest
2168.R42 Recourse. Regress. Rückgriff
2168.S97 Suretyship. Wechselbürgschaft
2168.U54 Unjust enrichment
2168.V64 Void and voidable bills
Procedure see KK3987
Stamp duties see KK7309+
Checks. Schecks
Including Inhaber- oder Namensscheck, Verrechnungs- oder Zahlungsscheck
2173 General (Table K11)
2174.A-Z Special topics, A-Z
2174.A22 Acceptance
2174.C35 Cancellation
2174.D72 Drawer
Postscheck see KK6959.P68
Letters of credit see KK2224+
Stock certificates and bonds see KK2474+
Trust investments see KK2254
Bills of lading (Land transportation) see KK2124
Maritime bills of lading see KK2264
Warehouse receipts see KK2119
2180 Mercantile order. Kaufmännische Anweisung
Including order of civil law
Promissory notes see KK1894+
2182 Bearer negotiable instruments. Schuldverschreibung auf den Inhaber
Criminal provisions see KK8868
2188 Banking. Stock exchange. Bankrecht. Börsenrecht (Table K11)
Including regulation of the banking business
2189 State supervision. Staatsaufsicht
2190 Accounting. Auditing
2191 Management. Directors
Types of banks and credit institutions
Banks of issue
2192 General works
2193 Reichsbank

Commercial law. Handelsrecht
Commercial transactions. Handelsgeschäfte
Banking. Stock exchange. Bankrecht. Börsenrecht
Types of banks and credit institutions
Banks of issue -- Continued
2194 Deutsche Rentenbank
Deutsche Bundesbank
Previously Bank Deutscher Länder
2195 General (Table K11)
Money see KK7090+
Discount policy
2196 General works
2197 Discount rate
2199 Kreditanstalt für Wiederaufbau
2200 Foreign banks
2201 Mortgage banks. Hypothekenbanken (Table K11)
Savings banks. Sparkassen
Including public and private banks
2203 General (Table K11)
2204 State supervision
Types of savings programs
2205 Special premiums. Prämiensparen
Investment savings see KK2245+
2206.A-Z Special topics, A-Z
2206.C73 Credit. Loans
Identification see KK2206.L44
2206.I58 Interest
2206.L44 Legitimation. Identification
2206.L5 Liability
Loans see KK2206.C73
2206.S39 Savings books
2208 Criminal provisions
Postsparkassen see KK6959.P69
2210 Building and loan associations. Bausparkassen (Table K11)
2212 Cooperatives. Kreditvereine
2214 Clearinghouses
2216 Warehouses
Banking transactions
2217 General works
2218 Security of deposits. Einlagensicherung
2220 Banking secret. Confidential communication. Bankgeheimnis
2221 Liability. Haftung und Sorgfaltspflicht

Commercial law. Handelsrecht
Commercial transactions. Handelsgeschäfte
Banking. Stock exchange. Bankrecht. Börsenrecht
Banking transactions -- Continued

2222 Contract
Including standardized terms of contract (Allgemeine Bankbedingungen) and clauses (e.g., storno clause, etc.)

Deposits see KK2232

Loans. Credit

2224 General (Table K11)

2225 Contract. Krediteröffnungsvertrag (Table K11)

2226 Interest rate
For usury see KK8732+

2227.A-Z Special types of loans, A-Z
Subarrange each by Table K12

2227.C65 Consumer credit. Small loans. Kleinkredit (Table K12)
Including credit cards

2227.C73 Credit by acceptance of bills of exchange. Akzeptkredit

2227.D62 Documentary evidence. Dokumenten-Akkreditiv

2227.I47 Import credit

Small loans see KK2227.C65

2229 Suretyship. Guaranty. Bankgarantien

Deposit banking. Depotgeschaft

2230 General (Table K11)

2232 Deposits. Custodianship accounts
Including Sonderverwahrung, Sammeldepot, Stückekonto, Stückeverzeichnis, etc.

2234 Trading of securities. Effektenhandel. Effektengiroverkehr
Including electronic data processing

2235 Supervision. Depotprüfung

2236 Criminal provisions

2237 Stockholders voting through bank holding stocks in deposit. Depotstimmrecht der Banken

2239 Discount

2240 Consortium. Konsortialgeschäft der Banken
Cf. KK2598+ Combinations. Industrial trusts

2242 Account current. Kontokorrent

2243 Collecting of accounts. Einzugsverfahren

Noncash funds transfer. Bargeldloser Zahlungsverkehr
Including electronic funds transfer

2244 General (Table K11)

2244.5 Bill paying services. Drafts. Lastschriftverkehr. Überweisungen

Commercial law. Handelsrecht
Commercial transactions. Handelsgeschäfte
Banking. Stock exchange. Bankrecht. Börsenrecht -- Continued
Investments
For tax measures see KK7120

2245 General (Table K11)
Foreign investments see KK6433
Stock exchange transactions. Securities
2247 General (Table K11)
2248 Stockbrokers
2248.5 Investment advisors
2249.A-Z Particular stock exchanges. By place, A-Z
2249.F72 Frankfurt stock exchange
Futures trading. Futures transactions
2249.2 General (Table K11)
2249.5 Commodity exchanges. Produce exchanges
Investment trust. Investmentgesellschaft
2250 General (Table K11)
2252 Real estate investment trust. Immobilienfondsgesellschaft
2254 Trust investments
2254.5 Criminal provisions (Table K11)
Including money laundering
2255 Foreign exchange. Devisengeschäft
Taxation of banking transactions see KK7306.B35
Taxation of stock exchange transactions see KK7306.S76
Maritime law. Seehandelsrecht
For regulatory aspects of water transportation, navigation, and pilotage see KK6927+
2256 General (Table K11)
Shipowners. Ship operators. Reeder und Reederei
2257 General works
2258 Liability
2259 Shipmasters. Kapitäne
Affreightment. Carriage of goods at sea and inland waters
2260 General (Table K11)
2262 Liability (General)
2263 Freight forwarders
2264 Ocean bills of lading. Konossoment
2265 Charter parties
2266 Act of God. War. Act of government
2267 Carriage of passengers at sea and inland waters
Including carriage of passengers' luggage
Average. Haverei

Commercial law. Handelsrecht
Commercial transactions. Handelsgeschäfte
Maritime law. Seehandelsrecht
Average. Haverei -- Continued

2268 General (Table K11)
2269 Havarie grosse
Special average. Collision at sea
Cf. KK6927+ Water transportation
2270 General works.
2271 Criminal provisions
Insurance see KK2285+
Salvage. Shipwreck
2272 General (Table K11)
2273 Criminal provisions
Ship creditors
2274 General (Table K11)
2275 Bottomry and respondentia. Ship mortgages
2276 Maritime liens
2277 Priority of claims
2278 Executions
2280 Shipbrokers. Schiffsmakler
2282 Ship registers
Admiralität see KK4690
2283 Maritime courts. Seeämter. Oberseeamt (Table K11)
Marine insurance. Seeversicherungsrecht
2285 General (Table K11)
2286 Contract
Including standardized terms of contract, policies, etc.
2287 Accidents. Average
2288 Seaworthiness
Maritime social insurance
Including legislation for merchant mariners for inland navigation
2289 General (Table K11)
Labor law for merchant mariners
2290 General (Table K11)
2291 Collective labor agreements. Maritime unions
Labor standards
2291.5 General works.
2292 Hours of labor
2293 Wages. Nonwage benefits
2294 Vacations
2295 Discipline
Social insurance
2296 General (Table K11)
2297 Health insurance (Table K11)
Including Seekrankenkassen

Commercial law. Handelsrecht
Commercial transactions. Handelsgeschäfte
Maritime law. Seehandelsrecht
Maritime social insurance
Social insurance -- Continued
2298 Workers' compensation (Table K11)
Including Seeberufsgenossenschaft
Insurance law. Privatversicherungsrecht. Versicherungswirtschaftsrecht
Including regulation of insurance business
2301-2310 General (Table K9c)
Insurance carriers. Versicherungsträger
2311 General works
2312 Institution of public law. Offentliche Anstalt
Private insurance associations. Private Versicherungsgesellschaften
Including cooperatives, mutual companies, etc.
2313 General (Table K11)
State supervision
2314 General (Table K11)
2316 Monopolies. Control of restraint of trade. Versicherungs-Kartellrecht
Standardized terms of contract see KK2320+
Contract
Including standardized terms of contract (Allgemeine Versicherungsbedingungen)
2320 General (Table K11)
Parties to contract
Including third parties
2322 General works
2324 Respondeat superior doctrine
2325 Liability
2327 Limitation of risk. Risikoabgrenzung
2329 Insurance policy
2330 Group insurance
Adjustment of claims. Schadensregelung
2333 General (Table K11)
2334 Regress
2335 Balance. Vorteils- und Schadensausgleich
2337 Agents. Brokers
Life insurance
2339 General (Table K11)
2340 Companies. Finance
2341 Parties
Including third parties
2342 Group insurance
2344 Old age pensions

Commercial law. Handelsrecht
Commercial transactions. Handelsgeschäfte
Insurance law. Privatversicherungsrecht. Versicherungswirtschaftsrecht
Life insurance -- Continued
2345 Survivors' benefits
Health insurance. Medical care insurance
2350 General (Table K11)
2352 Risk
Accident insurance
2356 General (Table K11)
2359 Contract (Table K11)
Including standardized terms of contract
2360.A-Z Special topics, A-Z
2360.T72 Travelers' insurance
2362 Business insurance (Table K11)
Including bank insurance
Property insurance
2364 General (Table K11)
2366 Transfer of insured object
2367 Multiple line insurance
Including home owners insurance
2368.A-Z Particular hazards, A-Z
Burglary see KK2368.T43
2368.B88 Business interruption
2368.F57 Fire
Robbery see KK2368.T43
2368.T43 Theft. Burglary. Robbery
2368.W38 Water damage
2370.A-Z Types of property and business, A-Z
2370.A36 Aircraft
2370.F55 Film
2370.J48 Jewelry
2370.M32 Machinery
2370.M68 Motor vehicles
2370.P52 Plate glass
2370.P76 Profit
Suretyship. Guaranty. Title insurance
2375 General (Table K11)
2378 Credit insurance
Pension trust insurance see KK2968
2383 Litigation insurance. Rechtsschutzversicherung
2385 Replacement insurance. Versicherung für Haushaltsersatz im Falle Invalidtät oder Tötung der Ehefrau (Mutter)
2387 Mortgage insurance. Hypothekenversicherung

Commercial law. Handelsrecht
Commercial transactions. Handelsgeschäfte
Insurance law. Privatversicherungsrecht.
Versicherungswirtschaftsrecht -- Continued
Liability insurance. Haftpflichtversicherung
Including both statutory and private insurance

2390 General (Table K11)
Contract
Including standardized terms of contract
2392 General (Table K11)
2393 Parties to contract
Including third parties
2397 Limitation of risk. Risikoabgrenzung
2400 Serienschaden
2402 Folgeschaden
Adjustment of claims. Schadensberechnung
2406 General (Table K11)
2408 Subrogation
2409 Regress
2410 Balance. Forteils- und Schadensausgleich
Risks and damages
Traffic. Verkehrshaftpflicht-Versicherung
2412 General works
Automobiles. Kraftfahrzeuge
2414 General (Table K11)
2415 Contract (Table K11)
Including standardized terms of contract
2417 Insurance policy
2418 Adjustment of claims
2419 Automotive transportation (General)
Including trucking, bus lines, etc.
2421 Aviation
2423.A-Z Other special, A-Z
2423.A22 Accidents
2423.H85 Hunting accidents
2423.M34 Malpractice
2423.P64 Pollution
2423.P73 Products liability
2423.P76 Property damage
2423.T73 Travel contracts
2425.A-Z Special topics, A-Z
2425.A22 Accident experts. Unfallsachverständige
2425.C37 Casualty insurance and inheritance
2428 Reinsurance. Rückversicherung
Business associations. Gesellschaftsrecht
2432 General (Table K11)

Commercial law. Handelsrecht
Business associations. Gesellschaftsrecht -- Continued
Personal companies. Unincorporated business associations. Personalgesellschaften
2435-2435.9 General (Table KK-KKC10)
Partnership. Offene Handelgesellschaft (OHG)
2437-2437.9 General (Table KK-KKC10)
2439.A-Z Special topics, A-Z
2439.C59 Civil procedure
2439.P37 Parties to action
2439.Q33 Quasi-juristic person
2439.R46 Reorganization
2439.R48 Res judicata
2442-2442.9 Limited partnership. Kommanditgesellschaft (KG) (Table KK-KKC10)
2446-2446.9 Silent partners. Stille Gesellschaft (Table KK-KKC10)
Including Gelegenheitsgesellschaften
2447 Joint ventures. Gemeinschaftsunternehmen
Stock companies. Incorporated business associations. Kapitalgesellschaften
2448 General (Table K11)
2449 Foreign corporations
Stock corporations. Aktiengesellschaft (AG)
2451-2455.8 General (Table K10)
Incorporation and promoters. Gründung. Gründungsgesellschaft
Including Nachgründung and Sachgründung
2456 General (Table K11)
2456.2 Articles of incorporation. Bylaws. Gründungsvertrag (Table K11)
Capital see KK2469+
2456.4 Liability before registration
2456.5 Defective incorporation
2456.6 Domicile
2458 State supervision
2459 Registration and publicity. Eintragung im Handelsregister
Organization and management
2460 General works
Director or executive board. Vorstand
2461 General works
2462 Election. Dismissal
2462.5 Legal status. Liability
Board of controllers and supervisors. Aufsichtsrat
2463 General works
2463.5 Legal status. Liability
2464 Resolutions

Commercial law. Handelsrecht
Business associations. Gesellschaftsrecht
Stock companies. Incorporated business associations. Kapitalgesellschaften
Stock corporation. Aktiengesellschaft
Organization and management
Board of controllers and supervisors. Aufsichtsrat -- Continued
Employees' representation in management see KK3030+
Stockholders' meetings see KK2496+
Auditors see KK2494.5

2465 Corporate legal departments
2467 Liability. Relationship to third parties
Corporate finance
2468 General works
Capital stock. Gründungskapital. Einlagen
2469 General works
2470 Increase of capital. Nachschuss
2472 Corporate ownership of its own stock or stock of other corporations
2473 Loans as shares. Loan capital. Eigenkapitalersetzende Gesellschafterleistung
Securities
2474 General (Table K11)
Stocks. Aktien
2475 General (Table K11)
2476 Bearer stock. Inhberaktie
Including personal share (Inscribed share. Namensaktie)
Common stock. Summenaktie. Nennwertaktie
2479 General works
2479.5 Without par value
Preferred stock. Vorzugsaktie
2480 General works
2481 Nonvoting
2482 Dividends and profits
Bonds. Schuldverschreibung
2483 General works
2485 Bearer bonds. Inhaberschuldverschreibung
Including personal bonds (Inscribed bonds. Namensschuldverschreibung)
2486 Convertible bonds. Wandelschuldverschreibung
2487 Jouissance share. Genusschein
2488 Mortgage bonds
2489 Trust investments

Commercial law. Handelsrecht
Business associations. Gesellschaftsrecht
Stock companies. Incorporated business associations. Kapitalgesellschaften
Stock corporation. Aktiengesellschaft -- Continued
Accounting. Financial statements. Auditing
Cf. KK7138+ Tax accounting
2491 General (Table K11)
2492 Valuation
2493 Corporation reserves
2494 Pension trusts
Cf. KK2968 Labor law
2494.5 Auditors. Wirtschaftsprüfer
Stocks and stockholders' rights. Stock transfer. Aktionärs- und Mitglieddschaftsrechte
2495 General (Table K11)
Stockholders' meetings
2496 General works
Voting
2497 General works
2498 Agency. Assignment of stock for voting. Legitimationszession
2499 Resolutions
Including void and voidable resolutions
2500 Confidential communication
2502 Minority stockholders. Minderheitenschutz
2504 Business report. Rendering of account
2505 Stockholders' pre-emption rights
2507 Loss of stockholders' rights
Including exclusion or leaving of shareholders and recall of stocks
Types of corporations
Subsidiary and parent companies see KK2621
2508 Family corporations
2509 One-person companies
Termination
2512 Dissolution
2513 Liquidation
Corporate reorganization see KK2625+
Consolidation and merger see KK2628
2514 Criminal provisions. Aktienstrafrecht
2518 Partnership partly limited by shares. Kommanditgesellschaft auf Aktien (Table K11)
Private company. Gesellschaft mit beschränkter Haftung (GmbH)
2520 General (Table K11)
Incorporation

Commercial law. Handelsrecht
Business associations. Gesellschaftsrecht
Stock companies. Incorporated business associations. Kapitalgesellschaften
Private company. Gesellschaft mit beschränkter Haftung (GmbH)
Incorporation -- Continued
2522 General (Table K11)
2522.2 Articles of incorporation. Bylaws. Grundungsvertrag
Capital see KK2534+
2522.4 Liability before registration
2522.5 Defective incorporation
2522.6 Domicile
2524 Registration and publicity
Organization and management
2526 General works
Directors. Geschäftsführer
2527 General works
2528 Election. Dismissal
2528.5 Legal status. Liability
2529 Board of controllers and supervisors. Aufsichsrat
Stockholders' meetings see KK2548+
2530 Liability
Company finance
2532 General (Table K11)
Capital stock. Stammkapital. Stammeinlage
2534 General works
2535 Increase. Decrease
2536 Company ownership of its own stock or stock of other companies
2538 Loans as shares. Loan capital
Accounting. Financial statements. Auditing
2540 General works
2542 Valuation
Stocks and stockholders' rights. Stock transfer
2544 General works
2546 Stocks. Geschäftsanteile
Including stock certificates (Anteilscheine)
Stockholders' meetings
2548 General works
2549 Voting. Resolutions
Including void and voidable resolutions
2550 Control of partners
2552 Succession. Inheritance
2553 Loss of stockholders' rights
Including exclusion or leaving of stockholders
Types of private companies

Commercial law. Handelsrecht
Business associations. Gesellschaftsrecht
Stock companies. Incorporated business associations. Kapitalgesellschaften
Private company. Gesellschaft mit beschränkter Haftung (GmbH)
Types of private companies -- Continued
2556 GmbH und Co.
2556.5 GmbH und Still
2557 Family corporations
2558 One-person companies
Termination
2558.5 Dissolution. Liquidation
2559 Legal status in civil procedure
2560 Criminal provisions
2561 Multi-national corporations
Kolonialgesellschaften (Colonial companies) see KK576
Cooperative societies. Wirtschafts- und Erwerbsgenossenschaften
2565 General (Table K11)
Incorporation and promoters. Gründung. Gründungsgenossenschaft
2566 General works
2567 Articles of incorporation. Bylaws. Satzung
2567.5 Registration and publicity. Genossenschaftsregister
Organization and management
2568 General works
2569 Executive board. Vorstand
2570 Board of controllers and supervisors. Aufsichtsrat
Membership meetings see KK2577
2572 Liability. Limited liability
Cooperatives' finance
2573 General (Table K11)
2574 Depositors fund
2574.5 Dividends
Accounting. Financial statements. Auditing
2575 General works
2575.5 Reserve fund
Membership. Mitgliedschaft und Geschäftsanteil
2576 General works
2577 Voting. Resolutions
2579 Leaving and entering of members
2580.A-Z Types of cooperative societies, A-Z
Building and loan associations see KK2210
2580.C65 Consumer cooperatives
Farm producers and marketing cooperatives see KK6636

Commercial law. Handelsrecht
Business associations. Gesellschaftsrecht
Cooperative societies. Wirtschafts- und Erwerbsgenossenschaften
Types of cooperative societies, A-Z -- Continued
2580.G76 Grocery cooperatives
2580.H34 Halte- und Pachtgenossenschaft
Housing cooperatives see KK1305
2580.P76 Producer cooperatives
2580.Z45 Zentralgenossenschaften
Termination
2584 Dissolution. Liquidation
Consolidation and merger see KK2628
Cooperative as partner or shareholder see KK2630
2586 Criminal provisions
Combinations. Industrial trusts. Freiwillige wirtschaftliche Zusammenschlüsse
For government control see KK6511+
2598 General (Table K11)
2602 Consortium. Arbeitsgemeinschaft
2604 Interessengemeinschaft
(2606) Joint ventures. Gemeinschaftsunternehmen
see KK2447
Business concerns. Konzernrecht
2613 General (Table K11)
2614 Organization and management
2615 Accounting. Financial statements. Auditing
2616 Liability
2620 Holding company
2621 Subsidiary and parent company
Corporate reorganization. Umwandlung
2625 General (Table K11)
2628 Consolidation and merger. Verschmelzung (Table K11)
For government control see KK6467+
2630 Corporations and companies as partners and shareholders
2633.A-Z Special topics, A-Z
2633.C65 Compensation to stockholders
2633.L32 Labor contracts
2633.L33 Labor-management relations
2633.L52 Liability
2633.M55 Minority stockholders
2633.T78 Trusts and trustees
Insolvency see KK4171+
Bankruptcy see KK4290+
Intellectual and industrial property. Urheberrecht und gewerblicher Rechtsschutz

Intellectual and industrial property. Urheberrecht und gewerblicher Rechtsschutz -- Continued
2636 General (Table K11)
Principles
2637 Intangible property. Immaterielle Güter. Immaterialgüterrecht
2638 Personality rights. Moral rights
Cf. KK1923+ Civil law
2640 Territory. Territoriale Begrenzung der Schutzwirkung
Copyright. Urheberrecht
2647 History
2649 Criticism. Reform
2655-2655.9 General (Table KK-KKC8)
Branches of copyright
2660-2660.9 Literary copyright. Literarisches Urheberrecht (Table KK-KKC8)
2665-2665.9 Musical copyright (Table KK-KKC8)
Fine art and photography. Bildende Künste und Photographie
2670-2670.9 General (Table KK-KKC8)
Violation of rights in one's own picture see KK1967
Motion pictures see KK2690+
2678 Designs and models. Geschmacksmuster (Table K11)
2685 Prints and labels
Including works of commercial art, catalogs, sample books, etc.
Motion pictures and television shows. Tonfilm und Television
2690-2690.9 General (Table KK-KKC8)
2692.A-Z Special topics, A-Z
2692.A39 Advertisements and commercials
Commercials see KK2692.A39
2695 Computer programs
2700 Quasi copyright and neighboring rights. Leistungsschutz und Nachbarrechte (Table K11)
Author and publisher. Verlagsrecht
Including the publishing contract (Verlagsvertragsrecht)
2706 General (Table K11)
2707 Plays and stage productions. Bühnenvertriebs- und Bühnenvertragsrecht
2708 Motion pictures. Filmverlagsrecht
2709 Music. Musikverlagsrecht
2710 Scientific literature. Wissenschaftliches Schrifttum
2712.A-Z Special topics, A-Z
2712.D45 Delicts. Torts
2712.I45 Immoral contracts
2712.P47 Personality rights and the publishing contract

Intellectual and industrial property. Urheberrecht und gewerblicher Rechtsschutz
Author and publisher. Verlagsrecht
Special topics, A-Z -- Continued
Torts see KK2712.D45
2712.W37 Warranty
2714 Litigation and execution
International copyright see K1411+
Patent law and trademarks
2721-2725.8 General (Table K10)
2726 Scope of protection
2727 Relation to antitrust law
Patent office
2728 General (Table K11)
2729 Reichspatentamt
2729.2 Patentamt
2730 Bundespatentamt
Patent practice and procedure. Entstehung des Patents. Erteilungsverfahren
2732 General works
Invention. Erfinderrecht
2734 General (Table K11)
2735 Priority. Erfindungspriorität
2737 Eligibility of invention for patent (Novelty). Patentfähigkeit
2738 Legal status of inventors. Community of inventors
Employees' inventions. Arbeitnehmererfindung
2739 General (Table K11)
2740 Suggestion system. Vorschlage wesen
2741 Pay. Incentive awards
Claim drafting. Anmeldung, Offenbarung und Identitätsprüfung
2743 General (Table K11)
2744 Collision of patents
2745 Use and previous use. Benutzungsrecht und Vorbenutzung
2746 Res judicata
2747 Fees
2749 Duration and renewal. Schutzdauer. Ablauf der Schutzfrist
2750.A-Z Types of patents, A-Z
2750.K75 Kombinationspatent
2751.A-Z Patented products, processes, and engineering methods, A-Z
Subarrange each by Table K12
2751.B56 Biotechnology
2751.C43 Chemicals

Intellectual and industrial property. Urheberrecht und gewerblicher Rechtsschutz
Patent law and trademarks
Patent office
Patented products, processes, and engineering methods, A-Z -- Continued
2751.D78 Drugs
2751.E43 Electron tubes
2751.N82 Nuclear engineering
2751.P42 Plants. Pflanzen
2753 Designs and utility models. Gebrauchsmuster (Table K11)
Licences. Lizenvertrag und Verwertung
Including compulsory licenses and fees
2755 General (Table K11)
2757 Foreign licensing agreements. Internationale Industrielizenzerträge
Including know-how Verträge
Taxation see KK7191.F67
Patent litigation and infringements. Patentstreit
2759 General (Table K11)
2759.5 Bundespatentgericht
2760.A-Z Special topics, A-Z
2760.I53 In forma pauperis
2763 Patent attorneys (Table K11)
International uniform law on patents and trademarks see K1501+
Trademarks. Markenrecht. Markenschutzrecht
2768 General (Table K11)
Types of trademarks
2769 Brand names and numerals
2770 Ausstattung
2772 Accompanying marks. Begleitmarken
2773 Defensiv- und Vorratszeichen
2774 Marks of corporations. Verband- und Konzernzeichen
2775 Famous and notorious marks
2776 Service marks. Dienstleistungszeichen
2777 Quality marks. Gütezeichen
Marks of origin (certificates). Ursprungszeugnis
2778 General works
2779.A-Z Particular marks, A-Z
2779.P55 Pilsner Bier (the phrase)
2780 Scope of protection
2781 Relationship to antitrust law
Practice and procedure. Anmeldungsverfahren
2783 General works
Claim drafting and registration. Anmeldung und Eintragung

Intellectual and industrial property. Urheberrecht und gewerblicher Rechtsschutz
Patent law and trademarks
Trademarks. Markenrecht. Markenschutzrecht
Practice and procedure. Anmeldungsverfahren
Claim drafting and registration. Anmeldung und Eintragung -- Continued
2784 General works
2785 Collision of trademarks
2786 Use and compelled use of trademarks
2787 Unused marks
2789 Transfer of trademarks. Übertragung
Licenses. Warenzeichen-Lizenzverträge
2792 General (Table K11)
2793 Foreign licensing agreements
2796 Litigation
Unfair competition. Unlauterer Wettbewerb
For restraint of trade see KK6456+
2799 General (Table K11)
2800 Public policy. Verkehrssitte
Advertising. Werbung
2802 General (Table K11)
Disparagement of goods. Herabsetzung. Diskreditierung
2803 General (Table K11)
2804 Comparative advertising. Vergleichende Werbung. Alleinstellungswerbung
Misleading representation. False claims. Irreführung
2805 General works
2806 Producer. Business name
2807 Superlative advertising. Superlativreklame
2808 Testing of commercial products
2809 Imitation. Sklavische Nachahmung
Pushing for sales. Beeinflussung der Willensentscheidung
2810 General works
2811 Unordered merchandise by mail. Zusendung unbestellter Waren
Cf. KK1663 Contracts
2812 Gifts. Werbegeschenke
2813 Combined sales. Koppelungsgeschäfte
2814 Special sales. Ausverkaufswesen
Rebates and premiums. Rabatt- und Zugabewesen
2815 General (Table K11)
2817.A-Z Special topics, A-Z
2817.C65 Combined merchandise. Warenkopplung
2817.T64 Toll-free telephone calls. Telefonieren zum Nulltarif
2822 Price cutting. Preisunterbietung
2824.A-Z By industry or occupation, A-Z

Intellectual and industrial property. Urheberrecht und gewerblicher Rechtsschutz
Unfair competition. Unlauterer Wettbewerb
By industry or occupation, A-Z
Accountants see KK2824.E26
Auditors see KK2824.E26
2824.A88 Automobile industry
2824.E26 Economic and financial advisers. Accountants. Auditors
2824.E46 Employees
Financial advisers see KK2824.E26
2824.F87 Furniture industry
2824.G69 Government business enterprises
Laborers and employees see KK2824.E46
Delicts. Torts
Cf. KK1922+ Civil law
2826 General works
2827.A-Z Protected rights, A-Z
Business enterprise see KK1928
2827.T72 Trade and industrial secrets. Geschäfts- und Betriebsgeheimnis
2828.A-Z Torts, A-Z
2828.B69 Boycott
2828.B73 Breach of contract. Evasion. Vertragsbruch und Rechtsumgehung
2828.B74 Bribery. Schmiergeld
2828.E58 Enticement. Abwerbung
2828.E86 Espionage, Industrial. Betriebsspionage
Evasion see KK2828.B73
2828.U54 Unjust enrichment
Practice and procedure
2830 General (Table K11)
2832 Warning. Schutzrechtsverwarnung
2833 Arbitration and award
Labor law. Arbeitsrecht
Including works on both labor law and social insurance, and private labor law as it applies to the labor-management relationship
2849 History
Criticism and reform see KK3270
2851-2860 General (Table K9c)
2862 Influence of international labor law on German labor law. International labor organization
2863 Right to work. Recht auf Arbeit
2864 Ideology and labor law
2865 Politics and labor
2867 Interpretation and construction

Labor law. Arbeitsrecht -- Continued

Organization and administration

Class here works on federal and state departments of labor or departments of labor of several states

For the department of labor of an individual state, see the state

For departments and subordinate regulatory agencies prior to 1949 see KK4867+

2868 General (Table K11)

2869 Bundesminister für Arbeit und Sozialordnung (Federal department of labor and social affairs)

2869.5 Subordinate agencies

Bundesverischerungssanstalt für Angestellte see KK3394+

Bundessozialgericht see KK3613

2869.7 Conflict of laws

Labor contract and employment. Arbeitsvertrag und Arbeitsverhältnis

2870 General (Table K11)

Types of employment

2871 Permanent employment. Dauerarbeitsverhältnis

2872 Temporary employment. Befristete Verträge

Including Kettenverträge, seasonal work (Saisonarbeit), etc.

2873 Double employment. Doppelbeschäftigung

2874 Part-time employment. Teilzeitbeschäftigung

2875 Supplementary employment. Nebenbeschäftigung

2876 Subcontracting (Table K11)

Including Leiharbeitsverhältnis, Arbeitnehmer- überlassung und Dienstverschaffungsvertrag

2877 Leave of absence without pay. Ruhendes Arbeitsverhältnis

2878.A-Z Other types of employment, A-Z

2878.S44 Self-employment. Selbständigkeit

2880 Constitutional rights in employment

2881.5 Personnel records (Table K11)

Individual labor contract and collective agreements. Liberty of contract

2882 General works

2883 Theories

Including Eingliederungstheorie and Vertragstheorie

Working standards see KK3070

Works agreements see KK3002

Principle of most favorable wage rate see KK3068

Freedom of employment and restraint on freedom of employment

2885 General works

Labor law. Arbeitsrecht
Labor contract and employment. Arbeitsvertrag und Arbeitsverhältnis
Freedom of employment and restraint on freedom of employment -- Continued
2886 Free choice of employment. Freie Wahl des Arbeitsplatzes
Cf. KK5173 Constitutional law
Preferential employment
Including people with severe disabilities (Schwerbeschädigte), Veterans (Heimkehrer), etc.
2888 General (Table K11)
2889 Sheltered workshops. Behindertenwerkstätte (Table K11)
Observance see KK2902
2892 Loyalty. Treuepflichten und Fürsorgepflichten
2894 Duty of employer to provide work. Beschäftigungspflicht
2896 Right of work assignment, supervision, and transfer. Weisungs- und Versetzungsrecht
Including transfer to branch of enterprise abroad
Formation of contract
2898 General (Table K11)
2900 State and labor contract. Mitwirkung öffentlicher Stellen
Clauses and terms
2901 General works
2902 Observance. Betriebsübung
2903 Covenants not to compete
Standardized labor conditions see KK3066+
Operational changes. Relocation of enterprise see KK2927
2904 Age limit. Altersgrenze
2905 On-the-job training
2906 Employment of relatives
2908 Formalities
Including hiring and selection practices, personnel questionnaires, and employment tests
Parties to contract
2910 General works
Parties to collective bargaining see KK3082+
Prohibition of discrimination in employment see KK2942+
Void and voidable contracts
Cf. KK1063+ Civil law
2911 General works
2912 Immoral contracts
Extinction of employment
2914 General works
Expiration see KK1576

Labor law. Arbeitsrecht
Labor contract and employment. Arbeitsvertrag und Arbeitsverhältnis
Extinction of employment -- Continued
2916 Contractual discharge. Vertragliche Auflösung
Avoidance see KK2912
Dismissal and resignation. Kündigung
2919 General (Table K11)
2922 Dismissal of employees. Ordentliche und ausserordentliche Kündigung durch Dienstherrn (Table K11)
Including economic crisis dismissal, layoff, short hours, suspension, reinstatement, dismissal wage, etc.
2923 Resignation of employees. Ordentliche und ausserordentliche Kündigung durch Arbeitnehmer
2924.A-Z Other special topics, A-Z
2924.B35 Bankruptcy. Composition
Composition see KK2924.B35
2924.D42 Death
Job security. Kündigungsschutz
2926 General (Table K11)
2927 Special provisions
Including changes of conditions, operational changes, automation, relocation of enterprise, etc.
2928 Procedure
2929.A-Z Protected groups, A-Z
2929.D58 Disabled persons
2929.D72 Draftees. Wehrdienstverpflichtete
2929.V48 Veterans
2929.W67 Work councils
Nonperformance
Cf. KK1580+ Civil law
2930 General (Table K11)
2931 Breach of contract. Arbeitsvertragsbruch
Cf. KK2828.B73 Unfair competition
Impossibility of performance
2932 General (Table K11)
2933 Difference to default
2934 Risk. Betriebsrisiko
Automation see KK2927
2935 Seasonal employment
Including weather conditions and seasonal industry
2936 Plant shutdown. Betriebsstillegung
Liability
Including liability of employer, employee, and liability toward co-worker and third parties
2938 General (Table K11)

Labor law. Arbeitsrecht
Labor contract and employment. Arbeitsvertrag und Arbeitsverhältnis
Liability -- Continued
2939 Hazardous occupations
2940 Accidents
Cf. KK3185+ Labor hygiene and industrial safety
Cf. KK6018+ Police and public safety
Prohibition of discrimination in employment. Equal opportunity
2942 General (Table K11)
2943 Wage discrimination. Equal pay for equal work
2945.A-Z Groups discriminated against, A-Z
2945.A33 Aged. Older people. Alternde Personen
2945.A44 Alien laborers. Fremdarbeiter
2945.D58 Disabilities, People with
2945.E84 Ethnic groups. Minorities
Minorities see KK2945.E84
Older people see KK2945.A33
People with disabilities see KK2945.D58
2945.W65 Women
Wages. Arbeitslohn
2950 General (Table K11)
Principle of most favorable wage rate see KK3068
2952 Method of computation
Including work-factor method, method-time measurement, REFA system, Bedaux system, etc.
Types of wages and modes of remuneration. Entlohnungsgrundsätze
2954 Daywork. Piecework. Zeitlohn. Zeitakkord
2955 Incentive wages
Including bonus system (Gratifikation) and profit sharing (Gewinnbeteiligung)
2956 Adjustments. Zulagen und Zuschläge
Including cost-of-living adjustments, Schmutzzulagen, Schwerarbeiterzulagen, etc.
2958 Family allowances
2959 Overtime payments
Including night differentials
2960 Payment during sick leave or leave of absence. Lohnfortzahlung bei Krankheit oder Arbeitssäumnis (Table K11)
Time, place, and mode of payment
2962 Noncash payment. Bargeldlose Zahlung
2963 Payment in advance. Vorschuss
2964 Verfallklausel and Rückzahlungsklausel
Nonwage payments and fringe benefits

Labor law. Arbeitsrecht
Wages. Arbeitslohn
Nonwage payments and fringe benefits
2965 General works
Pension and retirement plans. Betriebsrenten
2967 General (Table K11)
2968 Pension trusts. Pensionskassen
Including insolvency insurance
2969 Health benefits and insurance plans
2972 Social (welfare) provisions. Wohlfahrtseinrichtungen
Naturalia. Deputat
2973 Coal for miners
Groups of employees or industries, A-Z
2976.A66 Apprentices
2976.B84 Building and construction industry
2976.H68 Hotels. Restaurants
Learners see KK2976.A66
Restaurants see KK2976.H68
2978 Employees' references. Dienstzeugnis. Arbeitspapiere
Labor-management relations. Betriebsverfassungsrecht
2981-2985.8 General (Table K10)
2987 Constitutional aspects. Private autonomy. Property rights
2988 Political activities. Limitations
Works councils. Betriebsrat
Including election, organization, parliamentary practice, etc.
2991 General (Table K11)
2994 Works assembly. Betriebsversammlung
2995 General works council. Gesamtbetriebsrat
2997 Union participation
Employee participation in management.
Mitbestimmungsrecht
3000 General (Table K11)
Constitutional aspects. Property rights see KK2987
3002 Works agreements. Betriebsvereinbarungen
Standardized labor conditions see KK3066+
Labor standards and protection of labor. Soziale
Angelegenheiten
3006 General (Table K11)
3008 Profit sharing. Employee ownership
(Vermögensbildung) (Table K11)
3010 Working hours
3012 Social (welfare) provisions. Wohlfahrtseinrichtungen
Including pension trusts, health insurance, housing,
cafeterias, etc.
3014 Employee rules and discipline. Arbeitsordnung (Table
K11)
Including procedure and penalties

Labor law. Arbeitsrecht
Labor-management relations. Betriebsverfassungsrecht
Employee participation in management. Mitbestimmungsrecht -- Continued
Personnel management
3019 General (Table K11)
3020 Hiring. Dismissal. Transfer
Including interdiction and veto of works council
For personal questionnaires and tests see KK2908
3022 Occupational training or retraining (Table K11)
Including apprenticeship
Economic policies
Including apprenticeship
3024 General (Table K11)
3026 Economic council. Wirtschaftsausschuss
3027 Control of operational changes. Kontrolle über betriebliche Änderungen
Employee representation on board of controllers and supervisors. Arbeitnehmer im Aufsichtsrat
Including unincorporated and incorporated business associations, cooperative societies, industrial trusts, etc., and elections, parliamentary practice, etc.
3030 General (Table K11)
3032 Antitrust aspects
3034 Representation during strikes
3036.A-Z Industries, A-Z
3036.M55 Mining industry
3038 Youth representatives. Betriebsjugendvertreter
3040.A-Z Industries and trades, A-Z
3040.F73 Franchises
3040.I53 Information display systems industry
3040.S47 Service industry. Dienstleistungsgewerbe
3040.T45 Theater
Exemptions
3042 Enterprises serving a special purpose. Tendenzbetriebe
3043 Religious societies. Religionsgesellschaften
3045 Public enterprises. Offentliche Betriebe
Schiedstellen. Conciliation board and permanent grievance committee. Procedure
3048 General (Table K11)
Judicial review see KK3238
3052 Criminal provisions
Collective bargaining and labor agreements. Tarifrecht
3056 General (Table K11)
3057 Constitutional aspects. Equality of social partners. Freedom of coalition
General provisions of civil law and public law

Labor law. Arbeitsrecht
Collective bargaining and labor agreements. Tarifrecht
General provisions of civil law and public law -- Continued
3060 Friedenspflicht
3062 Gemeinsame Einrichtungen und Wohlfahrtseinrichtungen
3064 Standards for conclusion of labor contracts. Abschlussnormen
Standardized labor conditions. Arbeitsbedingungen
3066 General (Table K11)
3067.A-Z By industry, A-Z
3067.C43 Chemical industry
3068 Most favorable wage. Günstigkeitsprinzip. Höchstnorm (Tariflohn)
3070 Working standards. Betriebsnorm
Formation of contract. Abschluss des Tarifvertrages
3076 General works
3078 Clauses. Conditions. Reservations
3080 Formalities
Parties to contract. Tarifvertrags-Parteien
3082 General works
Autonomy. Tariffähigkeit und Tarifhoheit
Including loss of autonomy (Tariffähigkeitsverlust)
3084 General works
3086 Delegation of power
Unions see KK3123+
Employers' associations see KK3136
3089 Third parties
Validity, applicability, and effectiveness. Geltungsbereich (räumlich und zeitlich) und Allgemeinverbindlichkeit
3092 General works
3094 Tarifverbandsauflösung
3097.A-Z By industry or occupation, A-Z
3097.B36 Banks
3097.B84 Building and construction industry
Cab drivers see KK3097.T39
Civil service see KK5958+
3097.C56 Clothing industry
3097.H68 Hospital and medical personnel
3097.I58 Insurance companies
Medical personnel see KK3097.H68
Merchant marine see KK2291
3097.M48 Metal industry
3097.M68 Motion picture industry
3097.O66 Opera chorus singers
3097.P42 Pharmacists
3097.P49 Physicians
3097.P74 Printing industry

Labor law. Arbeitsrecht
Collective bargaining and labor agreements. Tarifrecht
By industry or occupation, A-Z -- Continued
3097.S25 Salaried employees. Angestellte
3097.S72 Stagehands
3097.T39 Taxicab drivers
Collective labor disputes. Arbeitskampfrecht
3100 General (Table K11)
Constitutional aspects see KK2987
3102 Arbitration. Conciliation. Schlichtungswesen
Strikes and lockouts. Boycotts
3104 General works
3105 Picketing. Streikposten
Wildcat strikes. Sympathy strikes. Political strikes
3106 General (Table K11)
3107 Damages. Unerlaubte Handlung und Schadensersatz
3109 Criminal provisions
3111 Nonparticipants. Strikebreakers
3113 Apprenticeship, vocational training, and strike
3116 National emergency and strike. Streik und Staatsnotstand (Arbeitskampfschutzklausel)
Corporate representation. Organisationen und Verbände
3118 General (Table K11)
3120 Constitutional aspects. Freedom of coalition
Union. Gewerkschaften
3123 General (Table K11)
3125 Personality and capacity
Autonomy see KK3084+
Union organization
3127 General (Table K11)
3129 Officers
Including election, legal status, etc.
3132 Dues. Beitragsrecht
3134.A-Z Unions. By name, A-Z
3136 Employers' associations. Arbeitgeberverbände (Table K11)
Protection of labor. Arbeitsschutz
3140 General (Table K11)
3143 Protection of human resource. Schutz der Arbeitskraft
Hours of labor. Arbeitszeitschutz
Including night work and Sunday labor
3145 General (Table K11)
3147 Overtime. Arbeitszeitverlängerung
Part-time employment see KK2874
3149 Readiness to work. Arbeitsbereitschaft
Including Bereitschaftdienst (Stand-by duty)
3151 Shifts. Schichtarbeit

Labor law. Arbeitsrecht
Protection of labor. Arbeitsschutz
Hours of labor. Arbeitszeitschutz -- Continued
Kurzarbeit see KK2922
3154.A-Z By industry or type of employment, A-Z
3154.A95 Aviation
3154.B35 Bakeries
3154.C43 Chemical workers
Highway transport workers see KK3154.T72
3154.H68 Hospitals
3154.I76 Iron and steel workers
Physicians, Hospital see KK3154.H68
3154.P82 Publishing houses
3154.R34 Railroad workers
Retail trade see KK6804
Shipping on inland waterways see KK2292
Steel workers see KK3154.I76
3154.T72 Transport workers, Highway
Vacations. Urlaub
Including employment and supplementary employment (Haupt- und Nebenbeschäftigung)
3157 General (Table K11)
3159 Recreation. Unpermitted work during vacation. Erholungsurlaub. Arbeitsverbot
3161 Leave of absence. Arbeitsbefreiung
Including Sonderurlaub und Bildungsurlaub (Sabbatical leave)
For wage payments see KK2960
For household day for women see KK3176
3163 Sick leave. Krankheitsurlaub
For wage payments see KK2960
3165 Holidays. Feiertage und Ersatzfeiertage
3167 Cash compensation and holiday pay. Urlaubsentgelt und Feiertagsbezahlung (Table K11)
3169.A-Z By industry or type of labor, A-Z
3172 Child labor. Jugendarbeitsschutz (Table K11)
Including hours of labor
Women's labor. Frauenarbeitsschutz
Including hours of labor
3175 General (Table K11)
3176 Women's household day. Hausarbeitstag
3179 Maternal welfare. Mutterschutz (Table K11)
3182 Home labor. Heimarbeiterschutz
Labor hygiene and industrial safety. Persönliche und technische Sicherheit
Including safety regulations for equipment and hazardous substances

Labor law. Arbeitsrecht
Protection of labor. Arbeitsschutz
Labor hygiene and industrial safety. Persönliche und technische Sicherheit -- Continued

3185 General (Table K11)
3186 Factory inspection
3187.A-Z By industry or type of labor, A-Z
3187.B35 Banks
3187.B54 Biotechnology industry
3187.B54 Biotechnology
3187.B84 Building and construction industry
3187.E86 Explosives industry
3187.I76 Iron and steel workers
3187.L42 Leather industry
Longshoremen see KK3187.S73
3187.M55 Miners
3187.S34 Salaried employees. Angestellte
Steel workers see KK3187.I76
3187.S73 Stevedores
White collar workers see KK3187.S34
3189.A-Z By machinery, equipment, material, etc. A-Z
3189.A73 Asbestos
3189.C65 Conveying machinery
Electric installations see KK6021
3189.P73 Pressure vessels
Steam boilers see KK6020
3189.V53 Video display terminals
3192.A-Z Labor law for particular industries or occupations, A-Z
3192.A37 Agricultural and farm laborers
3192.A44 Alien laborers. Fremdarbeiter
3192.A84 Aviation industry
3192.B84 Building and construction industry
3192.C47 Church employees
3192.C54 Clerks
3192.D45 Dentistry
3192.D65 Domestics. Haushaltsangestellte und Gesinde
Draftees see KK2929.D72
3192.E58 Entertainers
3192.E83 Executives. Leitende Angestellte
Farm laborers see KK3192.A37
3192.F67 Foreign armed forces, Employees of
3192.F73 Franchises
3192.H67 Hospitals and medical personnel
3192.H69 Hotels, taverns, and restaurants
3192.I53 Independent contractors
3192.J68 Journalists
Medical personnel see KK3192.H67

Labor law. Arbeitsrecht
Labor law for particular industries or occupations, A-Z -- Continued
Office clerks see KK3192.S25
3192.P74 Prisoners
Restaurants see KK3192.H69
3192.S25 Salaried employees. Angestellte
Servants see KK3192.D65
3192.T45 Theater
3192.T73 Transportation workers
Veterans see KK2929.V48
3192.V65 Volunteers. Volontärsverhätnis
White collar workers see KK3192.S25
Labor supply. Manpower control. Arbeitsvermittlung
3195 General (Table K11)
Bundesanstalt fur Arbeitsvermittlung und Arbeitslosenversicherung see KK3422
Arbeitsämter (local employment offices) see KK3422
3200 Criminal provisions
Labor courts and procedure
Class here works on federal courts, federal and state courts, or courts of several jurisdictions
For courts (several or individual) or an individual jurisdiction, see the state or municipality
History
Class here works on the law prior to 1953
For the later period see KK3211+
3205 General (Table K11)
3206 Gewerbegerichte (1890)
3207 Kaufmannsgerichte (1890)
3208 Schlichtungsausschüsse (1918)
3209 Reichsarbeitsgericht
3211-3215.8 General (Table K10)
3218 Arbeitsgerichte
Including judges, lay judges, etc.
3221 Landesarbeitsgerichte (Labor courts of the states)
Including senates, presidents, judges, lay judges, etc.)
3223 Bundesarbeitsgericht (Federal labor court)
Procedural principles
3225 General (Table K11)
3226 Due process of law. Rechtsschutz. Gesetzlicher Richter. Rechtliches Gehör
Including frivolous suits (Querulantenklagen)
3227 Parties to action
Pretrial procedures. Vorverfahren
3230 General works
3232 Time periods. Deadlines. Fristen. Termine

Labor law. Arbeitsrecht
Labor courts and procedure -- Continued
Procedure at first instance. Verfahren im ersten Rechtszug
Including Urteilsverfahren (procedure leading to judgment) and Beschlussverfahren (procedure leading to resolution)
3233 General works
3234 Jurisdiction
Including competence in subject matter and venue (sachliche und örtliche Zuständigkeit)
Actions and defenses
3237 General works
3238 Judicial review of grievance procedures. Überprüfung von Entscheidungen betriebsverfassungsrechtlicher Stellen
3240 Settlement. Güteverfahren
3243 Set-off and counterclaim. Aufrechnung und Gegenklage
3246 Evidence. Burden of proof. Beweisverfahren
Judgements. Judicial decisions. Urteile und Beschlüsse
3250 General works
3253 Res judicata
3257 Remedies. Rechtsmittel
3261 Execution
3263 Costs (Table K11)
Arbitration. Schiedsgerichte und Schiedsvertrag
3267 General (Table K11)
3269.A-Z By trade or profession, A-Z
3269.A28 Actors
Competence conflicts between labor and social courts see KK3646
Social legislation. Sozialrecht
3270 Social reform and policies. Sozialreform und Sozialpolitik
Including all branches of social legislation
3270.5 General (Table K11)
3271-3275.8 Administrative process. Sozialverwaltungsrecht (Table K10)
Social insurance. Sozialversicherungsrecht
For works on both labor law and social insurance see KK2851+
Criticism and reform see KK3270
Information retrieval and electronic data processing see KK82.S62
3281 General (Table K11)
3282 Constitutional aspects. Private autonomy and compulsory insurance

Social legislation. Sozialrecht
Social insurance. Sozialversicherungsrecht -- Continued
Organization and administration
Including insurance carriers (Versicherungsträger), both corporations of public law (Körperschaften des öffentlichen Rechts), and cooperatives (Berufsgenossenschaften)
For the federal department of labor and social affairs see KK2869

3285 General works
3285.2 Corporate rights and personality. Rechte und Rechtsfähigkeit
Autonomy. Self-government
3285.3 General works
3285.33 Organs (Table K11)
Including elections
e.g. Geschäftsführer
Officials and employees
3285.4 General (Table K11)
3285.42 Labor-management relations
Finance
3285.5 General (Table K11)
3285.52 Accounting and auditing. Rechnungsführung und Betriebsprüfung
Dues. Beitrage
3285.53 General works
3285.54 Employers' and employees' contributions. Arbeitgeber- und Arbeitnehmeranteile
3285.55 Collection. Einzug
3285.56 Hortatory procedures and execution. Mahn- und Beitreibungsverfahren
3285.57 Stamps and insurance certificates. Beitragsmarken und Versicherungskarte
3285.6 Practice and procedure
3285.8 State supervision. Staatsaufsicht
Coverage and benefits
3287 General works
3288.A-Z Groups of beneficiaries, A-Z
3288.A45 Alien laborers
3288.A66 Apprentices
Artisans see KK3411.A78
3288.A76 Artists
Civil servants see KK5950+
3288.D78 Drug addicts. Süchtige
3288.E93 Executives
Mariners see KK2296+
Monks see KK3288.R47

Social legislation. Sozialrecht
Social insurance. Sozialversicherungsrecht
Coverage and benefits
Groups of beneficiaries, A-Z -- Continued
Nuns see KK3288.R47
3288.P36 Part-time, temporary, and intermittent employees
3288.P75 Prisoners
3288.R45 Relatives. Spouses
3288.R47 Religious orders. Monks. Nuns
3288.S44 Self-employed
Spouses see KK3288.R45
Special subjects applying to all branches of social insurance
3290 Liability
Including insurance carriers, the insured, employers, etc.
3294 Collective labor disputes and social insurance
3296 Wages
Including transfer, attachment and garnishment (Gehaltsabtretung und Pfändung)
3300 Subrogation
3302 Restitution between social agencies. Kostener-stattung zwischen Sozialhilfeträgern (Ausgleich)
3304 Criminal provisions
3305 Conflict of laws
Health insurance. Krankenversicherung
For private health insurance see KK2350+
For health insurance plans see KK2969
3308 General (Table K11)
3310 Compulsory insurance
Including exemptions
3312 Right to insurance
3316 Organization and administration
Including Ortskrankenkassen, Landkrankenkassen, Innungskrankenkassen, Betriebskrankenkassen and Ersatzkassen
For Seekrankenkassen see KK2297
For Knappschaften see KK6724+
Coverage and benefits
For public employees and officials see KK5951
3319 General works
3322 General and specialist care. Krankenpflege
Including expenses for medications, dental care, hospital inpatient care, care in skilled nursing facilities, long-term care, etc.

Social legislation. Sozialrecht
Social insurance. Sozialversicherungsrecht
Health insurance. Krankenversicherung
Coverage and benefits -- Continued

3324 Cash sickness benefits. Krankengeld und Hausgeld (Table K11)
Including employers' contribution to cash sickness benefits

3328 Maternity benefits. Mutterschaftshilfe

3329 Funeral grants. Sterbegeld

3331 Sickness and medical benefits for dependents. Familienhilfe

3333.A-Z Groups of beneficiaries, A-Z

3333.A55 AIDS patients

3333.L32 Laborers. Arbeiter

3333.P45 Pensioners. Rentner

3333.S25 Salaried employees. Angestellte

3333.U53 Unemployed. Arbeitslose

3336 Cash settlement (lump-sum payment and cancellation of insurance). Aussteuerrecht der Krankenkase

The medical profession and health insurance

3337 General works

3338 Physicians employed by the health administration. Amtsärzte. Vertrauensärzte (Table K11)

3340 Physicians under contract with and paid by the sickness fund. Kassenärzte (Table K11)

3344 Hospitals and pharmacies under contract with the sickness fund (Table K11)

3346 Criminal provisions

Workers' compensation. Gesetzliche Unfallversicherung
Including occupational diseases (Berufskrankheiten)

3350 General (Table K11)

3355 Compulsory insurance and statutory insurance
Including exemptions

Organization and administration
Including Gewerbliche und Landwirtschaftliche Berufsgenossenschaften (Industrial and agricultural accident insurance funds), and federal, state, and municipal insurance carriers
For Seeberufsgenossenschaft see KK2298

3358 General works

3358.2 Corporate rights and personality. Rechte und Rechtsfähigkeit

Autonomy. Self-government

3358.3 General works

3358.33 Organs (Table K11)
Including elections

Social legislation. Sozialrecht
Social insurance. Sozialversicherungsrecht
Workers' compensation. Gesetzliche Unfallversicherung
Organization and administration -- Continued
Officials and employees
3358.4 General (Table K11)
3358.42 Labor-management relations
Finance
3358.5 General
3358.52 Accounting and auditing. Rechnungsführung und Betriebsprüfung
Dues. Beitrage
3358.53 General works
3358.54 Employers' and employees' contributions. Arbeitgeber- und Arbeitnehmeranteile
3358.55 Collection. Einzug
3358.56 Hortatory procedures and execution. Mahn- und Beitreibungsverfahren
3358.57 Stamps and insurance certificates. Beitragsmarken und Versicherungskarte
3358.6 Practice and procedure
3358.8 State supervision. Staatsaufsicht
Coverage and benefits
3360 General works
3362 Accident prevention. Factory inspection. Unfallverhütung
Compensation. Damages. Schadensersatz
Including injury at work, accident on the way to and from work
3363 General works
3364 Medical benefits. Rehabilitation
3364.5 Cash benefits
3366 Temporary and continuous disability pensions
Survivor benefits
3367 General works
3368 Funeral grants
3370 Widows' and orphans' pensions
3374.A-Z Groups of beneficiaries
3374.C59 Civil servants
3374.F37 Farmers. Farmhands. Landarbeiter. Landwirte
Farmhands see KK3374.F37
Landarbeiter see KK3374.F37
Landwirte see KK3374.F37
3377 Liability
Including employer and other persons
3379 Relationship between health insurance and accident insurance

Social legislation. Sozialrecht
Social insurance. Sozialversicherungsrecht
Workers' compensation. Gesetzliche Unfallversicherung -- Continued
3381 Conflicting claims. Konkurrierende Ersatzansprüche
3383 Criminal provisions
Social security. Rentenversicherungen
Including old age pensions (Altersversorgung), invalidity and disability pensions (Erwerbsunfähigkeit and Berufsunfähigkeit), and survivor benefits (Hinterbliebenenversorgung)
For pensions and retirement plans of private enterprise see KK2967+
Social reform see KK3270
3387 General (Table K11)
3390 Compulsory insurance. Exemptions
3392 Nachversicherung (Retroactive insurance)
Organization and administration
Including Landesversicherungsanstalten (State insurance office), Bundesversicherungsanstalt für Angestellte (Federal employees' insurance office), and Bahnversicherungsanstalt (Railroad insurance institute)
For Seekasse see KK2296+
For Knappschaften see KK6724+
3394 General works
3394.2 Corporate rights and personality. Rechte und Rechtsfähigkeit
Autonomy. Self-government
3394.3 General works
3394.33 Organs (Table K11)
Including elections
Officials and employees
3394.4 General (Table K11)
3394.42 Labor-management relations
Finance
3394.5 General
3394.52 Accounting and auditing. Rechnungsführung und Betriebsprüfung
Dues. Beitrage
3394.53 General works
3394.54 Employers' and employees' contributions. Arbeitgeber- und Arbeitnehmeranteile
3394.55 Collection. Einzug
3394.56 Hortatory procedures and execution. Mahn- und Beitreibungsverfahren
3394.57 Stamps and insurance certificates. Beitragsmarken und Versicherungskarte

Social legislation. Sozialrecht
Social insurance. Sozialversicherungsrecht
Social security. Rentenversicherungen
Organization and administration -- Continued

3394.6 Practice and procedure
3394.8 State supervision. Staatsaufsicht
Social security taxes see KK7185
Coverage and benefits
3396 General works
3397 Medical benefits. Rehabilitation
3397.5 Cash benefits
Pensions. Renten
3398 General (Table K11)
3401 Calculation. Adjudication
3403 Qualifying period. Expectancies. Wartezeit. Anwartschaft
Types of period
3405 Old age pensions
3407 Occupational disability. Berufsunfähigkeit
3408 Invalidity and death. Erwerbsunfähigkeit und Tod
3409 Fremdrenten. Auslandsrenten
3411.A-Z Groups of beneficiaries, A-Z
3411.A44 Alien laborers. Fremdarbeiter
3411.A78 Artisans. Handwerker
3411.C45 Clergy
Cottage industries see KK3411.H65
3411.D58 Divorced people
3411.F37 Farmers. Farmhands. Landwirte. Landarbeiter
3411.H65 Home laborers. Cottage industries. Heimarbeiter. Hausgewerbetreibende
3411.L32 Laborers. Arbeiter
Laborers, Alien see KK3411.A44
3411.M55 Miners. Bergarbeiter
Orphans see KK3411.S87
3411.P35 Parents
3411.P76 Professionals. Freiberuflich Tätige
3411.S35 Salaried employees. Angestellte
3411.S45 Self-employed
Spouses see KK3411.S87
3411.S87 Survivors
3413 Relationship between social security and private life insurance
Unemployment insurance. Arbeitslosenversicherung
For pension trusts see KK2968
For civil service pensions see KK5955
3418 General (Table K11)

Social legislation. Sozialrecht
Social insurance. Sozialversicherungsrecht
Unemployment insurance. Arbeitslosenversicherung -- Continued
3420 Compulsory insurance
Including exemptions
3422 Organization and administration
Including Bundesanstalt für Arbeitsvermittlung und Arbeitslosenversicherung (Federal placement and unemployment insurance institute), Landesarbeitsämter, Arbeitsämter (regional and local employment offices), and Hilfskassen (friendly societies)
Coverage and benefits
3424 General works
3425 Unemployment cash benefits. Arbeitslosengeld (Table K11)
3426 Health insurance. Workers' compensation
3427 Compensation for shutdown, short hours, etc.
Measures against unemployment see KK3195+
3428.A-Z Groups of beneficiaries, A-Z
3428.A44 Alien laborers. Fremdarbeiter
3428.S42 Seasonally unemployed
Social services. Public welfare. Sozialfürsorge. Sozialhilfe
History
3430 General (Table K11)
3430.5 Amt für Heimatwesen
Criticism and reform see KK3270
3431-3435.8 General (Table K10)
Organization and administration. Träger der Sozialhilfe
History see KK3430+
3437 General (Table K11)
3438 Practice and procedure
Including Domicile (Unterstützungswohnsitz)
Coverage and benefits
3442 General works
3443 Institutional care (continuous or one-time). Laufende oder einmalige Leistungen in Anstalten
For old age homes and nursing homes see KK6227.O42
3445 Educational assistance and allowances. Ausbildungshilfe und Hilfe zum Aufbau einer Existenz (Table K11)
Including vocational training
3446 Nursing aid. Pflegehilfe
3447 Maternal and infant welfare. Mutterschutz (Table K11)
3448 Rent subsidies. Wohnungsgeld

Social legislation. Sozialrecht
Social services. Public welfare. Sozialfürsorge. Sozialhilfe
Coverage and benefits -- Continued
3450 Medical care for tuberculosis
Cf. KK6180.T82 Public health
3451 Replacement aid. Hilfe zur Weiterführung des Haushalts
3452 Spending money. Taschengeld
Subjects applying to various branches of social services
3454 Priority and subsidiarity of public welfare and social services
3456 Restitution and subrogation between agencies and persons responsible for support. Erstattungsrecht
Social work and social workers. Sozialhelfer
3458 General (Table K11)
3460 Organization and administration
3462 Volunteers for social work. Freiwilliges soziales Jahr
3464 Rural social services. Dorfhelfer
Social service beneficiaries. Sozialleistungsempfänger
3468 General works
3470 The poor and destitute. Arme. Hilfsbedürftige (Table K11)
3473 Older people. Alte (Table K11)
3476 Pensioners. Kleinrentner
Large families. Kinderreiche
3480 General (Table K11)
3483 Kindergeldkasse (Child's supplement fund)
Cf. KK3560 Federal department for family and children
Coverage and benefits
3485 General works
3486 Child's supplements
People with disabilities. Behinderte
Including people with physical, mental, and emotional disabilities
3490 General (Table K11)
Coverage and benefits
3492 General works
3494 Rehabilitation. Einliederungshilfe
Cf. KK2889 Sheltered workshops
3496.A-Z Beneficiaries, A-Z
3496.B54 Blind
3496.D42 Deaf-mute. Taubstumme
3496.M44 Mental disabilities, People with
People with mental disabilities see KK3496.M44
People with severe disabilities see KK3496.S38
3496.S38 Severe disabilities, People with. Schwerbeschädigte
3498.A-Z Asocial types. Gefährdete, A-Z

Social legislation. Sozialrecht
Social services. Public welfare. Sozialfürsorge. Sozialhilfe
Social service beneficiaries. Sozialleistungsempfänger
Asocial types. Gefährdete, A-Z -- Continued
3498.A52 Alcoholics
3498.D78 Drug addicts. Süchtige
3498.P76 Prostitutes
3502 Evacuated and homeless persons. Evakuierte und Obdachlose
War-related groups of beneficiaries
3503 General (Table K11)
Organization and administration
3503.5 General works
Bundesminister für Vertriebene, Flüchtlinge und Kriegsgeschädigte (Department for expatriated, refugees, and war victims)
3504 General (Table K11)
Bundesausgleichsamt see KK7073
3504.5 Agencies and camps for admission of refugees
Versorgungsamter see KK3538
Refugees. Expelled or forcefully repatriated persons. Flüchtlinge und Heimatvertriebene
Including German-stock refugees, homeless (stateless) foreigners, and political refugees
3506 General (Table K11)
3508 Right of asylum
Coverage and benefits
3510 General (Table K11)
3512 Refugee housing projects. Flüchtlingssiedlung
Ausgleich fur Vertreibungsschäden
3514 General (Table K11)
Restitution and indemnification see KK7642+
Soforthilfe see KK7277+
Lastenausgleich see KK7277+
3516 Debtors' relief. Composition
3520.A-Z Beneficiaries, A-Z
3520.E18 East German refugees
3525 Prisoners of war and political prisoners. Veterans. Kriegsgefangene, politische Gefangene und Heimkehrer (Table K11)
Services for war victims and war invalids. Kriegsopferversorgung und Kriegsopferfürsorge
3530 General (Table K11)
3532 Constitutional aspects
3538 Versorgungsämter
Practice and procedure
3540 General (Table K11)

Social legislation. Sozialrecht
Social services. Public welfare. Sozialfürsorge. Sozialhilfe
Social service beneficiaries. Sozialleistungsempfänger
War-related groups of beneficiaries
Services for war victims and war invalids. Kriegsopferversorgung und Kriegsopferfürsorge
Practice and procedure -- Continued

3542 Expert opinion. Gutachterwesen

Coverage and benefits

3544 General (Table K11)

3545 Pensions. Cost-of-living adjustments. Renten un Zusatzrenten

3547 Medical and cash sickness benefits. Krankegeld und Pflegegeld

3548.A-Z Other, A-Z

3550.A-Z Beneficiaries, A-Z

Disabled veterans see KK3550.W37

3550.S87 Survivors. Hinterbliebene

3550.W37 War invalids and war victims. Kriegsbeschädigte und Kriegsopfer

3552 Cash settlement (lump-sum payment). Kapitalisierung der Rente

Children. Youth. Jugendwohlfahrt. Jugendhilfe

3556 General (Table K11)

3558 Constitutional aspects

Organization and administration

3559 General (Table K11)

3560 Bundesminister für Familie und Jugend (Federal department for family and children)

3562 Jugendwohlfahrtsausschuss (Child welfare board)

Jugendämter

3563 General works

3564 Stadtjugendamt (Municipal child welfare agency)

3565 Landesjugendamt (State child welfare agency)

Including supervision of juvenile detention homes

Measures and provisions

3566 General works

3567 Protection of children in public. Schutz der Jugend in der Offentlichkeit (Table K11)

Including restaurants, taverns, theaters, gambling, etc.

3569 Protection of children against obscenity. Schutz gegen jugendgefährdende Schriften

3571 Government guardianship. Amtsvormundschaft

Custodial education. Fürsorgeerziehung

3573 General (Table K11)

3574 Homes for custodial education. Erziehungsheime

3575 Foster homes. Pflegefamilien

Social legislation. Sozialrecht
Social services. Public welfare. Sozialfürsorge. Sozialhilfe
Social service beneficiaries. Sozialleistungsempfänger
Children. Youth. Jugendwohlfahrt. Jugendhilfe
Measures and provisions
Custodial education. Fürsorgeerziehung -- Continued
3577 Orphanages. Waisenhäuser
3579 Priority or subsidiarity in child welfare. Rangverhältnisse in der Jugendhilfe
Disaster relief see KK6066
Social courts and procedure. Sozialgerichtsbarkeit
Class here works on federal courts, federal and state courts, or courts of several jurisdictions
For courts (several or individual) of an individual jurisdiction, see the state or municipality
History
Class here works on the law prior to 1958
For the later period see KK3591+
3587 General (Table K11)
3587.2 Bundesamt für Heimatwesen (1871)
3589 Criticism. Reform
3591-3595.8 General (Table K10)
3604 Sozialgerichte
Including Fachkammern, judges, lay judges, etc.
3609 Landessozialgerichte (Social courts of the states)
Including senates, presidents, judges, lay judges, etc.
3613 Bundessozialgericht (Federal social court)
Including senates (Fachsenate, Grosser Senat), judges, etc.
Procedural principles
3617 General works
3618 Due process of law. Rechtsschutz. Gesetzlicher Richter. Richterliches Gehör
Including frivolous suits (Querulantenklage)
3619 Oral procedures. Mündlichkeit
Including frivolous suits (Querulantenklage)
3619.5 Speedy trial. Court congestion and delay. Prozessökonomie. Prozessverschleppung
3620 Parties to action
Pretrial procedures. Vorverfahren
3621 General works
3622 Safeguarding evidence. Beweissicherungsverfahren
3623 Administrative remedies. Rechtsbehelfe
Procedure at first instance. Verfahren im ersten Rechtszug
3624 General works
Jurisdiction
Including competence in subject matter and venue (sachliche und örtliche Zuständigkeit)

Social legislation. Sozialrecht
Social courts and procedure. Sozialgerichstbarkeit
Procedure at first instance. Verfahren im ersten Rechtszug
Jurisdiction -- Continued
3625 General works
3626 Domicile. Place of employment. Wohnsitz
3628 Evidence. Burden of proof. Beweisverfahren
3630 Judicial decisions and judgments. Urteile und Beschlüsse
Remedies. Rechtsmittel
3633 General works
3634 Recourse. Rechtsmittel
Appellate procedures
3635 General works
3636 Berufung
3638 Revision
3640 New trial. Reopening a case. Wiederaufnahme des Verfahrens
3642 Execution
3644 Costs (Table K11)
Competence conflicts between administrative, labor, and social courts see KK5760
3646 Competence conflicts between social and labor courts
Courts and procedure
Administration of justice. Organization of the judiciary. Justizverwaltung und Rechtspflege
For the administration of criminal justice see KK9429.2+
Criticism. Reform (Justizreform) see KK942
3655 General works
Judiciary and politics (Rechtspflege und Politik) see KK942
3658 Judiciary and administration. Justiz und Verwaltung
3660 Judiciary and foreign relations. Justiz und Aussenpolitik
Organization and administration
Class here works on federal and state departments of justice or departments of justice of several states
For the department of justice of an individual state, see the state
For departments of justice and subordinate regulatory agencies prior to 1949, see KK4688; KK4880
For Justizprufungsämter (Examination boards) see KK3707
3664 General (Table K11)
3665 Bundesminister der Justiz (Federal department of justice) (Table K11)
Judicial statistics see KK61+
Courts. Gerichtsverfassung
3666 General (Table K11)

Courts and procedure
Courts. Gerichtsverfassung -- Continued

3668 Principle of self-government. Gerichtliche Selbstverwaltung und Geschäftsverteilung

3670 Präsidialprinzip

3671 Kollegialitätsprinzip

Regular courts. Ordentliche Gerichte

Class here works on federal courts, federal and state courts, or courts of several jurisdictions

For courts (several or individual) of an individual jurisdiction, see the state or municipality

3673 General (Table K11)

Amtsgerichte (Magistrate courts)

3674 General (Table K11)

Courts of assizes see KK9455+

Jurisdiction (Civil procedure) see KK3872+

Jurisdiction (Criminal procedure) see KK9576+

Landgerichte (State district courts)

3676 General (Table K11)

Juries and jurors see KK9459+

3678 Kammer für Handelssachen

3682 Oberlandesgerichte (State supreme courts) (Table K11)

National supreme courts

3684 Reichsoberhandelsgericht (1869-1879)

3685 Reichsgericht (Imperial court, 1879-1945)

Including senates for civil and criminal matters

3686 Bundesgerichtshof (Federal supreme court)

Including senates for civil and criminal matters

Bundesverwaltungsgericht see KK5663+

Bundesarbeitsgericht see KK3223

Bundessozialgericht see KK3613

Bundesverfassungsgericht see KK5461+

Bundesfinanzhof see KK7441

3688 Gemeinsamer Senat der obersten Gerichtshöfe des Bundes (Joint senate of the federal supreme courts)

Military government courts and other temporary courts, boards, etc. (Germany under Allied occupation, 1945-1955)

Including procedure

3690 General (Table K11)

3691 Jurisdiction

Including competence in subject matter and venue (sachliche und örtliche Zuständigkeit)

3691.5.A-Z Courts. By name, A-Z

3691.5.D48 Deutsches Obergericht

Courts of special jurisdiction. Special tribunals

3692 General works

Courts and procedure
Courts. Gerichtsverfassung
Courts of special jurisdiction. Special tribunals -- Continued
3693 Consular courts. Konsulargerichte
3695 Competence conflict courts. Konsulargerichte
Cf. KK3646 Competence conflicts between social and labor courts
Cf. KK5760 Competence conflicts between administrative, labor, and social courts
3696 Courts of honor. Ehrengerichtsbarkeit
Class here general works
For individual courts, see KK122; KK6862; KK7047
Other courts of special jurisdiction
see the subject, e.g. KK3205+ Labor courts; KK3587+ Social courts; KK5647+ Administrative courts; KK7900+ Military courts, etc.
3697.A-Z Special tribunals within a court. Spruchkörper innerhalb eines Gerichtes. By name, A-Z
Deliberating and voting. Secrecy
3697.5 General works
Jury room procedure see KK9462
3698 Court decorum and discipline. Conduct of court proceedings. Mass media
3700 Terms of court. Gerichtsferien
3703 Judicial opinions. Advisory opinions. Gerichtliche Gutachtertätigkeit
The legal profession
Including judicial officers and personnel
3704 General (Table K11)
Law school education see KK89+
Post-law school education. Justinzausbildung für den höheren Justizdienst und Rechtsanwaltschaft
Including examinations, Vorbereitungsdienst, admission to the bar, etc.
3706 General (Table K11)
3707 Boards and commissions. Justizprüfungsämter
Class here general works
For boards and commissions of a particular state, see the state
3708 Judicial personnel other than lawyers. Unterer und mittlerer Justizdienst
3710 Nationality and citizenship
3712.A-Z Minorities, A-Z
3712.J49 Jews
3712.W65 Women
3713 Salaries, allowances, pensions, etc.

Courts and procedure
The legal profession -- Continued
Judges. Richter
3716 General (Table K11)
Women as judges see KK3712.W65
3718 Independence of judges. Richterliche Unabhängigkeit
3720 Liability
Disqualification of judges see KK3804.D58
3721 Honorary judges. Ehrenamtliche Richter
3722 Political activity of judges
3723 Ethics and discipline
3725 Lawyers as research aides at supreme courts. Juristische Hilfsarbeiter
Staatsanwaltschart (Office of the public prosecutor)
Class here works on federal prosecution offices, federal and state prosecution offices, or prosecution offices of several states
For prosecution offices (several or individual) of an individual state, see the state
3728 General (Table K11)
3732 Oberstaatsanwalt (at the Landgericht)
Including Staatsanwälte and Amtsanwälte
3735 Generalstaatsanwalt (at the Oberlandesgericht)
Federal prosecution office
3739 Oberreichsanwalt (at the Reichsgerichtshof, until 1945)
Including Reichsanwälte
3743 Oberbundesanwalt (at the Bundesgerichtshof)
Including Bundesanwälte
3745 Supervision. Dienstaufsicht und Weisungsgebundenheit
3747 Jurisdiction
Notaries see KK4070+
Auxiliary personnel. Clerk's office
3752 General (Table K11)
Clerks to the court. Rechtspfleger. Gerichtsschreiber
3754 General (Table K11)
3755 Accounting. Gerichtskasse
3757 Business administration. Court records. Geschäftsstelle. Aktenverwaltung
For personal data protection in information retrieval systems see KK1968.5
3759 Bailiffs. Gerichtsvollzieher
Experts and expert witnesses. Sachverständige
3762 General (Table K11)
3765 Medical examiners
For forensic medicine see RA1001+
Practice of law
3769 General (Table K11)

Courts and procedure
The legal profession
Practice of law -- Continued
Attorneys. Rechtsanwälte
3770 General (Table K11)
Admission to the bar see KK3706+
3772 Attorney and client
Including liability
Law office management
3775 General (Table K11)
3776 Accounting
3777 Clerks, etc. Anwaltsgehilfen
3779 Costs. Anwaltskosten (Table K11)
For in forma pauperis (Armensachen) see KK3792
Corporate representation see KK122+
Courts of honor. Disbarment see KK122+
3782.A-Z Special topics, A-Z
3782.P55 Pleading
3790 Legal consultants. Rechtsberater (Table K11)
3792 Legal aid. Beratungshilfe (Table K11)
Professional associations see KK132.A+
Judicial assistance. Rechtshilfe
For judicial assistance in criminal matters see KK9432+
3795 General (Table K11)
3797 International judicial assistance
3799 Interzonal judicial assistance
3800 Foreign judgments (Conflict of laws)
Judicial review see KK3804.J833
Procedure in general
3802 General (Table K11)
3804.A-Z Special topics, A-Z
3804.A28 Actions and defenses
Appellate procedures see KK3804.R45
3804.A66 Applicability of the law. Gesetzesanwendung
Burden of proof see KK3804.E84
Competence conflict see KK3804.J87
3804.C64 Conduct of court proceedings. Decorum
3804.C65 Conflict of judicial decisions. Befangenheit und Unparteilichkeit des Richters
Correction of judgments see KK3804.J83
Court congestion and delay see KK3804.S63
3804.C68 Court records. Gerichtsakten
Deadlines see KK3804.T55
Decorum see KK3804.C64
Defenses see KK3804.A28
3804.D58 Disqualification of judge

Courts and procedure
Procedure in general
Special topics, A-Z -- Continued

3804.D83 Due process of law. Rechtsschutz. Gesetzlicher Richter und Rechtliches Gehör

Error of judgment see KK3804.J83

3804.E84 Evidence. Burden of proof

Expert witnesses see KK3762+

3804.G66 Good faith. Vertrauensschutz im Prozess

3804.J83 Judgments and grounds of judgments. Urteil und Urteilsgründe

3804.J832 Judicial discretion. Richterliches Ermessen

3804.J833 Judicial review of legislative acts. Richterliches Prüfungsrecht. Normenkontrolle

3804.J87 Jurisdiction. Competence conflicts

Juristic persons see KK3804.P37

3804.L39 Law and fact. Tatsachenforschung

3804.L58 Lis pendens. Rechtshängigkeit

Minutes see KK3804.C68

Mistake of judgments see KK3804.J83

3804.O28 Oath

Oral procedures see KK3804.P82

3804.P37 Parties to action. Prozessparteien
Including juristic persons (Verbände)

3804.P73 Preclusion

3804.P76 Provisional remedies. Vorbeugender Rechtsschutz

3804.P82 Publicity and oral procedure. Offentlichkeit und Mündlichkeit

3804.R42 Recourse. Beschwerde

3804.R45 Remedies. Appellate procedures. Rechtsmittel. Berufung und Revision

3804.R48 Res judicata. Rechtskraft

Revisibility of judgments see KK3804.J83

3804.S63 Speedy trial. Court congestion and delay. Prozessökonomie. Prozessverschleppung

Stare decisis see KK3804.U54

3804.S87 Suspension. Aussetzung. Unterbrechung

3804.T55 Time periods. Deadlines. Fristen. Termine

3804.U54 Uniformity of law application. State decisis. Einheitlichkeit der Rechtsanwendung

Withdrawal of judgment see KK3804.J83

3804.W58 Witnesses. Zeugen

Civil procedure. Zivilprozess

3809 History
Class here works on recent history and development of the law beginning ca. 1850
For works on the law prior to 1850 see KK722+

Courts and procedure
Civil procedure. Zivilprozess -- Continued
3810 Criticism. Reform. Rechtserneuerung. Polemik
3811-3827 General (Table K9a)
3831 Civil procedure law relating to other branches of the law
Procedural principles
3832 Due process of law. Rechtsschutz. Gesetzlicher Richter. Rechtliches Gehör
Including frivolous suits (Querulantenklagen)
3833 Uniformity of law application. Stare decisis
Prohibition of abuse of legal procedure and chicanery see KK887.7
3834 Bona fides. Good faith
3835 Party autonomy versus inquiry ex officio. Verhandlungsmaxime versus Offizialmaxime
3836 Publicity and oral procedure. Grundsatz der Offentlichkeit und Mündlichkeit
Principles of evidence see KK3927
3839 Speedy trial. Konzentrationsprinzip (Prozessökonomie)
3840 Truthfulness and falsehood. Discovery (disclosure). Wahrheitspflicht und Aufklärungspflicht
3842 Prejudicial actions. Bindung des Richters an Urteile und Verwaltungsakte
Parties to action. Prozessparteien
3846 General (Table K11)
3847 Juristic persons. Verbände
3848 Privileged parties
Litigant. Plaintiff. Defendant
3850 General (Table K11)
Parteifähigkeit und Prozessfähigkeit
3852 General works
Juristic persons see KK3847
3855 Unborn children. Nasciturus
Joinder of parties see KK3909
Change of parties see KK3915
Succession into procedure see KK3915
3857 Judges
State prosecutor see KK3739+
Pretrial procedures. Vorbereitung und Prozesshandlungen
3859 General (Table K11)
3860 Summons, service of process, subpoena, etc. Ladungen, Zustellung, etc.
Time periods. Deadlines. Fristen. Termine
3862 General works
3864 Default and restitution. Saümnis und Wiedereingsetzung in den vorigen Stand

Courts and procedure
Civil procedure. Zivilprozess
Pretrial procedures. Vorbereitung und Prozesshandlungen -- Continued

3866 Suspension of procedure. Ruhen und Aussetzung des Verfahrens
3868 Mistakes. Errors in procedural acts. Correction
Procedure at first instance. Verfahren im ersten Rechtszug
3870 General works
3871 Standing. Klagerecht
Jurisdiction
3872 General works
3873 Admission of a case to the civil court. Zulässigkeit des Rechtsweges
Competence in subject matter and venue. Sachliche und örtliche Zuständigkeit
3874 General (Table K11)
Value or amout at issue see KK4036
3875 Forum rei sitae
3876 Prorogation
3877 Venue for corporate bodies
3878 Domicile or place of business
3880 Capacity to sue and to be sued. Aktiv- und Passivlegitimation
3882 Right to litigate. Prozessführungsbefugnis
3884 Accepting service. Prozesstandschaft
Representation. Power of attorney. Vertretung und Prozessvollmacht
3886 General (Table K11)
3888 Attorney
Lis pendens see KK3907.L58
Res judicata see KK3907.R48
3890 Object at issue. Streitgegenstand
3892 Forfeiture. Verwirkung prozessualer Befugnisse
Time periods. Deadlines see KK3862+
Actions and defenses. Klage und Einlassung
3896 General works
Classification of actions see KK3960+
3897 Form requirements
3899 Prayer in complaint. Klageantrag
3900 Matter of complaint. Klagerund
Facts see KK3929
Value or amount at issue see KK4036
3902 Joinder of actions. Compounded claims. Klagenhäufung und Anspruchshäufung
3904 Amendment. Withdrawal. Klageänderung. Klagerücknahme

Courts and procedure
Civil procedure. Zivilprozess
Procedure at first instance. Verfahren im ersten Rechtszug
Actions and defenses. Klage und Einlassung -- Continued
Defense and exceptions. Verteidigung. Einwendungen und Einreden
3906 General works
3907.A-Z Defenses, A-Z
3907.C65 Confession. Geständnis und Annahme
Counterclaim see KK3907.S48
3907.L55 Limitation of actions. Verjährung
3907.L58 Lis pendens. Rechtshängigkeit
3907.R48 Res judicata. Rechtskraft
3907.S48 Set-off. Counterclaim (Cross action). Aufrechnung im Prozess. Widerklage
Particular proceedings. Besondere Gestaltung des Verfahrens
3908 General works
3909 Joinder of parties. Mehrheit der Parteien
Including einfache, notwendige, and besondere Streitgenossenschaft
3911 Intervention (Table K11)
Including Haupt- und Nebenintervention
3913 Interpleader. Streitverkündung
3915 Change of parties. Parteienwechsel
Including death of party
3916 Change of ownership of res litis. Eigentümerwechsel der streitbefangenen Sache
3919 Default judgments. Versäumnisverfahren
3920 Decision without trial. Verfahren ohne mündliche Verhandlung
3922 Dismissal and nonsuit. Erledigung des Rechtsstreits in der Hauptsache (Table K11)
3923 Settlement before trial. Güteverfahren
3924 Compromise. Prozessvergleich (Table K11)
Evidence. Beweisverfahren
3926 General
3927 Principles of evidence. Free evaluation of evidence
3928 Burden of proof. Proof of foreign law. Beweislast
3929 Facts. Tatsachen. Sachverhalt
3930 Prima facie. Beweis des ersten Anscheins
Admission of evidence. Zulässigkeit des Beweises
3931 General works
3932 Physical examinations. Blood tests
For forensic medicine see RA1001+
Witnesses. Zeugen

Courts and procedure
Civil procedure. Zivilprozess
Procedure at first instance. Verfahren im ersten Rechtszug
Evidence. Beweisverfahren
Witnesses. Zeugen -- Continued
3934 General works
3936 Privileged witnesses (Confidential communication)
3938 Expert testimony. Sachverständigengutachten
3940 Documentary evidence. Urkundenbeweis
3942 Circumstantial evidence. Indizienbeweis
3944 Testimony of party
3946 Presumptions. Gesetzliche Vermutungen
3947 Inspection by official person. Augenscheinseinnahme
3949 Oath. Eidesrecht
Including oath of witnesses and parties
Judicial decisions
3952 General works
3954 Injunctions. Arrest. Einstweilige Anordnung
Judgment. Urteil
3956 General works
3958 Judicial discretion. Richterliches Ermessen
Including equity
Types of judgments
3960 Leistungsurteil (to do, to tolerate, to refrain from doing)
3961 Declaratory judgment. Feststellungsurteil
3962 Gestaltungsurteil
3963 Prozessurteil und Sachurteil (Motion to dismiss and judgment in rem)
3964 Anerkenntnisurteil (Agreed judgment)
3966 Abänderungsurteil
Judgment by default see KK3919
Decision without trial see KK3920
Dismissal and nonsuit see KK3922
3968 Interlocutory decision. Zwischenurteil
3969 Vorbehaltsurteil
3970 Teilurteil
3972 Void judgments and nonjudgments. Nichtige Urteile und Nicht-Urteile
3974 Form
3976 Mistakes (error)
Including correction or withdrawal of faulty decision
3978 Res judicata. Rechtskraft (Table K11)
3980 Court records. Minutes of evidence. Gerichtsprotokoll
Including clerks' mistakes and corrections
3982 Advisory opinions. Rechtsgutachten
Particular procedures. Besondere Verfahrensarten

Courts and procedure
Civil procedure. Zivilprozess
Particular procedures. Besondere Verfahrensarten -- Continued
3985 General works
3987 Procedure concerning documents and bills of exchange. Urkundenprozess. Wechselprozess (Table K22)
3990 Matrimonial actions. Ehesachen
3993 Procedures in parent and child cases. Kindschaftsachen
For procedures in guardianship cases see KK4130+
3996 Interdiction. Entmündigungsverfahren
3999 Public summons. Aufgeborsverfahren
Settlement before trial see KK3923
4002 Hortatory procedures. Mahnverfahren. Zahlungsbefehl
4006 Small claims. Procedures before the justice of the peace or magistrate
Remedies. Rechtsmittel und Rechtsbehelfe
4010 General works
4012 Gravamen. Beschwer
4014 Reformatio in peius
4016 Recourse. Beschwerde
Appellate procedures
4018 General works
4019 Berufung
4020 Revision
4024 New trial. Reopening of a case. Wiederaufnahme des Verfahrens
4026 Waiver of appeal. Rechtsmittelverzicht und Rechtsmittelrücknahme
4030 Arbitration. Schiedsgerichtsbarkeit (Table K11)
Including commercial arbitration
Costs. Gerichtskosten
4034 General (Table K11)
4036 Evaluation of object at issue. Streitwertfestsetzung
4038 In forma pauperis
Noncontentious jurisdiction. Freiwillige Gerichtsbarkeit
4044 General (Table K11)
4048 Inquiry ex officio. Offizialmaxime
4050 Parties to action. Beteiligte
Procedure
4052 General works
4053 Evidence. Beweisaufnahme
4055 Decisions. Beschlüsse und Verfüngen
Remedies and special procedures
4057 General works
4059 Beschwerde und special procedure
4061 New trial. Wiederaufnahme des Verfahrens

Courts and procedure
Noncontentious jurisdiction. Freiwillige Gerichtsbarkeit
Procedure -- Continued
4063 Res judicata. Rechtskraft
Notaries
Class here works on notaries of several jurisdictions
For notaries (several or individual) of an individual state, see the state
4070 General (Table K11)
4072 Legal status
4074 Liability. Haftungsrecht
4076 Legal instruments. Certification
4078 Costs (Table K11)
Registration. Recording
Class here works on registers of several jurisdictions
For registers (several or individual) of an individual state, see the state
For data protection (torts) see KK1968.5
For data protection (access to public records) see KK6071.5
4084 General (Table K11)
4085 Publicity. Rechtsschein
Civil register. Standesamt
4087 General (Table K11)
The officer. Der Standesbeamte
4089 General (Table K11)
4091 Legal status
4093 Regulations. Discipline
4095 Recordkeeping
Registration of civil status. Personenstand
4100 General (Table K11)
4102 Family names
For change of name see KK1024
4105 Marriage
4107 Birth
4110 Death
For absence and presumption of death see KK1014
4114 Aliens. Stateless foreigners. Fremde und staatenlose Ausländer
4116 Costs (Table K11)
4117 Register of matrimonial property. Güterrechtsregister
Land registers see KK1410+
Ship registers see KK2282
Commercial registers see KK2083+
Business associations see KK2459
Vereinsregister see KK1032.5

Courts and procedure

Noncontentious jurisdiction. Freiwillige Gerichtsbarkeit -- Continued

Domestic relations. Family

4120 General works

4122 Distribution of household after divorce. Hausrat-Teilungssachen (Table K11)

4126 Adoption procedures (Table K11)

Guardianship courts. Vormundschaftsgericht

4130 General (Table K11)

Jurisdiction

4137 General works

4138 Custody of children. Personensorge

Appointment of guardian

4139 General works

4140 Qualifications of guardian

4141 Co-guardians. Supervisory guardians

4143 Family council

4145 Orphan council of community. Gemeindewaisenrat

Guardians' responsibilities

4146 General works

4147 Education

4149 Legal transactions

Government guardianship see KK3571

Interdiction see KK3996

4152 Inheritance (Probate court). Nachlassgericht

4154 Wertpapierbereinigung

4156 Condominium. Wohnungseigentum

4160 Arrest and detention (Review)

4165 Judicial review of administrative acts of the administration of justice

4168 Costs

Class here general works

For costs of a particular branch of noncontentious jurisdiction, see the branch

Insolvency

4171-4175.8 General (Table K10)

4177 State of insolvency. Zahlungseinstellung. Uberschuldung

Execution. Zwangsvollstreckungsrecht

4180 General (Table K11)

Parties to execution

Including executors and administrators

4182 General (Table K11)

4185 Succession during execution

Third parties see KK4284.T44

Bailiffs see KK3759

Courts and procedure
Insolvency
Execution. Zwangsvollstreckungsrecht -- Continued
Titles for execution. Vollstreckungstitel
Including judgments (res judicata), documents of title, etc.
4187 General works
4189 Vorläufige Vollstreckbarkeit
Procedure in execution
4192 General (Table K11)
4194 Discovery proceedings. Poor debtors oath. Offenbarungseid und Verfahren
Including inventory (Vermögensvertzeichnis)
4196 Judicial decisions (Res judicata). Beschlüsse und Rechtskraft
Execution for payment due. Vollstreckung wegen Geldforderungen
4200 General works
Hortatory procedures see KK4002
Attachment and garnishment of personal property. Pfändung und Verstrickung von beweglichem Vermögen
4203 General works
Exemptions see KK4276+
Attachment and garnishment of rights and choses in action. Pfändung von Forderungen und Rechten
4205 General works
4207 Pledges. Expectancies. Pfandrechte und Anwartscahftsrechte
4209.A-Z Other, A-Z
4209.A33 Account current
4209.A54 Animals
4209.B35 Bank deposits
4209.E73 Escrows
4209.I57 Intellectual property
4209.L48 Letters of credit
4209.L53 Life insurance
Negotiable instruments see KK4209.S42
4209.S34 Salaries and wages
4209.S42 Securities. Negotiable instruments
4211 Pfandungspfandrecht
Judicial sale. Offentliche Versteigerung
4214 General (Table K11)
4216 Good faith. Gutgläubigkeit
4218 Transfer of ownership
4220 Distribution. Verteilungsverfahren
4222 Detention of debtor. Haft
Poor debtors oath see KK4194

Courts and procedure
Insolvency
Execution. Zwangsvollstreckungsrecht
Procedure in execution
Execution for payment due. Vollstreckung wegen Geldforderungen -- Continued
Remedies see KK4252+
Execution in real property. Zwangsvollstreckung in das unbewegliche Vermögen
4225 General (Table K11)
4227 Zwangshypothek
Foreclosure sale. Judicial sale. Receivership. Zwangsversteigerung und Zwangsverwaltung
4229 General (Table K11)
4231 Receiver. Zwangsverwalter (Table K11)
4233 Mortgage and land charger (Table K11)
4234 Condominium. Cooperative housing
Execution against tenants see KK1781+
Exemptions and restrictions see KK4276+
4240 Enforcement of surrender of goods or documents
4243 Enforcement of acts (commissions or omissions)
4245 Executions against associations, personal companies, and corporations
Including execution against juristic persons of public law
4250 Injunction. Arrest. Seizure. Einstweilige Verfügung und Arrest
Cf. KK3954 Procedure at first instance
4251 Fine for debtor's delay. Zwangsgeld
Remedies
4252 General (Table K11)
4254 Vollstreckungsgegenklage
4259 Objections of third party claiming ownership and seeking release. Drittwiderspruchsklage
4265 Costs
Protection against abuse of claims enforcement. Vollstreckungsschutz
4270 General (Table K11)
Moratorium see KK4384
4272 Suspension. Accord and satisfaction. Vollstreckungsaussetzung
4274 Compromise
Exemptions and restrictions
4276 General (Table K11)
4277 Salaries. Wages. Pensions
4278 Support (Domestic relations)
4280 Minimum income. Beneficium competentiae
4282 Damages. Compensation for unjustified execution

Courts and procedure
Insolvency
Execution. Zwangsvollstreckungsrecht
Protection against abuse of claims enforcement.
Vollstreckungsschutz -- Continued
4284.A-Z Special topics, A-Z
4284.C65 Conditional sales. Installment plans
Cf. KK1713+ Civil law
Installment plans see KK4284.C65
4284.P74 Priorities of claims and liens
4284.T44 Third parties
Bankruptcy. Konkursrecht
4290 General (Table K11)
4295 Insolvent estate. Konkursmasse
4297 Court. Konkursgericht (Table K11)
Parties to action. Parteien des Konkursverfahrens
4300 General works
4302 Referee. Konkursrichter
4305 Gemeinschuldner
Including legal status, liability, etc.
4307 Konkursgläubiger
Trustee in bankruptcy. Konkursverwalter
4308 General works
4309 Legal status. Liability
Third parties
4311 General works
4312 Spouses. Matrimonial property
Procedure. Konkursverfahren
4314 General (Table K11)
4315 Konkursantrag
4316 Konkurseröffnung
Feststellungsverfahren
4317 General works
4319.A-Z Priority claims and privileged claims, A-Z
4319.B35 Banks and credit institution claims
4319.B38 Baukostenzuschüsse
4319.T38 Tax liens
4323 Aussonderung und Absonderung (Severance and separate performance)
4325 Distribution. Verteilungsverfahren
4327 Aufhebung. Einstellung
4330 Composition to end bankruptcy. Zwangsvergleich
Judicial review of voidable transactions.
Gläubigeranfechtung während Konkurs
4332 General (Table K11)
Fraudulent conveyances see KK8750+
Effect of bankruptcy on obligations and rights

Courts and procedure
Insolvency
Bankruptcy. Konkursrecht
Effect of bankruptcy on obligations and rights -- Continued

4336 General (Table K11)
4337.A-Z Special topics, A-Z
4337.A22 Account current
Conditional sale see KK4337.S25
4337.C66 Contracts and other obligations
4337.H96 Hypotheca
Industrial property see KK4337.I58
4337.I58 Intellectual and industrial property
4337.L42 Lease
Pensions see KK4337.W34
4337.R48 Retention of ownership
Salaries see KK4337.W34
4337.S25 Sale. Conditional sale
4337.S48 Set-off. Aufrechnung
4337.W34 Wages. Salaries. Pensions
4339 Nachlasskonkurs
4340 Anschlusskonkurs
4343 Costs (Table K11)
4348 Gläubigeranfechtung nach dem Anfechtungsgesetz (ausserhalb des Konkurses) (Table K11)
Debtors' relief
For wartime debtors' relief see KK7521+
4353 General (Table K11)
Composition to avoid bankruptcy. Deferment of execution
4357 General (Table K11)
Receivership. Vergleich (nach der Vergleichsordnung) und Geschäftsaufsicht
4360 General works
4362 Receivers
4367 Richterliche Vertragshilfe (nach dem Vertragshilfegesetz)
4373 Schuldenbereinigung (nach dem Schuldenbereinigungsgesetz)
4378 Corporate reorganization
4384 Moratorium. Stundung
4389 Tax privileges. Sanierung im Steuerrecht
Collection agencies see KK6823
Costs. Kostenrecht
Including bookkeeping and accounting
4394 General (Table K11)

Courts and procedure
Costs. Kostenrecht -- Continued
4396 Courts
Including witnesses and expert witnesses, and Prozesskostenhilfe (In forma pauperis)
Costs in special proceedings or special courts
see the subject, e.g. KK3779 Attorneys; KK4034+ Civil procedure; KK4116 Civil registers; KK5762+ Administrative courts; KK9798 Criminal courts, etc.
4399 Execution. Enforcement. Kostenbeitreibung (Table K11)
Public law. Offentliches Recht
Class here works on all aspects of public law, including early works
For civics see KK156
4413 General (Table K11)
The State. Staatsphilosophie. Staats- und Verwaltungslehre
For nonlegal works on political theory, see JC
4420 General (Table K11)
Law and the state see KK890
Empire see KK291.E46
4425 Sovereignty
Federalism see KK5075+
Rule of law. Rechtsstaatlichkeit
4426 General (Table K11)
4427 Sozialstaat
4429 Sozialer Rechtstaat
4430 Annexation of territory
4432 Succession of states. Continuity. Staatennachfolge
4434.A-Z Special topics, A-Z
Constitutional law. Staats- und Verfassungsrecht
Class here works on constitutional law of the Federal Republic of Germany (Bundesrepublik Deutschland), which is composed of the three Western Zones of Occupation and the Saarland under the Constitution of 1949
For works on constitutional law of the German Democratic Republic (Deutsche Demokratische Republic, previously the Russian Zone of Occupation) under its own constitution of 1949, see KKA
For works on the constitutional aspects of a subject, see the subject
For works on constitutional law of Germany prior to 1949 see KK4455+
History see KK4455+
4436 Constitutional reform. Criticism. Verfassungsreform. Polemik
For works on a particular constitution, see the constitution

Constitutional law. Staats- und Verfassungsrecht -- Continued

4441 Bibliography

Including bibliography of constitutional history

Sources

Including 19th century constitutions and related material

For sources prior to 1806 see KK250+

4443.6 Collections. Compilations

Including federal sources, federal and state sources, and sources of several states

Constitutions. Verfassungen

Collections see KK4443.6

Individual constitutions

4444 Rheinbundakte, 1806 (Table K17)

4444.2 Deutsche Bundesakte, 1815 (Table K17)

4444.22 Wiener Schlussakte, 1820 (Table K17)

4444.23 Constitution, 1848 (Table K17)

4444.24 Norddeutsche Bundesakte, 1867 (Table K17)

4444.25 Constitution of the Empire (Kaiserreich), 1871 (Table K17)

4444.26 Weimar constitution, 1919 (Table K17)

4444.3 Constitution of the Federal Republic, 1949 (Table K17)

Individual sources other than constitutions

Including legislative documents

4444.6 Karlsbader Beschlüsse

4444.63 Ermächtigungsgesetz, 1933

4444.65 Gesetz über Gleichschaltung der Länder, 1933

4444.67 Gesetz über Neuaufbau des Reiches, 1934

4444.69 Charter of the Allied High Commission, 1949

4444.7 Occupation Statute, 1949

4444.72 First instrument of revision of the Occupation statute for Germany, 1951

4444.75 Protocol on the termination of the occupation regime in the Federal Republic of Germany, 1954

Comparative state constitutions

4445 Collections

4445.6 General works. Treatises

Court decisions

4446 Indexes and tables

4446.3 Serials

4446.5 Monographs. By date

4446.7 Digests. Analytical abstracts

4449 Conferences. Symposia

Collected works (nonserial) see KK4450

4450 General works. Treatises

Compends. Outlines. Examination aids. Popular works see KK4450

Addresses, essays, lectures see KK4450

Constitutional law. Staats- und Verfassungsrecht -- Continued
Constitutional history. Verfassungsgeschichte
For works on constitutional history prior to 1806 see KK190
For individual constitutions see KK4444+
4455 General works
By period
Early period. Germanic tribes see KJ160+
Frankish period, ca. 500-ca. 919 see KJ160+
German empire. Holy Roman Empire, ca. 919-1806 see KK290
Period of confederation, 1806-1871
4460 General works
Confederation of the Rhine. Rheinbund, 1806-1815
4462 General (Table K22)
4465 Bundestag (Legislature) (Table K22)
4468 Press laws. Censorship
German Confederation. Deutscher Bund, 1815-1866
4470 General (Table K22)
Constitutional principles
4473 General works
4475 Particularism
4477 Separation and delegation of powers
Intergovernmental relations. Jurisdiction
4479 General works
4481 Particular states and estates in relation to the German Confederation. Execution
4483 Territory
4485 Foreign relations
Individual and state
4487 General works
4488 Nationality and citizenship
Fundamental rights and constitutional guaranties. Grundrechte und Verfassungsgarantien
4489 General works
Equality before the law. Gleichheit vor dem Gesetz
Including antidiscrimination
4490 General works
Minorities (ethnic, religious, racial)
4493 General works
4495.A-Z By region, state, or city, A-Z
4495.F72 Frankfurt
Freedom. Freiheit des Meschen
4500 General works
4502 Freedom of religion and conscience. Religious-, Glaubens- und Gewissensfreiheit

Constitutional law. Staats- und Verfassungsrecht
Constitutional history. Verfassungsgeschichte
By period
Period of confederation, 1806-1871
German Confederation. Deutscher Bund, 1815-1866 -- Continued

4504 Political parties and pressure groups
4505 Election law. Wahlrecht
Church and state see KK5520+
Organs of the German Confederation
4506 General works
Bundesversammlung. Bundestag (Legislature)
4508 General works
4510 Engerer Rat. Bundesregierung (Executive branch)
4511 Zentraluntersuchungsausschuss in Mainz
Competence. Jurisdiction
4513 General works
4515 Succession conflicts of ruling dynasties
4517 Austrägalinstanz. Bundesschiedsgericht (Arbitral court, 1834)
4519 Zollverein (Custom Union, 1834)
4521 Military organization. Military law
North German Confederation. Norddeutscher Bund, 1867-1871
Including works on both North German Confederation and Empire of 1871
4525 General (Table K11)
4529 Constitutional principles
Bundesrat. Bundespräsidium (Council of princes and rulers of German states)
Including free cities
4533 General (Table K11)
Organization and procedure. Standing order
4534 General (Table K11)
4536 Bundeskanzler
Duties and powers
4537 General works
4538 Treatymaking power
4540 Legislative power
War and emergency power
4541 General (Table K11)
4542 Execution against member states. State of siege
4544 Reichstag (Legislature)
Empire of 1871. Kaiserreich, 1871-1918
General works see KK4525

Constitutional law. Staats- und Verfassungsrecht
Constitutional history. Verfassungsgeschichte
By period
Empire of 1871. Kaiserreich, 1871-1918 -- Continued
Constitutional principles
4552 General works
Rulers. Princes. Dynasties. Regierende Häuser
4553 General works
Dynastic rules. Hausgesetze see KK295.5+
Legal status and juristic personality see KK301.J87
4555 Privileges of classes and particular groups
4558 Privileges, prerogatives, and immunities of states or estates
Rule of law (Rechtsstaatsprinzip) see KK4426+
Separation and delegation of power see KK4565+
4562 Amending process
Separation and delegation of powers
4565 General works
4567 Incompatibility of offices
Cf. KK4652 Reichstag
4569 Executive privilege
Sources and relationships of law. Lehre vom Gesetz
4572 General works
4573 Statutory law and delegated legislation
The Kaisers' ordinance power see KK4660
Intergovernmental relations
4574 General works
4575 Particularism
Federal-state controversies
4576 General works
4577 Secession
4578 Execution against member states. State of siege
Privileges, prerogatives, and immunities of particular states or estates see KK4558
Federal and state jurisdiction
4579 General works
4580 Sedition
4582 Foreign relations. Treaties
4584 Imperial territory. Reichsgebiet
4586 Foreign relations
Individual and state
4588 General works
Nationality and citizenship
4590 General works
4592 Natural and juristic persons
4594 Allegiance of citizen towards the state or ruler
Acquisition and loss

Constitutional law. Staats- und Verfassungsrecht
Constitutional history. Verfassungsgeschichte
By period
Empire of 1871. Kaiserreich, 1871-1918
Individual and state
Nationality and citizenship
Acquisition and loss -- Continued

4596 General (Table K22)
4598 Naturalization. Einbürgerung
For procedure see KK6046
4600 Expatriation. Ausbürgerung
Emigration see KK6048
Passports see KK6040
4602.A-Z Particular groups, A-Z
Fundamental rights and constitutional guaranties. Grundrechte und Verfassungsgarantien
4603 General works
Equality before the law. Gleichheit vor dem Gesetz
Including antidiscrimination
4604 General works
4606.A-Z Particular groups, A-Z
4606.W65 Women
Freedom. Freiheit des Menschen
4608 General works
4610 Freedom of religion and conscience. Religions-, Glaubens- und Gewissensfreiheit
Freedom of thought and speech. Freiheit der Meinungsbildung und Meinungsäusserung
4614 General works
4616 Freedom of the press and information
4618 Right of opposition
4620 Freedom of coalition
4622 Freedom of movement. Freizügigkeit
Family see KK1112
Cultural affairs see KK6258
4624 Political parties
4625 Internal security. Staatsschutz und Verfassungsschutz
Election law. Wahlrecht. Wahlverfahrensrecht
4626 General (Table K11)
4627 Proportional representation. Majority (Table K11)
4628 Direct and indirect election
Election to a particular office
4628.5 Reichstag
Organs of government
4629 General works
Bundesrat (Council of princes and rulers of the German states)

Constitutional law. Staats- und Verfassungsrecht
Constitutional history. Verfassungsgeschichte
By period
Empire of 1871. Kaiserreich, 1871-1918
Organs of government
Bundesrat (Council of princes and rulers of the German states) -- Continued

4630 General works
Organization and procedures. Standing order
4631 General (Table K22)
4632 Standing committees
Powers and prerogatives
4633 General works
4634 Legislative power
Execution against member states. State of siege see KK4578
4636 Method of appointment. Membership
Reichstag (Legislature)
4637 General works
4638 Representation of classes and social groups
4639 Relation to other branches of government
Organization and procedures. Standing order
4642 General (Table K22)
4643 President
4644 Powers and prerogatives
4645 The legislative process
Legal status of legislators
Including privilege of membership
4647 General (Table K11)
Election see KK4628.5
4651 Parliamentary immunity
4652 Incompatibility of offices
4653 Prerogation and dissolution of assemblies
Including duration of session
Kaiser
4654 General works
Legal status
4655 General works
4656 Succession to the crown
Powers and prerogatives of the crown
4657 General works
4658 Treatymaking power
4660 Legislative power
4662 War and emergency power

Constitutional law. Staats- und Verfassungsrecht
Constitutional history. Verfassungsgeschichte
By period
Empire of 1871. Kaiserreich, 1871-1918
Organs of government
Kaiser
Powers and prerogatives of the crown -- Continued
4664 Administration of colonies (Table K22)
Including finance, taxes, officials, companies, criminal provisions, etc.
For Kolonialamt see KK4692.K65
Reichskanzler
4667 General works
4669 Powers and office
Kabinett und Ministerien (Cabinet and departments)
Including rules and regulations, parliamentary practice, etc.
4671 General (Table K11)
4673 Relation to other branches of government
Auswärtiges Amt (Department of state)
4684 General (Table K11)
Foreign service. Auswärtiger Dienst
4685 General (Table K11)
4686 Legal status of personnel
Including allowances, salaries, retirement pensions, etc.
4687 Reichsamt des Innern (Department of the Interior, 1879)
Previously Reichskanzleramt
4688 Reichsjustizamt (Department of justice)
4689 Reichsfinanzministerium (Department of finance)
Previously Reichsschatzamt
4690 Reichsmarineamt (Department of the navy, 1889)
Previously Admiralität (1872)
For Maritime courts see KK2283
4692.A-Z Other departments, A-Z
4692.K65 Kolonialamt
4692.R42 Reichseisenbahnamt
4692.R43 Reichsgesundheitsamt (Health department)
4692.R45 Reichspostministerium (Post office department)
4692.R47 Reichswirtschaftsamt (Department of commerce)
4692.S72 Statistisches Reichsamt
4693 Beiräte (Advisory boards and councils)
Civil service see KK5930+
4696 The Judiciary. Judicial power
Class here general works on constitutional status

Constitutional law. Staats- und Verfassungsrecht
Constitutional history. Verfassungsgeschichte
By period
Empire of 1871. Kaiserreich, 1871-1918 -- Continued
4697 Statsgerichtshöfe (Constitutional tribunals)
For the constitutional tribunal of an individual state, see the state
National emblem. Flag. Seal. Seat of government.
National anthem see KK5505
Patriotic customs and observances see KK5509
Decorations of honor. Awards. Dignities see KK5511
Commemorative medals see KK5513
National defense. Military law
4700 General (Table K22)
Kontingentsherrlichkeit
4701 General works
4702 Command. Police
4703 Military criminal courts. Courts martial
4704 Military administration. Militarverwaltung
4705 Inspection. Chief of staff
Weimar Republic and Third Reich. Deutsches Reich unter Weimarer Verfassung und National-Sozialismus, 1919-1945
4710 General (Table K22)
Constitutional principles
4713 General works
Rule of law (Recht- und Gesetzmässigkeit see KK4426+
Separation and delegation of powers see KK4718
4716 Amending process
For particular amendments see KK4444.26
4718 Separation and delegation of powers
Sources and relationships of law. Lehre vom Gesetz
4719 General works
4720 International and municipal law
4721 Statutory law and delegated legislation. Gesetz im formellen und materiellen Sinn
Including ordinances and regulations (Verordnungen und Satzungen)
Intergovernmental relations
4723 General works
4724 Particularism
Federal-state disputes
4725 General works
4726 Execution against member states. State of siege
4727 State-state disputes

Constitutional law. Staats- und Verfassungsrecht
Constitutional history. Verfassungsgeschichte
By period
Weimar Republic and Third Reich. Deutsches Reich unter Weimarer Verfassung und National-Sozialismus, 1919-1945
Intergovernmental relations -- Continued

4728 Centralization of federal government. Reorganization. Neuaufbau des Reiches
Including works on the Reichsstatthalter and abolition of state parliaments
For Gesetz uber Gleichschaltung der Länder (1933) see KK4444.65
For Gestz uber Neuaufbau des Reiches (1934) see KK4444.67

4730 National territory
4732 Foreign relations
Individual and state
4733 General works
Nationality and citizenship
4734 General (Table K22)
4735 Allegiance of citizen towards the state
Acquisition and loss
4736 General (Table K22)
4737 Naturalization. Einbürgerung
For procedure see KK6046
4739 Expatriation. Ausbürgerung
Emigration see KK6048
4740 Marriage to a foreigner
Passports see KK6040
Minorities (ethnic, religious, racial)
4742 General (Table K22)
4743 Jews. Nürnberger Gesetze
Aliens. Homeless foreigners. Non-German refugees see KK6050+
Internal security see KK4784+
Fundamental rights and constitutional guaranties. Grundrechte und Verfassungsgarantien
4745 General (Table K22)
Equality before the law. Gleichheit vor dem Gesetz
Including antidiscrimination
4746 General works
4747.A-Z Particular groups, A-Z
4747.M55 Minorities (ethnic, religious, racial)
4747.W65 Women
Freedom. Freiheit des Menschen
4748 General works

Constitutional law. Staats- und Verfassungsrecht
Constitutional history. Verfassungsgeschichte
By period
Weimar Republic and Third Reich. Deutsches Reich unter Weimarer Verfassung und National-Sozialismus, 1919-1945
Individual and state
Fundamental rights and constitutional guaranties. Grundrechte und Verfassungsgarantien
Freedom. Freiheit des Menschen -- Continued
4749 Freedom of religion and conscience. Religions-, Glaubens- und Gewissensfreiheit
Freedom of thought and speech. Freiheit der Meinungsbildung und Meinungsäusserung
4750 General works
4751 Freedom of the press and information
4752 Prohibition of censorship
Official secrets and information see KK7026
4753 Freedom of movement. Freizügigkeit
4754 Freedom of assembly, association, and demonstration. Versammlungs- und Vereinsfreiheit
4755 Privacy of home
Privacy of communication
4756 General works
4757 Postal services. Telecommunication. Post- und Fernmeldegeheimnis
Property rights
For private property and right to inherit see KK1261+
4759 General works
Expropriation and confiscation of property
4759.5 General works
4760 Unwanted minorities. Enemy property
4761 Jews
Including Aryanization
Procedure see KK5778
4762 Right to asylum. Asylrecht
Prohibition against extradition see KK9571
4763 Right to resistance against government. Widerstandsrecht
Constitutional safeguards. Sicherung der Grundrechte
4764 General works
Process and procedure before constitutional court see KK4883+
4766 Civic duties. Staatsbürgerpflichten

Constitutional law. Staats- und Verfassungsrecht
Constitutional history. Verfassungsgeschichte
By period
Weimar Republic and Third Reich. Deutsches Reich unter Weimarer Verfassung und National-Sozialismus, 1919-1945
Individual and state -- Continued
Political parties

4770 General works
4772 Dissolution and interdiction
4773 Sozialistische Reichspartei
4774 Deutsche Demokratische Partei
4774.5 Kommunistische Partei Deutschlands (KPD)
Cf. KK5485.5.K65 Outlawing of political parties
Nationalsozialistische Deutsche Arbeiter Partei (NSDAP)
4775 General works
Subordinate or connected units
4776 Sturm-Abteilung (SA)
Schutz-Staffel (SS)
Including relation to police and Gestapo
4777 General works
4778 Discipline
Including courts and procedure
Hitler-Jugend (HJ)
Including Jungvolk, Jungmädchen, Bund Deutscher Mädel, etc.
4780 General works
4781 Discipline
Internal security. Staats- und Republikschutz
4784 General (Table K22)
Sicherheitsdienst (SD)
4785 General works
4786 Reichssicherheitshauptamt
4788 Geheime Staatspolizei (Gestapo)
Organs of government
4790 General works
The people. Das Volk
4791 General works
4792 Initiative and referendum. Plebiscite
Political parties see KK4770+
Election law. Wahlrecht. Wahlverfahrensrecht
4795 General (Table K22)
4796 Proportional representation. Majority
4797 Direct and indirect election
Suffrage (active and passive). Subjektives Wahlrecht

Constitutional law. Staats- und Verfassungsrecht
Constitutional history. Verfassungsgeschichte
By period
Weimar Republic and Third Reich. Deutsches Reich unter Weimarer Verfassung und National-Sozialismus, 1919-1945
Organs of government
The people. Das Volk
Election law. Wahlrecht. Wahlverfahrensrecht
Suffrage (active and passive). Subjektives Wahlrecht -- Continued

4799 General (Table K22)
4800 Women
4802 Auslandsdeutsche
Election to a particular office
4804 Reichstag
4805 Reichsrat
4806 Reichspräsident
4807 Election contest. Wahlprüfung
Including judicial review
Election crimes see KK9145+
The legislature
4810 General works
Reichstag
4812 General works
4813 Organization and procedures. Standing order
4814 Powers and prerogatives
4815 The legislative process
Legal status of legislators
Election see KK4804
4817 Incompatibility of offices
4819 Dissolution. Duration of session
Reichsrat
4820 General works
4821 Organization and procedures. Standing order
4822 Powers and prerogatives
Method of appointment. Election see KK4805
4824 Duration of session
Reichswirtschaftsrat (National economic council)
4825 General works
4826 Powers and prerogatives
The executive
4828 General works
Executive power over states
4829 General works
4830 Reichsstatthalter
Reichspräsident (to 1934)

Constitutional law. Staats- und Verfassungsrecht
Constitutional history. Verfassungsgeschichte
By period
Weimar Republic and Third Reich. Deutsches Reich unter Weimarer Verfassung und National-Sozialismus, 1919-1945
Organs of government
The executive
Reichspräsident (to 1934) -- Continued
4831 General works
Election see KK4806
4832 Term of office. Disability. Succession
Powers and duties
4833 General works
4834 Treatymaking power
War and emergency power
4835 General works
Against states. State of siege see KK4726
4837 Legislative power
4838 Appointing and removing power
4839 Impeachment
Reichskanzler
Beginning with 1934 Führer und Reichskanzler
4842 General works
4845 Powers and duties
Kabinett und Ministerien (Cabinet and departments)
Including rules and regulations, parliamentary practice, etc.
4850 General (Table K22)
4851 Relations to other branches of government
Auswartiges Amt (Department of state)
4853 General (Table K11)
4855 Legal status of personnel
Including tenure, salaries, pensions, etc.
4858 Reichsministerium des Innern (Department of the interior)
Reichsfinanzministerium (Department of finance)
4860 General (Table K11)
4860.2.A-Z Subordinate agencies, A-Z
Hauptkassen see KK7079
Rechnungshöfe see KK7083
Reichsfinanzhof see KK7428
Reichswehrministerium (Department of defense) see KK4897
Reichsmarineleitung see KK4899
4865 Reichswirtschaftsministerium (Department of commerce)

Constitutional law. Staats- und Verfassungsrecht
Constitutional history. Verfassungsgeschichte
By period
Weimar Republic and Third Reich. Deutsches Reich unter Weimarer Verfassung und Nationalsozialismus, 1919-1945
Organs of government
The executive
Kabinett und Ministerien (Cabinet and departments)
Reichsarbeitsministerium (Department of labor)

4867 General (Table K22)
4869.A-Z Subordinate agencies, A-Z
4869.D48 Deutsche Arbeitsfront
4869.G45 Generalbevollmächtigte für den Arbeitseinsatz
4869.T73 Treuhänder der Arbeit
4872.A-Z Other departments, A-Z
Kolonialamt see KK4692.K65
4872.R44 Reichsministerium Ernährung und Landwirtschaft (Department of agriculture)
4872.R443 Reichsministerium besetzte Gebiete (Department for administration of occupied countries)
4872.R448 Reichsverkehrsministerium (Department of transportation)
Reichsstatthalter in particular states see KK4728
4875 Reichsprotektor
The civil service see KK5930+
The judiciary. Judicial power
Class here general works on constitutional status
For judicial review see KK4889
4879 General works
4880 Reichsjustizministerium (Department of justice)
Constitutional tribunals. Staatsgerichtshöfe
Including procedure
Class here works on federal courts, federal and state courts, or courts of several jurisdictions
For courts (several or individual) of an individual jurisdiction, see the state
4883 General (Table K22)
Staatsgerichtshof of the Weimar Republic (Federal constitutional court)
4884 General (Table K22)
Jurisdiction
Including exclusive and concurrent jurisdiction on subject matter
4887 General works
4888 Political questions

Constitutional law. Staats- und Verfassungsrecht
Constitutional history. Verfassungsgeschichte
By period
Weimar Republic and Third Reich. Deutsches Reich unter Weimarer Verfassung und Nationalsozialismus, 1919-1945
Constitutional tribunals. Staatsgerichtshöfe
Staatsgerichtshof of the Weimar Republic (Federal constitutional court)
Jurisdiction -- Continued
4889 Judicial review of legislative acts
National emblem. Flag. Seal. Seat of government.
National anthem see KK5505
Patriotic customs and observances see KK5509
Decorations of honor. Awards. Dignities see KK5511
Commemorative medals see KK5513
National defense. Military law
4895 General (Table K22)
Reichswehrministerium (Department of defense)
4897 General (Table K22)
4899 Marineleitung (Department of the navy, 1919)
4900 Command. Police
Germany under Allied Occupation. Militärregierung, 1945-1955
4902 General (Table K22)
4905 Supreme Headquarters Allied Expeditionary Force (AHAEF), V-E Day to July, 1945 (Table K22)
Office of Military Government in Berlin (OMGB), 1946
4912 General (Table K22)
4914 Military Governor
4916.A-Z Administrative divisions, A-Z
4916.C59 Civil Administration Division
4916.C65 Control Office
4916.E26 Economic Division
4916.E29 Education and Cultural Relations Division
4916.F55 Finance Division
4916.I54 Information Control Division
4916.L44 Legal Division
4920 Interallied Control Council. Kontrollrat, 1945-1948 (Table K22)
Comprising the four zonal commanders-in-chief
Allied High Commission (Trizonal). Allierte Hohe Kommission, 1949-1955
4925 General (Table K22)
Sources
Charter of the Allied High Commission, 1949 see KK4444.69

Constitutional law. Staats- und Verfassungsrecht
Constitutional history. Verfassungsgeschichte
By period
Germany under Allied Occupation. Militärregierung, 1945-1955
Allied High Commission (Trizonal). Allierte Hohe Kommission, 1949-1955
General
Sources -- Continued
Occupation Statute, 1949 see KK4444.7
Regional subdivisions. Zones of occupation and Greater Berlin. Besatzungszonen
4928 General
Western zones. Trizonia
United States Zone
4930 General (Table K22)
Organs of military government
4932 General works
4934 Zonal military commander-in-chief (Military governor). Zonenbefehlshaber
4938 High Commissioner of Zonal Sector. Hohe Kommissar der Zone
Civilian councils and agencies
4942 Länderrat (Prime minister conference of the states. Delegation of the states) (Table K22)
British Zone
4945 General (Table K22)
Organs of military government
4947 General works
4949 Zonal military commander-in-chief (Military governor). Zonenbefehlshaber
4954 High Commissioner of Zonal Sector. Hohe Kommissar der Zone
Civilian councils and agencies
4956 General works
4957 Zonenbeirat (Advisory council consisting of the delegates of the state governments, political parties, and unions)
4958 Zentralämter (Advisory agencies)
French Zone
4964 General (Table K22)
Organs of military government
4966 General works
4967 Zonal military commander-in-chief (Military governor). Zonenbefehlshaber

Constitutional law. Staats- und Verfassungsrecht
Constitutional history. Verfassungsgeschichte
By period
Germany under Allied Occupation. Militärregierung, 1945-1955
Regional subdivisions. Zones of occupation and Greater Berlin. Besatzungszonen
Western zones. Trizonia
French Zone
Organs of military government -- Continued

4971 High Commissioner of Zonal Sector. Hohe Kommissar der Zone
Civilian councils and agencies
4973 General works
4974 Generaldirektionen

East Zone. Russian Zone
For the constitutional law of East Germany beginning with 1949, see KKA

4979 General (Table K22)
Organs of military government
4982 General works
4983 Sowjetische Militär-Administration in Deutschland (SMAD)
4984 Sowjetische Kontrollkommission (SKK), 1949
Civilian councils and agencies
4985 General works
4986 Deutsche Zentralverwaltungen
Deutsche Wirtschaftskommission, 1947-1948
Previously Ständige Wirtschaftskommission
4987 General (Table K22)
4988 Wirtschaftliche Zentralverwaltungen
Previously Deutsche Zentralverwaltungen

Vereinigtes Wirtschaftsgebiet, 1946-1949 (Bizonal: British Zone and United States Zone combined)
4992 General (Table K11)
4996 Allied (bipartite) Control Board
4998 Wirtschaftsrat (Legislative branch)
Including first (1947) and second (1948) Wirtschaftsrat
5000 Länderrat (Conference of delegates of state governments)
Previously Ministerpräsidenten-Konferenz der Westlichen Besatzungszonen
Verwaltungsrat (Executive branch)
5002 General (Table K11)
5004 Oberdirektor

Constitutional law. Staats- und Verfassungsrecht
Constitutional history. Verfassungsgeschichte
By period
Germany under Allied Occupation. Militärregierung, 1945-1955
Regional subdivisions. Zones of occupation and Greater Berlin. Besatzungszonen
Vereinigtes Wirtschaftsgebiet, 1946-1949 (Bizonal: British Zone and United States Zone combined)
Verwaltungsrat (Executive branch) -- Continued

5008.A-Z Subordinate agencies, A-Z
Including directors
Amt für Heimatvertriebene see KK3504
5008.H38 Hauptverwaltung für Post- und Fernmeldewesen
Patentamt see KK2729.2
5008.P47 Personalamt
Rechnungshof see KK7083
5008.R42 Rechtsamt
Statistisches Amt see KK6352.S73
5008.V27 Verwaltung für Arbeit
5008.V37 Verwaltung für Ernährung, Landwirtschaft und Forsten
5008.V74 Verwaltung für Verkehr
5008.V85 Verwaltung für Wirtschaft
Bank Deutscher Länder see KK2195+
Deutsches Obergericht see KK3691.5.D48
Greater Berlin
5015 General (Table K22)
Organs of military government
5016 General works
5017 Allied Command. Allierte Komandantur
5019 Regional subdivisions. Zonal sectors
International Authority for the Ruhr
5022 General (Table K22)
5024 Intergovernmental Working Party to Draft an Agreement for the Establishment of an International Authority for the Ruhr
5034 Interpretation and construction. Verfassungsauslegung
Constitutional principles
Rule of law (Recht- und Gesetzmässigkeit) see KK4426+
Rechtsstaat see KK4426+
Sozialstaat see KK4427
Sozialer Rechtsstaat see KK4429
Separation of powers see KK5049+
5041 Legitimationsprinzip
5043 Legitätsprinzip

Constitutional law. Staats- und Verfassungsrecht
Constitutional principles -- Continued
5044 Subsidiaritätsprinzip
5047 Amending process
For a particular amendment, see the appropriate constitution
Separation of powers. Gewaltentrennung
5049 General works
5051 Conflict of interests (General). Incompatibility of offices. Ethics in government
5052 Executive privilege
5053 Judicial review of legislative acts. Richterliches Prüfungsrecht und Normenkontrolle
Class here general works
For procedure see KK5475+
Parliament and Federal government see KK5413
Sources and relationships of the law
5055 Preconstitutional law and constitutional law
For judicial review of preconstitutional law see KK5476
5057 International and municipal law. Treaties and agreements
5059 Constitutional aspects of international cooperation, membership in supranational organizations, etc.
5061 Conflict of laws and international law
Statutory law and delegated legislation. Lehre vom Gesetz. Gesetz im formellen und materiellen Sinn
Including statutory orders (Verordnungen) and skeleton laws (Rahmengesetze)
5063 General works
Nullity. Nichtigkeit. Teilnichtigkeit see KK5479
5066 Retroactivity. Rückwirkung
5068 Repeal of legislation. Anderung oder Abbau
5070 Customary law. Ungeschriebenes Verfassungsrecht. Gewohnheitsrecht
Criminal law and constitutional law see KK7992
Federalism. Intergovernmental relations. Bundesstaatlichkeit
5075 General (Table K11)
Federal comity. Bundestreue
Including federal-state or state-state disputes
5077 General works
5079 Secession
5082 Cooperation of the states. Gemeinschaftseinrichtungen der Lander. Gemeinschatsaufgaben von bund und Ländern
Including works on cooperation of the Federal Republic and the states
Jurisdiction and concurring jurisdiction. Zuständigkeiten
Including federal and state jurisdiction

Constitutional law. Staats- und Verfassungsrecht
Federalism. Intergovernmental relations. Bundesstaatlichkeit
Jurisdiction and concurring jurisdiction. Zuständigkeiten -- Continued
5086 General (Table K11)
Execution of federal laws by the states
Including Auftragsverwaltung und Ausführung als eigene Angelegenheit
5087 General works
5088 Supervision by federal government and execution against the states. Bundesaufsicht und Bundeszwang
5090.A-Z States' jurisdiction in special fields. By field, A-Z
5090.C84 Culture
Education see KK5090.C84
5090.F67 Foreign relations
Kulturabkommen see KK5090.C84
Science and the arts see KK5090.C84
Interstate compacts and agreements. Staatsverträge und Verwaltungsabkommen
Including compacts and agreements between the Federal Republic and states or between states
5092 General (Table K11)
5093.A-Z By subject, A-Z
5093.C64 Culture
Federal (National) territory. Bundesgebiet
5095 General works (Table K11)
5096 Division into East and West Germany
For reunification claim see KK5109
States. Political subdivisions
5097 General works
Boundary disputes. Neugliederung und Eingliederung
5099 Südwest-Staat
5102 Saarland
Foreign relations. Auswärtige Gewalt
5105 General works
Foreign service see KK5445+
5106 Treatymaking power
Cf. KK5398+ Bundespräsident
5107 Executive agreements
Foreign assistance program see KK6435
5109 Relationship with East Germany
Including Bundesminister für Gesamtdeutsche Fragen and Bundesminister für innerdeutsche Beziehungen
5110 Neutrality
5111 Culture. Education and exchange. Kulturhoheit

Constitutional law. Staats- und Verfassungsrecht -- Continued
Individual and state
Nationality and citizenship. Staatsangehörigkeits- und Staatsbürgerrecht
5114 General (Table K11)
Acquisition and loss
5116 General (Table K11)
5116.5 Loyalty. Allegiance
Naturalization (Immigration). Einbürgerung
5118 General works
Procedure see KK6046
Temporary admission see KK6052
5120 Expatriation
Cf. KK5199 Protection against expatriation
5122 Criminal sentence
5123 Acquisition of different citizenship
5124 Marriage to a foreigner
Emigration see KK6048
Passports and identification see KK6040
5126.A-Z Particular groups, A-Z
Aliens see KK6050+
5126.A87 Austrians in Germany. Osterreich-Deutsch
5126.G47 German-stock refugees and expellees from non-German countries. Deutschstämmige, Heimatvertriebene und Flüchtlinge
Including Sudetendeutsche, Volksdeutsche, Ostdeutsche, Ungarndeutsche, etc.
5126.G48 Germans without citizenship. Statusdeutsch (Deutscher im sinne Art. 116, Abs. I, GG)
Homeless foreigners see KK6050+
Non-German refugees see KK6050+
5126.T87 Turks
Internal security see KK5245+
Human rights. Fundamental rights and constitutional guaranties. Menschenrechte. Grundrechts und Verfassungsgarantien
For rights or guaranties pertaining to a particular subject, see the subject
For the Convention for the protection of human rights and fundamental freedoms see K3236+
5132 General (Table K11)
5134 Natural and juristic persons
5135 Third parties. Drittwirkung
5136 Retention of power to infringe upon civil rights by law. Gesetzesvorbehalt
5137 Human dignity. Würde des Menschen

Constitutional law. Staats- und Verfassungsrecht
Individual and state
Human rights. Fundamental rights and constitutional guaranties. Menschenrechte. Grundrechts und Verfassungsgarantien -- Continued
Equality before the law. Antidiscrimination in general. Gleichheit vor dem Gesetz
5142 General (Table K11)
5144.A-Z Groups discriminated against, A-Z
Civil servants see KK5933
Jews see KK5144.M56
5144.M56 Minorities (ethnic, religious, racial)
Soldiers see KK7802
5144.W65 Women
Cf. KK1134+ Family law
5146.A-Z Special subjects, A-Z
5146.L36 Language
Freedom. Freiheit des Menschen
5149 General (Table K11)
Personal (individual) freedom. Persönliche Freiheit
5150 General works
5151 Life and health
5152 Protection against forced and compulsory labor
5154 Freedom of expression. Freie Entfaltung der Persönlichkeit
5156 Freedom of religion and conscience. Religions-, Glaubens-, und Gewissensfreiheit
For freedom of worship see KK5529
For separation of state and church see KK5535+
Freedom of thought and speech. Freiheit der Meinungsbildung und Meinungsäusserung
5160 General (Table K11)
Freedom of information. Informationsfreiheit
5162 General works
Freedom of the press see KK6947
Freedom of radio communication see KK6947
Protection of personality rights see KK1923.5
Official secrets and information see KK7026
Freedom of science and the arts. Academic freedom see KK6258
5167 Prohibition of censorship
5169 Right of opposition to government
Cf. KK5411 Parliamentary opposition
5171 Freedom of movement. Freizügigkeit
5173 Freedom of employment. Free choice of occupation. Anstellungsfreiheit. Berufsfreiheit

Constitutional law. Staats- und Verfassungsrecht
Individual and state
Human rights. Fundamental rights and constitutional guaranties. Menschenrechte. Grundrechts und Verfassungsgarantien
Freedom. Freiheit des Menschen -- Continued
5176 Freedom of assembly, association, and demonstration. Versammlungs-, Vereins- und Demonstrationsfreiheit (Table K11)
Freedom of coalition. Koalitionsfreiheit
5179 General
Labor-management relations see KK2987
Collective labor agreements and collective bargaining see KK3057
Labor unions see KK3120
Cartels and monopolies see KK6458
5183 Due process of law. Rechtsweggarantie. Gesetzlicher Richter und rechtliches Gehör
Class here general works
For works on due process of law in general procedure, see KK3804.D83; civil procedure, see KK3832; criminal procedure, see KK9485; administrative process, see KK5672; procedure before the Federal constitutional court, see KK5471
Ne bis in idem see KK9699
Retroactivity of law see KK8028
Family and marriage see KK1112
Parent and child see KK1190
Education see KK6268
5186 Privacy of home. Unverletzlichkeit der Wohnung
Privacy of communication. Official and private secrets
5190 General works
Mail and telecommunication see KK6947
Mail and telecommunication see KK9320
Personal privacy see KK8492
Private property and right to inherit see KK1261+
Private property and right to inherit see KK1451
5197 Right to national self-determination. Recht auf Heimat
5199 Protection against expatriation. Ausbürgerungsverbot
Right to enjoyment of nature see KK6255.5
5202 Right of asylum. Asylrecht (Table K11)
Protection against extradition see KK9571
5205 Right to petition. Petitionsrecht (Table K11)
5207 Right to resistance against government. Widerstandsrecht

Constitutional law. Staats- und Verfassungsrecht
Individual and state
Human rights. Fundamental rights and constitutional guaranties. Menschenrechte. Grundrechts und Verfassungsgarantien -- Continued

5212 Constitutional safeguards. Sicherung der Grundrechte
For forfeiture of civil rights and Beschwerde, see KK5487; KK5493

5216.A-Z Particular groups, A-Z

5216.A44 Aliens. Ausländer

5216.H64 Homosexuals

5219 Civic duties. Staatsbürgerpflichten

Political parties

5222 General (Table K11)

5223 Party affiliation. Mitgliedschaft

5227 Subordinate or connected organizations. Neben- und Sonderorganisationen

5229 Finance

Outlawing and dissolution see KK5485+

5239 Parliamentary practice

5240.A-Z Other political organizations, pressure groups, etc. By name, A-Z

5240.B85 Bund der Vertriebenen (Table K11)

5240.D48 Deutsche Jungdemokraten

Internal security. Staatsschutz und Verfassungsschutz
Including control of subversive activities or groups

5245 General (Table K11)

5247 Protection of official secrets
For freedom of the press and information see KK6947
For treason see KK7026

5251 Amter fur Verfassungsschutz
Including procedure

5253.A-Z Groups of parties, A-Z

5253.F38 Fascist and neo-Nazi groups

Kommunistische Partei Deutschlands see KK5485.5.K65

Neo-Nazi groups see KK5253.F38

Political oath see KK5507

Organs of government. Representation

5259 General (Table K11)

The people. Das Volk

5262 General works

5263 Constituent power. Verfassungsgebende Gewalt

5267 Initiative and referendum. Plebiscite. Volksbegehren und Volksabstimmung

Resistance against government see KK5207

Political parties see KK5223

Election law. Wahlrecht. Wahlverfahrensrecht

Constitutional law. Staats- und Verfassungsrecht
Organs of government. Representation
The people. Das Volk
Election law. Wahlrecht. Wahlverfahrensrecht -- Continued

5272 General (Table K11)
5274 Proportional representation
5276 Majority. Direct and indirect election
Suffrage. Subjektives Wahlrecht
Including active and passive suffrage and voting age
5279 General (Table K11)
5280.A-Z Groups of voters, A-Z
5280.A38 Aged. Older people
5280.A44 Aliens
5280.C58 Civil servants
Older people see KK5280.A38
5280.S64 Soldiers
5280.W65 Women
5282 Registration. Qualifications
Including procedure
5284 Absentee voting
5287 Election districts
Election to particular office
5289 President
5291 Bundestag. Bundesversammlung (Table K11)
5295 State, local, and municipal offices
Class here general works
For works on elections of a particular state, locality, or municipality, see the jurisdiction
5299 Campaign expenditures
5299.5 Equal time rule (Broadcasting). Sendezeitvergabe an Parteien
5300 Election contest. Wahlprüfung
Including judicial review (Wahlanfectung)
Election crimes see KK9145+
The legislature. Legislative power. Gesetzgebung
5310 General works
5312 Special and local legislation
Legislature and federal government see KK5413
Bundestag
Organization and procedures. Standing order
5318 General (Table K11)
5322 President of the Bundestag
5323 Publicity of sessions
5324 Hearings
5325 Voting
5327 Minority

Constitutional law. Staats- und Verfassungsrecht
Organs of government. Representation
The legislature. Legislative power. Gesetzgebung
Bundestag -- Continued
Powers and duties
5329 General works
5330 Legislative functions and limitations
5332 Obligation to legislation. Gesetzgebungsgebot
5334 Representation
5336 Investigative power
Including committees (Untersuchungsausschüsse)
Control of government
Cf. KK5416 Ministerial responsibility
5337 General works
5338 Auditing. Budgetary expenditure control
5340 Zivilbeauftragte (non-government mandatory)
Exclusive and concurrent legislative power
5343 General works
5344 Implied power. Ungeschriebene Gesetzgebungskompetenz
The legislative process
5349 General (Table K11)
Rechtsinformatik see KK79+
5352 Interpellation. Anfrage
5354 Bill drafting. Gesetzgebungstechnik
For legal composition see KK84
Consent of other organs or corporate bodies
5356 General works
5357 Bundesrat
Committees. Fachausschüsse
5359 General works
5361.A-Z Particular committees. By name, A-Z
5361.G45 Gemeinsamer Verteidigungsausschuss (Joint defense committee)
5361.S73 Ständiger Ausschuss (Standing committee)
5361.V47 Vermittlungsausschuss
5364 Lobbying
Beirate (Advisory councils)
5365 General works
5366 Beirat des Bundestages für handelspolitische Vereinbarungen
Parliamentary opposition see KK5411
5368 Impeachment
Legal status of legislators. Bundestagsmitglieder
5369 General (Table K11)
Election see KK5291
5370 Parliamentary immunity

Constitutional law. Staats- und Verfassungsrecht
Organs of government. Representation
The legislature. Legislative power. Gesetzgebung
Bundestag
Legal status of legislators. Bundestagsmitglieder -- Continued

5371 Incompatibility of offices
5373 Salaries, pensions, privileges, etc. (Table K11)
5375 Dissolution. Auflösung
5378 Bundesversammlung

Bundesrat (Council of representatives of state governments)
Organization and procedure
5382 General works
5384 President of the Bundesrat
5385 Fachausschüsse (Committees)
Powers and duties
5387 General works
5388 Legislative power. Consent
Supervision of states in executing federal law see KK5088

Bundespräsident
5392 General works
Election see KK5289+
5393 Term of office
5394 Disability. Succession
5395 Incompatibility of offices
Powers and duties
5396 General works
5397 Representation
Treatymaking power
5398 General works
5398.2 International relations
Cf. KK5105+ Foreign relations
5398.3 Executive agreements. Verwaltungsabkommen
Legislative power
5400 General works
5401 Ordinance power
5402 Veto
5403 Review of legislative acts. Promulgation. Prüfung, Ausfertigung und Verkündung
5404 Appointive and removal power
5406 Impeachment

Bundesregierung (The federal government)
Constitutional principles
5410 Coalition government. Koalitionsregierung
5411 Opposition

Constitutional law. Staats- und Verfassungsrecht
Organs of government. Representation
Bundesregierung (The federal government)
Constitutional principles -- Continued
Parliamentary system
5412 General works
5413 Federal government and Bundestag
5414 President and federal government. Countersignature
5416 Cabinet system. Ministerial responsibility
Bundeskanzler und Kabinett
5418 General works
5419 Appointment. Term of office
Disability. Succession
5420 General works
5421 Vice-chancellor
5422 Incompatibility of offices
5424 Vote of confidence. Mistrauensvotum
Powers and duties
5425 General works
5426 Political decision making. Richtlinien der Politik
Including Regierungserklärungen
5428 War and emergency power
Including Notverordnungsrecht
Legislative power
5429 General works
5430 Initiative
5432 Consent to consent-legislation. Zustimmungsgesetzgebung
5433 Ordinance power
5434 Gesetzgebungsnotstand
Supervision over states executing federal laws and Bundeszwang (Execution) see KK5088
5437 Consent to budgetary appropriations and expenditures
Economic policymaking see KK6417+
Bundesministerien. Oberste Bundesbehörden (Federal departments)
Class here works on several departments not related to a particular branch of the law or subject
Including Staatssekretäre, administrative divisions, Beiräte, etc.
For works on several departments related to a branch of law or subject, as well as an individual department or its regulatory agencies, see the branch of law or the subject
For departments and their regulatory agencies prior to 1949, see KK4671+; KK4850+

Constitutional law. Staats- und Verfassungsrecht
Organs of government. Representation
Bundesregierung (The federal government)
Bundesministerien. Oberste Bundesbehörden (Federal departments) -- Continued

5440 General (Table K11)

Auswärtiges Amt (Federal department of the exterior)

5443 General (Table K11)

The foreign service. Auswärtiger Dienst

5445 General (Table K11)

5446 Legal status of foreign service personnel

Including tenure, salaries, allowances, pensions, etc.

Bundesminister für gesamtdeutsche Fragen (Federal department for reunification problems) see KK5109

Bundesminister für innerdeutsche Beziehungen see KK5109

5448 Bundesminister für Angelegenheiten des Bundesrates und der Länder (Federal department for problems concerning the Bundesrat and the states)

5449.A-Z Subordinate regulatory agencies. Bundesoberbehörden

Class here works on several agencies

For an individual agency, see the branch of law or the subject

5450.A-Z Special bureaus and agencies. By name, A-Z

5450.P73 Presse- und Informationssamt der Bundesregierung (Press and information agency of the federal government)

5451 Executive advisory bodies. Commissions

5452 The judiciary. Judicial power

Class here works on constitutional aspects

For judicial review see KK5475+

Cf. KK3654.2+ Administration of justice

Cf. KK9429.2+ Administration of criminal justice

Constitutional courts and procedure. Verfassungsgerichtsbarkeit

Class here works on federal courts, federal and state courts, or courts of several jurisdictions

For courts (several or individual) of an individual jurisdiction, see the state

History see KK4883+

5454 Criticism. Reform. Rechtserneuerung. Polemik

5456 General (Table K11)

Bundesverfassungsgericht (Federal constitutional court)

5461-5470 General (Table K9c)

Procedural principles

5471 Due process of law. Rechtsweggarantie

5471.3 Offizialmaxime (Investigation ex officio)

Constitutional law. Staats- und Verfassungsrecht
Constitutional courts and procedure.
Verfassungsgerichtsbarkeit
Bundesverfassungsgericht (Federal constitutional court)
Procedural principles -- Continued
5471.5 Constitutional court as court of last resort. Erschöpfung des Rechtsweges
5471.7 Parties to action
Time periods. Deadlines. Fristen
5471.8 General works
5471.85 Default and restitution. Säumnis und Wiedereinsetzung
Jurisdiction
Including exclusive and concurrent jurisdiction of the federal court and the state constitutional courts, as well as political questions
5472 General works
5473 Organstreitigkeit (Powers and duties of organs of federal government)
Judicial review of legislative acts. Normenkontrollverfahren
Cf. KK3804.J833 Procedure in general
Cf. KK5713 Administrative procedure
5475 General works
5476 Preconstitutional law as federal law. Fortgeltung früheren Rechts als Bundesrecht
5477 International law as municipal law. Völkerrecht als bindendes innerstaatliches Recht
5478 Unconstitutionality of law (federal and state). Verfassungswidrigkeit von Gesetzen
5479 Nullity. Nichtigkeit von Gesetzen
5480 Controversies concerning federal supervision and execution of federal laws by states
5482 Public law suits between federal government and states where no other jurisdiction in subject matter is given
5483 Impeachment of federal president. Präsidentenanklage
Election contest (Wahlanfectung) see KK5300
Outlawing of political parties. Parteiverbot
5485 General works
5485.5.A-Z By group or party, A-Z
5485.5.K65 Kommunistische Partei Deutschlands (KPD)
5486 Indictment of judges. Richteranklage
5487 Forfeiture of civil rights. Grundrechtsverwirkung
5492 Popularklage (Class or representative action)

Constitutional law. Staats- und Verfassungsrecht
Constitutional courts and procedure. Verfassungsgerichtsbarkeit
Bundesverfassungsgericht (Federal constitutional court) -- Continued
5493 Verfassungsbeschwerde (Constitutional tort)
Including comparisons between federal and state procedures (Landesverfassungsbeschwerde)
For constitutional court as court of last resort see KK5471.5
Actions and defenses
Provisional remedies. Vorbeugende Rechtsmittel
5495 General works
5496 Injunction. Einstweilige Anordnung
5497 Evidence. Beweis
Judicial decisions. Judgments
5498 General (Table K11)
5500 Res judicata (State decisis). Wirkung und Bindung der Urteile. Gesetzeskraft
5503 Execution. Vollstreckung (Table K11)
5505 National emblem. Flag. Seal. Seat of government. National anthem (Table K11)
5507 Political oath (Table K11)
5509 Patriotic observances and customs (Table K11)
5511 Decorations of honor. Awards. Dignities (Table K11)
5513 Commemorative medals (Table K11)
Economic constitution see KK6417+
Secular ecclesiastical law. Staatskirchenrecht
Class here works on the relationship of church and state, regardless of denomination
For works on the internal law and government of a church, see KBR+
History see KK379+
Treaties between church and state. Concordats (Catholic Church) and contracts (Protestant church). Kirchenverträge
Including related material such as court decisions, official reports, memoranda, etc.
For treaties relating to a particular region or state, see the region or state
For treaties on a particular subject, see the subject
For treaties in general, see KZ
5520 Collections. Compilations
5522 Individual concordats. By date
5524 Individual contracts. By date
5525 General works
5527 General (Table K11)

Secular ecclesiastical law. Staatskirchenrecht -- Continued
Constitutional guaranties
5528 General works
5529 Freedom of religion. Freedom of worship. Glaubensfreiheit. Kultusfreiheit
5530 Freedom of speech of the clergy
5532 Protection of church property. Financial support
Separation of church and state. Independence of church
5535 General works
5536 Church and state jurisdictions. Policymaking. Zuständigkeiten und Kirchenpolitik
Religious corporations and societies. Kirchen. Religiöse Orden und Religionsgesellschaften
5538 General works
5539 Legal status. Corporations of public law. Juristic personality
5540.A-Z By denomination, A-Z
5540.J83 Judaism
Church autonomy and state supervision
5541 General works
5541.5 Education and training of the clergy. Degrees
Salaries, pensions, etc., of the clergy
see KBR+
Officials and employees other than the clergy (according to civil service rules, including labor contract and social legislation)
see KBR+
Church property and the administration and maintenance of church property
see KBR+
Religious education in schools see KK6278
Marriage laws and marital rites
see KBR+
5545 Protection of holidays. Kirchliche Feiertage
Cemetery regulations see KK6175
Church taxes see KK7266
5548 Secession from a church. Staatliches Kirchenaustrittsrecht
5549 Church and military establishment
Administrative process and procedure. Verwaltungsverfahrensrecht
5550 General works
5551 Due process of law. Rechtsweggarantie
5552 Jurisdiction. Gerichtsbarkeit
Including conflict of jurisdictions (Kompetenzkonflikte)
5556 Control of ecclesiastical administrative acts. Judicial review

Secular ecclesiastical law. Staatskirchenrecht
Administrative process and procedure. Verwaltungsverfahrensrecht -- Continued
Ecclesiastical courts and tribunals
see KBR+
Disciplinary measures. Disciplinary courts
see KBR+
Administrative law. Verwaltungsrecht
5569 History
Class here works on recent history and development of administrative law beginning 1800
For works on the law prior to 1800 see KK376+
5570 Criticism. Reform. Rechtserneuerung. Polemik
5571-5580 General (Table K9c)
Sources of administrative law
5581 Customary law. Gewohnheitsrecht
5582 Statutes. Ordinances. Regulations and guidelines
5582.2 Executive agreements. Contracts
5583 Interpretation and construction. Legal hermeneutics
Administrative principles
5586 Rule of law. Gesetzmässigkeit der Verwaltung
5587 Autonomy. Rulemaking power
Limitation and freedom of administration. Gebundenheit und Freiheit der Verwaltung
5588 General works
5589 Administrative discretion. Ermessen und Ermessensfreiheit
5590 Abuse of administrative power. Ombudsman
Judicial review see KK5673
5592 Classification of administration
Including Leistungsverwaltung, Planungsverwaltung, Erwerbswirtschaftliche Verwaltung, etc.
5593 Government monopoly. Verwaltungsmonopol
Class here general works
For particular commodities and services, see KK5918; KK7305
5594 Offentlich (the word)
5595 Offentliches Interesse (Public interest)
5596 Offentliche Sache (Public property)
5597 Gemeinwohl. Gemeines Bestes (Public good)
5598 Subjektiv-öffentliches Recht
5599 Benevolentia. Wohlwollen
Legal relations in administrative law. Coordination and subordination
5600 General works
5601 Private persons acting for or in behalf of government
5602 Succession into rights or positions

Administrative law. Verwaltungsrecht -- Continued
Relationship to other branches of law or subjects
Civil law
5603 General works
5603.2.A-Z Special topics, A-Z
Good faith see KK945.G66
5603.2.J87 Juristic persons of private law
5603.2.P73 Prescription
5603.2.U54 Unjust enrichment
The judiciary and administration. Verwaltung und Justiz
Including conflict of jurisdictions (Kompetenzkonflikte)
5604 General works
Kompetenzkonfliktgerichtshofe see KK3695
5605 Judicial review
5606 Executive power and legislative branch
5607 Conflict of laws
Administrative process
5607.5 General (Table K11)
Acts of government. Hoheitliches Handeln. Fiskalisches Handeln
5608 General works
5608.5 Form
Administrative acts. Lehre vom Verwaltungsakt
5610 General
5611 Befehl (Superior order)
5612 Begünstigende Verwaltungsakte (Beneficial acts)
5613 Belastende Verwaltungsakte (Unfavorable acts)
5614 Feststellende Verwaltungsakte (Declaratory acts)
5615 Gestaltende Verwaltungsakte (Creative acts)
Bilateral acts. Zweiseitige, mitwirkungsbedürftige Verwaltungsakte
5616 General works
5616.2 By request. Antrag
5616.3 Submission. Unterwerfung
5617 Stillschweigende Verwaltungsakte (Silence)
5618 Promise. Information. Zusagen und Auskünfte
Including reliance (Vertrauensschutz)
5619 Conditions. Bedingungen. Auflagen
Defective acts. Fehlerhafter Verwaltungsakte
5621 General (Table K11)
5622 Correction. Heilung
5623 Restitutio in integrum. Folgenbeseitigung
5624.A-Z Special topics, A-Z
5624.B74 Bribery
5624.E77 Error
5624.F67 Force. Threat
5624.F68 Form, Lack of. Formmangel

Administrative law. Verwaltungsrecht
Administrative process
Administrative acts. Lehre vom Verwaltungsakt
Defective acts. Fehlerhafter Verwaltungsakte
Special topics, A-Z -- Continued

5624.F73 Fraud
5624.J87 Jurisdiction, Lack of. Unzuständigkeit
Threat see KK5624.F67
5624.U56 Unofficially performed act
5624.V64 Void and voidable acts
Judicial review of administrative act see KK5715+
Reliance see KK5618
5626 Reinterpretation. Umwandlung
5627 Revocation. Rücknahme und Widerruf
5628 Res judicata. Rechtskraft
5629 Recognition of foreign administrative acts. Conflict of laws. Anerkennung ausländischer Verwaltungsakte
Legal transactions. Offentlich-rechtliche Rechtsgeschäfte
5631 General (Table K11)
Public contracts. Offentlich-rechtliche Verträge
5632 General (Table K11)
5633 Price regulation. Preisprüfrecht
5634 Nondiscrimination clause
5635.A-Z Special topics, A-Z
5635.B84 Building, construction, and engineering contracts
5635.C55 Computer contracts
Construction contracts see KK5635.B84
5635.D43 Defense contracts
Engineering contracts see KK5635.B84
5635.P75 Professional services contracts
5635.R47 Research and development contracts
Unilateral acts. Einseitige Rechtsgeschäfte
5636 General works
5637 Renunciation. Verzicht
5638 Set-off. Aufrechnung
5639 Nonperformance. Leistungsstörungen
Enforcement of administrative sanctions. Verwaltungszwangsverfahren
Including Beitreibung, Ersatzvornahme, Zwangsstrafe, and unmittelbarer Zwang
5640 General (Table K11)
5642 Remedies. Protection against law enforcement
5643 Form requirements. Summons. Protocols. Minutes
5644 Time periods. Deadlines. Fristen. Termine
5645 Costs. Verwaltungsgebühren

Administrative law. Verwaltungsrecht -- Continued
Administrative courts and procedure.
Verwaltungsgerichtsbarkeit
Class here works on federal courts, federal and state courts, or courts of several jurisdictions
For courts (several and individual) or an individual jurisdiction, see the state or municipality
History
Class here works on the law and courts prior to 1960
5647 General (Table K11)
5648 Reichsverwaltungsgericht (1941)
5649 Criticism and reform
5651-5655.8 General (Table K10)
5659 Verwaltungsgerichte
5661 Oberverwaltungsgerichte (Administrative courts of the states)
Bundesverwaltungsgericht (Federal administrative court)
5663 General (Table K11)
5664.A-Z Particular senates, A-Z
5664.S77 Spruchsenat für Soforthilfe
5665 Kompetenzkonfliktgerichtshofe
5669 Judicial assistance
Procedural principles
5672 Due process of law. Rechtsweggarantie
5673 Generalklausel (Admission of judicial review for administrative acts)
5675 Offizialmaxime (Investigation ex officio)
Parties to action
Including Beigeladene, Beteiligte, und Vertreter
5678 General works
Litigant. Plaintiff. Defendant
5680 General works
5681 Parteifähigkeit. Prozessfähigkeit
5684 Judges
5686 Other representatives of public interest. Vertreter des öffentlichen Interesses
Pretrial procedures. Administrative remedies. Vorverfahren. Rechtsbehelfe
5689 General (Table K11)
5690 Gegenvorstellung (Remonstration)
5692 Widerspruchsverfahren (Administrative appeal)
5694 Suspensive effect (Administrative remedies)
5696 Summons, service of process, subpoena, etc. Ladungen, Zustellungen, etc. (Table KK-KKC4)
Time periods. Deadlines. Fristen. Termine
5698 General works

Administrative law. Verwaltungsrecht
Administrative courts and procedure. Verwaltungsgerichtsbarkeit
Pretrial procedures. Administrative remedies. Vorverfahren. Rechtsbehelfe
Time periods. Deadlines. Fristen. Termine -- Continued

5699 Restitutio in integrum. Wiedereinsetzung in den vorigen Stand

Procedure at first instance. Judicial review

5700 General works

Jurisdiction

5701 General works

5702 Admission of case to the administrative court as the exclusive court. Zulässigkeit des Rechtswegs

5704 Competence in subject matter and venue. Sachliche and örtliche Zuständigkeit

5706 Capacity to sue and to be sued. Aktiv- und Passivlegitimation

5707 Right to litigate. Prozessführungsbefugnis

5708 Representation. Power of attorney. Vertretung

5709 Object at issue. Streitgegenstand

Actions and defenses. Klage und Einlassung

5711 General works

5713 Judicial review of legislative act. Normenkontrollverfahren

Anfechtungsklage (Action against voidable administrative act)

5715 General works

Pretrial procedures see KK5689+

5717 Statement of illegal action of administration

5718 Declaratory action. Feststellungsklage

Leistungsklage und Unterlassungsklage (Action for specific performance or refraining from doing)

5720 General works

5721 Verpflichtungsklage (Officers or agency charged to issue a particular administrative act)

5722 Actio negatoria

5723 Nachbarklage (Action of adjoining landowner)

5723.5 Actionable nuisances

5724 Form requirements

5725 Klageantrag (Prayer in complaint)

5726 Klagegrund (Matter of complaint)

Value or amount at issue see KK5763

Exemption from judicial review

5727 General works

5728 Acts of state

5729 Political questions

Administrative law. Verwaltungsrecht
Administrative courts and procedure.
Verwaltungsgerichtsbarkeit
Procedure at first instance. Judicial review
Actions and defenses. Klage und Einlassung
Exemption from judicial review -- Continued
Quasi-judicial procedures of a more political nature
5730 General works
Denazification see KK7612+
5730.5 Set-off. Counterclaim. Aufrechnung
Particular proceedings. Besondere Gestaltung des Verfahrens
5731 Dismissal and nonsuit. Erledigung des Rechtstreits in der Hauptsache
5732 Compromise. Vergleich
5734 Evidence. Beweisverfahren
Judicial decisions
5738 General works
5739 Injunctions. Einstweilige Anordnung. Arrest
Judgment. Urteil
5741 General works
Anfechtungsklage see KK5715+
Declaratory judgment see KK5718
Leistungsklage und Unterlassungsklage see KK5731+
Dismissal and nonsuit see KK5731
5744 Interlocutory decisions. Zwischenurteil
5746 Res judicata. Rechtskraft
5748 Provisional remedies. Vorbeugender Rechtsschutz
Remedies
5750 General works
5750.5 Reformatio in peius
5751 Gravamen. Beschwer
Appellate procedures
5752 Berufung
5754 Revision
5756 New trials. Reopening a case. Wiederaufnahme des Verfahrens
5757 Execution (Table K11)
5758 Arbitration. Verwaltungsschiedsverfahren
5760 Competence conflicts between administrative, labor, and social courts
Costs
5762 General (Table K11)
5763 Evaluation of object at issue. Streitwertfestsetzung
Indemnification for acts performed by government.
Offentlich-rechtliche Entschadigung

Administrative law. Verwaltungsrecht
Indemnification for acts performed by government. Offentlich-rechtliche Entschadigung -- Continued
Indemnification for lawful interference with property or person. Rechtmässige Eingriffe
5765 General (Table K11)
Eminent domain. Public restraint on private property. Enteignung. Enteignungsgleiche Eingriffe und Eigentumsbeschränkungen
Including authority (Enteignungshoheit)
5769 History
Including classical system (prior to 1919), system of the Weimar Republic (1919-1933), system of National Socialism (1933-1945), and system of the German Federal Republic
5772 General (Table K11)
5773 Public good and individual sacrifice. Gemeinwohl und Sonderopfer
5777 Compensation. Junctim clause
5778 Practice and procedure
5779.A-Z Special topics, A-Z
5779.B84 Building. Zoning. Regional and city planning
5779.B87 Business enterprise
City planning see KK5779.B84
5779.D43 Defense
5779.E53 Energy. Power lines
Goods see KK5779.S25
5779.H54 Highway construction
Power lines see KK5779.E53
5779.R34 Railroads
5779.R43 Real property
Regional planning see KK5779.B84
5779.R54 Rights granted by public law. Offentlichrechtliche Rechtspositionen
5779.S25 Sales. Goods
Zoning see KK5779.B84
Necessity compensation. Notstandsentschädigung
Including Aufopferung oder Sonderopfer (individual sacrifice)
5782 General works
5784 Assistance in emergencies. Nothilfe
Government liability. Staatshaftung
For municipal corporations see KK5921
5786 General (Table K11)
5787 Strict liability
5788 Acts of government. Staatsakt
Administrative and judicial acts
5789 General works

Administrative law. Verwaltungsrecht
Indemnification for acts performed by government. Offentlich-rechtliche Entschadigung
Government liability. Staatshaftung
Administrative and judicial acts -- Continued
Tort liability of civil servants and judges (Beamtenhaftung) see KK2020+
5790 Compensation for criminal prosecution. Entschädigung für Strafverfolgungsmassnahmen (Table K11)
Including compensation for pretrial detention, search and seizure, withholding of a driver's license, imprisonment, etc., as well as judicial error
5791 Legislative acts
5791.5 Fiscal acts. Fiskalisches Handeln
5792.A-Z Other, A-Z
5792.A35 Administrative acts relating to economic control. Wirtschaftslenkung
5792.A37 Administrative acts relating to pollution control
5792.A44 Aliens
5792.A88 Automatenhaftung
Including vending machines, computers, etc.
Judicial decisions see KK5789+
5792.M55 Military personnel
Restitution and indemnification for Nazi victims see KK7642+
5792.V52 Victims of crimes, Compensation to
Administrative organization. Strukturen und Aufbau der Staatsverwaltung
5795 Centralization and decentralization in government. Abgestuftes Behördensystem und Zuständigkeitsverteilung
Including regional and functional jurisdiction
5797 Administration through autonomous bodies. Self-government. Mittelbare Staatsverwaltung und Selbstverwaltung
5799 Delegation. Mandate. Auftragsverwaltung
5801 State supervision and enforcement. Staatsaufsicht
5803 Government agencies. Interagency relations. Behörden- und Beamtenapparat (Table K11)
5805 Collegial structure. Kollegialitätsprinzip
Juristic persons of public law. Juristische Personen des öffentlichen Rechts
5807 General works
Körperschaften des öffentlichen Rechts (Public corporations)
5809 General works
5810 Body and members. Verband und Mitgliederbestand

Administrative law. Verwaltungsrecht
Administrative organization. Strukturen und Aufbau der Staatsverwaltung
Juristic persons of public law. Juristische Personen des öffentlichen Rechts
Körperschaften des öffentlichen Rechts (Public corporations) -- Continued

5812 Autonomy

5813 Corporate rights and personality. Rechte und Rechtsfähigkeit

5814 Foundation. Creation. Termination

5815 State supervision
Including Rechts-, Fach- und Dienstaufsicht

5816 Disciplinary power. Criminal jurisdiction. Verbandsstrafgewalt

Types of corporations

5817 Gebietskörperschaften (Administrative and political divisions). Regional corporations
Class here general works
For local government see KK5870
For municipal corporations see KK5922+
For special districts see KK5925+

Genossenschaften des öffentlichen Rechts (Cooperative societies of public law)

5820 General works

Berufsgenossenschaften see KK3285+

Innungen see KK6840

5826 Churches and religious societies. Kirchen und Religionsgesellschaften
For religious orders see KK5538+

5827 Leitungsverbände
Including syndicates (e.g. coal and kali syndicates), Reichskohlenverband, Reichskulturkammer, Reichsnährstand, etc.

5829 Lastenverbande

Anstalten des öpffentlichen Rechts (Public institutions)
Class here general works
For particular institutions, see the subject

5831 General works

5832 Objective. Anstaltszweck
Cf. KK5912+ Municipal services

5833 Public institution and founding body. Rechtsfähige Anstalt und Muttergemeinwesen

Public institution without personality see KK6070+

5834 Foundation. Creation. Termination

5835 Use and user. Anstalt-Benutzer-Verhältnis

Administrative law. Verwaltungsrecht
Administrative organization. Strukturen und Aufbau der Staatsverwaltung
Juristic persons of public law. Juristische Personen des öffentlichen Rechts
Anstalten des öpffentlichen Rechts (Public institutions) -- Continued

5837 Enforced use. Monopoly. Benutzungszwang und Anschlusszwang
5838 Administrative fee. Benutzungsgebühr
5839 Anstaltsgewalt (Authority over user)
5840.A-Z Types of institutions
5840.S34 Schools
5840.V47 Versorgungsanstalt der Post

Stiftungen des öffentliches Rechts (Foundations of public law)
Cf. KK1037+ Foundations in civil law

5842 Rights and personality. Rechte und Rechtsfähigkeit
5843 Objective. Property. Zweck und Vermögen
5844 Foundation. Creation. Termination
5845 State supervision. Staatsaufsicht

Government business enterprises
Including government controlled business enterprises
For particular business enterprises, see the subject

5847 General works
5848 Legal status and liability
5849 State supervision. Auditing and inspection
5851.A-Z Particular business enterprises, A-Z
5853 Monopolies
5853.5 Fiscus

Social insurance carriers see KK3285+

Administrative departments of the federal government. Verwaltungsbehörden des Bundes
General works see KK5440

5856 Bundesminister des Innern (Federal department of the interior) (Table K11)
For departments of the interior prior to 1949, see KK4687; KK4858

5858 Subordinate regulatory agencies. Obere (nachgeordnete) Bundesbehörden (Table K11)
Class here general works
For particular agencies, see the subject

Special councils, commissions, etc.

5860 General works

Ombundsman see KK5590

Administrative departments and divisions of the states. Verwaltungsbehörden der Bundesländer

Administrative law. Verwaltungsrecht
Administrative organization. Strukturen und Aufbau der Staatsverwaltung
Administrative departments and divisions of the states. Verwaltungsbehörden der Bundesländer -- Continued
5866 General works
5868 Landesinnenministerium (Department of the interior)
5870 Regierungsbezirke (District government)
Including Regierungspräsidien und Regierungspräsident
Gemeindeverbände (Local government other than municipal)
5873 General works
5874 Kreise (Landkreise. Stadtkreise). Ämter. Landschaftsverbände
Including Landrat, Oberkreisdirecktor, etc.
5875 State supervision
Including Dienst-, Fach- und Rechtsaufsicht
Municipal government. Gemeinderecht
5876 History
5877 General (Table K11)
5877.5 Autonomy and rulemaking power. Stazungsgewalt und Organisationsrecht
5878 Self-government. Selbstverwaltung
5879 Delegated jurisdiction. Auftragsverwaltung
Including Weisungsangelegenheiten and Pflichtaufgagen
5880 State supervisions. Komunalaufsicht
Including boundaries (Gemeindegrenzen) and incorporation (Eingemeindung)
5882 Municipal territory. Gemeindegebiet
Including boundaries (Gemeindegrenzen) and incorporation (Eingemeindung)
5883 Names. Flags. Insignia. Seals (Table K11)
5884 Citizens and residents. Bürger und Einwohner (Table K11)
Constitution and organization of municipal government. Gemeindeordnung
Including Magistratsverfassung, Bürgerversammlung, Bezirksvertretung, Stadtverordnetenversammlung, Gemeindevertreter, etc.
5887 General (Table K11)
5890 Councils and civic associations
Including Gemeinderat, Bürgerversammlung, Bezirksvertretung, Stadtverordnetenversammlung, Gemeindevertreter, etc.

Administrative law. Verwaltungsrecht
Administrative organization. Strukturen und Aufbau der Staatsverwaltung
Municipal government. Gemeinderecht
Constitution and organization of municipal government. Gemeindeordnung -- Continued
Officers and employees. Beamte und Angestellte
For works on officers and employees of an individual municipality, see the municipality
For general works on municipal civil service see KK5968+
5893 General works
5895 Elected and honorary officers. Wahlbeamte und Ehrenbeamte
5897 Beigeordnete
5898 Mayor. Bürgermeister
5899 City director. Stadtdirektor
5900.A-Z Special topics, A-Z
Allowances see KK5969.3
Discipline see KK5968.5
Incompatibility of offices see KK5968.3
Pensions see KK5969
Salaries see KK5969
Tenure see KK5968.2
Municipal economy. Gemeindewirtschaftsrecht
5903 General (Table K11)
5904 Property
Including foundations, trusts, and charitable uses
Government business enterprises
Including government controlled business enterprises
5905 General works
Utilities see KK5913+
5906 Government as merchant. Kaufmannseigenschaft der Gemeinde
5907 Aussenvertretung
5909 Municipal ownership and management. Eigenbetrieb
Savings banks see KK2203+
Debts and loans see KK7389
Budget see KK7387
Municipal public services. Gemeindliche Daseinsvorsorge
5912 General works
Public utilities. Versorgungsbegtriebe
For liability see KK5921
For regulation of energy industries see KK6848+
5913 General (Table K11)
Electricity. Gas see KK6852+

Administrative law. Verwaltungsrecht
Administrative organization. Strukturen und Aufbau der Staatsverwaltung
Municipal government. Gemeinderecht
Municipal public services. Gemeindliche Daseinsvorsorge
Public utilities. Versorgungsbegtriebe -- Continued
5914 Water. Sewerage. Wasser. Abwasser
For ecological aspects see KK6251+
5915 Trash collection. Müllabfuhr
5916 Public transportation. Offentliche Verkehrsmittel
Municipal public institutions
Including cultural affairs, health, and welfare institutions
5917 General works
5918 Use and enforced use. Anschluss- und Benutzungszwang Monopol
Cf. KK5593 Government monopoly
Administrative fees see KK7099
Chambers of commerce see KK6550
Boards of trade see KK6842
5920 Administrative practice and procedure. Gemeindliches Verwaltungsverfahren
5921 Liability of municipal corporation
Supramunicipal corporations and cooperation
5922 General (Table K11)
Boundary question see KK5882
Gemeindeverbände see KK5873+
Gemeindezweckverbände (Special districts)
For special districts within a state, see the state
5925 General works
5926.A-Z Particular districts, A-Z
Water districts see KK6116.A+
5927 Municipal services and powers beyond corporate limits. Ubergemeindliche Zusammenarbeit
Gemeindespitzenverbände
5928 General works
5929.A-Z Individual, A-Z
5929.G45 Deutscher Gemeindetag
5929.L35 Deutscher Landkreistag
5929.S72 Deutscher Städtebund
5929.S74 Deutscher Städtetag
Civil service. Offentlicher Dienst
Including civil servants (Beamte), salaried employees without tenure, and wage earners without tenure
5932 General (Table K11)
5933 Constitutional aspects. Freedom of speech. Nondiscrimination

Civil service. Offentlicher Dienst -- Continued

5934 Tenure. Wohlerworbene Beamtenrechte

5935 Official (superior) order. Weisungsgebundenheit

5936 Incompatibility of offices

5937 Official secrets. Amtsgeheimnis

5937.3 Protection of the law. Rechtsschutz

5937.5 Liability of officials toward the government

5938 Appointment. Ernennung

Conditions of employment

5939 General works

Career

Including education, titles, promotions, etc.

5940 General works (Table K11)

Nondiscrimination see KK5933

5942 Performance rating. Dienstliche Beurteilung

Loyalty see KK5947+

Conduct of private life see KK5944+

Discipline

5944 General (Table K11)

5945 Courts. Disziplinargerichte und Disziplinarhöfe

Including procedure

Illicit political activities

5947 General works

5947.5 Denazification

Types of modes of employment

5947.8 Part-time employment (Table K11)

5948 Preferential employment (Table K11)

Including veterans, refugees, and displaced civil servants (persons covered by Constitution Art. 131)

5948.5 Supplementary employment. Nebentätigkeit (Table K11)

5949 Remuneration. Besoldungsrecht der Beamten (Table K11)

Including judges and military personnel

For salaried employees and wage earners see KK5963

Allowances. Beihilfenrecht

Including federal and state regulations or regulations of several states

For regulations of an individual state, see the state

5950 General (Table K11)

5951 Comparison to social insurance benefits

5951.3 Health benefits. Krankenfürsorge und Krankenbeihilfe

5952 Housing. Dienst- und Werkdienstwohnungen

5953 Cost-of-living adjustments. Travel and moving expenses (Table K11)

5953.3 Survivor benefits (Table K11)

Additional insurance see KK5955

Compensation for injuries see KK3374.C59

Civil service. Offentlicher Dienst -- Continued
Retirement. Ruhestand
For forced retirement (disciplinary measures) see KK5944+
5954 General (Table K11)
5955 Retirement pensions
Including additional pensions or insurance (Zusatzversorgung)
5956 Dismissal. Amtsenthebung. Entlassung
5957 Reinstatement
Labor law and collective labor law
5958 General (Table K11)
Labor-management relations
5958.3 General works
5958.5 Works councils. Personalvertretungsrecht (Table K11)
5958.7 Employee participation in management
5959 Collective bargaining and labor agreement. Tarifrecht
5960 Collective labor disputes. Strikes
5961 Corporate representation. Unions Gewerkschaften
Labor standards and protection of labor
5962 General works
5963 Salaries
Including salaried employees and wage earners
For civil servants see KK5949
5964 Investment wages and employee ownership. Vermögensbildung
Social welfare provisions see KK5950+
Discipline see KK5944+
5965 Vacation and leave regulations (Table K11)
5967 State civil service
For works on the civil service of an individual state, see the state
Municipal civil service. Kommunalbeamtenrecht
For works on the civil service of an individual municipality, see the municipality
5968 General works
5968.2 Tenure
5968.3 Incompatibility of offices
5968.5 Discipline
5969 Remuneration
5969.3 Allowances
5969.5 Retirement
Labor law and collective labor law
5970 General works
Labor-management relations
5971 General works
5972 Work councils. Personalvertretungsrecht

Civil service. Offentlicher Dienst -- Continued
Civil service of public corporations other than state or municipal
For works on a particular public corporation, see the subject
5973 General works
Social insurance carriers see KK3285.4+
Police and public safety. Polizei- und Ordnungsrecht
For military law see KK7690+
For civil defense see KK7806+
5977 General (Table K11)
5978 Law and order
5979 Generalklausel
Opportunitatsprinzip see KK5991.5
5981 Imminent danger. Gefahrenlage
5982 Necessity. Assistance in emergencies. Polizeilicher Notstand
Polizeiwidrigkeit. Polizeipflichtigkeit
5984 General works
5985 Disturber of the peace. Störer
Organization and administration
Including Ordnungsämter, etc.
5987 General (Table K11)
5988 Licenses, concessions, and permits
For particular licenses, permits, etc., see the subject
Police magistrates. Ordnungswidrigkeitenrecht
5989 General (Table K11)
5990.A-Z Violations, A-Z
Begging see KK5990.V34
5990.C65 Concubinage
Construction and building see KK6165+
Health and hygiene see KK6172+
Homeless persons see KK3502
Industry, trade, and commerce see KK6864
5990.M34 Malicious mischief. Grober Unfug
5990.P34 Palmistry
Prostitution see KK3498.P76
Traffic violations see KK6890
5990.V34 Vagrancy. Begging
Procedure
5991 General (Table K11)
5991.5 Opportunitätsprinzip
Bagatellstrafsachen see KK9645
Penal orders and penal mandates see KK9715+
5992 Bussgeldverfahren
5993 Res judicata
Including time periods, deadlines, etc.
5994 Remedies

Police and public safety. Polizei- und Ordnungsrecht
Police magistrates. Ordnungswidrigkeitenrecht -- Continued
5994.5.A-Z Penalties and measures of safety, A-Z
5994.5.C65 Confiscation of corpus delicti
5994.5.F55 Fines
5994.5.R48 Revocation of licenses
5994.5.V37 Verwarnung. Verwarnungsgeld
Police measures. Polizeimassnahmen
5995 General (Table K11)
5996 Ordinances, regulations, and bans. Polizeiverordnungen. Polizeiverfügungen und Polizeibefehl
5997 Personalienfeststellung (Identification). Vorführung
5998 Arrest. Gewahrsam und Sicherstellung
Search and seizure see KK9553+
Law enforcement. Polizeizwang
5999 General (Table K11)
6000 Use of arms. Waffengebrauchsrecht (Table K11)
6002 Police information system (INPOL)
For data protection see KK6071.5
Police force. Polizeivollzugsdienst
6004 General
Police officers
6005 General (Table K11)
6006 Qualifications. Education. Training
6007 Tenure, salaries, pensions, etc.
6008.A-Z Police forces, A-Z
Ämter für Verfassungsschutz see KK5251
6008.B85 Bundesgrenzschutz
6008.C74 Criminal police
Including Bundeskriminalamt
Forest and rural police see KK6256.5
Geheime Staatspolizei (Gestapo) see KK4790+
6008.P75 Private police
Railroad police see KK6918.5
Schutz-Staffel (SS) see KK4777+
Sicherheitsdienst (SD) see KK4785
Water police see KK6118
Public safety. Offentliche Sicherheit
6009 General works
6010 Weapons. Explosives. Waffen- und Sprengstoffrecht (Table K11)
Including manufacturing, import, and trade of firearms and ammunition
Hazardous articles and processes
Including transportation by land
For transportation by sea see KK6932.D35
6011 General (Table K11)

Police and public safety. Polizei- und Ordnungsrecht
Public safety. Offentliche Sicherheit
Hazardous articles and processes -- Continued
6012 Nuclear power. Reactors. Radiation.
Strahlenschutzrecht (Table K11)
Including nuclear waste disposal
Cf. KK1978 Torts
Flammable materials
6013 Fireworks
6014 Petroleum
6016.A-Z Poisons and toxic substances, A-Z
6016.A85 Asbestos
Cf. KK3189.A73 labor hygiene and safety
Herbicides see KK6016.P47
6016.P34 Paint
6016.P47 Pesticides. Herbicides
Accident control. Unfaallverhütung. Technisches Hilfswerk
6018 General (Table K11)
6020 Steam boilers
6021 Electric installations. Electric engineering
Elevators see KK6168.E43
6022.A-Z Other, A-Z
Fire prevention and control. Brandverhütung
6024 General (Table K11)
6025 Fire departments. Firefighters. Feuerwehr
6026 Forest fires. Waldbrand
Theaters. Auditoriums
6028 General (Table K11)
6029 Motion picture theaters. Safety film
Flood control see KK6113
Weather bureau. Meteorological stations see KK7031+
Deutsches Hydrographisches Institut see KK6927.5+
Statistical services see KK6352.S73
Control of individuals
6032 General (Table K11)
Identification and registration of Germans. Pass- und Meldewesen für Inländer
6034 General (Table K11)
Registration of birth, marriage, and death see KK4087+
6036 Registration of residence. Einwohnermeldewesen
6038 Identity cards. Personalausweise
6040 Passports. Reisepasse
6042.A-Z Other, A-Z
Immigration and naturalization. Einwanderung und Einbürgerung
6044 General (Table K11)
6046 Procedure (Table K11)

Police and public safety. Polizei- und Ordnungsrecht
Control of individuals
Immigration and naturalization. Einwanderung und Einbürgerung -- Continued
Citizenship see KK5114+
6048 Emigration. Abzug und Auswanderung (Table K11)
For freedom of movement see KK5171
Particular groups
Aliens. Fremdenrecht. Ausländerpolizeirecht
Including citizens of European Community countries, homeless aliens, and non-German refugees
6050 General (Table K11)
6052 Temporary admission and residence. Aufenthaltserlaubnis und Niederlassung
6053 Identification. Ausweispflicht (Table K11)
6054 Restrictions in political activities
Employment. Business enterprises
6055 General works
6056 Alien laborers. Fremdarbeiter
Naturalization see KK6044+
6057 Deportation. Abschiebung. Ausweisung
Minorities (ethnic, religious, racial)
6058 General works
6059.A-Z Groups, A-Z
6059.G96 Gypsies. Romanies. Zigeuner
Romanies see KK6059.G96
Control of social activities
6060 General (Table K11)
6061 Amusements (Table K11)
Sports activities
6062 General (Table K11)
Corporate representation. Sportverbandsrecht
6063 General works
6063.3 Disciplinary measures. Sportsgerichtsbarkeit
Including tribunals and procedure
6063.5.A-Z Sports, A-Z
6063.5.F58 Fishing. Angelsport
Fussball see KK6063.5.S62
Hunting see KK6681+
6063.5.I23 Ice hockey
6063.5.S56 Skiing
6063.5.S62 Soccer. Fussball
6064 Demonstrations. Processions (Table K11)
6065 Gambling. Glücksspiel (Table K11)
Including lotteries, games of chance, etc.
6066 Disaster control. Disaster relief. Katastropenschutz
Public property. Public restraint on private property

Public property. Public restraint on private property -- Continued

6068 General (Table K11)

Government property. Finanzvermögen und Verwaltungsvermögen

Including public institutions without capacity (Sondervermögen)

6070 General (Table K11)

Administration. Powers and control

6071 General (Table K11)

6071.5 Records management. Access to public records (Table K11)

Including data bases (Dateien) and general data protection (Datenschutz), as well as works on the Deutsche Vereinigung für Datenschutz (DVD)

For violation of privacy see KK1968.5

For criminal provisions see KK8825

Res publicae. Offentliche Sachen

6072 General works

6073 Dedication. Widmung

6075 Res communies omnium. Things in common use. Sachen in Gemeinbebrauch

Environmental planning see KK6245

Eminent domain see KK5769+

Roads and highways. Strassen- und Wegerecht

6079 General

Bundesanstalt für Strassenwesen see KK6868.7

6082 Interstate highways and expressways. Autobahnen und Fernstrassen

6083 State highways. Landstrassen

6085.A-Z Other, A-Z

6085.P43 Pedestrian areas

6085.P74 Private paths

6086 Dedication. Widmung

6087 Common use. Intense use. Gemeingebrauch. Gesteigerter Gemeingebrauch

6088 Construction and maintenance. Baulast

Including regional planning (Planungsfeststellung)

Safety see KK2008+

6090 Abutting property. Anliegerrecht

Including special assessment (Beitragsrecht)

Water resources. Wasserrecht und Wasserhaushaltsrecht

Including rivers, lakes, watercourses, etc.

6094 General (Table K11)

6095 Common use. Intense use

6096 Water rights. Rechte und Berechtigungen

Cf. KK1334 Riparian rights in civil law

6097 Abutting property. Anliegerrecht

Public property. Public restraint on private property
Water resources. Wasserrecht und Wasserhaushaltsrecht -- Continued

6098 Damages. Haftung für Gewässerschaden

Protection against pollution (Gewässerschutz) see KK6251+

Development and conservation of water resources. Erschliessung

Cf. KK6870.B85 Bundesanstalt Gewässerkunde, Koblenz

6099 General (Table K11)

6112 Registers. Wasserbücher

Including water rights, conservation districts (Wasserschutzgebiete), flood control district (Überschwemmungsgebiete), etc.

6113 Flood control

Including dams and dikes

Particular inland waterways and channels see KK6942+

6116.A-Z Particular bodies and districts. Wasserverbände. By name, A-Z

6118 Water police. Wasserschutzpolizei

National preserves. Forests

6120 General (Table K11)

Constitutional right to recreation see KK6255.5

6123 Common use

Wilderness preservation see KK6255+

Forest and rural police see KK6256.5

Architectural landmarks and historic monuments see KK6405

Public land law. Boden- und Bodennutzungrecht

6130 Land reform and land policy legislation. Bodenpolitik und Bodenreform

For agricultural land law see KK6593+

6132 General (Table K11)

Regional planning. Raumordnungsrecht. Landesplanung

6135 General (Table K11)

6137 Jurisdiction

Including federal, state, and local organization

6138 Ecological aspects. Fragen der Umweltbelastung

Including Immissionsschutz and procedure

City planning and redevelopment. Bauleitplanung und Städtebauförderung

6140 General (Table K11)

6142 Bundesminister für Wohnungswesen und Städtebau (Federal department for housing and city redevelopment) (Table K11)

Public property. Public restraint on private property
Public land law. Boden- und Bodennutzungrecht
Regional planning. Raumordnungsrecht. Landesplanung
City planning and redevelopment. Bauleitplanung und Städtebauförderung -- Continued

6143 Consolidation of urban land holdings. Baulandumlegung
Including procedure

6145 Zoning. Baunutzung (Table K11)
Including procedure
For variances see KK6156

6148 Valuation of real property. Wertermittlung (Table K11)

Assessment of utilities. Erschliessung und Erschliessungsbeiträge
Cf. KK5912+ Municipal public services

6149 General (Table K11)

6150 Sanitation. Städtesanierung

Building and construction. Baurecht und Bauordnungsrecht

6155 General (Table K11)

6156 Practice and procedure. Baugenehmigungsverfahren (Table K11)
Including application, permit, conditions, variances, etc.

6158 Design. Baugestaltung

6161 Adjoining landowners. Baunachbarrecht

6163 Building materials

Safety inspection. Bauaufsicht

6165 General (Table K11)

Fire prevention see KK6024+

6168.A-Z Buildings and structures, A-Z

Air conditioning see KK6168.H43

6168.A47 Air raid shelters

Architectural landmarks see KK6405

6168.C48 Churches

6168.C64 Commercial buildings. Stores

6168.E43 Elevators

6168.F37 Farm buildings

6168.G37 Garages

6168.H43 Heating and air conditioning
Including energy conservation provisions

Historic monuments see KK6405

6168.P74 Prefabricated buildings

Stores see KK6168.C64

6168.U85 Utility plants

6170 Criminal provisions (Table K11)

Housing see KK1791+

Homestead law see KK1321+

Public property. Public restraint on private property
Public land law. Boden- und Bodennutzungrecht
Regional planning. Raumordnungsrecht. Landesplanung -- Continued
Entail see KK6613+
Fideicommissum see KK454+
Workers' gardens see KK6627
6171 Public works (General)
Including public works contracts
Public health. Gesundheitswesen
Class here works on federal departments and boards, federal and state departments and boards, or departments and boards of several states
For departments and boards (several or individual) of an individual state, see the state
For the department of health prior to 1949 see KK4692.R43
6172 General (Table K11)
6173 Bundesminister für Gesundheitswesen (Federal department of health)
Subordinate agencies and boards
6174 Bundesgesundheitsamt. Gesundheitsämter (Health boards)
Including physicians (Amtsärzte)
6175 Burial and cemetery laws. Bestattungs- und Friedhofsrecht
Including dead bodies and disposal of dead bodies
6176 Cremation. Einäscherung
Contagious and infectious diseases. Seuchenbekämpfung
6178 General (Table K11)
6180.A-Z Diseases, A-Z
6180.A34 AIDS
6180.T82 Tuberculosis
6180.V45 Venereal diseases
Public health measures
Including compulsory measures
6181 General works
Immunization. Vaccination
6182 General (Table K11)
6183.A-Z Diseases, A-Z
6183.P65 Poliomyelitis
6183.S62 Smallpox
6185 Quarantine
Eugenics see KK6230+
Environmental pollution see KK6247+
6187.A-Z Other public health hazards and measures, A-Z
6187.R43 Refuse disposal
6187.S77 Street cleaning

Public health. Gesundheitswesen -- Continued

6189 Drinking water standards. Fluoridation (Table K11)

Food laws see KK6750+

Drug laws

6191 General (Table K11)

6192 Pharmaceutical products. Heilmittel

Narcotics. Betäubungsmittel

Including psychopharmaca

6193 General (Table K11)

Criminal provisions see KK8975

6195 Poisons. Gifte

Pharmacists and pharmacies. Apotheken und Drogerien

6197 General (Table K11)

6198 Leasing of pharmacies

6199 Professional representation. Apothekerkammer

6200 Auxiliary professions. Technical assistants

6201 Trade regulation. Advertising. Heilmittelverkehr und Heilmittelwerbung (Table K11)

Including consumer protection

6203 Alcohol. Alcoholic beverages. Liquor laws (Table K11)

For alcoholic beverage industries see KK6774+

6204 Cosmetics

Medical legislation

6206 General (Table K11)

6207 Patient's rights (Table K11)

The health professions. Recht der Heilberufe

Class here works on education, licensing, professional representation, ethics, fees, and liability

For malpractice, see individual professions

6208 Physicians in general. Ärzte

6209 Dentists. Dental hygienists. Zahnärzte, Dentisten, Hygienisten

6211 Radiologists. Röntgenärzte

6213.A-Z Other, A-Z

6213.F32 Factory physicians. Werkärzte

6213.H42 Healers. Heilpractiker

Including herbalists, homeopathic physicians, naturopaths, etc.

Herbalists see KK6213.H42

6213.M43 Medical research personnel

6213.N32 Naval physicians. Marineärzte und Hafenärzte

6213.Q32 Quacks. Quacksalber

Auxiliary medical professions. Paramedical professions. Medizinische Hilfsberufe

6215 General (Table K11)

6216 Nurses and nursing. Krankenpfleger. Krankenschwestern

Medical legislation
The health professions. Recht der Heilberufe
Auxiliary medical professions. Paramedical professions. Medizinische Hilfsberufe -- Continued

6217 Psychotherapists

6218 Midwives. Hebammen

6219 Physical therapists. Krankengymnasten

6220 Laboratory assistants. Medizinisch-technische Assistenten

6221.A-Z Health organizations. By name, A-Z

6221.R43 Red Cross. Rotes Kreuz
Cf. KK6066 Disaster relief

Hospitals and other medical institutions or health services

6222 General (Table K11)

6223 Health resorts and spas. Kurorte

6224 Blood banks
Including Blutspende- und Transfusionsdienst (blood donation)

6226 Institutions for the mentally ill. Irrenswesen

6227.A-Z Other health organizations, institutions, or services, A-Z
Ambulance service see KK6227.E43

6227.E43 Emergency medical services. Ambulance service. Ärztlicher Notfalldienst
Nursing homes see KK6227.O42

6227.O42 Old age homes. Nursing homes. Altenheime. Pflegeheime, etc.
Including invalid adults (behinderte Volljährige)

Biomedical engineering. Medical technology. Medizintechnik
Including human experimentation in medicine (Humanexperimente)
Cf. KK8410+ Criminal aspects of medicine

6228 General (Table K11)

6228.3 Genetic engineering. Gentechnik. Humangenetik (Table K11)
For artificial insemination (Human reproductive technology) see KK6229.A78

6228.4 Transplantation of organs, tissues, etc. Organ-und Gewebeübertragungen (Table K11)
Including donation of organs, tissues, etc.

Human reproductive technology. Fortpflanzungsmedizin see KK6229.A78

6229.A-Z Special topics, A-Z

Medical legislation
Special topics, A-Z -- Continued
6229.A78 Artificial insemination. Künstliche Befruchtung. Fortpflanzungsmedizin
Including fertilization in vitro (Extrakorporale Befruchtung)
Cf. KK1229+ Family law
Cf. KK8422 Criminal law
6229.A83 Aufklärungspflicht. Informing the patient. Patient's right to know
6229.A85 Autopsy. Postmortem examination
6229.C65 Confidential communications. Arztgeheimnis
(6229.D65) Donation of organs, tissues, etc.
see KK6228.4
(6229.E86) Experiments with the human body
see K6228+
Fertilization in vitro see KK6229.A78
Human reproductive technology see KK6229.A78
6229.M43 Medical instruments and apparatus. Medical devices
Professional ethics see KK7047
Transplantations see KK6228.4
Eugenics. Sterilization and castration. Erbgesundheitsrecht. Ehegesundheitsrecht
Including race hygiene (Rassen- und Blutschutz. Nürnberger Gesetze) of the Third Reich
6230 General (Table K11)
Criminals see KK8294
6232 Unwanted minorities (Table K11)
For marriage impediments see KK1124.E84
6234 Criminal provisions
Euthanasia see KK8364
6235 Disaster medicine. Katastrophenmedizin
Veterinary medicine and hygiene. Veterinary public health Veterinarsrecht. Viehseuchenverhütung
6236 General (Table K11)
6237 Veterinarians. Tierärzte
6239 Removal of animal cadavers
Animal protection. Animal welfare. Animal rights
Including prevention of cruelty to animals
For animal rights as a social issue see HV4701+
6239.2 General works (Table K11)
6239.3 Animal experimentation and research (Table K11)
Including vivisection and dissection
6239.4 Slaughtering of animals (Table K11)
6239.6.A-Z Other special topics, A-Z
Criminal aspects see KK8616

6240 Birth control. Family planning. Population control. Gerburtenkontrolle. Familienpolitik. Bevölkerungspolitik (Table K11)

Environmental law. Umweltschutz

For civil liability see KK2024

6242 General (Table K11)

Organization and administration

6243 General (Table K11)

6244 Umweltbundesamt (Environmental protection agency)

6245 Environmental planning. Conservation of environmental resources (Table K11)

For ecological aspects of regional planning see KK6138

Environmental pollution. Umweltgefährdung. Umweltbelastung

6247 General (Table K11)

6249 Air pollution. Luftverunreinigung (Table K11)

Including control of smoke, noxious gases, automobile emissions, etc.

Water and ground water pollution. Wasser- und Grundwasserverseuchung

Including sewage control

6251 General (Table K11)

6252.A-Z Pollutants, A-Z

6252.C45 Chlorohydrocarbons

6252.D48 Detergents

6252.D73 Dredging spoil

6252.P48 Petroleum

6252.R33 Radioactive substances

6252.T69 Toxic substances

6253 Noise control. Lärmbekämpfung (Table K11)

Including traffic noise

Cf. KK1308 Property

6254 Recycling of refuse. Abfallverwertung

Wilderness preservation. Naturschutz

Including natural monuments (Landschaftsschutz)

6255 General (Table K11)

6255.5 Constitutional right to recreation. Recht auf Naturgenuss und Erholung

6255.7 Plant protection. Pflanzenschutz (Table K11)

Wildlife conservation. Tierschutz

Including game, birds, and fish

6256 General (Table K11)

Game laws and hunting see KK6681+

Fishery laws see KK6695+

Land reclamation in mining see KK6733

6256.5 Forest and rural police. Forst- und Feldpolizei

Environmental law. Umweltschutz -- Continued

(6256.7) Criminal provisions. Umweltstrafrecht

see KK8879+

Cultural affairs. Kulturrecht und Kulturverwaltungsrecht

6257 General (Table K11)

6258 Constitutional aspects. Freedom of science and the arts. Academic freedom

6259 Cultural policy. State encouragement of science and the arts. Kulturpolitik und Wissenschaftsförderung

Organization and administration

Class here works on the departments of cultural affairs of several states

For the department of cultural affairs of an individual state, see the state

6260 General (Table K11)

6260.5 Bundesminister für wissenschaftliche Forschung (Federal department for science and research)

Special boards, commissions, councils, etc.

6261 Ständige Konferenz der Kultusminister der Länder

6262 Wissenschaftsrat

Deutscher Bildungsrat

6263 General works

6264 Bildungskommission

Education. Schulverwaltungsrecht

6266 General (Table K11)

6268 Constitutional safeguards. Parental rights and decision-making

6269 Schulhoheit of the state

6271 Boards and commissions

Including Schulämter und Oberschulämter

6271.5 Parent-teacher associations. Elternbeiräte

6272 School districts

School government

Including curriculum and participation in school government in general

For parent-teacher association see KK6271.5

For student participation see KK6281

6274 General (Table K11)

6276 Administrative acts and judicial review

Including Zeugnisse (reports)

6277 School discipline

6278 Religious instruction

Including public schools and denominational schools and concordats

6278.3 Political science

Students. Schüler

6279 General (Table K11)

Cultural affairs. Kulturrecht und Kulturverwaltungsrecht
Education. Schulverwaltungsrecht
Students. Schüler -- Continued

6280 Constitutional aspects
Including right to education, freedom of speech and expression, etc.

6280.5 Compulsory education. Schulpflicht

6281 Student participation in administration. Schülermitverwaltung

6282 Political activity
Including strikes

6283 Student magazines and periodicals. Schülerzeitung
For freedom of speech see KK6280

Teachers. Lehrer
For elementary teachers see KK6296+
For vocational teachers see KK6302
For university teachers see KK6324+

6286 General (Table K11)

6287 Constitutional aspects
Including freedom of speech

6289 Education and training
Including religious education

6290 Tenure, salaries, pensions, etc.

6291 Duties. Amtspflichten

6292 Disciplinary power. Züchtigungsrecht
Cf. KK8398 Corporal punishment in criminal law

School liability. School playground accidents see KK2026.S34

Elementary education. Volksschulwesen

6295 General (Table K11)

Teachers

6296 General (Table K11)

6296.5 Tenure, salaries, pensions, etc.

6296.7 Disciplinary power

Education of children with disabilities. Sonderschulwesen

6298 General (Table K11)

6298.5 Children with social disabilities
Including orphans, outcasts, paupers, etc.

6298.7 Children with physical disabilities

6299 Children with mental disabilities

Vocational education. Berufsschulwesen

6300 General (Table K11)

6302 Teachers (Table K11)

6304 Landliche Fortbildungsschulen

Secondary education. Mittelschulen. Höhere Schulen

6307 General (Table K11)

6308.A-Z Special topics, A-Z

Cultural affairs. Kulturrecht und Kulturverwaltungsrecht
Education. Schulverwaltungsrecht
Secondary education. Mittelschulen. Höhere Schulen
Special topics, A-Z -- Continued
Abitur see KK6308.M38
Examination see KK6308.M38
6308.M38 Matura. Abitur. Hochschulreife
6309 Gesamtschule (Combined elementary and secondary education)
6311.A-Z Teaching methods and media, A-Z
6311.C67 Correspondence courses. Fernunterricht
6311.E38 Educational radio programs. Schulfunk
6311.T48 Textbooks
Higher education. Universities. Hochschulrecht
For legal education see KK89+
For research policies in higher education see KK6345+
6313 General (Table K11)
6313.6 Constitutional aspects. Numerus clauses
Administration. Industrial management in higher education
6314 General (Table K11)
6315 Self-government and autonomy. Grundordnungen und Selbstverwaltung
Student participation in administration see KK6330
6316 Disciplinary power and tribunals. Disziplinarrecht
6317 Degrees. Akademische Grade
Including Promotionsordnunge, Druckzwang, etc.
For law degrees see KK112+
6318.A-Z Special topics, A-Z
6318.A35 Admission. Zulassung
6318.E94 Examinations
Federal aid to higher education see KK6318.F54
6318.F54 Finance
Including federal aid to higher education
Numerus clausus see KK6318.A35
Faculties. Institutes
For law schools see KK118.A+
6320 General (Table K11)
6322.A-Z Particular. By place, A-Z
Teachers. Lehrkörpfer
Including professors (ordinarii, extraordinarii, and emeriti), assistants, Dozenten, Wissenschaftliche, Räte, Akademische Räte, etc.
6324 General (Table K11)
6326 Tenure, salaries, pensions, etc.
Students
6329 General (Table K11)

Cultural affairs. Kulturrecht und Kulturverwaltungsrecht
Education. Schulverwaltungsrecht
Higher education. Universities. Hochschulrecht
Students -- Continued

6330 Student participation in administration. Student parliament

6331 Fellowships. Grants
For general educational assistance see KK3445

6332 Political activities
Including strikes

6333 Student societies. Studentische Korporationen

6334.A-Z Universities. By place, A-Z

6335.A-Z Other schools or institutions of higher education. By place, A-Z
Including colleges or institutes of technology, schools or music, art, drama, etc.
For academies see KK6347.A+

6335.H43 Heidelberg. Pädagogische Hochschule

6335.S78 Stuttgart. Technische Hochschule

6337 Costs of education. Social insurance, etc.

Private schools

6339 General (Table K11)

6340.A-Z Types, A-Z

6340.K35 Kindergartens

6340.L39 Law schools

Denominational schools see KK6278

6341 Adult education. Erwachsenenbildungsrecht. Volkshochschulen

6342 Physical education. Sports. Leibesübungen. Sport (Table K11)
For liability for sports accidents see KK1982+
Cf. KK6062+ Sports activities

Science and the arts
For constitutional guaranties see KK6258

6345 Public policies in research. Forschungspolitik
Including research in higher education

Public institutions. Akademien und Anstalten

6346 General (Table K11)

6347.A-Z Academies. By name, A-Z
Akademie für deutsches Recht see KK137.A32

6347.A37 Akademie für Raumforschung und Landesplanung

6349.A-Z Research institutes. By name, A-Z
Deutscher Wetterdienst see KK7031+
Deutsches Hydrographisches Institut see KK6927.5+

6352.A-Z Branches and subjects, A-Z

6352.A72 Archaeology

Cultural affairs. Kulturrecht und Kulturverwaltungsrecht
Science and the arts
Public institutions. Akademien und Anstalten
Branches and subjects, A-Z -- Continued

6352.C37 Cartography
For cadastral surveys see KK1437
Meteorology see KK7031+
Oceanography see KK6927.5+
6352.S62 Social sciences
6352.S73 Statistical services
Including statistisches Bundesamt
For data protection, see KK1968.5; KK6071.5

The arts
6353 General works
6354 Fine arts
Performing arts
6355 General (Table K11)
Music. Musicians
6357 General (Table K11)
6358 Labor contracts
Corporate representation
6359 General works
6360 Reichsmusikkammer
Theater. Theaterrecht
For copyright see KK2707
6363 General (Table K11)
6365 Personnel
Including managerial, performing, and technical staff
For labor contracts and collective labor agreement of stagehands see KK3097.S72
6367 Playwrights. Contracts (Table K11)
Motion pictures. Filmrecht
6369 General (Table K11)
6371 Labor contracts
6372 Regulation of industry
Including trade practice and censorship
6373 Screenwriters. Contracts

Public collections. Recht der öffentlichen Sammlungen
6377 General (Table K11)
6378 Archives. Historic documents. Archivrecht (Table K11)
Libraries. Bibliotheksrecht
6382 General (Table K11)
6385 Research libraries. Wissenschaftliche Bibliotheken
6387.A-Z Other types of libraries, A-Z
Librarians and other library personnel
6389 General (Table K11)
6391 Education

Cultural affairs. Kulturrecht und Kulturverwaltungsrecht
Public collections. Recht der öffentlichen Sammlungen
Libraries. Bibliotheksrecht
Librarians and other library personnel -- Continued
6392 Tenure, salaries, pensions, etc.
6393 Legal deposit of books. Abgabe von Druckwerken. Pflichtexemplare
6395 Inter-library loan
Including national and international loan
6397 Criminal provisions
Cf. KK3569 Protection of children against obscenity
6399 Museums and galleries. Museumsrecht (Table K11)
6405 Historic buildings and monuments. Architectural landmarks. Baudenkmalschutz. Sonstige Kulturdenkmaler
Including vessels, battleships, archaeological sites (Bodenaltertümer), etc.
6409 Educational, scientific, and cultural exchange
Economic law. Wirtschaftsrecht
6411-6415.8 General (Table K10)
Economic constitution. Wirtschaftsverfassung. Wirtschaftsverwaltung
6417 General works
6418 Theories and concepts
Including liberalism, national planning (Planification), socialization, Soziale Marktwirtschaft, Wirtschaftsdemokratie, etc.)
Organization and administration
Class here works on federal departments of commerce, federal and state departments of commerce, or departments of commerce of several areas
For the department of commerce of an individual state, see the state
For departments of commerce prior to 1949, see KK4692.R47; KK4865
6420 General (Table K11)
6422 Bundesminister für Wirtschaft (Federal department of commerce) (Table K11)
Subordinate agencies and courts
6423 Bundesaufsichtsamt für das Kreditwesen
6424 Bundesamt für gewerbliche Wirtschaft
6425 Bundesstelle für Aussenhandelsinformation
Bundesanstalt für Materialprüfung see KK6555.5
Physikalisch-technische Bundesanstalt see KK6555
Institut für chemisch-technische Untersuchungen see KK6555.7
Bundeskartellamt see KK6515+

Economic law. Wirtschaftsrecht
Economic constitution. Wirtschaftsverfassung. Wirtschaftsverwaltung
Organization and administration -- Continued

6427 Bundesminister für wirtschaftliche Zusammenarbeit (Federal department for economic cooperation with developing countries)

Government control and policy. Wirtschaftslenkung und Wirtschaftspolitik

6428 General (Table K11)

6431 Expansion control. Stabilitätskontrolle
Including business cycles

6433 Investment control. Investitionskontrolle
Including foreign investments
For tax measures see KK7120

6435 Assistance to developing countries. Entwicklungshilfe
For tax measures see KK7121

Economic assistance

6436 General works

Subsidies. Subventionen

6437 General works

6438 Investment credits. Investitionshilfe (Table K11)

6439 Criminal provisions

Agricultural credits see KK6639+
Mining industry see KK6713
Tax measures see KK7118+
Berlin-Hilfe see KK7122
Assistance to Zonen-Randgebiete see KK7123

6440 Marketing orders. Marktordnungen
Class here general works
For particular marketing orders, see the subject, e.g. Agriculture

Prices and price control. Preisbildung und Preisüberwachung

6442 General (Table K11)

6444.A-Z Industries, services, or products, A-Z

Agricultural products see KK6663.A+

6444.A72 Architects

6444.B52 Blacksmiths

6444.B84 Building and construction industry

Construction industry see KK6444.B84

6444.D78 Drugs. Pharmaceutical products

Food processing industry see KK6750+

6444.F87 Furniture industry

6444.H68 Hospitals

Pharmaceutical products see KK6444.D78
Premiums see KK2815+

Economic law. Wirtschaftsrecht
Government control and policy. Wirtschaftslenkung und Wirtschaftspolitik
Prices and price control. Preisbildung und Preisüberwachung
Industries, services, or products, A-Z -- Continued
6444.P82 Public contracts
6444.P84 Public utilities
6444.R43 Real property
Rebates see KK2815+
Rent control see KK1816
6446 Price delicts. Preisstrafrecht
Including price fixing, hoarding, discrimination, etc.
6447 Distribution
6449 Licenses. Lizenzbedürftigkeit
Money see KK7090+
Foreign exchange control see KK7095+
Business enterprises owned or controlled by government see KK5847+
Industrial priorities and allocations in wartime. Economic recovery measures see KK7520+
Rationing see KK7520+
6452 Protection of the law against acts of economic control. Rechtsschutz gegen Massnahmen der Wirtschaftsverwaltung
For indemnification see KK5792.A35
Control of contracts and combinations in restraint of trade. Competition rules. Wettbewerbsrecht
For unfair competition see KK2799+
6456 General (Table K11)
6458 Constitutional aspects
Including freedom of association and freedom on contract
6462 Antidiscrimination
6464 Abuse of rights. Missbrauch
Horizontal and vertical combinations
6465 General works
Corporate consolidation, merger, etc. Unternehmenszussammenschlüsee
6467 General (Table K11)
6469 Fusionskontrolle
Cartels. Kartelle
6471 General (Table K11)
6472 Contract. Kartellvertrag
Including rescission and cancellation
Notification to cartel agency see KK6523
Registration see KK6517
Control of abuse of rights see KK6524

Economic law. Wirtschaftsrecht
Government control and policy. Wirtschaftslenkung und Wirtschaftspolitik
Control of contracts and combinations in restraint of trade. Competition rules. Wettbewerbsrecht
Horizontal and vertical combinations
Cartels. Kartelle -- Continued

6474.A-Z Types of cartels, A-Z
Absatzsyndikat see KK6474.S97
Breakfast cartel see KK6474.G45
6474.E96 Export cartel
Frühstückskartell see KK6474.G45
6474.G45 Gentlemen's agreement. Breakfast cartel
6474.I46 Importkartell
6474.K65 Konditionskartell
6474.M56 Mittelstandskartell
6474.N67 Normenkartell. Typenkartell
6474.R32 Rabattkartell
6474.R38 Rationalisierungskartell
6474.S34 Schlichtungskartell
6474.S92 Submissionskartell
6474.S97 Syndicates. Absatz- und Verkaufssyndikate
Typenkartell see KK6474.N67
Verkaufssyndikat see KK6474.S97
6474.Z82 Zwangskartell
(6476) Particular industries, occupations, financial institutions, etc.
see the subject, e.g. KK2188+ Banking; KK6743.A95 Automobile industry
6478 Exclusive dealing or use arrangements. Requirement contracts. Knebelverträge
6480 Restraint-of-competition clause in labor relations
Including collective labor agreement clauses
6482 Restraint-of-competition clause in business concern contracts and in articles of incorporation and partnership
6484 Price maintenance and open price system. Preisbindung und Preisempfehlung (Table K11)
(6486) Particular industries, products, etc.
see the subject
6488 Voluntary chain stores. Freiwillige Handelsketten
6490 Licensing contracts
6492 DIN-norms
6494 Standardized forms of contract

Monopolies. Oligopolies. Antitrust law. Marktbeherrschende
For government monopolies, see KK5593; KK5918

Economic law. Wirtschaftsrecht
Government control and policy. Wirtschaftslenkung und Wirtschaftspolitik
Control of contracts and combinations in restraint of trade. Competition rules. Wettbewerbsrecht
Monopolies. Oligopolies. Antitrust law. Marktbeherrschende -- Continued

6497 General (Table K11)
Constitutional aspects see KK6458
6501 Market. Market structure
6503 Market dominance. Marktbeherrschung
6504 Kontrahierungszwang
Abuse of rights see KK6524
Cartel agencies and procedure
6511 History
6512 General (Table K11)
6514 Kartellreferate der Wirtschaftsminister der Länder (State agencies)
For the cartel agency of a particular state, see the state
Reichswirtschaftsgericht see KK6511+
Kartellgericht see KK6511+
Bundeskartellamt (Federal cartel agency)
6515 General (Table K11)
6517 Cartel register
Including procedure
6519 Offizialmaxime (Investigation ex officio)
Procedure
6521 General works
6522 Jurisdiction
Including procedures according to EEC-legislation (conflict of laws)
6523 Anmeldeverfahren
6524 Missbrauchsaufsicht
6525 Procedure in antitrust cases
Decisions
6526 General works
6527 Permit. Kartellerlaubnis
Including conditions
6528 Interdiction. Verbot und Aufhebung
6529 Judicial review of decisions of cartel agencies
6530 Damages (Private law) and indemnification (Public law)
6533 Criminal provisions
6534.A-Z Mergers, cartels, business concerns, etc., A-Z
6535 Small business. Mittelständisches Gewerbe
Corporate representation of industry, trade, and commerce. Wirtschaftsorganisationsrecht. Wirtschaftsverbände
6538 General (Table K11)

Economic law. Wirtschaftsrecht
Corporate representation of industry, trade, and commerce. Wirtschaftsorganisationsrecht. Wirtschaftsverbände -- Continued
6540 Autonomy
6542 Self-government and state supervision
6544 Membership
6550 Chambers of commerce. Industrie- und Handelskammern
Boards of trade see KK6842
Agricultural societies see KK6665
Einfuhr- und Vorratsstellen see KK6650
Werberat der Deutschen Wirtschaft see KK6585
Professional associations see KK7033
Money, currency, and foreign exchange control see KK7090+
Standards. Norms. Quality control. Normenwesen. Materialsprüfung
For standards, grading, and quality control of agricultural products or consumer products, see the product
6554 General (Table K11)
6555 Physikalisch-technische Bundesanstalt (Table K11)
6555.5 Bundesanstalt für Materialprüfung
6555.7 Institut für chemisch-technische Untersuchungen
Weights and measures. Containers. Mess- und Eichwesen
6556 General (Table K11)
6557.A-Z By instrument, A-Z
Standardization
6558 General (Table K11)
Engineering standards
6559 General (Table K11)
6560.A-Z By material, A-Z
6561.A-Z By instrument, A-Z
6561.E43 Electric apparatus and appliances
Time see KK6959.S72
6564 Labeling. Warenauszeichnung. Etikettierung (Table K11)
Class here general works
For special subjects, see the subject
Regulation of industry, trade, and commerce. Gewerberecht
6569 General (Table K11)
6570 Constitutional aspects
Including freedom of trade and commerce (Gewerbefreiheit)
For freedom of choice of occupation or profession see KK7032.5
6573 Licensing. Zulassung eines Gewerbes. Bedürfnisprüfung
6574 Right of objection of adjoining landowner. Nachbarrecht

Economic law. Wirtschaftsrecht
Regulation of industry, trade, and commerce. Gewerberecht -- Continued
6576 State supervision of installations. Genehmigung und Aufsicht über Anlagen
6577 Consumer protection. Verbraucherschutz
Advertising agencies. Werbewirtschaft
6580 General (Table K11)
6582 Advertising agencies. Werbeagenturen
6583 Trade fairs and expositions. Messewesen und Ausstellungen
Including national and international fairs and expositions
6585 Corporate representation for advertising matters. Werberat der Deutschen Wirtschaft
6586.A-Z By industry or product, A-Z
6586.H4 Health services. Medicine
6586.I57 Insurance
Medicine see KK6586.H4
6586.T63 Tobacco
By medium
6588 Broadcasting
6589 Publishing
Including newspapers and magazines
Testing of commercial products see KK2808
Primary production. Extractive industries. Urproduktion
Agriculture
Land reform and agrarian land policy legislation. Landwirtschaftliche Bodenreform und Agrarpolitik (Agrarstruktur)
6593 General (Table K11)
Restraint on alienation of agricultural land. Landwirtschaftliches Grundstückverkehrsrecht
6595 General (Table K11)
Criminal provisions see KK6669
6598 Consolidation of landholdings. Commasation. Flurbereinigung (Table K11)
Homestead law see KK1321+
6601-6605.8 General (Table K10)
Organization and administration
Class here works on federal departments of agriculture, federal and state departments of agriculture, or departments of agriculture of several states
For the department of agriculture of an individual state, see the state
For the department of agriculture prior to 1949 see KK4872.R44
6606 General (Table K11)

Economic law. Wirtschaftsrecht
Regulation of industry, trade, and commerce. Gewerberecht
Primary production. Extractive industries. Urproduktion
Agriculture
Organization and administration -- Continued

6607 Bundesminister für Ernährung, Landwirtschaft und Forsten (Department of agriculture and forestry)

Subordinate regulatory agencies

6608 Bundesamt für Ernährung und Forstwirtschaft
6609 Bundessortenamt
6610 Biologische Bundesanstalt für Land- und Forstwirtschaft
6611.A-Z Bundesforschungsanstalten. By specialization, A-Z
6611.F48 Fettforschung
6611.F58 Fischerei
6611.F63 Fleischforschung
6611.F67 Forst- und Holzwirtschaft
6611.G48 Getreideverarbeitung
6611.H38 Hauswirtschaft
6611.K63 Kleintierzucht
6611.L42 Lebensmittelfrischhaltung
6611.Q35 Qualitätsforschung pfanzlicher Erzeugnisse
6611.T32 Tabakforschung

Entail. Anerbenrecht und Erbhofrecht

6613 General (Table K11)
6614 Registration and transfer. Höferolle und Rechtsverkehr
6615.A-Z Special topics, A-Z
6615.A66 Appurtenances
6615.C65 Conveyance. Life annuities. Leibrenten. Leibzucht. Altenteil
6615.D42 Debts. Execution

Execution see KK6615.D42

6615.H44 Heirs
6615.H88 Husband and wife. Relatives
6615.I54 Inheritance and entail

Life annuities see KK6615.C65

6615.M67 Mortgages
6615.O95 Ownership

Relatives see KK6615.H88

6615.U88 Usufructuary lease
6615.W55 Wills

Courts and procedure

6616 General (Table K11)
6617 Anerbengerichte
6618 Erbhofgerichte
6619 Reichserbhofgericht

Economic law. Wirtschaftsrecht
Regulation of industry, trade, and commerce. Gewerberecht
Primary production. Extractive industries. Urproduktion
Agriculture -- Continued
Entailed estates of the greater nobility see KK454+
Agricultural contracts
6622 General (Table K11)
Leasing of rural property. Farm tenancy. Landwirtschaftliche Pacht
Class here civil law provisions as well as legislation aimed at protection and stability for tenants
6624 General (Table K11)
6625 Farm equipment leasing
6627 Workers' gardens. Community gardens. Kleinlandpacht. Kleingartenwesen (Table K11)
Agricultural business enterprise
6630 General (Table K11)
Corporate structure
6632 General (Table K11)
6634 Cartels
6636 Cooperatives. Landwirtschaftliche Genossenschaften
Including producers and marketing cooperatives
Marketing orders. Marktordnungen
6637 General (Table K11)
Economic assistance
6638 General works
Agricultural credits, loans, mortgages, etc.
6639 General (Table K11)
6640 Pachtkredite
6642 Osthilfe
6644 Production control and quotas. Price support and regulations (Table K11)
6646 Standards and grading. Qualitätsbestimmungen und Handelsklassen
Importing and stockpiling. Einfuhrkontrolle und Vorratshaltung
6648 General (Table K11)
6650 Einfuhr- und Vorratsstellen
Rationing see KK7520+
Livestock industry and trade. Fleisch- und Viehwirtschaft
6652 General (Table K11)
6653 Cattle
6655 Swine
6657 Sheep
6659 Poultry. Eggs. Geflügl- und Eierwirtschaft

Economic law. Wirtschaftsrecht
Regulation of industry, trade, and commerce. Gewerberecht
Primary production. Extractive industries. Urproduktion
Agriculture -- Continued

6661 Milk production. Dairy farming. Milchwirtschaft
6663.A-Z Products, A-Z
6663.F38 Fats
6663.F63 Fodder and grain. Futtermittel und Getreide
6663.F78 Fruits and vegetables. Obst und Gemüse
Grain see KK6663.F63
6663.S43 Seeds. Saatgut
6663.T62 Tobacco
Vegetables see KK6663.F78
6665 Corporate representation. Agricultural societies. Landwirtschaftskammern
6667 Agricultural courts and procedure (Table K11)
6669 Criminal provisions
Viticulture. Weinbau. Weinwirtschaft
6671 General (Table K11)
6673 Criminal provisions
6674 Apiculture. Beekeeping. Bienenrecht
6675 Horticulture. Gartenbau
Forestry. Forstwirtschaftsrecht
Including timber laws
6676 General (Table K11)
Common use see KK6123
6678 Seedlings
Game laws. Jagdrecht und Jagdschutzrecht
6681 General (Table K11)
6682 Games leases and licenses. Jagdpacht und Jagdschein
6684 Damges. Wildschadenrecht
Fishery. Fischerei- und Fischereipachtrecht
6695 General (Table K11)
6696 Fishing leases and licenses. Fischereipacht
6697.A-Z Particular fish or marine fauna, A-Z
Sport fishing see KK6063.5.F58
Mining and quarrying. Bergrecht
Including metallurgy (Hüttenwesen)
6700 General (Table K11)
Continental shelf. Festlandsockel
6705 General (Table K11)
Rights see KK6706.2+
Rights to mines and mineral resources. Abbauberechtigungen. Gewinnungsrechte
Including procedure (Verleihungsverfahren)
History see KK554

Economic law. Wirtschaft
Regulation of industry, trade, and commerce. Gewerberecht
Primary production. Extractive industries. Urproduktion
Mining and quarrying. Bergrecht
Rights to mines and mineral resources. Abbauberechtigungen. Gewinnungsrechte -- Continued

6707 General (Table K11)
6709 Public restraint on property rights and positions
6710 Adjoining landowners. Bergnachbarrecht

Mining industry
6712 General works
6713 Economic assistance

Corporations and cooperatives. Bergrechtliche Gewerkschaften
6715 General (Table K11)
6716 Securities. Kux

Social legislation
6717 General works

Labor law for miners
6718 General (Table K11)
6719.A-Z Special topics, A-Z
6719.C45 Children
6722 Unions. Knappschaftsvereine
6723 Mine safety regulations. Rescue work
Including equipment

Social insurance. Knappschaftsversicherung
Including all branches of social insurance
6724 General (Table K11)
6725 Organization and administration (Table K11)
Including Reichsknappschaft und Bundesknappschaft

6727.A-Z Resources. Bodenschatze, A-Z
6727.A44 Alkalies
6727.C62 Coal
6727.G38 Gas
Metals, Nonferrous see KK6727.N65
6727.N65 Nonferrous metals
6727.P48 Petroleum
6729 Subsidences. Earth movement. Bergschadenrecht
6732 Eminent domain
6733 Environmental laws. Land reclamation

Manufacturing industries
Including heavy and light industries
6739 General (Table K11)
6743.A-Z Types of manufacture, A-Z
6743.A95 Automobile industry

Economic law. Wirtschaft
Regulation of industry, trade, and commerce. Gewerberecht
Manufacturing industries
Types of manufacture, A-Z -- Continued
6743.B56 Biotechnology industries
6743.C39 Cement industry
6743.C43 Chemical industry
6743.E43 Electrical industry
Energy industry see KK6848+
6743.F47 Fertilizer industry
6743.S45 Shipbuilding industry
6743.T49 Textile industry
Food processing industries
Class here works on trade practices, economic assistance, labeling, sanitation and quality inspection
Including regulation of adulteration and additives
6750 General (Table K11)
6751 Labeling
6752 Purity
Including regulation of adulteration and food additives
6754 Cereal products. Getreideerzeugnisse
6756 Fruits and vegetables
6758 Confectionary industry. Susswaren
6760 Meat
6762 Poultry products
6764 Egg products
Dairy products
6766 General
6768 Cheese
6770 Fishery products. Seafood
6772 Oils and fats
Beverages. Getranke
6774 Brewing
6776 Winemaking
6778 Distilling
For taxation see KK7306.D58
6780 Mineral waters
6781 Coffee
6782 Storage. Tavern equipment. Getränkeanlage (Table K11)
6784.A-Z Related industries and products, A-Z
6784.S23 Saccharin
Building and construction industry
Including contractors
For building laws see KK6155+
6786 General (Table K11)
6788 Contracts and specifications (Table K11)

Economic law. Wirtschaft
Regulation of industry, trade, and commerce. Gewerberecht -- Continued
International trade. Aussenhandelsrecht
6791 General (Table K11)
Export and import controls
Including foreign trade practice and procedure
6792 General works
Foreign exchange control see KK7095+
Trade agreements see KK7315+
Export trade
6794 General (Table K11)
6795 Criminal provisions
Economic assistance and tax measures see KK7124
6796 Commercial agents for foreign corporations
6798.A-Z By region or country, A-Z
e.g.
6798.E28 East Germany
6798.E87 European Economic Community countries
Domestic trade. Binnenhandel
For consumer protection see KK6577
6799 General works
Cartel aspects see KK6471+
6800 Wholesale trade. Grosshandel (Table K11)
Retail trade. Einzelhandel
Cf. KK6836 Artisans as merchants
6802 General (Table K11)
Conditions of trading
6803 Licensing
6804 Sunday legislation (Table K11)
6805 Store hours
Price maintenance see KK6484
6808.A-Z Modes of trading, A-Z
Chain stores see KK6808.D46
6808.D46 Department stores. Chain stores. Kaufhäuser. Filialen
Fairs see KK6808.M37
6808.M34 Mail-order business. Versandgeschäft. Teleshopping
6808.M37 Markets. Fairs. Märkte und Jahrmärkte
For trade fairs and expositions see KK6583
6808.O98 Outlet stores
6808.P43 Peddling. Gewerbe im Umherziehen
Teleshopping see KK6808.M34
6808.V45 Vending machines. Warenautomaten
6810.A-Z Products, A-Z
6810.A88 Automobiles

Economic law. Wirtschaft
Regulation of industry, trade, and commerce. Gewerberecht
Domestic trade. Binnenhandel
Retail trade. Einzelhandel
Products, A-Z -- Continued
6810.C68 Cotton. Baumwolle
6810.G76 Groceries. Lebensmittel
6810.M48 Metals
Metals, Precious see KK6810.P73
6810.P73 Precious metals
Second hand trade. Gebrauchtwarenhandel
6813 General (Table K11)
6815.A-Z Types of trade, A-Z
6815.A82 Auction houses
6815.P39 Pawnbrokers
Service trades. Dienstleistungsgewerbe
6819 General (Table K11)
Old age homes (Altenheime) see KK6227.O42
Hotels, taverns, and restaurants
6821 General (Table K11)
Railroad dining cars see KK6908.D55
Railroad sleeping cars see KK6908.S43
6822 Liability
Adjoining landowners see KK1337+
6823 Collection agencies. Inkassobüros
6824 Travel agencies. Tourist trade. Reisebüros
6826 Private security guards. Wachgewerbe
6828 Undertakers
Cf. KK6175 Burial and cemetery laws
Artisans. Handwerksrecht
6830 General (Table K11)
6832 Apprentices. Lehrlinge und Gesellen
6834 Licensing and registration. Zuluassung. Handwerksrolle
Including examinations (Gesellen- und Meisterprüfung)
6836 Artisans as merchants
Corporate representation. Autonomous bodies
6838 General (Table K11)
6840 Trade associations. Innungen (Table K11)
For guilds in a particular province or state, see the province or state
For guilds (Zünfte) see KK578+
6842 Boards of trade. Handwerkskammern
6844.A-Z Crafts, A-Z
6844.B34 Bakers. Confectioners. Bäcker und Konditor
6844.B74 Bricklayers. Maurer
6844.C45 Chimney sweeps. Kaminfeger
Confectioners see KK6844.B34

Economic law. Wirtschaft
Regulation of industry, trade, and commerce. Gewerberecht
Artisans. Handwerksrecht
Corporate representation. Autonomous bodies
Crafts, A-Z -- Continued

6844.F87 Furriers. Kürschner
6844.M38 Masons. Steinmetzen
6844.M42 Mechanics. Mechaniker
6844.M63 Model makers. Modellbauer
6844.P37 Papermakers
6844.P48 Plumbers. Klempner. Installateure

Energy policy. Power supply. Energiewirtschaftsrecht
Including publicly and privately owned utilities

6848 General (Table K11)
6848.15 Federal, state, and local jurisdiction
6848.2 State supervision
6848.25 Licensing
6848.3 Ratemaking. Tarife
6848.4 Corporate structure
6848.5 Monopolies. Freedom of contract. Vertragsfreiheit und Anschlusszwang
6848.6 Accounting. Taxation
6848.7 Engineering

Particular sources of power
Electricity

6852 General (Table K11)
6852.15 Federal, state, and local jurisdiction
6852.2 State supervision
6852.25 Licensing
6852.3 Ratemaking. Tarife
6852.4 Corporate structure
6852.5 Monopolies. Freedom of contract. Vertragsfreiheit und Anschlusszwang
6852.6 Accounting. Taxation
6852.7 Engineering

Gas. Natural gas

6854 General (Table K11)
6854.15 Federal, state, and local jurisdiction
6854.2 State supervision
6854.25 Licensing
6854.3 Ratemaking. Tarife
6854.4 Corporate structure
6854.5 Monopolies. Freedom of contract. Vertragsfreiheit und Anschlusszwang
6854.6 Accounting. Taxation
6854.7 Engineering

Water see KK5914

Economic law. Wirtschaft
Energy policy. Power supply. Energiewirtschaftsrecht
Particular sources of power -- Continued
Heat. Steam distributed by central plant
6856 General (Table K11)
6856.15 Federal, state, and local jurisdiction
6856.2 State supervision
6856.25 Licensing
6856.3 Ratemaking. Tarife
6856.4 Corporate structure
6856.5 Monopolies. Freedom of contract. Vertragsfreiheit und Anschlusszwang
6856.6 Accounting. Taxation
6856.7 Engineering
Atomic energy
For protection from radiation see KK6012
6858 General (Table K11)
6858.15 Federal, state, and local jurisdiction
6858.2 State supervision
6858.25 Licensing
6858.3 Ratemaking. Tarife
6858.4 Corporate structure
6858.5 Monopolies. Freedom of contract. Vertragsfreiheit und Anschlusszwang
6858.6 Accounting. Taxation
6858.7 Engineering
6859.A-Z Other sources of power, A-Z
6860 Industrial arbitral courts and procedure. Schiedsgerichte und Wirtschaftsgerichte (Table K11)
6862 Business ethics. Courts of honor. Ehrengerichtsbarkeit der Gewerblichen Wirtschaft
6864 Criminal provisions. Wirtschaftsstrafrecht
Including fines (Ordnungsstrafen)
Transportation. Verkehrsrecht
6868 General (Table K11)
6868.5 Bundesminister für Verkehr (Federal department of transportation)
For departments of transportation prior to 1949, see KK4692.R42; KK4872.R448
Subordinate regulatory agencies
6868.7 Bundesanstalt für Strassenwesen
Kraftfahrt-Bundesamt, Flensburg see KK6876
Bundesanstalt Flugsicherung Frankfurt a/M see KK6920.3
Luftfahrt-Bundesamt, Braunschweig see KK6920.5
Bundeswasser- und Schiffahrtsverwaltung. Bundeswasserstrassen
6869 General works

Transportation. Verkehrsrecht
Subordinate regulatory agencies
Bundeswasser- und Schiffahrtsverwaltung.
Bundeswasserstrassen -- Continued

6870.A-Z Individual agencies. By name, A-Z
Bundesamt fur Schiffsvermessung, Hamburg see KK6930.3
6870.B85 Bundesanstalt Gewässerkund, Koblenz
6870.B88 Bundesanstalt Wasserbau, Karlsruhe
Bundesoberseeamt, Hamburg see KK2283
Deutsche Hydrographisches Institut, Hamburg see KK6927.5+
6870.S72 Staatswerft Rendsburg-Staatsee

Road traffic. Automotive transportation. Strassenverkehr
6871-6875.8 General (Table K10)
6876 Kraftfahrt-Bundesamt, Flensburg
Motor vehicles
6877 General (Table K11)
6878 Registration. Zulassung
6879 Inspection. Technische überwachung
Including engineers, Technischer Überwachungsverein, etc.
6880 Safety equipment
6881 Drivers' licenses (Table K11)
Including driving schools and instructors
6882 Compulsory insurance
6883.A-Z Vehicles, A-Z
6883.B5 Bicycles. Fahrräder
6883.C66 Company automobiles
6883.G68 Government automobiles. Dienstfahrzeuge. Fahrbereitschaft
6883.R43 Recreational vehicles. Wohnmobile
6883.T72 Trailers. Anhänger
6883.T78 Trucks

Traffic regulations and enforcement
6885 General (Table K11)
Traffic accidents see KK2002
Traffic violations
For criminal interference with street traffic see KK8940+
6887 General (Table K11)
Driving while intoxicated see KK8944
Hit-and-run drivers see KK8950
6888 Unauthorized use of a motor vehicle
6889 Police investigation
6890 Traffic courts and procedure
Including fines

Transportation. Verkehrsrecht
Road traffic. Automotive transportation. Strassenverkehr
Traffic regulations and enforcement
Traffic violations -- Continued
Verkehrszentralregister, Flensburg (Central register for traffic delinquents) see KK6876
Highway safety. Strassensicherheit
6893 General (Table K11)
6894 Traffic signs. Verkehrszeichen
6895 Crossings
Snow removal, etc. see KK2012
Traffic noise see KK6253
Carriage of passengers and goods
6897 General (Table K11)
6898 Passenger carriers. Bus lines. Taxicabs. Personenbeförderung (Table K11)
Cf. KK6959.P38 Post bus lines
Goods carriers. Güternahverkehr und Güterfernverkehr
6900 General (Table K11)
6901 Ratemaking. Tarife
Wages and hours of labor see KK3154.T72
6902 Sunday legislation. Sonntagsfahrverbot
Railroads. Eisenbahnverkehrsrecht
6903 General (Table K11)
6904 Corporate structure. Government ownership (Table K11)
Operation of railroads. Eisenbahnverwaltungsrecht
6905 General works
6906 Construction and maintenance. Bau- und Betriebsrecht
6907 Railroad land. Right-of-way
6907.A-Z Rolling stock and equipment, A-Z
6908.D55 Dining cars
6908.S43 Sleeping cars
6909 Railroad safety (Table K11)
Including railroad crossings, etc.
6910 Officials and employees
Including tenure, salaries, pensions, labor law, etc.
6911 Ratemaking. Tarife
Carriage of passengers and goods
6913 General (Table K11)
Liability see KK1988
6917 Private sidings. Privatgleisanschlüsse
6918.A-Z Kinds of railroads or railways, A-Z
6918.C32 Cable railways. Drahtseilbahn
Private-track railroads see KK6918.S42
6918.S42 Secondary railroads. Private-track railroads. Nebenbahn und Privatbahn

Transportation. Verkehrsrecht
Railroads. Eisenbahnverkehrsrecht
Kinds of railroads or railways, A-Z -- Continued
6918.S98 Suspended railways. Schwebebahn
Criminal provisions see KK8935
6918.5 Railroad police. Bahnpolize
Postal services. Telecommunication see KK6946+
6919 Pipelines. Fernleitungsrecht (Table K11)
Aviation. Air law. Luftfahrt
6920 General (Table K11)
6920.3 Bundesanstalt Flugsicherung Frankfurt a/M
6920.5 Luftfahrt-Bundesamt, Braunschweig
6921 Air traffic rules
Including air safety and airworthiness
6922 Airports
6923 Pilots. Flight crew
Including licensing, wages, etc.
Liability see KK1994
Crimes aboard aircraft see KK8960
6925 Space law. Weltraumrecht
Water transportation. Schiffahrtsrecht
Including Wasserstrassenverwaltung
6927 General (Table K11)
Deutsches Hydrographisches Institut, Hamburg
6927.5 General (Table K11)
6927.7 Inspection of compasses, barometers, thermometers, etc.
Seewetteramt see KK7031.2
Ships
6928 General (Table K11)
6929 Ship's papers
For registry see KK2282
Safety regulations
6930 General (Table K11)
6930.3 Bundesamt fur Schiffsvermessung, Hamburg
6930.5 Fire prevention
6931 Ship crew
6932.A-Z Types of cargo, A-Z
6932.D35 Dangerous articles
Navigation and pilotage
6933 General (Table K11)
Deutsches Hydrographisches Institut see KK6927.5+
6935 Rule of the road at sea. Seestrassenordnung (Table K11)
6936 Coastwise and inland navigation. Seewasserstrassenordnung und Seeschiffahrtsstrassenordnung (Table K11)

Transportation. Verkehrsrecht
Water transportation. Schiffahrtsrecht -- Continued
Harbors and ports of entry
6937 General works
6938.A-Z By name, A-Z
6938.B73 Bremen
6938.H35 Hamburg
Coastwise and inland shipping. Binnenschiffahrtsrecht
Including rafting (Flösserei)
6939 General (Table K11)
6941 Carriage of passengers and goods
Cf. KK2260+ Affreightment (Commercial law)
Individual waterways. Wasserstrassen
6942 Moselle River
Rhine River
6943 General works
6943.2 Courts. Rhein-Schiffahrtsgerichte
Elbe River
6944 General works
6945 Customs courts
Marine labor law see KK2290+
Marine insurance see KK2296+
6945.5 Combined transportation. Multimodaler Transport
Communication. Mass media
6946 General (Table K11)
6947 Constitutional aspects. Freedom of communication
6948 Policy. Competition between media
Postal services. Telecommunication. Post- und Fernmeldewesen
6950 General (Table K11)
Privacy of mail and telecommunication see KK6947
6952 Bundesminister für das Post- und Fernmeldewesen (Federal post office department)
Subordinate agencies
6953 Oberpostdirektionen
6954 Fernmeldetechnisches Zentralamt
6955 Officials and employees
Including tenure, salaries, pensions, labor law, etc.
6956 Government monopoly. Postmonopol und Postzwang
6958 Particular kinds of transportation (not A-Z)
Including airmail, surface mail, ocean mail, etc.
6959.A-Z Other services, A-Z
Bus lines see KK6959.P38
Money orders see KK6959.P68
Normalzeit see KK6959.S72
6959.P38 Passenger carriers. Bus lines

Communication. Mass media
Postal services. Telecommunication. Post- und Fernmeldewesen
Other services, A-Z -- Continued
6959.P68 Postal notes. Money orders. Postscheckverkehr. Zahlungsanweisungen
6959.P69 Postal savings. Postsparkassenwesen
6959.S72 Standard time. Normalzeit
Rates. Postage. Modes of collection
6960 General works
6961 Postage stamps. Briefmarken
6962 Liability
Telecommunication. Fernmeldewesen
6964 General (Table K11)
6966 Installations and interference
6968 Telegraph
6970 Teletype and data transmission systems. Fernschreibnetz und Datennetz (Table K11)
Including Telex, Datex, etc.
Telephone
6972 General (Table K11)
6972.5 Rates. Gebühren
Including local and long distance rates
6973 Telephone lines. Auschlüsse
Including extensions (Nebenanschlüsse)
6974 Lease
Radio and television communication
6976 General (Table K11)
Freedom of radio communication see KK6947
Competition between different media see KK6948
Organization and administration
Including federal and state jurisdiction, and federal-state controversies
6978 General (Table K11)
6979 Private and public institutions. Privatunternehmungen und Anstalten öffentlichen Rechts
Boards. Administrative organs
6981 Intendant
6982 Verwaltungsrat
6983 Rundfunkrat
Supra-regional boards
6984 Arbeitsgemeinschaft (Table K11)
6985 Autonomy. Self-government. Selbstverwaltung
6986 Horizontal and vertical combinations. Konzentration
6987 State supervision. Staatsaufsicht
Stations. Networks
Including frequency allocations and licensing

Communication. Mass media
Radio and television communication
Stations. Networks -- Continued
6989 General (Table K11)
6990 Post monopoly
6991 Wire broadcasting
6992 Interference
6993 Amateur stations
Broadcasting
6995 General (Table K11)
Programming
6996 General works
6996.3 Censorship
6997.A-Z Programs, etc., A-Z
Election campaigns see KK5299.5
6997.F34 Fahndungssendungen
6997.N48 News broadcasting
6997.R44 Religious broadcasting
Schulfunk see KK6311.E38
6997.S66 Sports broadcasting
6997.W47 Werbefunk
6997.W57 Wirtschaftsfunk
6998 Labor law
Including collective labor law
6999.A-Z Stations, A-Z
6999.D48 Deutsche Welle
6999.N67 Norddeutscher Rundfunk
6999.S84 Südwestrundfunk
6999.W47 Westdeutscher Rundfunk
6999.Z83 Zweites Deutsches Fernsehen
Criminal provisions
7000 General (Table K11)
7002 Pirate stations. Piratensender
7003 Illegal operation of a station. Schwarzsender
7004 Illegal reception. Schwarzhörer
Press law
7005 General (Table K11)
Freedom of the press and censorship see KK6947
7007 Right to information
7010 Publishers and publishing. Verlagswesen
7011 Editors. Schriftlieter. Redakteure
Including liability
7011.5 Journalists. Domestic and foreign correspondents
Including liability
Corporate representation
7013 Deutscher Pressrat
7015 Horizontal and vertical combinations. Konzentration

Communication. Mass media
Press law -- Continued
7016 Right to obtain retraction or restatement of facts by offender (or an opportunity to reply)
7017.A-Z Special topics, A-Z
7017.P37 Party press
7017.P65 Political advertising
7017.R48 Resistance. Underground press
Underground press see KK7017.R48
7017.Y68 Youth press
Press and criminal justice
7018 General (Table K11)
7019 Newspaper court reporting
Press delicts
7020 General (Table K11)
7021 Liability
Libel and slander
7022 General works
7023 Privilege. Wahrnehmung berechtigter Interessen
Right to obtain retraction or restatement of facts (or an opportunity to reply) see KK7016
7026 Treason by publishing official secrets. Publizistischer Landesverrat (Table K11)
Cf. KK9084+ Treasonable espionage
7028 Contempt of court. Verunglimpfung des Gerichts
7030 Criminal procedure
Including pretrial procedures
Search and seizure see KK9555
Jurisdiction and venue see KK9578
Privileged witnesses and confidential communication see KK9622.P73
Deutscher Wetterdienst. Weather bureau
7031 General (Table K11)
7031.2 Seewetteramt
Professions. Freie Berufe
Including education, licensing, liability, etc.
7032 General (Table K11)
7032.5 Constitutional aspects
Including freedom of choice of occupation (Freiheit der Berufswahl)
7033 Professional associations
For particular professional associations, see the profession
Individual professions
Class here works on education, licensing, professional representation, ethics, fees, and liability
Health professions see KK6208+
Pharmacists see KK6197+

Professions. Freie Berufe
Individual professions -- Continued
Veterinarians see KK6237
Attorneys see KK3770+
Economic and financial advisors
7035 Accountants. Buchhalter
7037 Auditors. Wirtschaftsprüfer. Revisoren. Treuhänder
7038 Business consultants
Tax consultants see KK7139
Engineering and construction
7039 Architects
7040 Engineers
7045.A-Z Other professions, A-Z
Journalists see KK7011.5
Librarians see KK6389+
Performing artists see KK6357+
7045.P74 Printers. Graphic artists
7045.R42 Real estate agents
Social workers see KK3458+
Teachers see KK6286+
7047 Professional ethics. Courts of honor. Ehrengerichtsbarkeit
For a particular court of honor, see the profession
Public finance. Offentliches Finanzrecht
Class here works on public finance law beginning with 1867
For works on the law prior to 1867 see KK362+
Finance reform and policies. Finanzreform und Finanzpolitik
Including federal and state finance and tax reforms
Cf. KK6428+ Government control and policy
7050 General (Table K11)
Monetary policies see KK7090+
7058 General (Table K11)
7059 Constitutional aspects
Organization and administration
7060 Bundesminister der Finanzen (Federal department of finance)
For departments of finance prior to 1949, see KK4689; KK4860+
Bundesminister für wirtschaftliche Zusammenarbeit (Federal department for economic cooperation with developing countries) see KK6427
Bundesschatzminister (Federal treasury department)
7062 General (Table K11)
7064 Administration of public property
7066 European Recovery Program fund. ERP-Sondervermögen
Public building construction
7068 General (Table K11)

Public finance. Offentliches Finanzrecht
Organization and administration
Bundesschatzminister (Federal treasury department)
Public building construction -- Continued
7070 Bundesbaudirektionen
Subordinate agencies and courts
Hauptkassen see KK7079
Finanzhöfe see KK7441
Oberfinanzdirektionen see KK7131
Hauptzollämter see KK7320
Administration of monopolies (Monopolverwaltung) see KK7305
7072 Bundesamt für äussere Restitutionen
Verwaltungsamt für innere Restitutionen see KK7649
Supreme court of claims see KK7656
7073 Bundesausgleichsamt (Lastenausgleich)
Budget. Government expenditure. Haushaltsrecht
7076 General (Table K11)
Constitutional aspects see KK7059
Accounting. Buchhaltung und Kassen
7077 General (Table K11)
7079 Hauptkassen (Table K11)
7080 Fund administration. Fondsverwaltung
Expenditure control. Auditing. Finanzrevision
7082 General (Table K11)
7083 Rechnungshöfe
Public debts. Loans. Bond issues. Staatsschuldenrecht, Anleiherecht und Notbewelligungsrecht
7085 General (Table K11)
7086 Bundesschuldenverwaltung (Federal administration of debts)
Revenue see KK7098+
7088 Intergovernmental fiscal relations. Vertikaler und horizontaler Finanzausgleich (Table K11)
Including revenue sharing (Verteilung des Steueraufkommens)
Money. Wahrung
7090 General (Table K11)
7091 Coinage. Mint regulations (Table K11)
7092 Bank notes. Banks of issue
Class here public law aspects of banks of issue
For banking law see KK2188
7093 Gold trading and gold standard
7094 Currency reforms. Revalorization of debts. Währungsreformen
Including revalorization of mortgages and land charges (Grundpfandumstellungen)

Public finance. Offentliches Finanzrecht
Money. Wahrung -- Continued
Foreign exchange control. Devisenrecht
7095 General (Table K11)
Valuta clause and gold clause see KK1557
7096 Criminal provisions. Devisenstrafrecht
7097 Conflict of laws
National revenue. Staatseinkommensrecht
7098 General (Table K11)
7099 Fees. Fines. Gebühren und Beiträge. Ordnungsstrafen
Taxation. Steuerrecht
Including taxes falling under the concurrent taxing power of the federal government and the states
Criticism and reform see KK7050+
7101-7105.8 General (Table K10)
7107 Constitutional aspects
Including equality
7109 Tax interpretation. Grundsätze der Auslegung. Steueranpassungsgesetze
7111 Tax obligation and tax liability. Schuld und Haftung
Equality see KK7107
7112 Capacity. Geschäftsfähigkeit und Rechtsfähigkeit
7113 Good faith. Treu und Glaube
Double taxation. Doppelbesteuerung
7114 General (Table K11)
7115 Domicile
7117.A-Z Special topics, A-Z
7117.A88 Assistance to developing countries. Entwicklungshilfe
7117.F67 Foreign corporations and foreign stockholders
7117.F68 Foreign exchange
7117.M85 Multi-national corporations
Taxation and tax exemption as a measure of social and economic policy. Sozial- und wirtschaftspolitische
7118 General (Table K11)
7120 Investments. Kapitalanlagen
Including foreign investments
7121 Assistance to developing countries. Entwicklungshilfe
7122 Berlin-Hilfe (Table K11)
7123 Assistance to Zonen-Randgebieten
7124 Export sales
7125 Housing reconstruction. Wohnraumschaffung
7126.A-Z Classes of taxpayers or lines of business, A-Z
7126.A44 Alien residents
7126.B84 Building and loan association accounts (Bausparkonten)
7126.C73 Credit institutions

Public finance. Offentliches Finanzrecht
National revenue. Staatseinkommensrecht
Taxation. Steuerrecht
Taxation and tax exemption as a measure of social and economic policy. Sozial- und wirtschaftspolitische
Classes of taxpayers or lines of business, A-Z -- Continued

7126.F67 Foreign military personnel
7126.G69 Government enterprises. Public utilities
Landlords see KK7126.R46
7126.M55 Military personnel. War invalids, war victims, and war veterans
Military personnel, Foreign see KK7126.F67
Public utilities see KK7126.G69
7126.R44 Refuse disposal
7126.R46 Rental housing
War invalids and victims see KK7126.M55
War veterans see KK7126.M55
7128 Tax saving. Tax avoidance. Steuerersparnisse und Steuervergünstigung (Table K11)
For tax planning relating to a particular tax, see the tax
Tax administration. Revenue service. Steuerverwaltung und Verfahren
7130 General (Table K11)
Bundesminister der Finanzen see KK7058
7131 Oberfinanzdirektionen. Oberfinanzpräsidien
7132 Finanzämter (Local agencies)
7133 Officers and personnel
Including tenure, salaries, pensions, etc.
7134 Administrative rules, guidelines, etc.
7135 Jurisdiction for tax allocation
Including concurrent taxing powers of federal, state, and local jurisdiction
Double taxation see KK7114+
Collection and enforcement
7136 General (Table K11)
Tax tables see KK7136+
Tax accounting. Financial statements. Bilanzsteuerrecht und Steuerbuchhaltung
Including personal companies and stock companies
For a particular tax, see the tax
7138 General (Table K11)
7139 Tax consultants. Steuerberater und Wirtschaftsprüfer (Table K11)
7140 Tax returns. Steuererklärungen
7141 Confidential communications. Steuergeheimnis
7142.A-Z Special topics, A-Z

Public finance. Offentliches Finanzrecht
National revenue. Staatseinkommensrecht
Taxation. Steurrecht
Tax administration. Revenue service. Steuerverwaltung und Verfahren
Collection and enforcement
Special topics, A-Z -- Continued
Buildings see KK7142.R42
7142.C68 Cost accounting
Currency reform of 1948 see KK7142.R49
Depreciation allowances see KK7142.R48
Factories see KK7142.R42
7142.I59 Inventories. Bilanz (Inventur)
Pension trusts see KK7200
7142.R42 Real property
7142.R48 Reserves. Depreciation allowances. Rückstellungen und Abschreibungen
7142.R49 Revalorization of debts. Currency reform of 1948 (DM-Bilanz)
Administrative acts. Steuerverwaltungsakte
7143 General (Table K11)
7143.2 Discretion
7143.3 Guidelines
Assessment. Steuerermittlung, Steuerfestsetzung und Steuerveranlagung
Including procedure
7144 General (Table K11)
7145 Discovery. Auskunftspflicht
7146 Lump-sum payments. Pauschbesteuerung
7147 Family property. Matrimonial property
7148 Notice of assessment. Steuerbescheid
7149 Withdrawal. Correction. Rücknahme. Änderung
7150 Tax remission. Delay granted for payment. Erlass, Senkung und Stundung
Administrative remedies see KK7445+
Judicial review see KK7449+
7151 Res judicata
7152 Tax auditing. Steuerprüfung. Betriebsprüfung (Table K11)
Cf. KK7504+ Tax and customs investigation
7153 Default. Steuersäumnis
Including penalties (Säumniszuschläge)
Cf. KK7512 Tax and customs delinquency
7154 Tax credit. Steuergutschein
7155 Refunds. Rückerstattung
Execution. Steuereinziehungsveerfahren
Cf. KK7504+ Tax and customs investigation

Public finance. Offentliches Finanzrecht
National revenue. Staatseinkommensrecht
Taxation. Steurrecht
Tax administration. Revenue service. Steuerverwaltung und Verfahren
Collection and enforcement
Execution. Steuereinziehungsveerfahren -- Continued

7156 General (Table K11)
Officers see KK7133
7157 Arrest
7158 Suspension. Accord and satisfaction. Vollstreckungsaussetzung
7160.A-Z Tax treatment of special activities, A-Z
7160.B35 Bankruptcy
7161.A-Z Classes of taxpayers or lines of business, A-Z
7161.A37 Agriculture. Horticulture
7161.A44 Aliens
7161.A78 Artisans
7161.A79 Artists
7161.A87 Attorneys
7161.C65 Commercial agents
7161.C66 Commission merchants
7161.C68 Construction industry
7161.F35 Families
7161.F73 Freight forwarders
7161.G49 Gewerbebetrieb
7161.H65 Homeowners
7161.H67 Hospitality industry
Including hotels and restaurants
Horticulture see KK7161.A37
7161.H68 Hospitals. Private hospitals
Hotels see KK7161.H67
7161.I58 Insurance agents
7161.M55 Mining and quarrying
7161.M85 Municipal corporations
7161.P36 Paper and pulp industry
Private hospitals see KK7161.H68
Pulp industry see KK7161.P36
Restaurants see KK7161.H67
7161.R48 Retail trade
Income tax. Einkommensteuer
7163 General (Table K11)
Tax tables see KK7163
7164 Tax planning. Estate planning
Accounting and financial statements. Bilanzsteuerrecht
7165 General works

Public finance. Offentliches Finanzrecht
National revenue. Staatseinkommensrecht
Taxation. Steurrecht
Income tax. Einkommensteuer
Accounting and financial statements. Bilanzsteuerrecht -- Continued

7166 Income tax consultants
7167 Assessment
Including liability
7168 Tax returns. Steuererklärungen
Including joint returns
For community property of husband and wife see KK7147
Taxable income. Exemptions. Einkommen und Freibeträge
7169 General
7170 Profits and capital gains. Gewinn, Wertzuwachs un Veräusserungsgewinn
7171 Tax-exempt securities. Steuerfreie Wertpapiere
7173 Deferred compensation. Ersatzeinziehung
Deductions. Abzuge
7174 General (Table K11)
7175 Amortization. Depreciation allowances. Abschreibungen
7176 Charitable or educational gifts and contributions
7177 Church tax
7178 Interest
Expenses. Geschäftsunkosten
7179 General (Table K11)
7180.A-Z Kinds of expenses, A-Z
7180.B88 Business expenses
7180.E38 Educational expenses
Entertainment expenses see KK7180.T73
7180.M43 Medical expenses
7180.R46 Repairs
7180.R48 Retirement contributions
7180.T72 Transportation
Including care and gasoline
7180.T73 Travel and entertainment
7181 Losses
Surtaxes see KK7268+
Salaries and wages. Lohnsteuer
Including fringe benefits, non-wage payments, etc.
7184 General
Tables see KK7184
7185 Social security tax
7186.A-Z Classes of taxpayers, A-Z

Public finance. Offentliches Finanzrecht
National revenue. Staatseinkommensrecht
Taxation. Steurrecht
Income tax. Einkommensteuer
Salaries and wages. Lohnsteuer
Classes of taxpayers, A-Z -- Continued

7186.E46 Employees
Including foreign and domestic laborers
7186.E93 Executives
Laborers see KK7186.E46
Capital investment. Kapitalanlage
Including foreign investment
Cf. KK7120 Taxation as a measure of economic policy
7187 General (Table K11)
7188 Dividends. Interest. Kapitalerträge
7190 Pensions and annuities. Renten
7191.A-Z Other sources of income, A-Z
7191.A44 Alimony and support
7191.C42 Charitable benefits
Commercial leases see KK7191.L42
Copyright see KK7191.I58
7191.D35 Damages
7191.F67 Foreign licensing agreements
7191.I58 Intellectual property
Including copyright, patents, and trademarks
7191.L42 Leases. Commercial leases
7191.L53 Life insurance proceeds
7191.N45 Negotiable instruments
Patents see KK7191.I58
7191.P76 Profit sharing. Gewinnbeteiligung
Support see KK7191.A44
Trademarks see KK7191.I58
7191.U88 Usufruct
Payment at source of income
Payroll deduction. Withholding tax. Lohnsteuerabzug
7193 General (Table K11)
Social security tax see KK7185
7195 Lump-sum payments. Pauschbesteuerung. Lohnsummensteuer
7196.A-Z Classes of taxpayers or lines of business, A-Z
7196.A37 Agriculture. Forestry. Horticulture
7196.A44 Aliens
7196.A77 Artists
7196.C65 Commercial agents. Insurance agents
7196.E44 Electronic commerce
7196.E93 Executives

Public finance. Offentliches Finanzrecht
National revenue. Staatseinkommensrecht
Taxation. Steuerrecht
Income tax. Einkommensteuer
Classes of taxpayers or lines of business, A-Z
Forestry see KK7196.A37
7196.H65 Homeowners
Horticulture see KK7196.A37
Insurance agents see KK7196.C65
Investment trusts see KK7257.I59
7196.M37 Married couples
7196.P76 Professions. Freie Berufe
7196.T4 Teachers. Lehrer
7196.U55 Unmarried couples
Corporation tax. Körperschaftsteuer
7198 General (Table K11)
7199.A-Z Special topics, A-Z
Subarrange each by Table K12
7199.L5 Liability. Territoriality
Territoriality see KK7199.L5
Nonprofit associations, nonprofit corporations, foundations (endowments), and pension trust funds. Gemeinnützige Vereine, Körperschaften, Stiftungen und Pensionsrückstellungen
7200 General (Table K11)
7202.A-Z Special topics, A-Z
7202.T39 Tax avoidance
Personal companies (Unincorporated business associations). Personalgesellschaften
7204 General (Table K11)
7205.A-Z Special topics, A-Z
Cooperatives
7207 General (Table K11)
7208.A-Z Special topics, A-Z
Stock companies (Incorporated business associations). Personalgesellschaften
7210 General (Table K11)
Tax tables see KK7210
7211 Liability. Territoriality
7212 Tax accounting. Financial statements
7213 Assessment. Veranlagung
7214 Disregard of corporate entity. Durchgriff
7215 Tax returns
Taxable income. Exemptions
7216 General works
7217 Capital stock
Inventories. Vorrate. Warenlager

Public finance. Offentliches Finanzrecht
National revenue. Staatseinkommensrecht
Taxation. Steurrecht
Income tax. Einkommensteuer
Corporation tax. Körperschaftsteuer
Stock companies (Incorporated business associations). Personalgesellschaften
Taxable income. Exemptions
Inventories. vorrate. Warenlager -- Continued

7218 General works
7219 Valuation. Bewertung
7220 Reserves. Rücklagen und Rückstellungen
7221 Profits
Dividends
7222 General works
7223 Schachtelprivileg und Organschaft
7224 Disguised profit distribution. Verdeckte Gewinnausschüttung
Deductions
7226 General (Table K11)
7227 Depreciation of property, plant, and equipment. Abschreibungen auf Anlagevermögen
7228 Pension reserves. Pensionsrückstellungen
Cf. KK7200 Pension trust funds
7229 Charitable, religious, or educational gifts and contributions
7229.5 Expenses
7230.A-Z Kinds of expenses, A-Z
Business gifts see KK7230.E58
Copyright royalties see KK7230.P38
7230.E58 Entertainment and travel expenses. Business gifts
Gifts, Business see KK7230.E58
7230.I58 Interest
7230.M35 Management costs
7230.P38 Patent and copyright royalties
7230.P39 Payment to directors
7230.R48 Reserves
Royalties, Patent and copyright see KK7230.P38
7230.T38 Taxes
Travel expenses see KK7230.E58
7231 Losses
Surtaxes see KK7268+
Corporate reorganization. Umwandlungssteuer
7237 General (Table K11)
7238 Conversions

Public finance. Offentliches Finanzrecht
National revenue. Staatseinkommensrecht
Taxation. Steurrecht
Income tax. Einkommensteuer
Corporation tax. Körperschaftsteuer
Corporate reorganization. Umwandlungssteuer -- Continued

7239 Merger, fusion, and consolidation
7241 Liquidation
7242 Recapitalization
7244 Limited partnership. Kommanditgesellschaft (KG)
7246 Stock corporation. Aktiengesellschaft
7248 Family corporation. Familiengesellschaft
7250 Private company. Gesellschaft mit beschränkter Haftung (GmbH)
Including GmbH & Co., GmbH & Still, etc.
7252 Partnership partly limited by shares. Kommanditgesellschaft auf Aktien
7254 Business concern, holding company, and industrial trust. Konzern, Interessengemeinschaft und Holdinggesellschaft
7256 Government corporations. Offentliche Unternehmen
7257.A-Z Lines of corporate business, A-Z
7257.B35 Banks. Credit institutions
7257.B76 Broadcasting. Television
Credit institutions see KK7257.B35
7257.I57 Insurance
7257.I59 Investment trusts. Real estate investment funds (Immobilienfonds)
7257.P82 Public utilities. Versorgungsbetriebe
7257.R42 Real estate business
Real estate investment funds see KK7257.I59
Television see KK7257.B76
Foreign corporations and stockholders
7258 General (Table K11)
Double taxation see KK7114+
Multi-national corporations
7259 General (Table K11)
Double taxation see KK7114+
Property tax and taxation of capital see KK7363+
Estate, inheritance, and gift taxes see KK7360
7266 Church tax. Kirchensteuer
7267 Capital gains tax. Kapitalertragsteuer. Kapitalrentensteuer
Development gains tax see KK7408
Surtaxes. Zuschlagsteuern
7268 General works

Public finance. Offentliches Finanzrecht
National revenue. Staatseinkommensrecht
Taxation. Steurrecht
Surtaxes. Zuschlagsteuern -- Continued
7268.5 Excess profits tax
Including war profits tax (Kriegsgewinn)
Poll tax see KK7424.P65
7269 Reichsfluchtsteuer
7270 Industriebelastungsgesetz. Aufbringungsumlage (1924)
7272 Aufbringungsumlage (1936-1946)
7273 Reichsnotopfer
7275 Wehrbeitrag. Ausserordentliche Kriegsabgaben
Lastenausgleich (1945). Soforthilfeabgabe
7277 General (Table K11)
7278 Vermögensabgabe (Levy on property)
7280 Kreditgewinnabgabe (Levy on gain from business debts)
7282 Hypothekengewinnabgabe (Levy on gain from business debts)
7283 Special assessments. Sonderabgaben
Excise taxes. Taxes on transactions.
Verbrauchssteuern. Verkehrssteurern
Including Kapitalverkehrsteuern
7284 General (Table K11)
Sales tax
7285 General (Table K11)
7286 Accounting
7287 Assessment. Veranlagung. Bemessung
7288 Tax returns. Steuererklärungen
Turnover tax. Umsatzsteuer
Including value-added tax (Mehrwertsteuer) and exemptions (Freibetrage)
7290 General (Table K11)
7291 Sales and services in Germany
7293 Private use. Expenses. Eigenverbrauch und Aufwendungen
7294 Selbstverbrauchssteuer
7295 Import sales
7296 Export sales
7297 Damages. Schadensersatz
Personal companies and stock companies.
Personal- und Kapitalgesellschaften
Including Organschaft
7299 General (Table K11)
7302 Municipal corporations
7304 Beforderungssteuer (Table K11)

Public finance. Offentliches Finanzrecht
National revenue. Staatseinkommensrecht
Taxation. Steurrecht
Excise taxes. Taxes on transactions.
Verbrauchssteuern. Verkehrssteurern
Sales tax -- Continued
Particular commodities, services, and transactions see KK7306.A+

7305 Government monopolies. Finanzmonopole. Monopolverwaltung (Table K11)
7306.A-Z Commodities, services, and transactions, A-Z
7306.A42 Alcoholic beverages (General)
Amusements see KK7424.A48
7306.A98 Automobile industry and service
7306.B35 Banking transactions
7306.B37 Bars and taverns. Weinstuben
Beer see KK7379
7306.B38 Betting (Bookmaking). Wetten. Lotterien
7306.B55 Bills of exchange tax. Wechselsteuer
Bonds see KK7306.S42
7306.B66 Book trade
Brandy (Branntwein) see KK7306.L57
7306.B94 Building and construction
Champagne see KK7306.W55
7306.C42 Charities
7306.C62 Coal
7306.D58 Distilleries
7306.E54 Electricity
7306.E96 Export-import sales
7306.F66 Food industry and trade
Gambling see KK7381
7306.H68 Hotels and motels
Import sales see KK7306.E96
7306.I58 Insurance policies
7306.L42 Leases
7306.L48 Leuchtmittel
7306.L57 Liquors
7306.M38 Matches. Zündwaren
Motels see KK7306.H68
7306.M68 Motor fuels. Treibstoffe
Motor vehicles (State tax) see KK7377+
Municipal corporations see KK7306.P82
7306.P48 Petroleum. Rohöl
7306.P52 Playing cards
7306.P68 Potash
7306.P74 Printing. Publishing
7306.P82 Public utilities

Public finance. Offentliches Finanzrecht
National revenue. Staatseinkommensrecht
Taxation. Steurrecht
Excise taxes. Taxes on transactions. Verbrauchssteuern. Verkehrssteurern
Commodities, services, and transactions, A-Z -- Continued
Publishing see KK7306.P74
7306.R33 Radio broadcasting
7306.R47 Restaurants
7306.R48 Retail trade
7306.S42 Securities and bonds. Wertpapiersteuer
7306.S76 Stock exchange transactions. Borsenumsatzsteuer
Taverns see KK7306.B37
7306.T62 Tobacco
Tourist trade see KK7306.T75
7306.T72 Transportation of persons or goods. Beförderungssteuer
7306.T75 Travel agencies. Tourist trade
7306.W46 Wholesale trade
7306.W55 Wine
Methods of assessment and collection
For assessment and collection of a particular tax, see the tax
7308 General works
Stamp duties. Stempelsteuer
7309 General works
Bills of exchange see KK7306.B55
Criminal provisions see KK7475+
Customs. Tariff. Zölle. Zolltarife
For foreign trade regulations, see KK6792+
For trade and tariff agreements not limited to a region, see K4600+
For regional trade and tariff agreements, see the appropriate region
For trade and tariff agreements with the United States, see KF6668
7312 General (Table K11)
Tables see KK7312
Trade agreements. Handelsabkommen
7315 General (Table K11)
7316 Favored nation clause. Meistbegünstigungsklausel (Table K11)
Customs organization and administration. Zollerverwaltung
7318 General (Table K11)
7320 Hauptzollämter

Public finance. Offentliches Finanzrecht
National revenue. Staatseinkommensrecht
Customs. Tariff. Zölle. Zolltarife
Customs organization and administration. Zollerverwaltung -- Continued

7321 Zollämter (Custom house)

7323 Officers and personnel
Including tenure, salaries, pensions, etc.

7325 Jurisdiction. Custom territory. Zollgebiet

Practice and procedure
Including remedies and enforcement

7328 General (Table K11)

7330 Duty by weight. Gewichtszoll

7332 Custom appraisal. Wertzoll

7334 Railroads

7336 Airlines

7338 Mail service

7340 Automobile transportation

7342 Bonded warehouses

7345.A-Z Commodities and services, A-Z

7345.B43 Beer. Breweries

Breweries see KK7345.B43

7345.C62 Coal

7345.C63 Cocoa

7345.M42 Meat inspection

7345.T48 Textiles

7348 Costs. Fees

Criminal provisions see KK7348

State and local finance
For the public finance of an individual state or municipality, see the state or municipality

7350 General (Table K11)

State finance

Finance reform see KK7058

7352 General (Table K11)

7354 Budget. Expenditure control
Including accounting and auditing

7356 Public debts. Loans

Intergovernmental fiscal relations see KK7088

7357 Fees. Fines. Beiträge. Ordnungsstrafen
Including license fees

Taxation
For local taxes shared by state and locality see KK7392

7358 General (Table K11)

Public finance. Offentliches Finanzrecht
State and local finance
State finance
Taxation -- Continued

7359 Jurisdiction for tax allocation
For concurrent taxing powers of federal government and states see KK7135
Tax administration see KK7130+
Income tax see KK7163+
Sales, turnover, and value-added taxes see KK7285+

7360 Estate, inheritance, and gift taxes. Erbschaft- und Schenkungsteuern (Table K11)

Property tax. Taxation of capital. Vermögensteuer
Including juristic persons and business enterprises
For real property tax see KK7400+

7363 General (Table K11)

Tax valuation. Bewertung

7365 General (Table K11)

7368.A-Z Particular industries or industrial properties, A-Z

7368.A35 Agriculture. Farms

7368.C32 Cables, pipelines, rail tracks, etc.

7368.C62 Coal

Farms see KK7368.A35

7368.F58 Fisheries

Pipelines see KK7368.C32

7368.P83 Publishing houses

7368.Q32 Quarries and quarrying rights

Rail tracks see KK7368.C32

7368.S54 Shipping

Soft coal see KK7368.C62

7370 Accounting. Financial statements. Vermögensaufstellung

7372 Assessment. Veranlagung

7373 Tax returns. Steuererklärung

7374 Taxable property. Exemptions

7375 Deductions. Abzüge und Abschreibungen

Motor vehicle tax. Kraftfahrzeugsteuer

7377 General (Table K11)

Motor vehicle emission fee (Kraftfahrzeugabgas-Abgabe) see KK6249

7379 Beer tax

7381 Taxes resulting from gambling tables. Casinos. Spielbanken (Table K11)

Local finance
Including municipalities, districts (Kreise), and special districts (Gemeindezweckverbände)
Finance reform see KK7050+

Public finance. Offentliches Finanzrecht
State and local finance
Local finance
7385 General (Table K11)
7387 Budget. Expenditure control
Including accounting and auditing
7389 Debts. Loans. Gemeindeschulden
7392 Intergovernmental fiscal relations
Including revenue sharing with the state
7393 Fees. Fines. Gebühren. Beiträge. Ordnungsstrafen
Including license fees
Taxation
For local ordinances and works on taxation of a particular locality or municipality, see the locality or municipality
7395 General (Table K11)
7396 Jurisdiction for tax allocation. Steuererfindungsrecht
Tax administration see KK7130+
Real property tax. Grundsteuer
Including Grunderwerbsteuer
7400 General (Table K11)
7404 Valuation of real property. Assessment. Bodeschätzung. Einheitswertfeststellung
7408 Capital gains tax. Wertzuwachssteuer
Including development gains
7410.A-Z Properties, A-Z
7410.B84 Buildings
7410.C65 Condominiums
7410.I53 Industrial properties. Office buildings. Industrienanlagen. Geschäftagebäude
Office buildings see KK7410.I53
Business tax. Gewerbesteuer
7412 General (Table K11)
7413 Assessment. Veranlagung
7415 Tax returns. Steuererklärung
7416 Taxable income. Gewerbeertrag (Table K11)
7418 Deductions. Abzüge und Abschreibungen
7420 Gewerbelohnsummensteuer
7422.A-Z Classes of taxpayers or lines of business, A-Z
7422.P49 Physicians
7422.P76 Professions (General)
7424.A-Z Other taxes, A-Z
Admission taxes see KK7424.A48
7424.A42 Alcoholic beverage tax. Gemeindegetränkesteuer
7424.A48 Amusement taxes. Admission taxes
7424.D64 Dog licenses
7424.F57 Fire protection tax
Fishing licenses see KK7424.H85

Public finance. Offentliches Finanzrecht
State and local finance
Local finance
Taxation
Other taxes, A-Z -- Continued
7424.H85 Hunting and fishing licenses
7424.P65 Poll tax. Bürgersteuer
Pollution by motor vehicles see KK6249
Sewage taxes see KK6251+
7424.T68 Tourism tax
Tax and customs courts and procedure. Finanzgerichtsbarkeit
Class here works on federal courts, federal and state courts, or courts of several states
For courts (several or individual) of an individual jurisdiction, see the jurisdiction
History
Class here works on the law and courts prior to 1960
7427 General (Table K11)
7428 Reichsfinanzhof (1918)
7430 Criticism. Reform
7431-7435.8 General (Table K10)
7439 Finanzgerichte (Tax and customs courts of the states)
Including senates, judges, etc.
7441 Bundesfinanzhof
Including Grosser Senat and other senates
7443 Procedural principles
7444 Parties to action
Pretrial procedures. Administrative remedies. Vorverfahren und Rechtsbehelfe
7445 General (Table K11)
7447 Einspruchsverfahren (Tax protest)
7448 Waiver of appeal. Rechtsmittelverzicht
Procedure at first instance. Judicial review
7449 General works
Jurisdiction
7450 General works
7451 Admission of case to the tax court as the exclusive court. Zulässigkeit des Finanzrechtswegs
7452 Competence in subject matter and venue. Sachliche und örtliche Zuständigkeit
7453 Actions. Defenses
7455 Dismissal and nonsuit. Erledigung in der Hauptsache
7457 Evidence. Beweisverfahren
Judicial decisions. Judgments
Including court records
7459 General (Table K11)

Public finance. Offentliches Finanzrecht
Tax and customs courts and procedure.
Finanzgerichtsbarkeit
Procedure at first instance. Judicial review
Judicial decisions. Judgments -- Continued
7460 Judicial discretion
7461 Res judicata
Remedies. Means of review
7463 General (Table K11)
Appellate procedures
7465 General works
7467 Revision to the Bundesfinanzhof
7469 Appeal to the Bundesverfassungsgericht
7470 Waiver of appeal. Rechtsmittelverzicht
7472 Costs
Refunds see KK7155
Tax credit see KK7154
Tax and customs crimes and delinquency. Procedure
7475 General (Table K11)
7479 Illegality and justification
7481 Criminal intent
7484 Liability
Including exculpation
7486 Error
7488 Completion and attempt
7489 Withdrawal and regret
7490 Perpetrators
Including principals and accomplices
7491 Compound offenses
7494 Statute of limitations
Individual offenses
7495 Tax evasion and avoidance
Including Steuerhinterziehung, Steuerunterschlagung und Steuerumgehung
7496 Receiving bootleg merchandise
7497 Violation of confidential disclosures. Bruch des Steuergeheimnisses
Including denunciation
Smuggling of contraband see KK7495
7498 Organized smuggling. Bandenschmuggel
7500 Forgery of seals, stamps, etc. Steuerzeichenfälschung
Procedure
For criminal procedure in general see KK9485+
General see KK7475+
Pretrial procedures
7502 General works

Public finance. Offentliches Finanzrecht
Tax and customs crimes and delinquency. Procedure
Procedure
Pretrial procedures -- Continued
Tax and customs investigation. Steuer- und Zollfahndung
7504 General (Table K11)
Officers (Zollfahndungsbeamte) see KK7133
7505 Evidence
7506 Special procedures in criminal tax cases before the Finanzamt (before 1967)
7508 Intervention of the Finanzamt. Nebenklage des Finanzamts
7510 Amnesty. Pardon
7512 Tax and customs delinquency. Ordnungswidrigkeiten (Table K11)
Including leichtfertige Steuerverkürzung, Steuergefährdung (faulty accounting and bookkeeping), unbefugte Hilfeleistung, etc.
Government measures in time of war, national emergency, or economic crisis. Emergency and wartime legislation. Notstands- und Kriegsnotrecht. Wirtschaftskrisenrecht
7520 General works
By period
7521-7540 1871-1918. Empire of 1871 (Table KK-KKC9)
7541-7560 1919-1933. Weimar Republic (Table KK-KKC9)
7561-7580 1933-1945. Third Reich (Table KK-KKC9)
Labor laws and organizations
7582 General (Table K11)
7584 Protection of labor in wartime
7586 Compulsory and forced labor in occupied countries or deportation for compulsory and forced labor
7588 Reichsarbeitsdienst. Reichskriegshilfsdienst
7591-7610 1945- (Table KK-KKC9)
Legislation for liberation from National Socialism and militarism. Denazification. Entnazifizierungsrecht
7612 General (Table K11)
Boards of denazification. Spruchkammern
7614 General (Table K11)
7617 American Zone of occupation (Table K11)
7620 British Zone of occupation (Table K11)
7624 French Zone of occupation (Table K11)
Legislation for economic and social recovery and restitution. Wiederaufbau- und Wiedergutmachungsrecht
7631-7635.8 General (Table K10)
7638 Reconstruction. Wiederaufbau

Government measures in time of war, national emergency, or economic crisis. Emergency and wartime legislation. Notstands- und Kriegsnotrecht. Wirtschaftskrisenrecht
By period
1945-
Legislation for economic and social recovery and restitution. Wiederaufbau- und Wiedergutmachungsrecht -- Continued
7639 Credit institute for reconstruction. Kreditanstalt für Wiederaufbau
Investititionshilfe see KK6438
Lastenausgleich und Soforthilfe see KK7277+
Restitution and indemnification for victims of the Nazi regime. Entschädigungs- und Rückerstattungsrecht
For benefits for refugees, expelled or repatriated persons, homeless (stateless) foreigners, prisoners of war, and war invalids see KK3503+
7642 General (Table K11)
7649 Verwaltungsamt für innere Restitution
Restitution courts and procedure. Rückerstattungsgerichte
7650 General (Table K11)
7651 Supreme Restitution Court (British Zone)
7652 Cour Superieure pour les Restitutions (French Zone)
7654 U.S. Court of Restitution Appeals (United States Zone)
7655 Supreme Restitution Court for Berlin (Western Zones)
7656 Oberstes Rückerstattungsgericht, 1955
7658 Councils of Jews
7660 Jewish Trust Corporation for Germany, Limited
7664 Minority groups (racial, religious, or other)
7667 Displaced scholars, civil servants, etc.
7670 Life and health damages
7672 Property damages
National defense. Military law. Wehrverfassungs- und Verwaltungsrecht
For emergency and wartime legislation see KK7520+
7690 General (Table K11)
Parliamentary control
7694 General (Table K11)
7696 Wehrbeauftragte des Bundestages (Legislative liaison officer for military affairs)
Organization and administration. Command
7700 General (Table K11)

National defense. Military law. Wehrverfassungs- und Verwaltungsrecht
Organization and administration. Command -- Continued
7702 Bundesminister der Verteidigung (Federal department of defense)
For departments of defense prior to 1949 see KK4897
7704 Subordinate agencies. Wehrverwaltung
Wehrbeauftragte des Bundestages see KK7696
The armed forces. Wehrmacht
7708 General works
Compulsory service. Militärdienstpflicht. Wehrersatzwesen
Including draft and selective service (Ziviler Ersatzdienst)
7710 General (Table K11)
Deferment. Aufschub
Including disqualification and exemption (Unabkömmlichstellung)
7714 General (Table K11)
7716.A-Z Particular groups, A-Z
7716.A44 Aliens
7716.C65 Conscientious objectors. Wehrdienstverweigerer
Ministers see KK7716.P74
7716.P74 Priests. Ministers. Geistliche
7720 Discharge. Entlassung
Education. Training. Career
7724 General (Table K11)
7726 Academies. Schools
Tenure, pay, and benefits. Wehrmachtversorgung und Wehrmachtfürsorge
Including drafted and career military personnel
7730 General (Table K11)
7735 Retirement pensions
7737 Social and health insurance. Indemnity
7740 Disability pensions. Rehabilitation
For war invalids, war victims, and prisoners of war see KK3525
Personnel
Including participation in management of the armed forces
7742 General (Table K11)
7743 Enlisted personnel. Freiwillige
7745 Officers
Including appointments, promotions, and retirement
7746 Women and children
Volkssturm see KK7790
7750 Equipment
Including weapons, plants, and installations
7754 Hospitals

National defense. Military law. Wehrverfassungs- und Verwaltungsrecht
The armed forces. Wehrmacht -- Continued
7758 Postal services
Air force. Luftwaffe
7767 General works
7768 Organization and administration
Personnel. Services
7770 General (Table K11)
7774 Tenure, pay, and benefits
Auxiliary services during war or emergency
7789 General works
7790 Volkswehr. Volkssturm
Civil status and rights of military personnel
7800 General (Table K11)
7802 Constitutional rights
Suffrage see KK5280.S64
Reemployment rights and rehabilitation see KK2929.V48
Civil defense. Ziviler Bevölkerungsschutz
7806 General (Table K11)
7810 Air defense. Air raid shelters. Luftverteidigung. Luftschutz
Cf. KK6168.A47 Building laws
7812 Evacuation
German participation in NATO
For NATO (General) see KZ5925+
7816 General (Table K11)
7818 Military expenditures and contributions of Germany. Verteidigungslasten
Cf. KK7520+ Military occupation and procurement
7821 Foreign armed forces in Germany. Stationierung
Including damages (Stationierungsschäden)
7825 German participation in United Nations peacekeeping forces (Table K11)
Military criminal law and procedure. Wehrstrafrecht. Kriegsstrafrecht
Cf. KK9174+ Crimes against national defense
7830 General (Table K11)
7832 Relationship between military criminal law and procedure and military discipline
7837 Commission and omission. Garantenpflicht
Illegality and justification
7839 General works
7842 Superior orders. Höherer Befehl
Liability
Including exculpation
7845 General works
7847 Necessity

National defense. Military law. Wehrverfassungs- und Verwaltungsrecht
Military criminal law and procedure. Wehrstrafrecht. Kriegsstrafrecht -- Continued

7850 Error
7853 Completion and attempt
7855 Perpetrators
Including principals and accessories
7857 Juveniles. Young adults
Individual offenses
7860 Desertion. Fahnenflucht
7862 Draft evasion. Wehrdienstverweigerung
7864 Incitement. Mutiny. Meuterei
7868 Insubordination. Gehorsamsverweigerung
7870 Self-mutilation. Malingering. Selbstverstümmelung
7873 Threats, constraint, or attacks against superiors. Bedrohung. Nötigung, Angriff gegen Vorgesetzte
7884 Calumny. Assault on subordinates. Vorsätzliche Misshandlung Untergebener
7885 Maltreatment of subordinates. Vorsätzliche entwürdigende Behandlung und böswillige Diensterschwerung
7887 Abuse of disciplinary authority. Missbrauch der Befehlsbefugnisse und Dienststrafgewalt
7889 Lack of surveillance. Mangelhafte Dienstaufsicht
7891 Nonreporting or noninterference in case of crimes committed. Unterlassung der Anzeige von geplanten oder ausgeführten Verbrechen
7893.A-Z Other offenses, A-Z
7893.D83 Dueling
Firearms, Illegal use of see KK7893.I45
7893.G38 Guard duty offenses. Wachverfehlungen
7893.I45 Illegal use of firearms. Rechtswidriger Gebrauch der Schusswaffe
7893.L52 Libel and slander. Privileged comment. Beleidigung
Privileged comment see KK7893.L52
Slander see KK7893.L52
Courts and procedure. Kriegsgerichte
7900 General (Table K11)
7908 Procedure in honor cases. Ehrengerichtsbarkeit
7913 Punishment. Execution. Strafe und Strafvollzug (Table K11)
7917 Probation and parole. Aussetzung zur Bewährung. Vollzugsaussetzung
7920.A-Z Particular trials. By name of defendant, A-Z
Military discipline. Law enforcement. Disziplinarrecht
Including all branches of the armed forces

National defense. Military law. Wehrverfassungs- und Verwaltungsrecht
Military discipline. Law enforcement. Disziplinarrecht -- Continued
7925 General (Table K11)
Constitutional aspects and freedom of speech see KK7802
7928 Superior orders. Enforcement of orders
7930 Procedure (Table K11)
7934 Remonstration. Beschwerde
7935.A-Z Other topics, A-Z
7935.M55 Military maneuvers
7935.R43 Rechtsextremismus
Criminal law. Strafrecht
7962 History
Class here works on recent history and development of criminal law beginning ca. 1800
For works on the law prior to 1800 see KK745+
7967 Reform of criminal law, procedure, and execution
Including reform of criminal justice administration (Strafjustizreform)
For works limited to a particular subject, see the subject
For works pertaining exclusively to the codes, see the code
Administration of criminal justice see KK9429.2+
7971-7987 General (Table K9a modified)
Federal legislation
Statutes. Strafrechtsgesetze
Particular acts
Codes. Gesetzbücher
7975.5<date> Individual codes
Arrange codes chronologically by appending the date of original enactment or revision of the code to KK7975.5 and deleting any trailing zeros. Subarrange each by Table K16
7975.5187 Code of 1870 (Table K16)
7975.51871 Code of 1871 (Table K16 modified)
Legislative papers and related works
Bills
Including records of proceedings and minutes of evidence
7975.51871.A14 Texts. By date
Including individual readings (first, second, and third), e.g., 1925 (Reichsratsvorlage); 1930 (Kahl); 1960 (Grosse Strafrechtskommission); 1962 (Bundesregierung)

Criminal law. Strafrecht
General
Federal legislation
Statutes. Strafrechtsgesetze
Particular acts
Codes. Gesetzbücher
Individual codes
Code of 1871
Legislative papers and related works -- Continued

7975.51871.A6-.Z8 Annotated editions. Commentaries. General works
e.g. Alternative-Entwurf der Strafrechtslehrer, 1966; Cormann, 1919/1920; Liszt, Kahl, Lilienthal, Goldschmidt, 1911; Lucas, 1909; Radbruch, 1922

7992 Constitutional aspects

Philosophy of criminal law. Strafrechtsphilosophie

7994 General (Table K11)

Theories of punishment and particular schools of thought see KK8233+

7996 Ideological theories of criminal law
Including Nazism, Fascism, etc.

7998 Free will and determinism

Criminal policy see KK8233+

8000.A-Z Special topics, A-Z

8000.J88 Justice. Morality of law. Gerechtigkeit

Morality of law see KK8000.J88

Relationship of criminal law to other disciplines, subjects, or phenomena

8004 Criminal law and ethics

8006 Criminal law and politics

8008 Criminal law and retaliation (revenge)
Cf. KK8235 Criminal policy

8010 Criminal law and society
Cf. HV6115+ Social pathology

8012 Criminal law and psychology
Cf. HV6080+ Criminal psychology

8014 Criminal law and hypnotism
Cf. HV6110 Criminal psychology

8016 Criminal law and public opinion

8018 Interpretation and construction. Legal hermeneutics

8020.A-Z Terms and phrases, A-Z

8020.D35 Danger. Gefahr

8020.D42 Death

Drugs see KK8020.F67

8020.F32 Facts

Criminal law. Strafrecht
Terms and phrases, A-Z -- Continued
8020.F67 Force. Gewaltanwendung
Including drugs and hypnosis
8020.H65 Honor
Hypnosis see KK8020.F67
8020.L34 Legal document. Urkundenbegriff
8020.P82 Public. Publicity. Offentlich. Öffentlichkeit
Concepts and principles. Allgemeiner Teil
8022 General
Applicability and validity of the law. Anwendbarkeit und Geltung des Gesetzes
8024 General works
Nulla poena sine lege. Nullum crimen sine lege
8026 General works
8028 Retroactivity. Ex post facto laws
8030 Interpretation. Analogy
8032 Customary law
Alternative conviction see KK9690
Territorial applicability. Räumliche Geltung
8034 General works
Place of commission of crime
8036 General works
8037 Press delicts
8038 Crimes aboard aircraft
Conflict of laws
8042 General works
8043 Interlocal (interstate) and interzonal law. Interlokales and interzonales Recht
Temporal applicability. Zeitliche Geltung
8044 General works
8045 Intertemporal law. Überleitungsrecht
8047 Personal applicability. Immunities
8048 Individuality. Individualisierung
Criminal offense. Verbrechenslehre
8054 General works
8056 Trichotomy
Including felony, misdemeanor, and transgression
8058 Crimes by commission or omission. Begehungs- und Unterlassungsdelikte
8060 Gefährdungsdelikte
8062 Delictum sui generis
8063 Eigenhändiges Delikt
8064 Crimes aggravated by personal characteristics. Sonderlikte
Criminal act. Handlung
8066 General works

Criminal law. Strafrecht
Concepts and principles. Allgemeiner Teil
Criminal offense. Verbrechenslehre
Criminal act. Handlung -- Continued
Corpus delicti. Fact-pattern conformity. Tatbestand und Tatbestandsmässigkeit
8067 General works
8068 Elements. Tatbestandsmerkmale und Unrechtselemente
Including negative, positive, and normative Tatbestandsmerkmale
8069 Objective Strafbarkeitsbedingungen
Omission. Unterlassungsdelikt
8071 General works
8072 Quasi-omission. Unenchtes Unterlassungsdelikt
8073 Obligation to avert harm. Rechtspflicht zum Handeln
Including legal duty and Garantenpflicht (Ingerenz)
For toleration of danger see KK8150
Causation. Kausalität und Kausalverlauf
8076 General works
8078 Theories
Including adequacy, relevancy, and equivalence
8079 Proximate cause. Überholende Kausalität
8082 Finalism. Finale Handlungslehre
Form of the act see KK8178+
Illegality. Justification of otherwise illegal acts. Rechtswidrigkeit und Rechtfertigung
8086 General (Table K11)
Self-defense or defense of another. Notwehr
8090 General (Table K11)
Defense of the state see KK9122
Necessity. Notstand
8094 General works
8096 Weighing of conflicting interests. Güterabwägung. Interessenabwägung
8098 Permit by public authority. Behördengenehmigung
Superior orders see KK8164
Corporal punishment see KK8398
Medical treatment see KK8410+
Duty to act (Legal authority or duty). Rechtspflicht zum Handeln
8104 General works
8105 Use of firearms
Consent of the injured party. Einwilligung
8106 General works
8107 Assumption of risk. Handeln auf eigene Gefahr
8109 Defective consent. Willensmängel

Criminal law. Strafrecht
Concepts and principles. Allgemeiner Teil
Criminal offense. Verbrechenslehre
Illegality. Justification of otherwise illegal acts. Rechtswidrigkeit und Rechtfertigung
Consent of the injured party. Einwilligung -- Continued
Presumed consent. Mutmassliche Einwilligung
8111 General works
8113 Willenserklärungs- und Willensrichtungstheorie
8115.A-Z Other grounds for justification, A-Z
Calculated risk see KK8115.R58
8115.C65 Conflicting duties. Pflichtenkollision
8115.R58 Risk. Erlaubtes Risiko
8115.S72 Standard of conduct in traffic. Verkehrsgerechtes Verhalten
Traffic conduct see KK8115.S72
Criminal intent. Mens rea. Vorsatz
8118 General (Table K11)
Purpose and scienter. Acting knowingly. Absicht und Unrechtsbewusstsein
8120 General works
8122 Error about prohibition (Presence of circumstances for which the law requires scienter). Verbotsirrtum
8124 Actio libera in causa
Negligence and wantonness. Fahrlässigkeit
8126 General (Table K11)
8128 Foresight. Standard of conduct. Voraussehbarkeit. Verkehrsgerechtes Verhalten
Criminal liability. Guilt. Schuld
8130 General (Table K11)
Capacity. Zurechnungsfähigkeit
8132 General (Table K11)
Incapacity and limited capacity. Unzurechnungsfähigkeit und verminderte Zurechnungsfähigkeit
8134 General (Table K11)
8136 Insane persons. People with mental or emotional disabilities. Geisteskranke. Geistesschwache und Psychopaten (Table K11)
Minors. Unmündige
8138 General works
8140 Infants. Kinder unter sieben Jahren
8142 Juveniles. Young adults. Jugendliche
8144.A-Z Special topics, A-Z
Affekt see KK8144.D58
8144.D58 Distemper. Affekt

Criminal law. Strafrecht
Concepts and principles. Allgemeiner Teil
Criminal offense. Verbrechenslehre
Criminal liability. Guilt. Schuld
Capacity. Zurechnungsfähigkeit
Incapacity and limite capacity. Unzurechnungsfähigkeit und verminderte Zurechnungsfähigkeit
Special topics, A-Z -- Continued
8144.L58 Litigious paranoia. Querulantentum
Passion see KK8144.D58
Exculpating circumstances. Schuldausschliessungsgründe
8148 General works
8150 Zumutbarkeit (Expectation to tolerate danger or act dutifully)
8152 Putative necessity. Putativ-Notstand
8156 Putative self-defense and exceeding self-defense. Putativ-Notwehr und Notwehr-Exzess
8158 Duress and putative duress. Nötigungsstand und Putativ-Nötigungsstand
Superior orders see KK8164
Conflicting duties see KK8115.C65
Incapacity see KK8134+
8164 Superior orders and justification or excusation. Höherer Befehl
Cf. KK7842 Military criminal law
Error. Irrtum
8168 General (Table K11)
8170 Error about fact. Tatsachenirrtum
8172 Error about grounds for justification or excusation
Error about prohibition see KK8122
8174 Error about extenuating circumstances
8176 Error in persona. Error in objecto. Aberratio ictus
Forms of the criminal act
Omission see KK8071+
Attempt. Versuchslehre
8178 General works
8180 Intent
8182 Preparation. Vorbereitungshandlung
8184 Inherently ineffective act. Untauglicher Versuch
Including unable perpetrator (Untauglicher Täter)
8185 Active repentance. Rücktritt und tätige Reue
Including attempted participation
Accessory at attempted crime see KK8206
8190 Attempted crimes with special consequences. Versuch erfolgsqualizierter Delikte

Criminal law. Strafrecht
Concepts and principles. Allgemeiner Teil
Criminal offense. Verbrechenslehre
Forms of the criminal act
Attempt. Versuchslehre -- Continued
8192 Attempted omission. Versuchtes Unterlassungsdelikt
Perpetrators. Täter
8194 General (Table K11)
Principals and accessories
8196 General works
8197 Liability of each participant
8198 Necessary participation. Notwendige Teilnahme
8199 Co-principles. Mittäter
8200 Mittelbare Täterschaft (Acting through innocent agent)
8201 Knowing agent. Arglistiges Werkzeug
8202 Accessory before the fact. Anstiftung (Table K11)
Including abettor (Anstifter)
8204 Accessory after the fact. Begünstigung (Table K11)
Cf. KK8752 Defeating rights of creditors
Cf. KK8776 Assisting the securing of benefits
8206 Accessory at attempted crime. Teilnahme am versuchten Verbrechen
8208 Complicity. Beihilfe (Table K11)
Agency see KK8201
8210 Agent provocateur
8212 Verbandsstrafrecht (Juristic persons)
Aggravating and extenuating circumstances (Sonderdelikte und Fahflässigkeitsdelikte) for principals and accomplices see KK8311+
Compound offenses and compound punishment. Konkurrenzen
8218 General (Table K11)
8220 Idealkonkurrenz. Tateinheit
8222 Realkonkurrenz. Tatmehrkeit
8224 Concurring statutes. Gesetzeskonkurrenz
Including priority, Vor- und Nachtat (acts before and after commission), etc.
8226 Continuing crime. Fortsetzungszusammenhang
Punishment
Including works on recent history and development of the law beginning ca. 1800
For works on the law prior to 1800 see KK758+
8230 General (Table K11)
8231 Constitutional aspects

Criminal law. Strafrecht
Punishment -- Continued
Theory and policy of punishment. Strafzweck. Kriminalpolitik
Including klassische and moderne Strafrechtsschulen

8233 General works

Commensurability of guilt and punishment see KK8306

8235 Retaliation. Retribution. Vergeltungstheorie

8236 Generalprävention. Abschreckungstheorie

8239 Spezialprävention. Besserungstheorie
Including rehabilitation and resocialization

Criminal anthropology see HV6035+

8244 Criminal sociology
For non-legal works see HV6035+

Penalties and measures of rehabilitation and safety. Strafen und Massregeln der Sicherung und Besserung (Zweispurigkeit)
For juveniles and young adults see KK9662
For execution of sentence see KK9759.2+

8250 General (Table K11)

8251 Capital punishment (to 1949). Todesstrafe

Imprisonment. Freiheitsstrafen
Including maximum and minimum terms

8253 General (Table K11)

Prisons and jails see KK9787

Reformatories see KK8280

Reformatories see KK9667

8260 Short-term sentence. Strafhaft

Fortress (Festungshaft) see KK760.F67

Fines. Geldstrafen

8264 General (Table K11)

8266 Per diem basis

8267 Subsidiarity of short-term sentence to fine. Ersatzfreiheitsstrafe

Bussen

8268 General (Table K11)

Bussgeldverfahren (Police magistrate) see KK5992

Compensatory damage (Adhäsionsprozess) excluding further claims of victim see KK9712

Bussauflage (Imposed payment of a sum of money) in case of probation see KK9792+

Voluntary payment for dismissal of trial (Bagatellverfahren) see KK9645+

Collateral punishment. Nebenstrafen

8269 General works

Criminal law. Strafrecht
Punishment
Penalties and measures of rehabilitation and safety. Strafen und Massregeln der Sicherung und Besserung (Zweispurigkeit)
Collateral punishment. Nebenstrafen -- Continued

8270 Loss of civil rights. Aberkennung bürgerlicher Ehrenrechte
Including infamy, disfranchisement, etc.

Measures of rehabilitation and safety

8274 General (Table K11)

Measures entailing deprivation of liberty

8276 General (Table K11)

8277 Commitment to medical or psychiatric treatment

8278 Commitment to medical or nursing institutions and reformatories. Unterbringung in Heil- und Pflegeanstalten oder sozialtherapeutischen Anstalten

8280 Commitment of addicts to institutions for withdrawal treatment. Entziehungsanstalten
Including commitment to halfway houses

8284 Protective custody. Sicherungsverwahrung
Including dangerous or habitual criminals

Workhouses see KK760.W47

8288 Protective surveillance. Führungsaufsicht

8290.A-Z Prohibition against practicing a profession. Berufsverbot. By profession, A-Z

8290.J68 Journalists

8290.L39 Lawyers

8290.P49 Physicians

8292 Revocation of driver's license. Führerscheinentzug

8293 Prohibition against keeping animals

8294 Sterilization. Castration

8295 Interdiction. Entmündigung

8296 Legal aid for rehabilitation of prisoners

8297 Publication of sentence

8299 Confiscation and destruction of corpus delicti. Einziehung und Unbrauchbarmachung

8300 Forfeiture. Verfall

Sentencing and determining the measure of punishment. Strafzumessungslehre

8304 General (Table K11)

8306 Commensurability of guilt and punishment. Verhältnismässigkeit und Strafmass

8308 Fixed and indeterminate sentence. Bestimmte und unbestimmte Verurteilung (Table K22)

8309 Conditional sentence. Bedingte Verurteilung

Criminal law. Strafrecht
Punishment
Sentencing and determining the measure of punishment. Strafzumessungslehre -- Continued
Juvenile delinquents see KK9656
Circumstances influencing measures of penalty
8310 General works
Aggravating and extenuating circumstances. Strafschärfungs- und Strafmilderungsgründe
Including principals and accessories
8311 General works
8312 Recidivism. Rückfall (Table K22)
8314 Special consequences. Qualifizierter Erfolg
8315 Motives
8316 Conduct after the act
8318 Detention pending investigation. Untersuchungshaft
Causes barring prosecution or execution of sentence
8322 General (Table K11)
8324 Lack of private complaint. Fehlen des Strafantrags für Antragsdelikte
8326 Active repentance. Rücktritt und tätige Reue
Pardon and amnesty. Clemency. Gnadenrecht
8328 General (Table K11)
8330 Abolition. Niederschlagung
8333 Remission. Straferlass
8335 Commutation of sentence. Strafumwandlung
Suspension of punishment see KK9790
Probation and parole see KK9792+
8338 Limitation of actions. Verjährung (Table K11)
Including Verfolgungsverjährung and Vollstreckungsverjährung and exemptions (e.g. crimes against humanity)
8338.6 Warning. Verwarnung
Criminal registers see KK9796+
Criminal statistics see KK62
Individual offenses. Einzelne Straftaten
8350 General. Besonderer Teil (Table K11)
Offenses against the person
Including aggravating circumstances
Homicide. Tötungsdelikte
8356 General (Table K11)
8357 Murder. Mord (Table K11)
8360 Manslaughter. Totschlag (Table K11)
8362 Killing on request. Tötung auf Verlangen (Table K11)
Eugenics see KK6234
8364 Euthanasia. Right to die. Living wills

Criminal law. Strafrecht
Individual offenses. Einzelne Straftaten
Offenses against the person
Homicide. Tötungsdelikte
8366 Suicide. Assisting suicide. Selbstmord und Beistand (Table K11)
8368 Parricide. Elternmord (Table K11)
8370 Infanticide. Kindestötung (Table K11)
8372 Negligent homicide. Fahrlässige Tötung
8374 Exposure. Exposing helpless person to mortal danger. Aussetzung
Crimes against inchoate life. Abortion. Abtreibungsdelikte
8377 General (Table K11)
8380 Justified abortion
Including ethical, social, medical, and eugenic aspects (Indikationen)
Crimes against physical inviolability
8384 General (Table K11)
8386 Battery. Körperverletzung
8388 Dangerous battery. Gefährliche Körperverletzung
8390 Battery with fatal consequences. Körperverletzung mit Todesfolge
8392 Maltreatment of defenseless persons or dependents. Mishandling abhängiger oder hilflower Personen
Consent. Justified assault
Cf. KK8107 Criminal law concepts
8394 General works
8396 Sports injuries
Cf. KK1982+ Torts
Medical treatment and operations see KK8410+
8398 Corporal punishment. Züchtigungsrecht
8399 Negligent physical harm. Fahrlässige Körperverletzung
8400 Compound offenses. Konkurrenzen
8402 Poisoning. Vergiftung (Table K11)
8405 Dueling. Zweikampf (Table K11)
8407 Brawling. Schlägerei. Raufhandel (Table K11)
Criminal aspects of surgical and other medical treatment. Arzt im Strafrecht
8410 General (Table K11)
8412 Malpractice. Ärztliche Kunstfehler
Cf. KK6208 Medical legislation
8416 Treatment without consent
8417 Experiments with the human body. Transplantations
8419 Gynecological treatment
Euthanasia see KK8364

Criminal law. Strafrecht
Individual offenses. Einzelne Straftaten
Offenses against the person
Criminal aspects of surgical and other medical treatment. Arzt im Strafrecht -- Continued

8422 Artificial insemination. Künstliche Befruchtung (Table K11)
8426 Transplantation
8429 Sterilization
8430 Stem cell research
8431 Autopsy
8433 Confidential communications
For confidential communications in criminal procedure see KK9622.P49
Psychopharmaca damages see KK8412

Crimes against personal freedom
8435 General (Table K11)
Danger see KK8020.D35
Force see KK8020.F67
8437 False imprisonment. Freiheitsberaubung
8439 Extortionate kidnapping. Erpresserischer Kindesraub
Abduction. Verschleppung. Entführung
Cf. KK8532 Parental kidnapping
8442 General (Table K11)
8444 Political abduction. Politische Entführung
8446 Abduction of a woman without her consent
8448 Abduction of a female minor
8451 Political accusation. Politische Verdächtigung
8453 Threats of felonious injury. Bedrohung
8455 Duress. Nötigung
8457 Unlawful entry. Hausfriedensbruch

Libel and slander. Defamation
Including juristic persons and families
8465 General (Table K11)
Honor see KK8020.H65
8467 Insult. Beleidigung
8469 Defamation. Üble Nachrede
8472 Calumny. Verleumdung
8474 Disparagement of memory of the dead. Verunglimpfung des Andenkens Verstorbener
8478 Defamatory statement and truth. Wahrheitsbeweis
8480 Privileged comment. Wahrnehmung berechtigter Interessen
Including criticism of scientific, artistic, or professional accomplishments
For press law see KK7022+

Criminal law. Strafrecht
Individual offenses. Einzelne Straftaten
Offenses against the person
Libel and slander. Defamation -- Continued
8482 Publication of conviction for libel, slander, or defamation. Bekanntmachungsbefugnis
8484 Mutual insult. Compensation. Wechselseitige Beleidigung
Violation of personal privacy and secrets. Verletzung des persönlichen Lebens- und Geheimbereiches
8490 General (Table K11)
8492 Constitutional aspects
8494 Violation of confidential disclosures by professional persons. Verletzung des Berufsgeheimnisses
8496 Opening of letters. Verletzung des Briefgeheimnisses
8498 Eavesdropping. Wiretapping. Verletzung der Vertraulichkeit des Wortes. Abhören
Offenses against the moral law. Verstösse gegen die Sittenordnung
Including aggravating circumstances
Crimes against religious tranquility and the peace of the dead. Störung des Religionsfriedens und der Totenruhe
8507 Blasphemy. Gotteslästerung (Table K11)
8510 Disturbing a religious observance. Störung des Gottesdienstes
8512 Reviling a religious society. Beschimpfung einer Religionsgesellschaft
8514 Disturbing the peace of the dead. Störung der Totenruhe
Including cemeteries and funerals
Crimes against marriage, family, and family status
8516 General (Table K11)
8526 Incest. Blutschande
8528 Adultery. Ehebruch (Table K11)
8530 Bigamy. Doppelehe
8532 Abduction of a minor from legal custodian. Parental kidnapping. Muntbruch
8534 Abandonment, neglect, or abuse of a child. Kindesvernachlässigung
8538 Breach of duty of support. Verletzung der Unterhaltspflicht
8540 Breach of duty of assistance to a pregnant woman. Unterlassene Hilfeleistung gegenüber einer Geschwängerten
Artificial insemination see KK8422
8542 Falsification of civil status. Personenstandsfälschung

Criminal law. Strafrecht
Individual offenses. Einzelne Straftaten
Offenses against the moral law. Verstösse gegen die Sittenordnung -- Continued
Sexual crimes. Straftaten gegen die Sittlichkeit
8550 General (Table K11)
8552 Indecent assault. Begriff der unzüchtigen Handlung
8554 Insult by violation of sexual integrity. Verletzung der geschlechtlichen Ehre und Beleidigung
8556 Rape. Notzucht
Compelling lewd acts
8564 Lewd acts with persons incapable of resistance. Schandung
8566 Abduction for lewd acts. Entführung zur Unzucht
8568 Lewd acts with children or charges. Unzucht mit Kindern oder Abhängigen
8570 Seduction. Verfuhrung
8572 Lewd acts by persons taking advantage of official position. Unzucht unter Ausnützung einer öffentlichen
8576 Lewd acts in institutions
8582 Sodomy. Homosexual acts. Unzucht zwischen Männern (Table K11)
8584 Bestiality. Unzucht mit Tieren
8588 Creating a public nuisance. Erregung öffentlichen Ärgernisses
8590 Obscenity
Including production, exhibition, performance, advertising, etc.
8592 Selling, exhibiting, or advertising contraceptives and remedies for venereal disease
8594 Advertising illicit relations. Werbung für unzüchtigen Verkehr
8596 Prostitution and solicitation. Gewerbsmässige Unzucht
Pandering and pimping. Kuppelei
8606 General (Table K11)
8610 White slave traffic. Menschenhandel
8612 Failure to render assistance. Unterlassene Hilfeleistung
8616 Tormenting animals. Tierquälerei (Table K11)
Offenses against property. Vermögensdelikte
Including aggravating circumstances
8643 Property and damages. Vermögensbegriff und Vermögensschaden
Including transaction (Vermögensverfügung)
8644 Possession. Gewahrsam
8645 Appropriation. Zueignungsbegriff
8646 Enclosed room. Umschlossener Raum

Criminal law. Strafrecht
Individual offenses. Einzelne Straftaten
Offenses against property. Vermögensdelikte -- Continued
Larceny and embezzlement
For relationship to fraud see KK8695
8648 General (Table K11)
8649 Tools. Diebeswerkzeuge
8650 Burglary. Einbruchsdiebstahl
8652 Armed theft and theft by gangs. Bewaffneter Diebstahl. Bandendiebstahl
8654 Pilfering. Mundraub
8656 Domestic and family theft. Haus- und Familiendiebstahl
8658 Automobile theft
Including automotive vehicles and their unauthorized use
8660 Energy theft
8662 Unauthorized use of savings books
Embezzlement. Unterschlagung
For relationship to breach of trust see KK8726
8670 General (Table K11)
8672 Embezzlement in office. Amtsunterschlagung
8675 Robbery and rapacious theft. Raub und räuberischer Diebstahl (Table K11)
For relationship to extortion see KK8716
8680 Destruction of property and conversion. Sachbeschädigung und Sachentziehung (Table K11)
Fraud. Betrug
8690 General (Table K11)
8695 Relationship to theft and embezzlement
8699 Fraudulent insurance claims. Versicherungsbetrug
8702 Fraudulently obtained credit. Kreditbetrug
8705 Obtaining benefits surreptitiously. Leistungserschleichung
8707 Fraudulently obtained employment. Anstellungsbetrug
8710 Fraud by litigation. Prozessbetrug
Fraudulent bankruptcy see KK8750+
Extortion. Erpressung
8714 General (Table K11)
8716 Use of force or threats. Relationship to robbery
Breach of trust. Untreue
8722 General (Table K11)
8726 Relationship to embezzlement
Usury. Wucher
8732 General (Table K11)
8734 Rents. Mietwucher
Defeating rights of creditors
8740 General (Table K11)

Criminal law. Strafrecht
Individual offenses. Einzelne Straftaten
Offenses against property. Vermögensdelikte
Defeating rights of creditors -- Continued

8743 Defeating rights of pledgees. Pfandkehr
8745 Defeating execution. Vollstreckungsvereitelung
Fraudulent bankruptcy. Konkursbetrug
8750 General (Table K11)
8752 Assisting debtors to defeat rights of creditors. Gläubiger- und Schuldnerbegünstigung
8759 Game and fish poaching. Wilderei (Table K11)
Aiding criminals in securing benefits
8764 General (Table K11)
Receiving stolen goods. Hehlerei
8768 General (Table K11)
8770 Deriving income from receiving stolen goods
8776 Assisting in the securing of benefits. Begünstigung
Money laundering see KK2254.5
Offenses against public order and convenience. Straftaten gegen die öffentliche Ordnung
Including aggravating circumstances
Crimes against the peace of the community. Straftaten gegen den Gemeinschaftsfrieden
Including terrorism
8780 General (Table K11)
8782 Inciting insubordination. Aufforderung zum Ungehorsam
8784 Inciting crime. Aufforderung zu Straftaten
8786 Rewarding or approving felonies
8788 Criminal societies. Verbrecherische Vereinigungen
8790 Breach of public peace. Landfriedensbruch
Demonstration and failure to disperse. Demonstrationsstrafrecht
8792 General (Table K11)
8793 Constitutional aspects
8794 Inciting acts against minorities. Volksverhetzung
8796 Threatening the community. Bedrohung der Allgemeinheit
8798 Misuse of titles, uniforms, and insignia
Crimes against security of legal and monetary transactions and documents. Straftaten gegen die Sicherheit des Rechts- und Geldverkehrs
8805 General (Table K11)
8810 Declaration (Documents). Erklärungsgehalt. Gedankenerklärung
8812 Evidence

Criminal law. Strafrecht
Individual offenses. Einzelne Straftaten
Offenses against public order and convenience. Straftaten gegen die öffentliche Ordnung
Crimes against security of legal and monetary transactions and documents. Straftaten gegen die Sicherheit des Rechts- und Geldverkehrs -- Continued
Forgery and suppression of documents. Urkundenfälschung und Urkundenunterdrückung
8818 General (Table K11)
8819 Forgery. Fälschungsbegriff
Including Geistigkeitstheorie
Declaration see KK8810
Evidence see KK8812
8825 Forgery and suppression of mechanical records. Fälschung und Unterdrückung technischer Aufzeichnungen (Table K11)
Including forgery of sound recordings (Tonträger) and electronic databases (Dateien)
8832 Physical and identifying marks. Beweiszeichen und Kennzeichen
8836 Blanks
8838 Telegrams. Money orders
False certification. Unwahre öffentliche Beurkundung
Including acting through innocent official (mittelbare Falschbeurkundung)
8840 General works
8842 False medical certificates. Unwahre Gesundheitszeugnisse
8846 Misuse of credentials. Missbrauch von Ausweisen
8848 Displacing boundaries. Grenzverrückung
8850 Forgery of art works. Kunstfälschung
Counterfeiting money and stamps. Geld- und Wertzeichenfälschung
Including postage stamps (Postwertzeichen)
8858 General (Table K11)
8862 Passing counterfeit money. Abschieben von Falschgeld
8868 Counterfeiting securities. Wertpapierfälschung
Including checks, bills of exchange, etc.
Customs crimes see KK7475+
Tax evasion see KK7495
Crimes involving danger to the community. Crimes against the environment. Gemeingefährliche Verbrechen. Umweltstrafrecht
For terrorism see KK8780+

Criminal law. Strafrecht
Individual offenses. Einzelne Straftaten
Offenses against public order and convenience. Straftaten gegen die öffentliche Ordnung
Crimes involving danger to the community. Crimes against the environment. Gemeingefährliche Verbrechen. Umweltstrafrecht -- Continued

8879 General (Table K11)
8880 Common danger Gemeingefahr
8885 Arson. Brandstiftung (Table K11)
8890 Causing explosion
Including explosives and nuclear energy
8897 Misuse of ionizing radiation
8900 Releasing natural forces. Entfesseln von Naturkräften
Including flood, avalanche, rockfall, etc.
8904 Dangerous use of poisonous substances
8906 Poisoning wells. Brunnenvergiftung
8909 Poisoning food, medicine, etc.
8910 Spreading communicable disease, morbific agents, or parasites
8911 Damaging water and power installations
8913 Impairing industrial safety appliances
8917 Sabotage of essential services and utilities
8920 Causing danger in construction
Including collapse, faulty gas or electric installation, etc.

Crimes affecting traffic. Verkehrsstraftaten
8930 Dangerous interference with rail, ship, or air traffic (Table K11)
8935 Unsafe operation of a rail vehicle, ship, or aircraft
Dangerous interference with street traffic
For minor traffic violations resulting in fines see KK6887+
8940 General (Table K11)
8942 Liability. Negligence
8944 Driving while intoxicated. Trunkenheitsfahrt
8948 Duress. Constraint
8950 Leaving the scene of an accident. Hit-and-run driving. Unfallflucht
Predatory assault on motorists. Räuberischer Angriff auf Kraftfahrer
8955 General (Table K11)
8957 Assault on taxicab drivers
8960 Crimes aboard aircraft. Air piracy
8964 Riots. Strassenschlachten
Misuse of intoxicants. Missbrauch von Rauschmitteln
8969 General (Table K11)
8970 Intoxication. Vollrausch (Table K11)

Criminal law. Strafrecht
Individual offenses. Einzelne Straftaten
Offenses against public order and convenience. Straftaten gegen die öffentliche Ordnung
Misuse of intoxicants. Missbrauch von Rauschmitteln -- Continued
8975 Illicit use of, possession of, and traffic in narcotics
Cf. KK6193+ Public health
Gambling. Glücksspiel
Cf. KK6065 Police and public safety
8984 Illegal operation of a lottery
8986 Illegal operation of games of chance
8988 Illegal participation in games of chance
Acts of annoyance to the public. Belästigungen
Malicious mischief see KK5990.M34
Palmistry. Fortune telling see KK5990.P34
9004 Theft of corpse. Secret burial. Leichendiebstahl (Table K11)
Vagrancy. Begging see KK5990.V34
Prostitution see KK8596
Offenses against the government. Political offenses
Including aggravating circumstances
9015 General (Table K11)
High treason and treasonable activities
9020 General (Table K11)
High treason against the state. Hochverrat
Including federal and state
9024 General (Table K11)
9026 Preparation of treasonable acts. Vorbereitung
9028 Negligence. Fahrlässige Förderung
9032 Treason against the constitution. Verfassungsverrat
9034 Assault on the head of state. Angriff auf das Staatsoberhaupt
9036 Inciting treason. Werbung
Treasonable activities. Staatsgefährdung
9040 General (Table K11)
9044 Preparation of a despotism. Vorbereitung einer Gewaltherrschaft
9047 Sabotage endangering the state. Staatsgefährdende Sabotage
9049 Undermining the state apparatus. Staatsgefährdende Zersetzung
9053 Propaganda endangering the state. Staatsgefährdende Werbung
9057 Subversive activities and relations. Staatsgefährdende Agententätigkeit und Beziehungen

Criminal law. Strafrecht
Individual offenses. Einzelne Straftaten
Offenses against the government. Political offenses
High treason and treasonable activities
Treasonable activities. Staatsgefährdung -- Continued
Crimes concerning political parties and associations
Cf. KK5485+ Outlawing of political parties

9060 General (Table K11)
9063 Contravening decisions of the federal constitutional court concerning political parties
9065 Contravening prohibition against associations. Verstoss gegen Vereinigungsverbot
9067 Using symbols of unconstitutional organizations
9070 Lese majesty. Beleidigung des Staatsoberhauptes
9073 Disparagement of the state and its symbols. Verunglimpfung des Staates und seiner Symbole
9076 Disparaging constitutional organs. Verunglimpfung von Verfassungsorganen

Treason. Landesverrat
9080 General (Table K11)
Treasonable espionage. Staatsgeheimnisschutz
9084 General (Table K11)
9088 Negligent disclosure of secrets. Fahrlässige Bekanntgabe von Staatsgeheimnissen
9092 Prying into state secrets. Eindringen in Staatsgeheimnisse
9094 Intelligence activities. Landesverräterischer Nachrichtendienst
9098 Treasonable use of false state secrets. Vortäuschen von Staatsgeheimnissen
Publication of official secrets by the press see KK7026
9104 Treasonable endangering of the peace. Friedensgefährdung
9109 Treasonable falsification and suppression of proof. Fälschung und Unterdrückung von Beweismitteln
9113 Treasonable deception. Landesverräterische Täuschung
9118 Treachery in conduct of state matters. Landesverräterische Untreue
9122 Necessity of action in defense of the state. Staatsnotstand. Staatsnothilfe

Crimes against constitutional organs
9126 General (Table K11)
9130 Constraining constitutional organs or their members. Nötigung eines Verfassungsorgans

Criminal law. Strafrecht
Individual offenses. Einzelne Straftaten
Offenses against the government. Political offenses
Crimes against constitutional organs -- Continued
9134 Violating curtilage of government buildings. Verletzung des Bannkreises eines Gesetzgebungsorgans
9138 Violating house regulations of legislative organs
Crimes in connection with election and voting. Wahlverbrechen
9145 General works. (Table K11)
9148 Bribery. Corrupt practices. Wahlbestechung. Abgeordnetenbestechung
9152 Coercing voters. Stimmnötigung
9156 Deceiving voters. Abstimmungstäuschung
9160 Violating secret ballot. Gefährdung freier Stimmabgabe
9162 Falsifying votes and voting results. Abstimmungsfälschung und Fälschung von Abstimmungsunterlagen
9170 Obstructing voting. Abstimmungshinderung
Crimes against national defense. Straftaten gegen die Landesverteidigung
9174 General (Table K11)
9176 Disruptive propaganda against the armed forces. Storpropaganda gegen die Wehrmacht
9179 Forbidden aerial photographs. Unerlaubte Luftaufnahme
9181 Recruiting for foreign military service. Anwerbung zu fremdem Wehrdienst
9183 Sabotaging and depicting means of defense. Wehrmittelsabotage
Self-mutilation see KK7870
9187 Violation of secrecy regulations. Verletzung von Geheimhaltungsvorschriften
Opposition to power of the state. Auflehnung wider die Staatsgewalt
9192 General (Table K11)
Constraining official action or inaction. Nötigung zu Diensthandlung oder Widerstand
9194 General works
9196 Legality of the official act
9198 Violation of directions given under protective surveillance. Verstoss gegen Weisungen bei Sicherungsaufsicht
9200 Violating prohibitions against practicing a profession or keeping animals. Verstoss gegen Berufsverbot oder Tierhaltungsverbot

Criminal law. Strafrecht
Individual offenses. Einzelne Straftaten
Offenses against the government. Political offenses
Opposition to power of the state. Auflehnung wider die Staatsgewalt -- Continued

9206 Prison escape. Mutiny. Freeing prisoners. Gefangenenmeuterei und Gefangenenbefreiung (Table K11)

9208 Interfering with official custody. Verwahrungsbruch

9212 Tampering with official seals and pawned articles. Siegelbruch. Verstrickungsbruch

9215.A-Z Other forms of opposition, A-Z

9215.D35 Damaging official announcements. Verletzung amtlicher Bekanntmachungen

Endangering the administration of justice. Obstruction of justice. Gefährdung der Rechtspflege

False testimony. Eidesdelikte

9220 General (Table K11)

9224 Attempt and participation. Versuch und Teilnahme

9226 Necessity and duress. Aussagennotstand und Nötigung

9229 Recklessness. Rücksichtslosigkeit

9233 False unsworn testimony. Falsche uneidliche Aussage

9237 Perjury. Meineid

9239 False affirmation. Falsche Versicherung an Eides Statt

9242 Causing false testimony. Herbeiführen einer falschen Aussage

9245 False accusation. Falsche Verdächtigung

9247 Bringing false complaint. Vortäuschung einer Straftat

9250 Thwarting criminal justice. Strafvereitelung

9253 Failure to report felony. Misprision. Unterlassene Verbrechensanzeige

9257 Public comment on criminal proceedings. Verbotene Mitteilung uber Gerichtsverhandlungen

9260 Coercion of testimony. Aussagenerpressung

9263 Intentional misconstruction by law officers. Rechtsbeugung

9267 Prosecuting innocent persons. Verfolgung Unschuldiger

Including execution (Vollstreckung)

Chicanery and abuse of legal process see KK887.7

9270 Repressing conflicting interests. Prevarication. Parteiverrat

9275 Contempt of court. Verunglimpfung des Gerichts

For contempt of court by the press see KK7028

Criminal law. Strafrecht
Individual offenses. Einzelne Straftaten
Offenses against the government. Political offenses -- Continued
Crimes against the civil service. Straftaten gegen den öffentlichen Dienst
9280 Performance and omission of official acts
Corruption. Bestechung und Bestechlichkeit
9285 General (Table K11)
9288 Corrupt acts by officials. Accepting benefits. Bestechlichkeit und Vorteilsanbietung
9292 Bribery. Granting benefits to civil servants. Bestechung und Vorteilsanbietung
9297 Illegal compensation to arbitrators. Schiedsrichtervergütung als Vorteilsannahme
Bribery in connection with election see KK9148
Embezzlement see KK8670+
Usurpation of office and securing appointment by false pretense. Amtsanmassung und Amtserschleichung
9303 General (Table K11)
9308 Unpermitted assistance at examination. Unerlaubte Hilfe bei Prüfungen
Violating official secrecy. Verletzung des dienstlichen Geheimbereiches
9311 General (Table K11)
9313 Constitutional aspects
9316 Disclosing official secrets. Bruch des Dienstgeheimnisses
Mail and telecommunication. Bruch des Post- und Fernmeldegeheimnisses
9319 General works
9320 Constitutional aspects
9324 Breach of duty in foreign service. Vertrauensbruch im auswärtigen Dienst
9328 Confidential information relating to taxes. Bruch des Steuergeheimnisses
9331 Levying undue taxes. Withholding tax payments. Erhebung nicht geschuldeter Steuern. Vorenthaltung von Zahlungen
Crimes against humanity. Straftaten gegen die Völkergemeinschaft
9339 General works
9345 Genocide. Völkermord (Table K11)
Crimes against foreign states, supranational institutions, or international institutions
9360 General works
9364 Attacks against agents

Criminal law. Strafrecht
Individual offenses. Einzelne Straftaten
Crimes against foreign states, supranational institutions, or international institutions -- Continued
9369 Insulting agents
9373 Public discussion of the private affairs of foreign heads of state
9376 Violation of flags, emblems, and national insignia
Offenses committed through the mail
9380 General (Table K11)
Obscenity see KK8590
Threats, extortion, and blackmail see KK8714+
Economic law criminal provisions see KK6864
Stock company criminal provisions (Stock corporations) see KK2514
Stock company criminal provisions (Private companies) see KK2560
Restraint of trade criminal provisions see KK6533
Labor law criminal provisions see KK3052
Social insurance criminal provisions see KK3383
Radio communication criminal provisions see KK7000+
Press law criminal provisions see KK7020+
Tax and customs crimes see KK7475+
Military criminal law see KK7830+
Criminal courts and procedure. Strafgerichtsbarkeit
For works on both criminal law and criminal procedure see KK7962+
9400 History
Class here works on recent history and development of the law beginning ca. 1800
For works on the law prior to 1800 see KK790+
Criticism and reform see KK7967
9401-9417 General (Table K9a)
9422 Constitutional aspects
9424 Criminal procedure and public opinion
Including trial by newspaper
9426 Sociology of criminal procedure
Including scandals
Administration of criminal justice. Strafjustizverwaltung. Strafrechtspflege
Criticism and reform see KK7967
9430 General (Table K11)
Bundesminister der Justiz see KK3665
Judicial statistics see KK61+
Judicial assistance. Rechtshilfe
9432 General works
9434 International judicial assistance (Table K11)

Criminal courts and procedure. Strafgerichtsbarkeit
Administration of criminal justice. Strafjustizverwaltung. Strafrechtspflege
Judicial assistance. Rechtshilfe -- Continued
9436 Interzonal judicial assistance
9438 Foreign judgments (Conflict of laws)
Judicial review of legislative acts see KK3804.J833
Criminal policy see KK8233+
Court organization. Gerichtsverfassung
9440 General (Table K11)
Amtsgerichte (Magistrate courts)
9445 General works
Courts of assizes see KK9457
Juvenile courts see KK9649+
Landgerichte (State district courts)
Including Kleine und Grosse Strafkammer, Direktoren, etc.
9450 General works
Jury see KK9459+
Courts of assizes
Including juries and lay judges
9455 General (Table K11)
9457 Schöffengerichte (Court of assizes)
Schwurgerichte (Jury)
9459 General (Table K11)
9462 Jury room procedure
9465 Oberlandesgerichte (State supreme courts)
Including senates, presidents, etc.
National supreme courts
Reichsgericht see KK3685
Bundesgerichtshof see KK3686
Courts of special jurisdiction
Schiffahrtsgerichte
see KK6943.2; KK6945
9475 Sondergerichte (Third Reich)
9480 Justices of the peace. Gemeindegericht und Friedensgericht
Class here general works
For an individual court, see the municipality
Jurisdiction see KK9576+
Procedural principles
9485 Due process of law. Rechtsschutz. Gesetzlicher Richter. Rechtliches Gehör
9488 Uniformity of law application. Stare decisis
Prohibition of abuse of legal process. Chicanery see KK887.7
Double jeopardy and ne bis in idem see KK9699

Criminal courts and procedure. Strafgerichtsbarkeit
Procedural principles -- Continued

9492 Offizialmaxime (Principle of prosecuting criminal matters solely through state prosecution)

9494 Accusation principle. Anklagegrundsatz. Akkusationsprinzip

9498 Legalitätsprinzip. Anklagezwang (Duty of accusation)

9500 Opportunitätsprinzip

9502 Principles of defense. Equality

Principles of evidence see KK9599

9504 Publicity and oral procedure. Grundsatz der Offentlichkeit und Mündlichkeit

9506 Speedy trial. Beschleunigung des Verfahrens

9507 Truthfulness and falsehood. Discovery (Disclosure). Wahrheitspflicht und Aufklärungspflicht

9508 Prejudicial actions. Bindung des Richters an Urteile un Verwaltungsakte

Including all branches of the law

Parties to action. Parteien des Strafprozesses

9510 General (Table K11)

9511 Suspect. Verdächtige

9512 Accused. Person charged. Defendant. Angeschuldigter. Beschuldigter. Angeklagter

State prosecutor. Staatsanwalt

Class here works on the legal status of the prosecutor in criminal procedure

For general works on the office of the public prosecutor see KK3728+

9515 General works

9516 Judicial review by judge. Richterliches Prüfungsrecht

9518 Defense attorney. Strafverteidiger (Table K11)

9520 Victim. Verletzter

9522 Criminal judge. Strafrichter

Pretrial procedures. Vorverfahren. Vorbereitung der Hauptverhandlung

9525 General (Table K11)

9527 Penal report. Charges brought against a person. Strafanzeige

Investigation. Ermittlungsverfahren. Vorbereitungsverfahren

9529 General (Table K11)

Techniques of criminal investigation see HV8073+

9533 Examination of the accused. Vernehmung und Untersuchung

Cf. KK9599 Principles of evidence

Cf. KK9604+ Admission of evidence

Criminal courts and procedure. Strafgerichtsbarkeit
Pretrial procedures. Vorverfahren. Vorbereitung der Hauptverhandlung -- Continued
9534 Preliminary judicial investigation. Gerichtliche Voruntersuchung
9536 Judicial order to prosecute. Klageerzwingungsverfahren
Public charges by prosecutor. Offentliche Klage
9538 General works
9540 Stare decisis. Bindung der Staatsanwaltschaft an höchstrichterliche Rechtsprechung
9542 Summons, service of process, and subpoena. Ladungen und Zustellungen
9544 Wanted notice. Streckbrief
9546 Time periods. Deadlines. Fristen. Termine
Compulsory measures against the accused. Securing of evidence. Zwangsmittel im Strafverfahren
9550 General (Table K11)
Search and seizure. Durchsuchung und Beschlagnahme
Including search of persons, buildings, institution's records, etc.
9553 General (Table K11)
9555 Press. Publishing houses
9557 Medical records
9559 Provisional apprehension. Vorläufige Festnahme
Detention pending investigation. Untersuchungshaft
Cf. KK9769+ Execution of sentence
9562 General (Table K11)
9564 Review of detention. Haftprüfungsverfahren
9568 Bail. Freilassung gegen Sicherheitsleistung
Extradition. Auslieferung
9570 General (Table K11)
9571 Constitutional aspects (Table K11)
Procedure at first instance. Hauptverfahren erster Instanz
9574 General (Table K11)
Jurisdiction
Including competence in subject matter and venue (sachliche und ortliche Zuständigkeit)
9576 General (Table K11)
9578 Venue for press delicts
9580 Action. Complaint. Strafantrag
9584 Lis pendens. Rechtshängigkeit
9586 Exclusion and challenge of court members
Time periods and deadlines see KK9546
Limitation of action see KK8338
9590 Procedure without trial. Plea bargaining
Trial. Hauptverhandlung
9595 General (Table K11)

Criminal courts and procedure. Strafgerichtsbarkeit
Procedure at first instance. Hauptverfahren erster Instanz
Trial. Hauptverhandlung -- Continued
Evidence. Beweisverfahren

9597 General (Table K11)

9599 Principles of evidence. Beweisgrundsätze
Including the principle of investigation (Ermittlungsgrundsatz); immediacy (Unmittelbarkeit); and free evaluation of evidence (freie Beweiswürdigung, in dubio pro reo)

9601 Burden of proof. Beweislast

Admission of evidence. Zulässigkeit, Unzulässigkeit des Beweises

9604 General (Table K11)

9606 Confession. Self-incrimination. Entrapment

9608 Informers. Official secrets

9610 Narcoanalysis

9614 Physical examinations
Including blood tests, urine tests, etc.
For forensic medicine see RA1001+

9616 Electronic listening and recording devices
Including wiretapping

9618 Previous testimony, police records, etc.

Witnesses. Zeugen

9619 General (Table K11)

9620 Oath

9620.5 Psychology of testimony. Lies

9622.A-Z Privileged witnesses (confidential communication), A-Z

9622.C68 Counselors

9622.G67 Government officials and employees

9622.P49 Physicians

9622.P73 Press

9622.R45 Relatives

9623.A-Z Other witnesses, A-Z

9623.A44 Aliens

9623.C44 Children

9623.P65 Police officers

9623.S73 State's witnesses. State's evidence

9625 Expert testimony. Sachverständigengutachten (Table K11)
For forensic medicine, chemistry, psychology, psychiatry, toxicology, etc. see RA1001+

Testimony of accused. Aussage des Angeklagten
Including silence (Schweigen), and truthfulness and falsehood (Wahrheitspflicht)

9636 General (Table K11)

Criminal courts and procedure. Strafgerichtsbarkeit
Procedure at first instance. Hauptverfahren erster Instanz
Trial. Hauptverhandlung
Evidence. Beweisverfahren
Testimony of accused. Aussage des Angeklagten -- Continued
9637 Errors (Declaration of intention)
9638 Documentary evidence. Urkundenvbeweis
9639 Circumstantial evidence. Indizienbeweis
9640 Alibi
9641 Illegal evidence. Rechtswidrige Beweismittel
9642 Presumptions. Vermutungen (Table K11)
9643 Summation. Closing argument
Particular proceedings. Besonderheiten des ordentlichen Verfahrens
9645 Bagatellstrafsachen
Including Busse und Verwarnung
9646 Summary proceedings. Summarisches (beschleunigtes) Verfahren
Proceedings against absentees. Verfahren gegen Abwesende
9647 General (Table K11)
9648 Restitutio in integrum. Wiedereinsetzung in den vorigen Stand
Juries and assizes see KK9455+
Procedure at juvenile courts. Jugendstrafverfahren
9649 History
9651-9655.8 General (Table K10)
9656 The juvenile delinquent. The young adult perpetrator. Jugendlicher Täter. Heranwachsender
9657 Juvenile crime. Jugendstraftat
Criminal liability and guilt see KK8130+
Punishment. Correctional or disciplinary measures. Jugendstrafe, Zuchtmittel und Erziehungsmassregel
Including measures of rehabilitation and safety
9662 General (Table K11)
9664 Custodial education. Fürsorgeerziehung
Cf. KK3573+ Social services
9665 Judicial orders. Richterliche Anweisung
9667 Detention homes. Reformatories. Jugendarrestanstalten. Jugendstrafanstalten
Cf. KK9789 Execution of sentence
Sentencing. Strafzumessung
9670 General works
9671 Fixed and indeterminate sentences
Execution of sentence see KK9759.2+

Criminal courts and procedure. Strafgerichtsbarkeit
Procedure at first instance. Hauptverfahren erster Instanz
Trial. Hauptverhandlung -- Continued
Judicial decisions
9674 General works
Judgment. Urteil
9679 General (Table K11)
Sentencing and determination of punishment see KK8304+
9681 Judicial discretion
Including opportunity and equity
Cf. KK9599 Principles of evidence
9683 Pronouncement and statement of grounds. Tenor und Gründe
9685 Change in legal classification. Änderung des rechtlichen Gesichtspunktes
9687 Acquittal. Freispruch
Conviction. Verurteilung
Including measures of rehabilitation and safety
9689 General works
9690 Alternative conviction. Wahlfeststellung. Alternativurteil
9692 Dismissal. Decision ab instantia. Einstellung des Verfahrens
Probation see KK9792+
9694 Void judgment. Nichtige Urteile
9696 Correction or withdrawal of faulty decisions (errors)
Res judicata. Rechtskraft
9698 General (Table K11)
9699 Ne bis in idem. Constitutional aspects
Waiver of appeal see KK9795
9701 Court records. Minutes of evidence. Sitzungsprotokoll
Including clerks, translators, and correction of records
Participation of injured party in criminal procedure
9705 General (Table K11)
9708 Private charge. Privatklage (Table K11)
Including public interest
9710 Intervention. Nebenklage
9712 Adhäsionsprozess (Civil suit of victim in connection with criminal proceedings)
Including compensatory damages (Busse)
Special procedures. Besondere Verfahrensarten
9715 Procedure in case of penal order and penal mandates. Strafbefehls- und Strafverfügungsverfahren
9718 Procedure before the justice of the peace. Verfahren vor dem Friedensrichter. Schiedsmannverfahren
Commitment of insane criminals see KK8277

Criminal courts and procedure. Strafgerichtsbarkeit
Special procedures. Besondere Verfahrensarten -- Continued
Procedure in confiscation of corpus delecti see KK8299
Other procedures
see the subject, e.g. KK7504+ Tax and customs criminal procedures; KK7900+ Military criminal procedure, etc.
9726 Sitzungspolizei (Maintaining order in court)
Remedies. Rechtsmittel und Rechtsbehelfe
9728 General works
9730 Gravamen. Beschwer
9732 Reformatio in peius
9736 Beschwerde
9738 Ruge
Appellate procedure
9739 General works
9740 Berufung
9743 Revision (Appeal for error)
9747 Widerklage
Restitutio in integrum see KK9648
9755 Waiver of appeal. Verzicht und Rücknahme des Rechtsmittels
Post-conviction remedies
9756 General works
9757 Reopening a case. New trial. Wiederaufnahme des Verfahrens
For procedure before the constitutional court see KK5493
Execution of sentence. Strafvollstreckung
Including execution of sentence of juvenile courts
Criticism and reform see KK7967
9760 General (Table K11)
Imprisonment
Including regulations of detention pending investigation (Untersuchungshaft) and short-term sentence (Strafhaft)
9769 General (Table K11)
9772 Administration of correctional institutions (Table K11)
Including discipline, hygiene, etc.
The prisoner. Der Strafgefangene
9774 General (Table K11)
9775 Legal status and rights of prisoners
9776 Juvenile prisoners
9778 Strafvollzugsuntaugliche
Including sick criminals
Dangerous criminals see KK8284
Insane criminals see KK8278
9779 Education of prisoners

Criminal courts and procedure. Strafgerichtsbarkeit
Execution of sentence. Strafvollstreckung
Imprisonment -- Continued
9780 Labor and industries in correctional institutions
Including wages
Rehabilitation and resocialization see KK8239
9787 Prisons and jails. Zuchthäuser und Gefängnisse
9788 Penal colonies. Strafkolonien
9789 Juvenile detention homes and reformatories. Jugendarrestanstalten und Jugendstrafanstalten
Including labor and wages
Pardon, amnesty, and clemency see KK8328+
9790 Suspension of punishment. Strafaufschub. Strafunterbrechung
9791 Restitution
Probation. Parole. Strafaussetzung zur Bewährung und vorläufige Entlassung
9792 General (Table K11)
9793 Probation and parole for juvenile delinquents
9794 Probation counselor. Bewährungshelfer
9795 Remission. Straferlass
Disability to stand execution see KK9778
Criminal registers. Strafregister. Führungslisten
9796 General (Table K11)
9796.5 Cancellation of entry. Strafeintragstilgung (Table K11)
Central register for traffic delinquents see KK6876
Judicial error and compensation see KK5790
Judicial assistance in criminal matters see KK9432+
Extradition see KK9570+
9798 Costs. Kostenrecht (Table K11)
Victimology. Opfer des Verbrechens
9799 General works
9799.3 Children and sexual crimes
Compensation to victims of crimes see KK5792.V52
Criminology and penology see HV6001+

Law of East Germany
Class here German statutory law as modified by socialist-communist doctrine, and East German statutory law from 1949 to 1991
For the law prior to 1949, see KK
For the law of a particular state, see KKB+
For law of a particular city see KKC5100+

3 General bibliography
Official gazettes
State, district, or city gazettes
see the issuing jurisdiction
Departmental gazettes
see the issuing department or agency
7 Indexes (General)
<8> Military government gazettes
see KK9.52
9 Ministerialblatt (1949-1952)
9.5 Indexes
9.7 Zentralblatt (1953-1954)
10 Gesetzblatt
10.3 Gesetzblatt-Sonderdruck
10.5 Indexes
<16-23> Legislative documents
see J351+
25 Other materials relating to legislative history
Legislation
Class here legislation from 1949 to 1991
For statutes, statutory orders, regulations, etc. on a particular subject, see the subject
For legislation prior to 1949 see KK27+
Indexes and tables. By date of publication
27 General
27.5 Chronological indexes
Statutes
Including statutory orders, regulations, etc.
Current and/or continuing collections and compilations
Including official and private editions
34 Comprehensive. By editor or compiler
35 Annotated. By editor
35.5 Selective. By editor or compiler
Codifications and related material
Class here collections of codes and related materials
For individual codes, see the subject
For codes before 1949 see KK36+
36 General
37 Legislative documents

Legislation
Codifications and related material -- Continued
38 Enactments
Class here collections of enactments
For enactments of an individual code, see the code
Treaties
General
see KZ
Treaties on uniform law not limited to a region
see subclass K
Treaties on uniform law of the European region
see KJC and KJE
Concordats see KK5520+
Court decisions and related material
Including authorized and private editions
For decisions and materials on a particular subject, see the subject
40 Several courts
Particular courts
Courts in Germany under Allied occupation (Russian Zone)
see KK49
41.A-Z Kreisgerichte (Local courts). By Kreis, A-Z
Subarrange each by Table KK-KKC6
42.A-Z Bezirksgerichte (District courts). By Bezirk, A-Z
Subarrange each by Table KK-KKC6
Oberstes Gericht der Republik (National supreme court)
Kollegium für Strafsachen see KKA3686+
Kollegium für Militärstrafsachen see KKA7900+
Kollegium für Zivil-, Familien- und Arbeitsrecht
see the subject
43 Indexes. Registers. By date of publication
44 General collections. By initial date of period covered
Other
46 Gesellschaftliche Gerichte
Including Schiedskommissionen und Konfliktkommissionen
Administrative decisions on a particular subject
see the subject
56 Legal dictionaries. Terms and phrases
For bilingual and multilingual dictionaries, see K52+
For law dictionaries on a particular subject, see the subject
Judicial statistics
61 General works
62 Criminal statistics
63 Other. By subject, A-Z
Trials
Criminal trials and judicial investigations
Collections. Compilations

Trials
Criminal trials and judicial investigations
Collections. Compilations -- Continued
65 General
67.A-Z Particular offenses, A-Z
69.A-Z Individual trials. By defendant, A-Z
Including records, briefs, commentaries, and stories on a particular trial
Legal research. Legal bibliography
Including methods of bibliographic research and how to find the law
76 General (Table K11)
Zentralinstitut für Information und Dokumentation see KKA6349.Z45
Electronic data processing. Information retrieval systems
79 General (Table K11)
80 Staatssekretär für Datenverarbeitung (Table K11)
88 Legal education
132 Law societies and associations. By name, A-Z
Including the journals, proceedings, annual reports, etc. of such societies
The legal profession see KKA3704+
137.A-Z Academies and institutes. By name, A-Z
137.A77 Akademie für Staats- und Rechtswissenschaft "Walter Ulbricht"
147 General works. Treatises
154 Popular works
156 Civics
158 Addresses, essays, lectures, Festschriften, etc.
Including single essays, collected essays of several authors, Festschriften, etc.
164.A-Z Works on diverse aspects of a particular subject and falling within several branches of the law. By subject, A-Z
164.P48 Photography
Biography
183 Collective
185.A-Z Individual, A-Z
Subarrange each by Table KK-KKC7
190 History (Table K11)
Philosophy, jurisprudence, and theory of East German law
Class here works on doctrines peculiar to East German legal institutions
For works by German authors on the philosophy of law in general, see K237+
For works on the philosophy of a particular branch of law (e.g. constitutional law, criminal law), see the branch
883 General (Table K11)

Philosophy, jurisprudence, and theory of East German law -- Continued
The socialist concept of law
Including the definition of law
885 General works
887 Socialist morality of law
890 Law and the socialist state. Legal order
891 Rights and duties
Legal science. Rechtswissenschaft
896 General works
Law reform and criticism see KKA942
907 Semantics
Schools of legal theory
911 General works
Modern political theory of law
925 General works
926 Socialist. Communist
942 Law reform and policies. Criticism
Including reform of administration of justice in general (Justizreform)
945.A-Z Concepts applying to several branches of the law, A-Z
Economic risk (Wirtschaftsrisiko) see KKA945.R58
945.R58 Risks in research, development, planning, and production. Forschungs- und Entwicklungsrisiko. Produktionsrisiko
Cf. KKA8114 Criminal law
Private international law. Conflict of laws. Internationales Privatrecht (IPR)
960 General (Table K11)
966 Interzonal law. Interzonales Recht
970 Retroactive law. Rückwirkendes Recht
Civil law. Zivilrecht
981-997 General (Table K9a)
National legislation
Statutes. Zivilrechtsgesetze
984 Collections. Compilations
Particular acts
Codes. Gesetzbücher
Collections see KKA984
985.5<date> Individual codes
Arrange chronologically by appending the date of original enactment or revision of the code to the number KKA985.5 and deleting any trailing zeros
Code of 1896/1900 see KK985.51896
985.51975 Code of 1975

Civil law. Zivilrecht
General -- Continued
Comparative legislation
Including works comparing federal law (Bürgerliches Recht) with socialist law, and comparisons of legislation by period
988 Texts. Unannotated editions. By date of publication
988.2 Annotated editions. Commentaries. By author of annotations or commentary, A-Z
988.6 General works
Concepts and principles. Grundsätze des sozialistischen Zivilrechte
1005 General (Table K11)
Morality of the law see KKA887
1006 Leistungsprinzips (Labor productivity)
1007 Sozialistische Gemeinschaftsbeziebungen
Including relationships of citizens to each other, to mass organizations, private and government enterprises (Betriebe), etc.
Persons
1011 General (Table K11)
Juristic persons. Juristische Personen
1026 General (Table K11)
Associations. Vereinsrecht
1031 General (Table K11)
1035 Rechtlich selbständige Vereinigungen. Incorporated associations
Including registration
1040.A-Z Other juristic persons, A-Z
Combinations (Kombinate) see KK6465+
Companies and business corporations see KKA2432+
Cooperative societies see KKA6630+; KKA6811+; KKA6837
Kominate see KKA6466+
Volkseigene Betriebe see KKA6454+
Legal transactions
1070 Agency
1078 Power of attorney
1081 Mandat
Domestic relations. Family law. Familienrecht
1100.5 Criticism. Reform
1101-1110 General (Table K9c)
1112 Constitutional guaranties
Marriage. Eherecht
1121 General (Table K11)
Constitutional guaranties see KKA1112

Civil law. Zivilrecht
Domestic relations. Family law. Familienrecht
Marriage. Eherecht -- Continued
Marriage bond. Persönliches Eherecht
1128 General works
1131 Name of husband or wife as family name
Legal status of married women
1132 General (Table K11)
Equal rights. Emancipation and decision-making. Gleichberechtigung
1134 General (Table K11)
Work and occupation of marital partners
1135 General (Table K11)
1135.5 Continuing education of women. Förderung der Frau
Including vocational, technical, and higher education
1135.7 Right to abortion. Recht auf Schwangerschaftsunterbrechung
Matrimonial actions. Dissolution of marriage
1139 General (Table K11)
1139.3 Family counseling to avoid matrimonial actions
Consanguinity and affinity. Verwandtschaft und Schwägerschaft
1185 General (Table K11)
Parent and child. Elternrecht
1189 General (Table K11)
1190 Constitutional guaranties
1194 Citizenship of children
Parental care. Elterliche Sorge
1200 General (Table K11)
Custody. Personensorge
1203 General (Table K11)
1205 Misuse. Negligence. Abuse
Including political irresponsibility of parents
Decisions over custody see KKA3572
Education see KKA6268
Custodial education see KKA3573+
Guardianship procedures see KKA3570
Adoption. Annahme an Kindes Statt
1212 General (Table K11)
1213 Procedures

Civil law. Zivilrecht -- Continued
Property and socialist property. Persönliches und sozialistisches Eigentum
Including genossenschaftliche Gemeineigentum (Property of cooperative societies) and property of socialist organizations
For Volkseigentum (Socialist public property) see KKA6068+
1251-1260 General (Table K9c)
1261 Right to private property. Constitutional guaranty
1261.5 Privileges of socialist property
1262.5.A-Z Types of private property, A-Z
Including intangible property
1262.5.C66 Copyright
1262.5.E27 Earnings. Wages. Arbeitseinkünfte
1262.5.I55 Innovations
1262.5.P38 Patents
1262.5.S29 Savings
Wages see KKA1262.5.E27
Real property. Grundstückstrecht
1315 General (Table K11)
1316 State policies and supervision
Land registration law see KKA1410+
Public and private restraint on real property
1318 General (Table K11)
Eminent domain see KKA5772+
Land reform and land policy legislation see KKA6130+
1323 Ownership. Eigentum. Rechtsträgerschaft
Land register and registration. Bodenbücher
1410 General (Table K11)
1419 Administration and procedure
1437 Cadastral surveys. Abteilung Kataster beim Kreisrat
1441 Inheritance. Succession upon death. Erbrecht
Obligations and contracts
1491 General (Table K11)
Agency see KKA1070
Power of attorney see KKA1078
Mandat see KKA1081
1640 Contracts. Verträge zur Gestaltung des materiellen und kulturellen Lebens (Table K11)
For socialist contract system (Verftragssystem) see KKA6432+
Parties
1680 General (Table K11)
1681 Government business enterprises and socialist economic organizations. Volkseigene Betriebe und sozialistische Wirtschaftsorganisationen

Civil law. Zivilrecht
Obligations and contracts
Parties -- Continued
Third parties
1682 General (Table K11)
1687 Third parties to government business enterprises
Lease. Landlord and tenant. Mietrecht
1741-1745.8 General (Table K10)
Buildings. Rooms. Raummiete
1789 General (Table K11)
Housing. Apartments. Wohnraummiete. Wohnungswirtschaft
1791-1795.8 General (Table K10)
Ministerium für Bauwesen see KKA6142
State policies and planning. Wohnraumplanung und Wohnraumlenkung
Including social measures
1796 General (Table K11)
1797 Distribution. Zuweisung
1798 Administration or sequestration of housing of persons who have left East Germany
1816 Rent control
1822 Publicly subsidized housing. Sozialwohnungen
Rent subsidies see KKA3448
1824.A-Z Housing provided for particular groups, A-Z
1824.L32 Laborers
Wohnungsbaugenossenschaftern (Cooperative societies for housing construction)
Including Arbeiterwohnungsbaugenossenschaften, Gemeinnützige Wohnungsbaugenossenschaften, etc.
1825 General (Table K11)
1825.5 Membership and use
Credit and banking see KKA2188+
Contracts of service and labor. Dienstleistungen
1844 General (Table K11)
1846 Persönliche Dienstleistungen
1853 Building contracts. Bauverträge
Maintenance and repair contracts
1854 General (Table K11)
1855.A-Z Particular services, A-Z
1857 Liability and warranty
1860 Travel and vacationing contracts. Reise und Erholung
Including transportation, hotels, etc.
1868 Gemeinschaften der Bürger (Civil companies)
1868.2 Freight forwarding, transportation, and communication
see KKA6868+ Transportation; KKA6946+ Communication

Civil law. Zivilrecht
Obligations and contracts -- Continued
Carriage by sea (Seeverkehrswirtschaft) see KKA6927+
Delicts. Torts. Unerlaubte Handlungen
1922 General
1941 Liability. Haftung für Verschuldung
Banks. Credit. Konto- und Kreditverträge
2188 General (Table K11)
Types of banks and credit institutions
Banks of issue
2192 General works
Reichsbank see KK2193
Deutsche Rentenbank see KK2194
2195 Deutsche Notenbank (Table K11)
For money see KKA7090+
2196 Deutsche Investitionsbank
2198 Deutsche Bauernbank
2198.5 Deutsche Landwirtschaftsbank
Local banks and credit institutions
2202 General works
Savings banks. Government savings banks. Sparkassen. Volkseigene Sparkassen
2203 General (Table K11)
Types of savings programs
2204.5 Building loans. Bausparwesen
2205 Special premiums. Prämiensparen
2205.5 Betriebssparkassen
2206.A-Z Special topics, A-Z
2206.S62 Sparkaufbrief
Postsparkassen see KKA6959.P685
2209 Genossenschaftsbanken für Landwirtschaft, Handwerk und Gewerbe
2256 Maritime law. Seehandelsrecht (Table K11)
2301-2305.8 Insurance law. Versicherungsrecht (Table K10)
For social insurance see KKA3270.52+
Business associations. Gesellschaftsrecht
2432 General (Table K11)
2433 Constitutional aspects. Interdiction of private business associations
Expropriation and nationalization of business associations. Verstaatlichung. Umwandlung in Volkseigene Betriebe
2434 General (Table K11)
Sequestrierkommissionen see KKA7678+
2434.3 Termination of business organizations

Business associations. Gesellschaftsrecht -- Continued

2442 Halbstaatliche Kommanditgesellschaften (Government investment and reorganization of private enterprise to part-public limited partnership)

Cf. KKA6438+ Investment credits

Cooperative societies

see KKA6630+ Agriculture; KKA6811 Retail trade; KKA6837 Artisans

Combinations (Kombinate) see KKA6466+

Grosshandelsgesellschaften see KKA6801.5

Intellectual and industrial property. Urheberrecht und gewerblicher Rechtsschutz

2636 General (Table K11)

2655 Copyright. Urheberrecht (Table K11)

Patent law and trademarks

2721-2725.8 General (Table K10)

Patent office

2728 General (Table K11)

2731 Amt für Erfindungs- und Patentwesen der Deutsche Demokratische Republik

Patent practice and procedure. Entstehung des Patents. Erteilungsverfahren

2732 General (Table K11)

Invention. Erfinderrecht

2734 General (Table K11)

2738 Legal status of inventors. Community of inventors

Employees' invention and technological innovations. Arbeitnehmererfindung und Neuererwesen

2739 General (Table K11)

2739.5 Neuererzentren

2740 Suggestion system. Vorschlagswesen

2741 Incentive awards

2742 Industrial arbitration. Schlichtungsverfahren nach der Neuererordnung

2751.A-Z Patented products, processes, and engineering methods, A-Z

2751.B84 Building and construction

Construction see KKA2751.B84

Patent litigation and infringements. Patentstreit

2759 General (Table K11)

2759.5 Patentgericht

Trademarks. Markenrecht. Markenschutzrecht

2768 General (Table K11)

Practice and procedure. Anmeldungsverfahren

2783 General (Table K11)

2784 Claim drafting and registration. Anmeldung und Eintrag

Intellectual and industrial property. Urheberrecht und gewerblicher Rechtsschutz
Patent law and trademarks -- Continued
Foreign licensing agreements
Including patents and trademarks
2792 General (Table K11)
2793 Zentrales Büro für internationalen Lizenzhandel
Labor law. Arbeitsrecht
Including works on both labor law and social insurance, and private labor law as it applies to the labor contract and to the labor-management relationship
Criticism and reform see KKA3270
2851-2860 General (Table K9c)
2863 Right and duty to work. Constitutional aspects
2864 Ideology and labor law
2865 Politics and labor
2866 Labor policies. Competition and incentives for high performance
Organization and administration
For departments and regulatory agencies prior to 1949 see KK4867+
2868 General (Table K11)
2869 Komitee der Arbeiter- und Bauern-Inspektion
2870 Labor contract and employment under the labor code. Arbeitsvertrag und Arbeitsverhältnis (Table K11)
Parties to contract
Including all employed persons such as wage earners (Arbeiter), salaried employees (Angestellte), members of the intelligentsia, home laborers, domestics in private homes, etc.
2910 General works
Parties to collective bargaining
see KKA3058.3 Rahmenkollektivverträge (Overall collective agreements); KKA3073 Betriebskollektivverträge für volkseigene Betriebe (VEB)
Socialist wage system. Arbeitslohn und Prämien
2950 General (Table K11)
2951 Equal pay for equal work
2952 Methods of evaluation
Including wage groups, work norms, time norms, tariff rates and tables, Von-Bis-Spannen, etc.
Types of wages and modes of remuneration. Entlohnungsgrundsätze
2954 Daywork. Piecework. Zeitlohn. Zeitakkord
2954.5 Collective wages. Kollektive Lohnformen
2955 Incentive wages. Leistungszuschläge. Prämien
Including bonus funds

Labor law. Arbeitsrecht
Socialist wage system. Arbeitslohn und Prämien
Types of wages and modes of remuneration. Entlohnungsgrundsätze -- Continued

2956 Adjustments. Zulagen und Erschwerniszuschläge. Entschädigungen
2956.5 Travel and moving expenses. Reise- und Umzugskosten
2962 Time, place, and mode of payment
Nonwage payments and fringe benefits
2965 General works
2972 Cultural and social provisions. Kulturelle und soziale Einrichtungen
Including culture and social funds
2976.A-Z Groups of workers or industries, A-Z
Labor-management relations. Betriebsverfassungsrecht
Including Volkseigene Betriebe, semigovernment-owned and private enterprises
2981 General (Table K11)
2982 Betriebsleiter (Director of the enterprise)
Including the duties of the director
2982.5 Managerial personnel. Leitende Mitarbeiter
2983 Works assembly. Vertrauensleutevollversammlung. Belegschaftsvollversammlung
2997 Union participation
2998 Employee participation in drawing up the annual enterprise collective agreement
Employee participation in planning and management
3000 General (Table K11)
3002 Works agreements. Betriebsvereinbarungen in Privatbetrieben
Production tasks
3003 General (Table K11)
3004 Produktionskomitee des volkseigenen Grossbetriebs
Okonomisches Aktiv des volkseigenen Grossbetriebs see KKA3026
3005 Maximum increase of labor productivity
3005.3 Technological improvements of enterprise. Innovations
3005.5 Rationalization. Rationalisierung
Labor standards and protection of labor. Soziale Angelegenheiten
3006 General (Table K11)
Social (welfare) provisions. Wohlfahrtseinrichtungen
Including social and cultural funds, housing, improvements of facilities of the enterprise, etc.
3012 General (Table K11)
3013 Cultural and sports activities

Labor law. Arbeitsrecht
Labor-management relations. Betriebsverfassungsrecht
Employee participation in planning and management
Labor standards and protection of labor. Soziale Angelegenheiten -- Continued
3013.5 Medals and incentive awards. Auszeichnungen und Prämien
Employee rules and discipline. Arbeitsordnung und Disziplinarordnung
3014 General
3015 Konfliktkommission (Dispute commission)
Including procedure and penalties
Personnel management
3019 General (Table K11)
3022 Occupational training or retraining (Table K11)
Including apprenticeship
Economic policies
3024 General (Table K11)
3026 Ökonomisches Aktiv des volkseigenen Grossbetriebs
Collective bargaining and labor agreements. Kollektivvertragsrecht
3056 General (Table K11)
3057 Constitutional aspects
Types of agreements
Rahmenkollektivverträge (Overall collective agreements)
3058 General (Table K11)
3058.3 Socialist parties to agreement
Including central organs of the state apparatus or Bezirksrate, Vereinigungen Volkseigener Betriebe, central organs of socialist cooperatives, and the national or district executives of the Freie Deutsche Gewerkschaftsbund, or national executive committees of industrial and trade unions
3058.5.A-Z By industry, A-Z
3058.5.A35 Agriculture. Forestry. Volkseigene Güter (VEG)
Forestry see KKA3058.5.A35
Volkseigene Güter see KKA3058.5.A35
3058.7 Musterkollektivvertrage (Model agreements)
Betriebskollektivverträge für volkseigene Betriebe (VEB)
3059 General (Table K11)
Betriebspläne. Arbeitsproduktivität. Arbeitswettbewerb
3061 General (Table K11)
3063 Aktive. Brigaden
3065 Innovaters movement. Neuererbewegung
3070 Working standards. Technisch begründete Arbeitsnormen (TAN)

Labor law. Arbeitsrecht
Collective bargaining and labor agreements. Kollektivvertragsrecht
Types of agreements
Betriebskollektivverträge für volkseigene Betriebe (VEB)
Betriebspläne. Arbeitsproduktivität. Arbeitswettbewerb -- Continued
3071 Qualification of laborers. Training. Qualifizierung und Weiterbildung
Including on-the-job training, Aktivistenschulen, education of union officials, etc.
3072 Produktionstechnische Propaganda
3073 Socialist parties to agreement
Including the director of the enterprise and the trade union committee of the enterprise
For unions in general see KKA3123+
Validity, applicability, and effectiveness. Geltungsbereich (räumlich und zeitlich) und Allgemeinverbindlichkeit
3092 General works
Beitriebskollektivverträge
3093 General works
3093.5 Perspektivplanzeitraum
Corporate representation. Organisationen und Verbände
3118 General (Table K11)
3120 Constitutional aspects. Freedom of coalition
Unions. Gewerkschaften
3123 General (Table K11)
Union organization
3127 General (Table K11)
3129 Officers
Including Bevollmächtigte für Arbeitsschutz, Bevollmächtigte für Sozialversicherung, Kulturorganisator, Gewerkschaftsgruppenorganisator and their election, legal status, etc.
3130 Gewerkschaftsgruppe. Brigade
3131 Freier Deutscher Gewerkschaftsbund (FDGB)
3135.A-Z Special topics, A-Z
Protection of labor. Arbeitsschutz
3140 General (Table K11)
3143 Protection of human resource. Schutz der Arbeitskraft
3144 Zentralinstitut für Arbeitsschutz
Hours of labor. Arbeitszeitschutz
3145 General (Table K11)
3154.A-Z By industry or type of employment, A-Z
Vacations. Urlaub
3157 General (Table K11)
3158 Constitutional aspects. Right to vacation and recreation

KKA

Labor law. Arbeitsrecht
Protection of labor. Arbeitsschutz
Vacations. Urlaub -- Continued
3160 Holiday facilities, services, and homes owned or provided by the Freie Deutsche Gewerkschaftsbund
3166 Additional holidays. Zusatzurlaub
Women's labor. Frauenarbeitsschutz
3175 General (Table K11)
3175.5 Advancement and promotion of women. Qualification
3176 Women's household day. Hausarbeitstag
Maternal welfare. Protection of expectant and breast-feeding mothers. Mutterschutz
Including hours of labor, paid maternity leave, special breaks during working hours, etc.
For maternity benefits see KKA3328
3179 General (Table K11)
3180 Constitutional guaranties
3181 Day care centers. Kinderkrippen
Including isolation wards for sick children
Labor hygiene and industrial safety. Persönliche und technische Sicherheit
3185 General (Table K11)
3187.A-Z By industry or type of labor, A-Z
3187.B85 Building and construction industry
3187.M48 Metal industry
Labor supply. Manpower planning. Arbeitskräftelenkung
3195 General (Table K11)
3196 Lenkung der Schulabgänger und Jugendlichen in Lehr- und Arbeitsstellen
Labor courts and procedure. Arbeitsgerichtsbarkeit
Class here works on national courts, national and district courts, or courts of several jurisdictions
For courts (several or individual) of an individual jurisdiction, see the jurisdiction
History see KK3205+
3211-3215.8 General (Table K10)
3218 Kreisgericht. Kammer für Arbeitsrechtssachen (Local court)
Including judges, lay judges, etc.
3221 Bezirkgericht. Senat für Arbeitsrechtssachen (District court)
Including judges, lay judges, etc.
3223 Oberstes Gericht. Senat für Arbeitsrechtssachen (National supreme court)
Including chairman, judges, lay judges, etc.
Parties to action
3227 General (Table K11)

Labor law. Arbeitsrecht
Labor courts and procedure. Arbeitsgerichtsbarkeit
Parties to action -- Continued
3228 State prosecutor. Staatsanwalt
3229 Union officers. Gewerkschaftsfunktionäre
Pretrial procedures. Vorverfahren
3230 General (Table K11)
3231 Konfliktkommission (Dispute commission)
For disciplinary measures see KKA3015
Social legislation. Sozialrecht
3270 Social reform and policies. Sozialreform und Sozialpolitik
Including all branches of social legislation and labor
3270.5 General (Table K11)
Social insurance. Sozialversicherungsrecht
For works on both labor law and social insurance see KKA2850.2+
Criticism and reform see KKA3270
3271-3275.8 General (Table K10)
3277 Constitutional guaranties of social insurance and pensions for working people
Compulsory insurance
3278 General works
Minimum pensions for old age and invalidity see KKA3399+
3279 Strict surveillance of the sick
Denial of pensions to widows under the age of sixty see KKA3400
Organization and administration
3281 General (Table K11)
3283 Zentralrat der Sozialversicherung (Central council of social insurance) (Table K11)
3285 Subordinate organs. Räte, Kommissionen und Bevollmächtigte
Including Bezirke, Kreise, Verwaltungen, volkseigene Betriebe, and private enterprises
3285.2 Corporate rights and personality. Rechte und Rechtsfähigkeit
3285.3 Autonomy. Self-government
3285.32 Election of organs. Selection from among officers of the Freie Deutsche Gewerkschaftsbund (FDGB)
Including Zentralrat der Sozialversicherung and subordinate organs
3285.4 Officials and employees
Finance
3285.5 General (Table K11)
3285.52 Accounting. Auditing by the FDGB
Dues. Beiträge

Social legislation. Sozialrecht
Social insurance. Sozialversicherungsrecht
Organization and administration
Finance
Dues. Beiträge -- Continued
3285.53 General works
3285.54 Employers' and employees' contributions. Arbeitgeber- und Arbeitnehmeranteile
3285.58 Staggered rate system
3285.8 State supervision by the Ministerium für Arbeit und Berufsbildung
3285.82 Supervision by the FDGB
Coverage and benefits
Health benefits
3308 General (Table K11)
3328 Maternity benefits. Schwangerschaftshilfe und Wochenhilfe
3333.A-Z Groups of beneficiaries, A-Z
Workers' compensation. Ersatz für Arbeitsunfälle
Including occupational diseases (Berufskrankheiten)
3350 General (Table K11)
3374.A-Z By industry or group of workers, A-Z
Social security. Rentenversicherungen
Including old age pensions (Altersversorgung), invalidity and disability pensions (Erwerbsunfähigkeit, Berufsunfähigkeit), and survivor benefits (Hinterbliebenenversorgung)
3387 General (Table K11)
3388 Constitutional right to social assistance in old age and invalidity
Pensions. Renten
3398 General (Table K11)
Policy
3399 Minimum pensions for old age and invalidity
3400 Denial of pensions to widows under the age of sixty
3400.5 Maximum pensions for workers of vitally important industries
3400.7 Additional pensions for the intelligentsia. Zusatzversorgung
3411.A-Z By industry or group of workers, A-Z
3411.C65 Collective farm workers
Farm workers, Collective see KKA3411.C65
Unemployment benefits. Arbeitslosenunterstützung
3418 General (Table K11)
3428.A-Z By industry or group of workers, A-Z
Social services. Public welfare. Sozialfürsorge. Sozialhilfe

Social legislation. Sozialrecht
Social service. Public welfare. Sozialfürsorge. Sozialhilfe -- Continued
Criticism and reform see KKA3270
3431-3435.8 General (Table K10)
Organization and administration
Including municipal, local, and district agencies
3437 General (Table K11)
3438 Practice and procedure
Coverage and benefits
3442 General works
Day care centers see KKA3447.5
3442.5 Family and sex counseling
3443 Aid for institutional care. Zuschüsse für Anstaltsunterbringung
Including older people, blind, and sick
3445 Educational assistance and allowances. Ausbildungshilfe und Hilfe zum Aufbau einer Existenz
Including vocational training
Maternal and infant welfare. Assistance for single mothers. Mutterschutz
3447 General (Table K11)
3447.5 Day care centers. Kinderkrippen
3448 Rent subsidies. Wohnungsgeld
Beneficiary groups. Sozialleistungsempfänger
3468 General (Table K11)
Single mothers see KKA3447+
Large families. Kinderreiche
3480 General (Table K11)
Coverage and benefits
3485 General works
3486 Child's supplements. Kindergeld
3487 Credit for housing
Including construction of single family houses
3489 Newly married couples. Junge Ehen
People with disabilities. Behinderte
Including people with physical, mental, and emotional disabilities
3490 General (Table K11)
Coverage and benefits
3492 General
3494 Rehabilitation. Eingliederungshilfe
Children. Youth. Jugendwohlfahrt. Jugendhilfe
3556 General (Table K11)
3556.3 Policy. Sozialistische Jugendpolitik
3556.5 Zentralinstitut für Jugendforschung
3557.A-Z Youth organizations and institutions. By name, A-Z

KKA

Social legislation. Sozialrecht
Social services. Public welfare. Sozialfürsorge. Sozialhilfe
Beneficiary groups. Sozialleistungsempfänger
Children. Youth. Jugendwohlfahrt. Jugendhilfe
Youth organizations and institutions. By name, A-Z -- Continued

3557.D48 Deutscher Jugendring
3557.K65 Kontos junger Sozialisten
Class here Kontos junger Sozialisten established in public enterprises, public institutes, public organs, and administrative agencies
3557.W62 Woche der Jugend und Sportler
3557.Z45 Zentralrat der Freien Deutschen Jugend
3557.5.A-Z State youth programs and facilities, A-Z
Ferienlager. Ferienheime see KKA3557.5.V32
Jugendherbergen see KKA3557.5.Y68
3557.5.P56 Pionierlager, Zentrale
3557.5.V32 Vacation camps and homes
3557.5.Y68 Youth hostels
Zentrale Pionierlager see KKA3557.5.P56
Organization and administration
3559 General (Table K11)
3560 Ministerium für Volksbildung. Zentraler Jugendhilfeausschuss
3560.5 Amt für Jugendfragen beim Ministerrat
3561 Referate Jugendhilfe und Jugendhilfekommissionen
Including Bezirke, Kreise, Stadtkreise, Stadbezirke and Gemeinden
3561.5 Vormundschaftsräte bei den Referaten Jugendhilfe
Measures and procedures
3566 General (Table K11)
3570 Guardianship procedures. Vormundschaftssachen
3572 Custodial decisions. Sorgerechtsentscheidungen
Custodial and collective education. Zwangserziehung und Kollektiverziehung
3573 General (Table K11)
3576 Jugendwerkhöfe
Social courts and procedure
3591 General (Table K11)
3604 Kreisbeschwerdekommission
Including commissioners, election, etc.
3609 Bezirksbeschwerdekommission
Including commissioners, election, etc.
3613 Zentrale Beschwerdekommission
Including commissioners, election, etc.

Social courts and procedure -- Continued
3621 Pretrial procedures. Vorverfahren
Including procedures in volkseigenen Betrieben and in social insurance administrations of the Freie Deutsche Gewerkschaftsbund (local chapters)
Courts and procedure
Administration of justice. Organization of the judiciary. Justizverwaltung und Rechtspflege
Criticism and reform see KKA942
3655 General works
3657 Judiciary and politics. Rechtspflege und politik
Organization and administration
For the department of justice (Empire of 1871 and Kaiserreich, 1871-1918) see KK4688
For the department of justice (Weimar Republic and Third Reich, 1919-1945) see KK4880
3664 General (Table K11)
3665 Ministerium der Justiz (National department of justice)
Including works on the supervision of regular courts and notaries
Judicial statistics see KKA61+
Courts. Gerichtsverfassung
3666 General (Table K11)
Regular courts. Ordentliche Gerichte
Class here works on national courts of several jurisdictions
For courts (several or individual) of an individual jurisdiction, see the jurisdiction
3673 General (Table K11)
Kreisgerichte (Local courts)
Including directors, judges, and assizes
3674 General (Table K11)
Jurisdiction
see KKA1139, Matrimonial actions; KKA3218+, Labor procedure; KKA3872, Civil procedure; KKA9576, Criminal procedure
3676 Bezirksgerichte (District courts)
Including Plenum, Präsidium, senates, and assizes
Oberstes Gericht (National supreme court)
Including Plenum, Präsidium, senates, judges, and assizes for labor procedure
3686 General (Table K11)
Jurisdiction
see KKA3223+, Labor procedure; KKA3872, Civil procedure; KKA9576, Criminal procedure; etc.
Courts of special jurisdiction. Special tribunals
3692 General works
Gesellschaftliche Gerichte

Courts and procedure
Courts. Gerichtsverfassung
Courts of special jurisdiction. Special tribunals
Gesellschaftliche Gerichte -- Continued
3694 General (Table K11)
3694.2 Konfliktkommissionen (Dispute commissions)
Class here commissions established in enterprises of more than fifty employees, that have jurisdiction for disciplinary measures, small claims, criminal transgressions, etc.
3694.3 Schiedskommissionen (Municipal arbitral boards)
3694.5 Sühnestelle mit Schiedsmann (Justice of the peace)
Staatliches Vertragsgericht see KKA6432.7
Other courts of special jurisdiction
see the subject
The legal profession
Including judicial officers and personnel
3704 General (Table K11)
3705 Analysis of personnel needs and planning for education, training, etc.
Including surveys conducted by the department of justice
Staatsanwaltschaft (Office of the public prosecutor)
Class here works on national and district prosecution offices, or prosecution offices of several districts
For prosecution offices (several or individual) of an individual jurisdiction, see the jurisdiction
3728 General (Table K11)
3729 Generalstaatsanwalt (National prosecution office)
3730 Staatsanwälte der Bezirke (District prosecution office)
3731 Staatsanwälte der Kreise (Local prosecution office)
3733 Militärstaatsanwaltschaft (Military prosecution office)
Including Militäroberstaatsanwalt
3734 Beigeordnete Staatsanwälte und Untersuchungsführer
Notaries see KKA4070+
Practice of law
3769 General works
Attorneys. Rechtsanwälte
3770 General (Table K11)
3771 Anwaltskollektive
Judicial assistance. Rechtshilfe
3795 General (Table K11)
3799 Interzonal judicial assistance
Civil procedure. Zivilprozess
3811-3815.8 General (Table K10)
3872 Jurisdiction
Particular procedures
3985 General works

Courts and procedure
Civil procedure. Zivilprozess
Particular procedures -- Continued
3990 Matrimonial actions
3993 Procedures in parent and child cases. Kindschaftssachen
For procedures in guardianship cases see KKA3570
4006 Small claims. Procedures before the Konfliktkommission and Sühnestelle
4030 Arbitration. Schiedsgerichtsbarkeit (Table K11)
Including commercial arbitration
Noncontentious jurisdiction. Freiwillige Gerichtsbarkeit
4044 General (Table K11)
Notaries
Class here works on notaries of several jurisdictions
Including staatliche Notare and freiberufliche Notare
For notaries (several or individual) of an individual jurisdiction, see the jurisdiction
4070 General (Table K11)
4077 Inheritance. Nachlassachen
Registration. Recording
4087 Civil registers
Land registers see KKA1410+
Ship registers see KKA6927+
Genossenschaftsregister see KKA6632
Geschmacksmusterregister see KKA2784
Adoption procedures (Domestic relations) see KKA1213
Guardianship procedures (Domestic relations) see KKA3570
4171 Insolvency (Table K11)
Including bankruptcy procedure and execution
Public law. Offentliches Recht
Class here works on all aspects of public law beginning with 1949
For works prior to 1949 see KK4413+
For civics see KKA156
4413 General (Table K11)
The State. Staatsphilosophie. Staats- und Verwaltungslehre
For nonlegal works on political theory, see JC
4420 General (Table K11)
Rule of law. Rechtsstaatlichkeit
4426 General (Table K11)
Socialist state. Sozialistische Staatsordnung
4427 General works
4428 Democratic centralism

Constitutional law. Staats- und Verfassungsrecht
Class here works on constitutional law of the Democratic Republic of Germany (Deutsche Demokratische Republik), which is composed of German states in the Russian Zone of occupation under the Constitution of 1949
For works on constitutional law of Germany before 1949 see KK4455+
4441 Bibliography
Sources
For sources before 1949 see KK4443.6+
4443.6 Collections. Compilations
For collections of state constitutions before the abolition of the five East German states in 1952 see KK4443.6
Constitutions. Verfassungen
Collections see KKA4443.6
Individual constitutions
4444 Verfassung der Deutschen Demokratischen Republik (DDR), 1949 (Table K17)
4444.2 Sozialistische Verfassung der Deutschen Demokratischen Republik, 1968 (Table K17)
4444.24 Verfassung der Deutschen Demokratischen Republik in der Fassung 1974 (Table K17)
Individual sources other than constitutions. Verfassungsgleiche Gesetze
Including legislative documents
Charter of the Allied High Commission, 1949 see KK4444.69
Occupation Statute, 1949 see KK4444.7
4444.76 Gesetz über die weitere Demokratisierung des Aufbaus und der Arbeitsweise der staatlichen Organe in den Ländern der DDR, 1952
4444.77 Gesetz über die Auflösung der Länderkammer der DDR, 1958
Comparative state constitutions
4445 Collections
4445.6 General works. Treatises
Court decisions
4446 Indexes and tables
4446.3 Serials
4446.5 Monographs. By date
4446.7 Digests. Analytical abstracts
4449 Conferences. Symposia
Collected works (nonserial) see KKA4450
4450 General works. Treatises
Compends. Outlines. Examination aids. Popular works see KKA4450

Constitutional law. Staats- und Verfassungsrecht -- Continued
Addresses, essays, lectures see KKA4450
4455 Constitutional history. Verfassungsgeschichte (Table K11)
5049 Centralization and concentration of powers. Zentralismus. Gewaltenvereinigung
5075 Federalism. Intergovernmental relations. Bundesstaatlichkeit (Table K11)
National territory
5095 General works
5096 Division into East and West Germany
For reunification claim see KKA5109
5097 Abolition of states and reorganization of territory. Auflösung der Staaten und Neugliederung
For legislation see KKA4444.76
Foreign relations. Auswärtige Gewalt
5105 General works
5108 Integration into East Block (East European socialist countries). Friendship and partnership with USSR
5109 Relationship with West Germany
Including Staatssekretariat für Westdeutsche Fragen
Foreign service see KKA5445
Individual and state
5114 Nationality and citizenship. Staatsangehörigkeit und sozialistische Staatsbürgerschaft
Internal security see KKA5245+
Constitutional guaranties. Socialist human rights. Socialist personality rights and civic duties. Verfassungsgarantien. Menschenrechte Sozialistische Personlichkeitsrechte und Grundpflichten
For guaranties, rights, or duties, pertaining to a particular subject, see the subject
5132 General (Table K11)
Retention of power to infringe upon civil rights by law see the individual civil right
Protection of human rights. Schutz der Staatsbürger- und Menschenrechte
For the Convention for the protection of human rights and fundamental freedoms, see K3236+
5138 General (Table K11)
5139 Komitee zum Schutz der Menschenrechte in der DDR
Right to co-determination and participation in government. Recht auf Mitbestimmung und Mitgestaltung
5140 General works
Eingabenrecht see KKA5601
Plebiscite see KKA5268
Right to elections see KKA5272+

Constitutional law. Staats- und Verfassungsrecht
Individual and state
Constitutional guaranties. Socialist human rights. Socialist personality rights and civic duties. Verfassungsgarantien. Menschenrechte Sozialistische Personlichkeitsrechte und Grundpflichten -- Continued
Equality before the law. Antidiscrimination in general. Gleichheit vor dem Gesetz

5142 General (Table K11)
5144.A-Z Groups discriminated against, A-Z
5144.S67 Sorbian nationale
5144.W65 Women

Freedom. Freiheit des Menschen

5149 General (Table K11)

Personal (individual) freedom. Persönliche Freiheit

5150 General works
5151 Health and physical fitness for work. Gesundheit und Arbeitskraft
5156 Freedom of religion and conscience. Religions-, Glaubens- und Gewissensfreiheit

Freedom of thought and speech. Freiheit der Meinungsbildung und Meinungsäusserung

5160 General (Table K11)

Freedom of the press see KKA6947
Freedom of radio communication see KKA6947

5171 Freedom of movement within East Germany. Freizügigkeit innerhalb der Deutsche Demokratische Republik
5173 Free choice of occupation according to the needs of society
5176 Freedom of assembly. Versammlungsfreiheit

Freedom of coalition. Koalitionsfreiheit

5179 General (Table K11)

Collective labor agreement and collective bargaining see KKA3057
Labor unions see KKA3120

Family and marriage see KKA1112
Motherhood see KKA3180
Parent and child see KKA1190
Right to social assistance in old age and invalidity see KKA3388
Right and duty to education and occupation see KKA6280
Right and duty to work see KKA2863
Right to vacation and recreation see KKA3158
Right to a clean environment and enjoyment of nature see KKA6248

Constitutional law. Staats- und Verfassungsrecht
Individual and state
Constitutional guaranties. Socialist human rights. Socialist personality rights and civic duties. Verfassungsgarantien. Menschenrechte Sozialistische Personlichkeitsrechte und Grundpflichten -- Continued
5186 Right to a home and to privacy of home. Recht auf Wohnung und Unverletzlichkeit der Wohnung
Private property, intangible property, and right to inherit see KKA1261
Privacy of communication. Official and private secrets
5190 General works
Mail and telecommunication see KKA6947
5219 Civic duties (Table K11)
Political parties and mass organizations
5225 General (Table K11)
5226 Sozialistische Einheitspartei Deutschlands (SED)
Including works on its individual organs and divisions, e.g. Zentralkomitee, Politbüro, Sekretariat, etc.
5226.5.A-Z Other parties. By name, A-Z
5227 Nationale Front der Deutschen Demokratischen Republik
5228.A-Z Other organizations. By name, A-Z
Internal security. Staatssicherheit
Including control of subversive activities
5245 General (Table K11)
5246 Ministerium für Staatssicherheit
Including subordinate agencies and special police forces
Central government and its organs
5259 General (Table K11)
The people. Das Volk
5262 General (Table K11)
Eingaben see KKA5601
5268 Plebiscite. Volksabstimmung
Political parties and mass organizations see KKA5225+
Election law. Wahlrecht
5272 General (Table K11)
5279 Suffrage
Class here works on active and passive suffrage
5287 Election districts
Election to particular office
5289 Volkskammer
5291 Local and municipal representatives. Ortliche Volksvertretungen
5293 Judges and assizes. Richter und Schöffen
Plebiscite see KKA5268
Legislative power. Gesetzgebung
5310 General (Table K11)

Constitutional law. Staats- und Verfassungsrecht
Central government and its organs
Legislative power. Gesetzgebung -- Continued
Volkskammer
Organization and procedures
5318 General (Table K11)
5319 Präsident und Präsidium
5319.5 Altestenrat
5320 Committees. Ausschusse
Powers and duties
5329 General works
5335 Appointive and removal power
Including Staatsrat, Ministerrat, chairman of the Nationale Verteidigungsrat, president and judges of the Oberste Gericht, and Generalstaatsanwalt
Control of government
5337 General works
5338 Staatsrat
5339 Ministerrat
5340 Nationaler Verteidigungsrat
5341 Oberstes Gericht
5342 Generalstaatsanwalt
5343 Exclusive and concurrent legislative powers
Legislative process
5349 General (Table K11)
5359 Committees. Ausschüsse
5382 Länderkammer (to 1958)
5389 Staatspräsident (to 1960)
Staatsrat. Kollektives Staatsoberhaupt
5392 General works
Powers and duties
5396 General works
5397 Representation
5398 Treatymaking power
5407 Supervision of activities of the Oberste Gericht and Generalstaatsanwalt
Nationaler Verteidigungsrat see KKA7701
Regierung der Republik
5408 General works
5416 Constitutional principles. Ministerial responsibility
5417 Ministerpräsident und Minister (to 1968)
Ministerrat (Council of ministers)
5418 General works
5418.5 Constitutional principles. Centralism
Powers and duties
5425 General works

Constitutional law. Staats- und Verfassungsrecht
Central government and its organs
Regierung der Republik
Ministerrat (Council of ministers)
Powers and duties -- Continued

5426 Political and economic policymaking. Richtlinien der Politik und Volkswirtschaft

5427 Foreign relations policies

5438 Kommissionen, Beiräte und selbständige Staatssekretariate

Ministerien

Class here works on several departments not related to a particular branch of law or subject

Including Staatssekretäre administrative divisions, Beiräte, etc.

For works on several departments related to a branch of law or subject, as well as an individual department or its regulatory agencies, see the branch of law or the subject

For departments and their regulatory agencies before 1949, see KK4671+ Empire of 1871 and Kaiserreich, 1871-1918; KK4850+ Weimar Republic and Third Reich, 1919-1945

5440 General (Table K11)

Ministerium für auswärtige Angelegenheiten (Department of state)

5443 General (Table K11)

5445 The foreign service. Gesandtschafts- und Konsularrecht

Staatssekretariat für Westdeutsche Fragen see KK5109

5450.A-Z Special bureaus and agencies. By name, A-Z

5450.P73 Presseamt

5456 Constitutional courts and procedure. Verfassungsgerichtsbarkeit

5505 National emblem. Flag. Seal. Seat of government. National anthem

Decorations of honor. Awards. Dignities

5511 General (Table K11)

5512.A-Z Particular decorations, awards, etc., A-Z

5512.K37 Karl-Marx-Orden

5527 Secular ecclesiastical law (Table K11)

Class here works on the relationship of church and state

Economic constitution see KKA6417+

Administrative law. Verwaltungsrecht

KKA

Administrative law. Verwaltungsrecht -- Continued
5570 Administrative reform and policies. Demokratisierung der Verwaltung
Including all branches of administration
5571-5580 General (Table K9c)
Administrative principles
5585 Control function of administration. Control organs
5593 Government monopoly. Zentralstaatliches Verwaltungsmonopol
5601 People's participation in administration. Eingaben
Administrative process
5610 Administrative acts. Lehre vom Verwaltungsakt (Table K11)
Legal transactions. Offentlich-rechtliche Rechtsgeschäfte
5631 General (Table K11)
5632 Public contracts. Offentlichrechtlicher Vertrag
Indemnification for acts performed by government. Offentlich-rechtliche Entschädigung
5765 General (Table K11)
Eminent domain. Nationalization. Public restraint on private property. Enteignung. Enteignungsgleiche Eingriffe und Eigentumsbeschränkungen
For agrarian land policy legislation (nationalization) see KKA6593+
For industrial reform (Nazi property) see KKA7674+
5772 General (Table K11)
5773 Public good and individual sacrifice. Gemeinwohl und Sonderopfer
5777 Compensation
Practice and procedure
5778 General (Table K11)
5778.2 Confiscation. Curator for refugee property. Abwesenheitspflegschaft
5778.6 Confiscation or expropriation of private property as criminal punishment
5779.A-Z Particular properties, A-Z
5779.A35 Agricultural estates. Fideicommissa
5779.E53 Energy industries
5779.I76 Iron and steel industries
Mineral resources see KKA5779.N38
5779.M55 Mines
5779.N38 Natural and mineral resources
Steel industries see KKA5779.I76
5790 Compensation for criminal prosecution
5793 Conflict of laws. Interzonal laws
Administrative organization. Strukturen und Aufbau des Staatsapparats

Administrative law. Verwaltungsrecht
Administrative organization. Strukturen und Aufbau des Staatsapparats -- Continued
Criticism and reform see KKA5570+
5795 Centralization of government. Zentralistischer Einheitsstaat
5801 State supervision and enforcement. Staatsaufsicht
5805 Collegial structure. Kollegialitätsprinzip
Juristic persons of public law. Juristische Personen des öffentlichen Rechts
5807 General (Table K11)
Genossenschaften des öffentlichen Recht. (Cooperative societies of public law)
5820 General works
Landwirtschaftliche Produktionsgenossenschaft (LPG) see KKA6631+
Handwerksproduktionsgenossenschaft see KKA6837
Volkseigene Betriebe (VEB). Business enterprises owned by government
5847 General (Table K11)
5848 Legal status
Administrative departments of the national government. Verwaltungsbehörden der Republik
General works see KKA5440+
5856 Ministerium des Innern (National department of the interior)
For departments of the interior, prior to 1949, see KK4687; KK4858
5858 Subordinate regulatory agencies
Class here general works
For particular agencies, see the subject
5860 Special councils, commissions, organs, etc. Beiräte, Kommissionen, zentrale Organe und Amter
Local organs of the national government. Ortliche Organe der Staatsgewalt
5869 General (Table K11)
Bezirke (Administrative districts)
5869.3 General (Table K11)
Bezirkstag
5869.5 General (Table K11)
5869.7 Ständige Kommissionen
Bezirksrat
5870 General (Table K11)
5870.5 Ständige Kommissionen
Elections see KKA5291
5871.A-Z Individual Bezirke, A-Z
5871.C43 Chemnitz

Administrative law. Verwaltungsrecht
Administrative organization. Strukturen und Aufbau des Staatsapparats
Administrative departments of the national government. Verwaltungsbehörden der Republik
Local organs of the national government. Örtliche Organe der Staatsgewalt
Bezirke (Administrative districts)
Individual Bezirke, A-Z -- Continued

5871.C68 Cottbus
5871.D73 Dresden
5871.E73 Erfurt
5871.F72 Frankfurt (Oder)
5871.G47 Gera
5871.H35 Halle
5871.L44 Leipzig
5871.M34 Magdeburg
5871.N48 Neubrandenburg
5871.P68 Potsdam
5871.R68 Rostock
5871.S35 Schwerin
5871.S94 Suhl

Kreise
5873 General (Table K11)
5874 Kreistag und ständige Kommissionen
5874.5 Kreisrat und ständige Kommissionen
Elections see KKA5291
Stadtkreise
5875 General (Table K11)
5875.3 Stadtverordnetenversammlung
5875.5 Stadtrat
5875.7.A-Z Individual Kreise, A-Z

Municipal government. Gemeinderecht
5877 General (Table K11)
Organization of municipal government
5887 General (Table K11)
Grosstädte (Cities with more than 100,000 inhabitants)
5888 General (Table K11)
5888.5 Stadtbezirke
5890 Councils and civic associations
Including Stadtbezirksversammlung, Stadtbezirksrat, etc.
Boards of trade see KKA6842
Chambers of commerce see KKA6550
Municipal economy. Gemeindewirtschaftsrecht
5903 General (Table K11)
5904 Property

Administrative law. Verwaltungsrecht
Administrative organization. Strukturen und Aufbau des Staatsapparats
Municipal government. Gemeinderecht -- Continued
5912 Municipal public services. Gemeindliche Daseinsvorsorge (Table K11)
Socialist officials and functionaries. Staats- und Wirtschaftsfunktionäre
5932 General (Table K11)
5932.5 Staatliche Stellenplankommission
5935 Official (superior) order. Weisungsgebundenheit
5937.5 Liability of officials towards the government
5938 Appointment. Ernennung
5938.5 Election. Wahl
Conditions of employment
5939 General (Table K11)
5939.5 Nomenklatur
Retirement. Ruhestand
5954 General (Table K11)
5955 Retirement pensions for civil servants retired before 1949
Social security see KKA3387+
5956 Dismissal. Abberufung
5958 Labor law and collective labor law (Table K11)
5966 Functionaries of central state organs
Including departments and subordinate regulatory agencies, Staatssekretariate, councils, committees, etc.
5967 Functionaries of local and municipal state organs
Including Bezirksräte, Kreisräte, Stadträte, Stadtbezirksräte, and subordinate agencies
5973 Functionaries of the economic administration. Funktionäre der Wirtschaftsverwaltungen
Police and public safety. Polizei- und Ordnungsrecht
For military law see KKA7690+
For civil defense see KKA7806
5977 General (Table K11)
Organization and administration
5987 General (Table K11)
Ministerium für Staatssicherheit see KKA5246
Police magistrates. Ordnungswidrigkeitenrecht
5989 General (Table K11)
5990.A-Z Violations, A-Z
Procedure. Ordnungsstrafverfahren
5991 General (Table K11)
5991.5 Jurisdiction
Including central state organs (Leiter und Stellvertreter), local organs of national government (Vorsitzende der örtlichen Räte), control organs and institutions, etc.

Police and public safety. Polizei- und Ordnungsrecht
Police magistrates. Ordnungswidrigkeitenrecht
Procedure. Ordnungsstrafverfahren -- Continued
5993 Res judicata
5994 Remedies
5994.5 Penalties and measures of correction and safety, A-Z
5994.5.C64 Compulsory labor
5994.5.C65 Confiscation of corpus delicti
5994.5.E38 Education of citizens
5994.5.F55 Fines. Ordnungsstrafen
5994.5.R46 Reparation of damage
5994.5.R48 Revocation of licenses
5994.5.V47 Verwarnungen
Police force. Polizeivollzugsdienst
Including education and training
6004 General (Table K11)
6008.A-Z Police forces, A-Z
Bereitschaftspolizei see KKA6008.K38
6008.C74 Criminal police
6008.D48 Deutsche Volkspolizei
6008.G73 Grenzpolizei
6008.K38 Kasernierte Volkspolizei
Public safety. Offentliche Sicherheit
6009 General (Table K11)
6010 Weapons. Explosives. Waffen- und Sprengstoffrecht (Table K11)
Including manufacturing, import, and trade of firearms and ammunition
Hazardous articles and processes
Including transportation by land
6011 General (Table K11)
6012 Nuclear power. Reactors. Radiation. Strahlenschutzrecht (Table K11)
Including nuclear waste disposal
Fire prevention and control. Brandschutz
6024 General
6025 Fire departments. Firefighters. Feuerwehr
Including volunteer firefighters
6027.A-Z Hazards of preventive measures, A-Z
6027.F45 Flammable liquids and gases
6027.F93 Fuel storage
6027.F94 Fueling of aircraft
Theaters. Auditoriums
6028 General (Table K11)
6029 Motion picture theaters
Meteorologischer Dienst see KKA7031
Hochwassermeldedienst see KKA7031

Police and public safety. Polizei- und Ordnungsrecht
Public safety. Offentliche Sicherheit -- Continued
Statistical services see KKA6352.S73
Seehydrographischer Dienst see KKA6927.7
Control of individuals
6032 General (Table K11)
Identification and registration. Pass- und Meldewesen
Including citizens and aliens
6034 General (Table K11)
Registration of birth, marriage, and death see KKA4087+
6036 Registration of residence. Einwohnermeldewesen
6038 Identify cards. Personalausweise
6040 Passports. Reisepässe
6042.A-Z Other, A-Z
6042.B48 Betriebsausweise
6042.D55 Dienstausweise
6042.S65 Sonderausweise
6048 Emigration. Abzug und Auswanderung (Table K11)
6049 Traveling and transit traffic. Reise- und Durchreiseverkehr
Including road traffic and traffic on inland waterways
Control of social activities
6060 General (Table K11)
6061 Vacationing. Ferienverkehr
Including campgrounds, hostels, outdoor swimming facilities, etc.
Sport activities
6062 General (Table K11)
6062.5 Mass events
Corporate representation. Sportverbandsrecht
6063 General (Table K11)
6063.2.A-Z Organizations. By name, A-Z
6063.2.A45 Allgemeiner Deutscher Motorsportverband
6063.2.D49 Deutscher Turn- und Sportbund
6063.2.G48 Gesellschaft für Sport und Technik
6063.5.A-Z Sports, A-Z
6064.5 Traveling shows. Wanderveranstaltungen
Including circuses, puppet theaters, air shows, open-air shows, etc.
Socialist public property. Public restraint on private property. Gesamtgesellschaftliches Volkseigentum
6068 General (Table K11)
Environmental planning see KKA6245
Eminent domain see KKA5772+

Socialist public property. Public restraint on private property.
Gesamtgesellschaftliches Volkseigentum -- Continued
Property of government organs and institutions.
Staatseigentum im Bereich staatlicher Verwaltungsorgane oder Einrichtungen
6070 General (Table K11)
6071.A-Z Particular, A-Z
6071.L52 Library holdings
6071.P8 Public records
Volkseigentum (Government property)
6076 General (Table K11)
6077 Interdiction of private ownership. Constitutional aspects.
Unzulässigkeit von Privateigentum
Roads and highways, roads, and bridges, etc.
6079 General (Table K11)
6081 Assessment of highways, roads, and bridges, etc.
Strassenbewertung
6087 Common use. Toll. Benutzung und Benutzungsgebühr
6088 Construction and maintenance. Baulast
Including winter maintenance
Water resources. Wasserrecht und Wasserverwaltung
Including rivers, lakes, watercourses, etc.
6094 General (Table K11)
6094.5 Amt für Wasserwirtschaft
Particular inland waterways and channels see KKA6943+
6120 National preserves. Forests
Architectural landmarks and historic monuments see KKA6405+
Continental shelf and its resources see KKA6705+
Natural resources and mines see KKA6700+
6126 Volkseigene Güter (Government agricultural enterprises)
6126.5.A-Z Other, A-Z
6126.5.A45 Airlines
6126.5.B35 Banks
6126.5.D35 Dams. Talsperren
6126.5.I58 Insurance institutions
6126.5.P68 Postal and telecommunication installations
6126.5.P69 Power stations. Kraftwerke
6126.5.R34 Railroads
6126.5.S45 Shipyards and ships
Telecommunications installations see KKA6126.5.P68
Public land law. Boden- und Bodennutzungsrecht
6130 Land reform and land policy legislation. Bodenpolitik und Bodenreform
For agricultural land law see KKA6593+
6132 General (Table K11)
Regional planning

Socialist public property. Public restraint on private property.
Gesamtgesellschaftliches Volkseigentum
Public land law. Boden- und Bodennutzungsrecht
Regional planning -- Continued

6135 General (Table K11)

City planning and redevelopment. Städtebau und Wiederaufbau

6140 General (Table K11)

6142 Ministerium für Bauwesen

6151 Wohnungsbaugenossenschaften

6152 Arbeiterwohnungsbaugenossenschaften

6154 Other regional and local development

Building and construction. Baurecht und Bauordnungsrecht

6155 General (Table K11)

Deutsche Bauakademie see KKA6786.5

Government building and construction enterprises see KKA6787

6163 Building materials

6165 Safety inspection. Bauaufsicht

Buildings and structures, A-Z

Industrial structures see KKA6168.I59

6168.I59 Investitionsbauten

Including iron and steel industries, shipyards (Werften), etc.

6168.K94 Kulturhäuser

6168.L52 Libraries

Shipyards see KKA6168.I59

Werften see KKA6168.I59

Public health. Gesundheitswesen

6172 General (Table K11)

6173 Ministerium für Gesundheitswesen. Hygiene-Inspektion

6173.5 Subordinate agencies and boards

6174.A-Z Other public institutions. By name, A-Z

6174.A42 Akademie für Sozialhygiene, Arbeitshygiene und ärzliche Fortbildung

6174.F67 Forschungsinstitut für Hygiene und Mikrobiologie

Contagious and infectious diseases. Seuchenbekämpfung

6178 General (Table K11)

6180.A-Z Diseases, A-Z

Public health measures

Including compulsory measures

6181 General (Table K11)

6181.5 Zentralstellen für Hygiene

Immunization. Vaccination. Impfung und Desinfektion

6182 General (Table K11)

6183.A-Z Diseases, A-Z

Public health. Gesundheitswesen -- Continued
Eugenics see KKA6230
Environmental pollution see KKA6247+
Drug laws
6191 General (Table K11)
6191.5.A-Z Public institutions and agencies. By name, A-Z
6191.5.D48 Deutsches Institut für Arzneimittelwesen
6191.5.S74 Staatliches Institut für Arzneimittelprüfung
6191.5.S78 Staatliches Versorgungskontor für Pharmazie und Medizintechnik
6191.5.Z45 Zentraler Gutachterausschuss für Arzneimittelverkehr
Pharmaceutical products. Heilmittel
6192 General (Table K11)
6192.5 Registration. Verzeichnis der Gesundheitspflegemittel
6192.7 Medicinal herbs and spices. Arznei- und Gewürzpflanzen
Animal glands and organs used for pharmaceutical products see KKA6192+
6195 Poisons. Gifte (Table K11)
6196 Medico-technical instruments
Pharmacists and pharmacies. Apothekerrecht
6197 General (Table K11)
6197.5 Deutsches Institut für Apothekenwesen
Medical legislation
6206 General (Table K11)
Ministerium für Gesundheitswesen see KKA6173
6207.A-Z Public institutions, agencies, and special bureaus. By name, A-Z
6207.D48 Deutsches Zentralinstitut für Arbeitsmedizin
6207.I58 Institut für Wissenschaftsinformation in der Medizin
6207.M43 Medizinisch-Statistische Büros (Statistical services)
6207.Z45 Zentralinstitut für medizinische Aufklärung
The health professions. Recht der Heilberufe
6208 Physicians (General). Ärzte
Including physicians in private practice (freiberufliche Ärzte) and physicians employed by the state (Ärzte in staatlichen Gesundheitseinrichtungen)
Auxiliary medical professions. Paramedical professions. Mittlere medizinische Berufe und Hilfsberufe
6215 General (Table K11)
6216 Nurses and nursing. Krankenpfleger. Schwestern
Including Gemeindeschwestern
6220 Arzthelfer
6221.A-Z Health organizations. By name, A-Z
6221.R43 Red Cross. Rotes Kreuz
Hospitals and other medical institutions or health services
6222 General (Table K11)

Medical legislation
Hospitals and other medical institutions or health services -- Continued
6223 Health resorts and spas. Kurorte, Erholungsorte und natürliche Heilmittel
6224 Blood banks
Including Blutspende- und Transfusionsdienst (blood donation)
6225 Polykliniken. Landambulatorien
6227.A-Z Other health organizations, institutions, or services, A-Z
6227.D39 Day care centers for infants and children
6227.F72 Frauenmilchsammelstellen. Milchküchen
6227.G45 Gemeindeschwesterstationen
6227.G48 Geschwulstbetreuungsstellan (Tumor treatment centers)
Including preventive measures
Kinderkrippen see KKA6227.D39
6227.M43 Medizinischer Dienst des Verkehrswesens
Milchküchen see KKA6227.F72
6227.M88 Mutter- und Säuglingsberstungsstellen (Mother and infant care services)
Including expectant and new mothers
Säuglings- und Kleinkinderheime see KKA6227.D39
6227.S66 Sportmedizinischer Dienst
Medical technology. Medizintechnik
6228 General (Table K11)
6228.2 Zentrale Begutachtungskommission für Medizintechnik
Staatliches Versorgungskontor für Pharmazie und Medizintechnik see KKA6191.5.S78
6228.5.A-Z Equipment and supplies, A-Z
6230 Eugenics
Veterinary medicine and hygiene. Veterinärsrecht. Viehseuchenverhütung
6236 General (Table K11)
6236.3 Veterinarhygiene-Inspektionen
6236.5 Veterinarhygienischer Verkehrsüberwachungsdienst
Environmental law. Landeskultur und Umweltschutz
6242 General (Table K11)
Organization and administration
6243 General (Table K11)
6244 Ministerium für Umweltschutz und Wasserwirtschaft
6245 Environmental planning. Conservation of environmental resources
Environmental pollution
6247 General (Table K11)
6248 Constitutional aspects. Right to a clean environment and the enjoyment of nature

Environmental law. Landeskultur und Umweltschutz
Environmental pollution -- Continued
6254 Recycling of refuse. Verwertung von Siedlungsabfällen. Abprodukte
Cultural affairs. Sozialistisches Kulturrecht und Kulturverwaltungsrecht
6257 General (Table K11)
6258 Constitutional aspects
6259 Cultural policy. Kulturpolitik
Organization and administration
6260 General (Table K11)
6260.2 Ministerium für Kultur
Including Hauptverwaltung Verlage und Buchhandel, Hauptverwaltung Film, etc.
6260.3 Ministerium für Volksbildung
Ministerium für Hoch- und Fachschulwesen see KKA6313.2
6260.4 Ministerium für Wissenschaft und Technik
6260.5 Kulturfonds
Special boards, commissions, councils, institutions, etc.
6262 Staatliche Kommission zur Gestaltung des einheitlichen sozialistischen Bildungssystems
6262.2 Forschungsrat der Deutschen Demokratischen Republik
6262.3 Institut für Technologie kultureller Einrichtungen
Regierungskommission für Fachschulen see KKA6313.3
Staatliches Komitee für Körperkultur und Sport see KKA6342.5
Staatliches Amt für Berufsausbildung see KKA6301
Zentralhaus für Kulturarbeit see KKA6345.3
Functionaries see KKA6345.5
Education. Schulrecht und Schulverwaltung. Einheitliches sozialistisches Bildungssystem
6266 General (Table K11)
6268 Constitutional aspects. Parental right to cooperation with state institutions
6268.3 Akademie der pädagogischen Wissenschaften
6271 Boards and commissions
Including Pädagogischer Rat, Pädagogisches Kreiskabinet, etc.
6271.7 Elternbeirate. Elternaktive
Students. Schüler
6279 General (Table K11)
6280 Constitutional aspects. Right and duty to education and occupation
Including adults
6280.5 Compulsory education. Schulpflicht
Including elementary, vocational, and secondary education

Cultural affairs. Sozialistisches Kulturrecht und Kulturverwaltungsrecht
Education. Schulrecht und Schulverwaltung. Einheitliches sozialistisches Bildungssystem -- Continued
Teachers. Lehrer und Erzieher
6286 General (Table K11)
6289 Education and training
6290 Salaries, pensions, etc.
6293 School functionaries. Schulfunktionäre
6294 Pre-school education. Vorschulerziehung. Kindergartenwesen
6298 Education of people with disabilities. Sonderschulwesen
Including children and adults
Vocational education. Berufsschulwesen
6300 General (Table K11)
6301 Staatliches Amt für Berufsausbildung
Teachers. Ausbildungsberufe
6302 General (Table K11)
6303.A-Z Systematik der Ausbildungsberufe. By vocation, A-Z
6304.A-Z Particular schools, institutions, etc. By place, A-Z
Secondary education. Allgemeinbildende polytechnische Oberschulen
Including erweiterte Oberschulen
6307 General (Table K11)
6308 Compulsory attendance of ten years
Higher education. Universities. Hochschulrecht. Fachschulrecht
For special schools in a particular field of study, see the field
6313 General (Table K11)
6313.2 Ministerium für Hoch- und Fachschulwesen
6313.3 Regierungskommission für Fachschulen
6313.4 Zentralamt für Forschung und Technik
6313.5 Intelligentsia (General)
Administration
6314 General works
6317 Academic degrees. Akademische Grade
Including Promotionsordnungen, Diplomordnungen, etc.
Teachers. Lehrkörper
Including professors, Fachschullehrer, Wissenschaftliche Mitarbeiter and Räte, assistants, etc.
6324 General (Table K11)
6326 Salaries, pensions, etc.
Students
6329 General (Table K11)
6329.5 Selection for higher education. Zulassungswesen
6331 Fellowships. Grants
Including assistance for foreign students

Cultural affairs. Sozialistisches Kulturrecht und Kulturverwaltungsrecht
Education. Schulrecht und Schulverwaltung. Einheitliches sozialistisches Bildungssystem
Higher education. Universities. Hochschulrecht. Fachschulrecht -- Continued

6334.A-Z Universities. By place, A-Z
Pädagogische Hochschulen oder Institute
6334.3 General (Table K11)
6334.4.A-Z By branch of science, A-Z
6334.4.E26 Economics
6334.4.E54 Engineering
6335.A-Z Other schools or institutions of higher education. (Hochschulen und Fachschulen). By place, A-Z
6335.H34 Halle. Hochschule für industrielle Formgestaltung Burg Biebichenstein
6337 Cost of education. Social insurance, etc.
6337.5 Placement of graduates. Absolventenlenkung
6338 Part-time studies. Teilstudium
Including Fernstudium (correspondence courses) and Abendstudium (night school)
6338.3 Sonderstudium
6338.5 Post-graduate studies
6341 Adult education. Erwachsenenbildungsrecht. Volkshochschulen
Physical education. Sports. Körperkultur. Sport
6342 General (Table K11)
6342.3 Staatssekretariat für Körperkultur und Sport
6342.5 Staatliches Komitee für Korperkultur und Sport
6343 Sport instructors and functionaries. Trainer und Funktionäre
Including labor law
6343.3 Athletes
Including labor law
6344.A-Z Particular institutions. By name, A-Z
For particular sports activities and mass events see KKA6062.5
For corporate representation see KKA6063+
Woche der Jugend und Sportler see KKA3557.W62
Sports medicine see KKA6227.S66
Science and the arts. Kunst und Wissenschaft. Kulturelle Massenarbeit
6345 General (Table K11)
6345.3 Zentralhaus, Bezirks- und Kreiskabinette für Kulturarbeit
Including subordinate divisions (Bezirks- und Kreiskabinette für Kulturarbeit)

Cultural affairs. Sozialistisches Kulturrecht und Kulturverwaltungsrecht
Science and the arts. Kunst und Wissenschaft. Kulturelle Massenarbeit -- Continued
6345.5 Functionaries. Leiter im künstlerischen Volksschaffen
Including labor law, social insurance, etc.
6345.7 Scientists and artists (General). Kunst- und Kulturschaffende
For individual professions, see KKA6353+ ; KKA7034.2+
Public institutions
6346 General (Table K11)
6347.A-Z Academies. By name, A-Z
6347.A485 Akademie der Künste zu Berlin
Akademie der Landwirtschaftswissenschaften see KKA6612.5.A42
Akademie der Pädagogischen Wissenschaften see KKA6268.3
6347.A692 Akademie der Wissenschaften zu Berlin
Akademie für ärztliche Fortbildung see KKA6174.A42
Akademie für Staats- und Rechtswissenschaft "Walter Ulbricht" see KKA137.A77
Bauakademie see KKA6786.5
6349.A-Z Research institutes or organizations. By name, A-Z
Agrarwissenschaftliche Gesellschaft see KKA6612.5.A37
6349.M48 Meteorologische Gesellschaft
Meteorologischer Dienst see KKA7031
6349.N38 Nationale Forschungs- und Gedenkstätten der klassischen deutschen Literatur in Weimar
Seehydrographischer Dienst see KKA6927.7
Zentrales Forschungsinstitut für Verkehrswesen see KKA6868.8
6349.Z45 Zentralinstitut für Information und Dokumentation
Zentralinstitut für Jugendforschung see KKA3556.5
6352.A-Z Branches and subjects, A-Z
6352.A72 Archaeology
6352.C37 Cartography
For cadastral surveys see KKA1437
For Seehydrographie see KKA6927.7
Meteorology see KKA7031
6352.S73 Statistical services
Including staatliche Zentralverwaltung für Statistik
The arts
Including Volkskunstkollektive
6353 General works
Performing arts
6355 General (Table K11)

Cultural affairs. Sozialistisches Kulturrecht und Kulturverwaltungsrecht
Science and the arts. Kunst und Wissenschaft. Kulturelle Massenarbeit
The arts
Performing arts -- Continued
Motion pictures. Film- und Lichtspielwesen
6369 General (Table K11)
Hauptverwaltung Film see KKA6260.2
6370 Wissenschaftlich-technischer Beirat des Filmwesens
6370.3 Zentralstelle für Filmtechnik
6370.5 Deutsche Hochschule für Filmkunst
Staatliches Filmarchiv see KKA6379.S72
6371 Labor contracts
Including labor law and social insurance
Regulation of industry
Including censorship, licensing, etc.
6372 General (Table K11)
6372.3 Government film studios DEFA
6372.5 Government enterprises for cinematography
6372.7 Regulations for motion picture theaters
Including personnel
For public safety see KKA6029
Public collections. Recht der öffentlichen Sammlungen. Kunst- und Kulturbesitz
6377 General (Table K11)
Archives. Historic and scientific documents. Archivwesen
6378 General (Table K11)
6378.5 Fachschule für Archivwesen
6379.A-.A Archives. By name, A-Z
6379.S72 Staatliches Filmarchiv
Libraries. Bibliotheksrecht
6382 General (Table K11)
6383 Deutscher Bibliotheksverband
6384 Government libraries. Staatliche allgemeine Bibliotheken
6387.A-Z Other types of libraries, A-Z
6387.E38 Education libraries
e.g. Pädagogische Zentralbibliothek
Museums and galleries. Museen und Kunstsammlungen
6399 General (Table K11)
6400.A-Z Institutions and museums. By place, A-Z
6400.B48 Berlin. Institut für Museumswesen
6400.B63 Berlin. Neue Berliner Galerie-Zentrum für Kunstausstellungen der Deutschen Demokratischen Republik

Cultural affairs. Sozialistisches Kulturrecht und Kulturverwaltungsrecht
Science and the arts. Kunst und Wissenschaft. Kulturelle Massenarbeit
Public collections. Recht der öffentlichen Sammlungen. Kunst- und Kulturbesitz
Museums and galleries. Museen und Kunstsammlungen
Institutions and museums. By place, A-Z -- Continued

6400.B75 Berlin. Staatliche Museen Berlin
6400.D75 Dresden. Staatliche Kunstsammlung
6401.A-Z By specialization, A-Z
6401.H44 Heimatmuseen (Local history)
6402 Education and training of museologists

Historic buildings and monuments. Architectural landmarks. Baudenkmalschutz. Nationale Gedenkstätten. Sonstige Kulturdenkmäler
Including archaeological sites (Bodenaltertümer)

6405 General (Table K11)
6406.A-Z Institutions and organizations. By name, A-Z
6406.I58 Institut für Denkmalpflege
6406.N38 Nationale Mahn- und Gedenkstätten
6406.S88 Staatliche Schlössr und Gärten Potsdam-Sanssouci
6408 Medals, honors, and awards for cultural achievements
6409 Educational, scientific, and cultural exchange

Economic law. Wirtschaftsrecht

6411-6415.8 General (Table K10)

Economic constitution. Staatswirtschaftssystem. Staatswirtschaftsverwaltung

6417 General works
6418 Socialist theory and concept
Including national planning, government ownership of resources, industries, distribution, etc.

Organization and administration
Class here works on national departments of commerce
For departments of commerce prior to 1949, see KK4692.R47 ; KK4865

6420 General (Table K11)

Ministerium für Aussenhandel see KKA6791.5
Ministerium für Handel und Versorgung see KKA6799.3
Ministerium für Kohle und Energie see KKA6702.3
Ministerium für Erzbergbau, Metallurgie und Kali see KKA6702.2

6422 Ministerium für Grundstoffindustrie
6425 Ministerium für Schwermaschinen und Anlagenbau
6426.A-Z Other ministries. By name, A-Z
6426.M295 Ministerium fur bezirksgeleitete Industrie und Lebensmittlindustrie

Economic law. Wirtschaftsrecht
Economic constitution. Staatswirtschaftssystem. Staatswirtschaftsverwaltung
Organization and administration
Other ministries. By name, A-Z -- Continued
6426.M345 Ministerium für chemische Industrie
6426.M363 Ministerium für Elektrotechnik und Elektronik
Ministerium für Geologie see KKA6702
6426.M435 Ministerium für Leichtindustrie
6426.M538 Ministerium für Materialwirtschaft
6426.M837 Ministerium für Verarbeitungsmaschinen- und Fahrzeugbau
Subordinate agencies and courts
6426.3 Arbeitsgruppe Staats- und Wirtschaftsführung beim Ministerrat
Amt für Standardisierung see KKA6558.5
Amt für Preise beim Ministerrat see KKA6442.5
Deutsches Amt für Messwesen und Warenprüfung see KKA6555
Staatliches Vertragsgericht see KKA6432.7
Government control and policy. Wirtschaftsleitung und Planung. Wirtschaftspolitik
6428 General (Table K11)
National planning. Zentralwirtschaftsplanung
For the planning of an individual branch of industry, trade, or commerce, see the branch
6429 General (Table K11)
Planning agencies and bureaus
6429.3 Staatlicher Plankommiission
Staatliche Zentralverwaltung für Statistik see KKA6352.S73
Deutsches Amt für Messwesen und Warenprüfung see KKA6555
Zentralamt für Forschung und Technik see KKA6313.4
6429.5 Deutsches Wirtschaftsinstitut
6429.6 Hochschule für Planökonomie
6430 Planning periods. Planungszeitraum
Including Seven-Year Plan, Five-Year Plan, Two-Year Plan, etc.
6430.5 Techniques and methods of planning. Planmethodik
Including projection, prognosis, statistics, etc., and bureaus (Projektierungsbüros, Projektierungsbetriebe)
Contract system. Kooperationsbeziehungen. Vertragssystem
Cf. KKA1640 Civil law
6432 General (Table K11)
6432.3 Auftragslenkung und Kontrolle

Economic law. Wirtschaftsrecht
Government control and policy. Wirtschaftsleitung und Planung. Wirtschaftspolitik
Contract system. Kooperationsbeziehungen. Vertragssystem -- Continued
6432.5 General- und Hauptauftragsnehmerschaft
6432.7 Staatliches Vertragsgericht (Table K11)
Including organization and procedure
Investments. Investitionskontrolle und Lenkung
Including foreign investments
6433 General (Table K11)
6434 Funds
6434.5.A-Z By industry or project, A-Z
6435 Assistance to developing countries. Entwicklungshilfe
Economic assistance
6436 General (Table K11)
Agricultural credits see KKA6639+
Investments. Credits
For credit institutions see KKA2192+
6438 General (Table K11)
6439 Planning. Policies
6439.5.A-Z Particular credits and subsidies, A-Z
Tax measures see KKA7118+
6440 Marketing orders. Marktordnungen
Class here general works
For particular marketing orders, see the subject, e.g., Agriculture
Prices and price control. Preisbildung und Preiskontrolle
6442 General (Table K11)
6442.5 Amt fur Preise
6444.A-Z Industries, services, or products, A-Z
6444.E97 Exquisiterzeugnisse
Price delicts see KKA8628
Distribution see KKA6450+
Industrial priorities, allocations, and circulation. Vorrang, Zuteilung und Zirkulation
Including organizations (Kontore)
For industrial priorities and allocations in wartime prior to 1949 see KK7520+
6450 General (Table K11)
6450.5.A-Z Raw materials, A-Z
6451.A-Z Industries or products, A-Z
Volkseigene Industriebetriebe (Government business enterprises)
Including formation and management
6454 General (Table K11)
6454.3 Registration

Economic law. Wirtschaftsrecht
Government control and policy. Wirtschaftsleitung und Planung. Wirtschaftspolitik
Volkseigene Industriebetriebe (Government business enterprises) -- Continued
Central administration of government business enterprises. Zentralgeleitete Industrien
6454.5 General (Table K11)
Vereiningungen (Verwaltungen) Volkseigener Betriebe
Including incorporation, consolidation, or liquidation
6455 General (Table K11)
6455.5.A-Z By industry, A-Z
Abwasserbehandlung see KKA6455.5.W38
Bergbau und Hüttenwesen see KKA6700+
6455.5.C43 Chemische Industrie
Energie see KKA6848+
6455.5.G46 Geologische Forschung und Erkundung
Gerätebau see KKA6455.5.R44
Kohle see KKA6711.5.C62
6455.5.L43 Lederwaren
6455.5.L44 Leichthchemie
6455.5.M38 Maschinenbau
6455.5.M62 Mobel
Optik see KKA6455.5.R44
6455.5.R44 Reglungstechnik, Gerätebau und Optik
6455.5.R64 Rohrleitungen
6455.5.V44 Vereinigung INTERHOTEL
Vereinigung Volkseigener Güter see KKA6628+
6455.5.V49 Vereinigung Volkseigener Warehäuser
6455.5.W38 Wasserversorgung und Abwasserbehandlung
Staatliche Kontore
6457 General (Table K11)
6457.5.A-Z By industry or product, A-Z
Exportkontore see KKA6791.7
Local administration of government business enterprises. Bezirksgeleitete Industrie
Including Bezirke, Kreise, etc.
6459 General (Table K11)
Ministerium für bezirksgeleitete Industrie und Lebensmittelindustrie see KKA6426.M295
Horizontal and vertical combinations
6465 General (Table K11)
6465.5 Joint ventures
Kombinate
6466 General (Table K11)
6466.5.A-Z By industry, A-Z

Economic law. Wirtschaftsrecht
Government control and policy. Wirtschaftsleitung und Planung. Wirtschaftspolitik
Volkseigene Industriebetriebe (Government business enterprises)
Horizontal and vertical combinations -- Continued
Vereinigungen (Verwaltungen) Volkseigener Betriebe see KKA6455
Produktionsgenossenschaften
6470 General
6470.5.A-Z By industry, A-Z
Handwerksproduktionsgenossenschaften see KKA6387.E38
Kreditgenossenschaften see KKA2209
Landwirtschaftliche Produktionsgenossenschaft see KKA6631+
6470.5.T49 Textiles Reinigungswesen
Werktätige See- und Küstenfischer see KKA6695.7
6550 Chambers of commerce. Industrie- und Handelskammern
Boards of trade see KKA6842
Money, currency, and foreign exchange control see KKA7090+
Standards. Norms. Quality control. Normenwesen. Materialprüfung
For standards, grading, and quality control of agricultural or consumer products, see the product
6554 General (Table K11)
6555 Deutsches Amt für Messwesen und Warenprüfung
6555.5 Institut für Leichtbau und ökonomische Verwendung von Werkstoffen
6555.7 Quality control. Gütekontrolle (Table K11)
Weights and measures. Containers. Mess- und Eichwesen
6556 General (Table K11)
6557.A-Z By instrument, A-Z
Standardization
6558 General (Table K11)
6558.5 Amt für Standardisierung
Engineering standards
6559 General (Table K11)
6560.A-Z By material, A-Z
6561.A-Z By instrument, A-Z
Materialverbrauchsnormen und Materialeinsparung (Rationalization)
Including Materialumsatzlisten (Inventories)
6562 General (Table K11)

Economic law. Wirtschaftsrecht
Government control and policy. Wirtschaftsleitung und Planung. Wirtschaftspolitik
Volkseigene Industriebetriebe (Government business enterprises)
Standards. Norms. Quality control. Normenwesen. Materialprüfung
Standardization
Materialverbrauchsnormen und Materialeinsparung (Rationalization) -- Continued
6562.5 Recycling of refuse
Including scrap metal, glass, paper, wood, etc.
For Altstoffwirtschaft in general see KKA6740
6563 Prohibition of industrial use of scarce materials
6563.5.A-Z By industry or product, A-Z
Price norms see KKA6442+
6564 Labeling. Warenauszeichnung. Etikettierung
Class here general works
For the labeling of particular goods or products, see the good or product
6577 Consumer protection. Verbraucherschutz
Advertising. Werbung
6580 General (Table K11)
Trade fairs. Expositions. Messewesen. Ausstellungen
6583 General (Table K11)
6584 Leipziger Messeamt
Agricultural and horticultural expositions see KKA6611.3.A+
6586.A-Z By industry or product, A-Z
Primary production. Extractive industries. Urproduktion
Agriculture
Land reform and agrarian land policy legislation. Bodenreform. Nationalisierung
6593 General (Table K11)
6594 Bondenfonds
6595 Restraint on alienation of agricultural land. Bodennutzung
Including Neubauernwirtschaften
6598 Consolidation of landholdings. Genossenschaftliches Bodeneigentum
For Landwirtschaftliche Produktionsgenossenschaft see KKA6631+
Volkseigene Güter see KKA6628+
6601-6605.8 General (Table K10)
Organization and administration
For the department of agriculture prior to 1949 see KK4872.R44

Economic law. Wirtschaftsrecht
Primary production. Extractive industries. Urproduktion
Agriculture
Organization and administration -- Continued

6606 General (Table K11)
6607 Landwirtschaftsrat
Subordinate agencies
Staatliches Komitee für Forstwirtschaft see KKA6677
6607.3 Staatliches Komitee für Landtechnik und materielltechnische Versorgung der Landwirtschaft
6607.5 Staatliches Komitee für Meliorationen
Staatliches Komitee für Erfassung und Aufkauf landwirtschaftlicher Erzeugnisse see KKA6645.3
6609 Sortenkommission
6609.3 Zentralstelle für Sortenwesen
6609.5 Zentralstelle für Futtermittelprüfung und Fütterung
Veterinarhygiene-Inspektion see KKA6236.3
6611 Local administration
6611.3.A-Z Other organizations. By name, A-Z
6611.3.I58 Internationale Gartenbauausstellung
6611.3.L35 Landwirtschafts- und Gartenbauausstellung
Agricultural science and research institutions. Landwirtschaftswissenschaften
6612 General (Table K11)
6612.5.A-Z Institutions. By name, A-Z
6612.5.A37 Agrarwissenschaftliche Gesellschaft
6612.5.A42 Akademie der Landwirtschaftswissenschaften
6612.5.H67 Hochschule für die Landwirtschaftliche Produktionsgenossenschaft
6612.5.I55 Institut für künstliche Besamung
6612.7 Agricultural technique. Landtechnik
Including transportation
6620 Planning and planning periods. Planung und Perspektivplanzeiträume
6621 Contract systems. Vertragssystem
6621.5 Finance. Funds
Production see KKA6644
Volkseigene Guter (Government agricultural enterprises)
Including central administration (previously Vereinigung Volkseigner Güter) and local administration (Bezirksräte)
6628 General (Table K11)
6628.5 Rechtsträgerschaft
Cooperative societies. Genossenschaften
6630 General (Table K11)

Economic law. Wirtschaftsrecht
Primary production. Extractive industries. Urproduktion
Agriculture
Cooperative societies. Genossenschaften -- Continued
Landwirtschaftliche und gärtnerische
Produktionsgenossenschaften (LPG, GPG)
6631 General (Table K11)
6632 Organization. Registration
6633 Planning. Production. Competition
Including Brigaden, Aktive, innovator's movement (Neuererbewegung), etc.
6635 Vereinigung der gegenseitigen Bauernhilfe. Bäuerliche Handelsgenossenschaft (VDGB. BHG)
6635.5 Maschinen-Traktoren-Stationen (MTS)
Inter-cooperative organizations.
Zwischengenossenschaftliche Organisationen
6636 General (Table K11)
6636.5 Meliorationengenossenschaft
Marketing orders. Marktordnungen
6637 General (Table K11)
Economic assistance. Förderungsmassnahmen
6638 General (Table K11)
Agricultural credits, loans, etc
6639 General (Table K11)
Deutsche Bauernbank see KKA2198
Deutsche Landwirtschaftsbank see KKA2198.5
Genossenschaftsbanken see KKA2209
6641 Credits for small and medium farms. Hilfe für Klein- und Mittelbauern
Including Entschuldung
6642 Assistance for farmers coming from West Germany
6643 Credits for LPGs
6644 Production control and quotas
6644.5 Prices. Price supports
Priorities, allocations, and distribution. Aufkauf. Lagerung
6645 General (Table K11)
6645.3 Staatliches Komitee für Erfassung und Aufkauf landwirtschaftlicher Erzeugnisse
6645.5.A-Z By product, commodity, etc., A-Z
6646 Standards and grading
Importing and stockpiling see KKA6645+
Livestock and trade. Fleisch- und Viehwirtschaft
6652 General (Table K11)
6652.5 Institut für künstliche Besamung

Economic law. Wirtschaftsrecht
Primary production. Extractive industries. Urproduktion
Agriculture
Livestock and trade. Fleisch- und Viehwirtschaft -- Continued
6657 Sheep
For Schafscherer-Genossenschaft see KKA6844.S34
6663.A-Z Products, A-Z
Horticulture. Gartenbau
6675 General (Table K11)
International Gartenbauausstellung see KKA6611.3.I58
Landwirtschafts- und Gartenbauausstellung see KKA6611.3.L35
Gartnerische Produktionsgenossenschaft see KKA6631+
Forestry. Forstwirtschaftsrecht
Including timber laws
6676 General (Table K11)
6677 Staatliches Komitee für Forstwirtschaft
6681 Game laws. Jagdrecht und Jagschutzrecht (Table K11)
Fishery. Fischerei- und Fischereipachtrecht
6695 General (Table K11)
6695.5 Institut für Hochseefischerei und Fischverarbeitung
6695.7 Produktionsgenossenschaft werktätiger Fischer
Including See- und Küstenfischer
Mining and quarrying. Bergrecht
Including metallurgy (Hüttenwesen)
6700 General (Table K11)
6701 Constitutional aspects
Organization and administration
6702 Ministerium für Geologie
6702.2 Ministerium für Erzbergbau, Metallurgie und Kali
6702.3 Ministerium für Kohle und Energie
6702.5 Oberste Bergbehörde beim Ministerrat
6702.7 Staatssekretariat für Geologie
Subordinate agencies
6702.8 Stahlberatungsstelle Freiberg
6702.9 Zentralinstitut für Metallurgie
Continental shelf. Festlandsockel
6705 General (Table K11)
Constitutional aspects see KKA6701
Government rights to mines and mineral resources see KKA6701

Economic law. Wirtschaftsrecht
Primary production. Extractive industries. Urproduktion
Mining and quarrying. Bergrecht -- Continued
6706 Planning and planning periods. Planung und Perspektivplanzeiträume
Including calculation of reserves (Berechnung des Lagerstättenvorrats)
Government mining enterprises. Volkseigene Betriebe
Including central administration (Verwaltung Volkseigener Betriebe)
6711 General (Table K11)
6711.5.A-Z Kombinate. Verwaltungen, A-Z
6711.5.B76 Brown coal
6711.5.C62 Coal (General)
Energy see KKA6848+
6711.5.G38 Gaskombinat Schwarze Pumpe
Power stations see KKA6848+
Social legislation
6717 General (Table K11)
6723 Mine safety regulations
Including Institut für Bergbausicherheit
6727.A-Z Resources. Bodenschätze, A-Z
6727.A44 Alkalies
6727.B58 Bitumen
6727.C62 Coal
6727.G38 Gas
Metals, Nonferrous see KKA6727.N65
6727.N65 Nonferrous metals
6727.P58 Petroleum
6729 Subsidences. Earth movement. Bergschadenrecht
6733 Environmental laws. Wiederurbarmachung
Manufacturing industries
Including heavy and light industries
6739 General (Table K11)
6740 Recycling industries (General). Altstoffwirtschaft. Altrohstoffwirtschaft. Altrohstoffwirtschaft
6743.A-Z Other types of manufacturing industries, A-Z
Including particular recycling industries
Ceramics industry see KKA6743.G52
6743.C43 Chemical industry
Including pharmacy
Energy industry see KKA6848+
6743.G52 Glass and ceramics industry
6743.M32 Machine industry
Paper industry see KKA6743.W66
Pharmacy see KKA6743.C43
6743.T49 Textile industry

Economic law. Wirtschaftsrecht
Manufacturing industries
Other types of manufacturing industries, A-Z -- Continued
6743.W66 Wood and paper industry
Food processing industries. Food products. Lebensmittelrecht
6750 General (Table K11)
Ministerium für bezirksgeleitete Industrie und Lebensmittelindustrie see KKA6426.M295
Building and construction industry
For building laws see KKA6155+
6786 General (Table K11)
Ministerium für Bauwesen see KKA6142
Other organizations and institutions
6786.5 Deutsche Bauakademie
6787 Government construction enterprises. Volkseigene Bauwirtschaft
Including volkseigene Entwurfbüros, Bezirksbauunionen, etc.
International trade. Aussenhandelsrecht
6791 General (Table K11)
6791.5 Ministerium für Aussenhandel
6791.7 Exportkontore
Export and import controls
6792 General (Table K11)
Trade agreements see KKA7315+
6798.A-Z By region or country, A-Z
6798.B85 Bulgaria
6798.E28 Eastern Europe (General)
6798.H85 Hungary
6798.P65 Poland
6798.S69 Soviet Union
6798.5.A-Z By product or industry, A-Z
6798.5.B84 Building and construction
Montage see KKA6798.5.B84
Domestic trade. Binnenhandel. Versorgung der Bevölkerung
6799 General (Table K11)
6799.3 Ministerium für Handel und Versorgung
Subordinate agencies
Zentrale Warenkontore see KKA6801.A+
6799.5 Versorgungsinspektionen
6799.7.A-Z Other organizations and institutions. By name, A-Z
6799.8.A-Z Funds, A-Z
6799.8.H35 Handelsfonds
6799.8.W37 Warenfonds

Economic law. Wirtschaftsrecht
Domestic trade. Binnenhandel. Versorgung der Bevölkerung -- Continued
6799.9 Planning and planning periods. Planung und Bedarfsforschung
Including techniques and methods of planning
Government wholesale trade. Volkseignener Grosshandel
Including zentralgeleitete Handelssysteme
6800 General (Table K11)
6801.A-Z Direcktionen. Hauptdirektionen. Zentrale Warenkontore. By product, A-Z
6801.B58 Bismuth
6801.C65 Consumer goods
6801.T49 Textiles
Waren täglicher Bedarf see KKA6801.C65
6801.5 Corporate structure. Grosshandelsgesellschaften
Retail trade. Einzelhandel
6802 General (Table K11)
Government retail trade. Volkseigener Einzelhandel
Including zentralgeleitete Handelssysteme
6805 General
6808.A-Z Modes of trading, A-Z
6808.I53 Industrieladen
6808.V47 Vereinigung Volkseigener Warenhäuser
6810.A-Z Products, A-Z
6810.G76 Groceries. Lebensmittel
6810.5 Private retail trade. Privater Einzelhandel
Cooperative retail trade. Genossenschaftlicher Einzelhandel
6811 General (Table K11)
6811.5.A-Z Products, A-Z
6812 Commission trade (semi-private). Kommissionshandel
Service trades. Dienstleistungsgewerbe
6819 General (Table K11)
Hotels, taverns, and restaurants
6821 General (Table K11)
6821.5 Government enterprises
Artisans. Handwerksrecht
6830 General (Table K11)
6837 Handwerksproduktionsgenossenschaften (Cooperative societies)
6842 Boards of trade. Handwerkskammern
6844.A-Z Crafts, A-Z
Including particular cooperatives
6844.S34 Schafscherer
Energy policy. Power supply. Energiewirtschaftsrecht
6848 General (Table K11)

Economic law. Wirtschaftsrecht
Energy policy. Power supply. Energiewirtschaftsrecht -- Continued

6848.15 Planning and rationalization
6848.2 Centralized administration. Verwaltungen Volkseigener Betriebe
6848.3 Ratemaking. Tarife
6848.6 Accounting. Taxation
6848.7 Operating. Engineering

Particular sources of power
Electricity

6852 General (Table K11)
6852.15 Planning and rationalization
6852.2 Centralized administration. Verwaltungen Volkseigener Betriebe
6852.3 Ratemaking. Tarife
6852.6 Accounting. Taxation
6852.7 Operating. Engineering

Gas. Natural gas

6854 General (Table K11)
6854.15 Planning and rationalization
6854.2 Centralized administration. Verwaltungen Volkseigener Betriebe
6854.3 Ratemaking. Tarife
6854.6 Accounting. Taxation
6854.7 Operating. Engineering

Heat

6856 General (Table K11)
6856.15 Planning and rationalization
6856.2 Centralized administration. Verwaltungen Volkseigener Betriebe
6856.3 Ratemaking. Tarife
6856.6 Accounting. Taxation
6856.7 Operating. Engineering

Transportation. Verkehrsrecht

6868 General (Table K11)
6868.5 Ministerium für Verkehrswesen

Subordinate agencies

6868.8 Zentrales Forschungsinstitut für Verkehrswesen

Kraftfahrzeugtechnische Anstalt see KKA6873

Wasser- und Schiffahrtsverwaltung. Wasserstrassen

6869 General (Table K11)
6870.A-Z Individual agencies. By name, A-Z
6870.F67 Forschungsanstalt für Schiffahrt, Wasser- und Grundbau

Hochwassermeldedienst see KKA7031

Seefahrtsamt see KKA6927.5

Transportation. Verkehrsrecht
Subordinate agencies
Wasser- und Schiffahrtsverwaltung. Wasserstrassen
Individual agencies. By name, A-Z -- Continued
Seehydrographischer Dienst see KKA6927.7
6870.3 Medizinischer Dienst des Verkehrswesens
6870.5 Hochschule für Verkehrswesen
Road traffic. Automotive transportation
6871 General (Table K11)
6873 Kraftfahrzeugtechnische Anstalt
6874 Bezirksdirektionen für Kraftverkehr
Traffic regulations and enforcement
6885 General (Table K11)
6893 Highway safety. Strassensicherheit
Carriage of passengers and goods
6897 General (Table K11)
6898 Passenger carriers. Personenbeförderung (Table K11)
Goods carriers. Güternahverkehr und Güterfernverkehr
6900 General (Table K11)
6901 Ratemaking. Tarife
Railroads. Eisenbahnverkehrsrecht
6903 General (Table K11)
6903.5 Staatliche Bahnaufsicht
6917 Sidings. Anschlussbahnen
6918.A-Z Kinds of railroads, A-Z
6918.W47 Werkbahnen (Coal mining)
6920 Aviation. Air law. Luftfahrt (Table K11)
Water transportation. Carriage by sea. Schiffahrtsrecht
Including Seeverkehrswirtschaft
6927 General (Table K11)
6927.5 Seefahrtsamt
6927.7 Seehydrographischer Dienst
Individual waterways. Wasserstrassen
6943 Oder. Westoder
6944 Lausitzer Neisse
Communication. Mass media
6946 General (Table K11)
6947 Constitutional aspects. Freedom of communication
6948 Government policies. Censorship
Postal services. Telecommunication. Post- und Fernmeldewesen
6950 General (Table K11)
Privacy of mail and telecommunication see KKA6947
6952 Ministerium für das Post- und Fernmeldewesen
Subordinate agencies
6953 Bezirksdirektionen für das Post- und Fernmeldewesen

Communication. Mass media
Postal services. Telecommunication. Post- und Fernmeldewesen
Subordinate agencies -- Continued
6954 Zentralamt für Fernleitungsanlagen
6956 Government monopoly. Postmonopol und Postzwang
Including the sale and distribution of newspapers, magazines, etc.
6959.A-Z Other services, A-Z
Hochwassermeldedienst see KKA7031
Money orders see KKA6959.P68
6959.P68 Postal notes. Money orders. Postscheckverkehr. Zahlungsanweisungen
6959.P685 Postal savings. Postsparkassenwesen
6959.P689 Postzeitungsvertrieb
Telecommunication. Fernmeldewesen
6964 General (Table K11)
6968 Telegraph
6970 Teletype. Telex
Telephone
6972 General (Table K11)
6973 Telephone lines
6975 Electronic data processing. Information retrieval systems. Datenübertragung im Fernmeldenetz
Radio and television communication
6976 General (Table K11)
6980 Staatliches Rundfunkkomitee
Freedom of radio communication see KKA6947
Broadcasting
6995 General (Table K11)
6995.3 Censorship
6997.A-Z Programs, etc., A-Z
6997.A42 Amateurfunkdienst
6997.E38 Eisdienst
Cf. KKA7031 Meteorologischer Dienst
6997.F48 Flugfunkdienst
6997.L35 Landfunkdienst
6997.S43 Seefunkdienst
Press law
7005 General (Table K11)
Freedom of the press see KKA6947
Government policies. Censorship
7006 General (Table K11)
7006.4 Special permits for importing West German or other Western literature
7006.5 Interdiction of transport or transit of neo-Nazi literature

Communication. Mass media
Press law
Government policies. Censorship -- Continued
7006.7 State encouragement for developing progressive literature
7008 Organization and administration
Presseamt see KKA5450.P73
Hauptverwaltung Verlage und Buchhandel see KKA6260.2
7008.5.A-Z Other organizations and institutions. By name, A-Z
7008.5.I58 Institut für Literatur
Planning and planning periods
7009 General (Table K11)
7009.5.A-Z Types of literature, A-Z
7009.5.P47 Periodicals
7009.5.S34 Schoolbooks
Including all levels of education
Sonderschulbücher see KKA7009.5.S34
Publishers and publishing. Verlagswesen
7010 General (Table K11)
7010.3 Licenses and permits. Lizensen und Druckgenehmigungen
7010.5 Government publishing enterprises. Volkseigene Betriebe
Including central administration
Bookdealers. Buchhandel
7013 General (Table K11)
7013.3 Volksbuchhandel
7013.5.A-Z Types of books, A-Z
7013.5.A58 Antique books
7031 Meteorological Dienst. Weather bureau
Including Hochwassermeldedienst, Eisdienst, etc.
For Seehydrographischer Dienst see KKA6927.7
Intelligentsia. Professions. Freie Berufe
Including the intelligentsia of scientific, medical, educational, and art institutions and the technical intelligentsia of government industrial enterprises
7032 General (Table K11)
7032.5 Constitutional aspects
7033 Professional associations
Individual professions
Class here works on education, licensing, professional representation, ethics, fees, and liability
Health professions see KKA6208+
Pharmacists see KKA6197+
Veterinarians see KKA6236+
Lawyers see KKA3769+

Intelligentsia. Professions. Freie Berufe
Individual professions -- Continued
Engineering and construction
7040 Engineers
7041 Technicians
7045.A-Z Other professions, A-Z
Book dealers see KKA7013+
7046 Assistants. Assistenten und Aspiranten
Public finance. Öffentliches Finanzrecht
Class here works on public finance law beginning with 1949
For works on the law prior to 1949, see KK362+, KK7055+
7050 Finance reform and policies. Finanzreform und Finanzpolitik
Cf. KKA6433+ Government control and policy
7058 General (Table K11)
Organization and administration
7060 Ministerium der Finanzen (National department of finance)
For departments of finance prior to 1949, see KK4689, KK4860+
7061 Finanzrat beim Ministerrat
Subordinate agencies and courts
Abgabenverwaltung see KKA7130+
Administration of public property. Verwaltung und Nutzung von Volkseigentum
Including central and local administrative organs
7064 General (Table K11)
7064.5.A-Z Particular properties, A-Z
7065 Administration of trust property. Treuhänderisch verwaltetes Eigentum
Including property of persons who have left East Germany
7065.5 Administration of alien property. Verwaltung von Ausländischem Vermögen
Finanzrevision see KKA7082+
Budget. Staatshaushalt
7075 Reform
7076 General (Table K11)
Accounting. Rechnungsführung und Kassen
Including central and local organs of national government
7077 General (Table K11)
Inventories
Including government enterprises
7078 General (Table K11)
7078.5.A-Z Particular agencies, institutions, businesses, etc., A-Z
Fund administration. Fondsverwaltung
7080 General (Table K11)
7081.A-Z Particular funds, A-Z
Expenditure control. Auditing. Finanzrevision
7082 General (Table K11)

Public finance. Offentliches Finanzrecht
Budget. Staatshaushalt
Expenditure control. Auditing. Finanzrevision -- Continued
7083 Organs
Public credits and investments see KKA6438+
7085 Public debts. Loans. Staatsschuldenrecht
7088 Intergovernmental fiscal relations. Finanzausgleich
Including Bezirke, Kreise, and communities and revenue sharing
Money. Währung
Including control of circulation
7090 General (Table K11)
7091 Coinage. Mint regulations (Table K11)
Including medallions and commemorative medals
7092 Bank notes. Banks of issue
Including regulations of paper and print
For Deutsche Notenbank see KKA2195
7094 Currency reform. Revalorization of debts. Währungsreform
Foreign exchange control. Devisenrecht
7095 General (Table K11)
7097 Conflict of laws
National revenue. Staatseinkommensrecht
7098 General (Table K11)
Fees. Fines. Gebühren. Beiträge. Ordnungsstrafen
Including rates and tables
7099 General (Table K11)
7099.3.A-Z Particular, A-Z
7100.3.A-Z Other income, A-Z
Taxation. Steuern und Abgaben
7101-7105.8 General (Table K10)
Taxation and tax exemption as a measure of social or economic policy. Steuerbefreiung oder Steuervergünstigung als sozial- oeder wirtschaftspolitische Massnahme
7118 General (Table K11)
7119.A-Z Exemption from turnover sales tax. By product, A-Z
7119.F66 Food. Groceries
7119.F87 Furs. Edelpelze
Groceries see KKA7119.F66
7119.O78 Orthopedic shoes
7126.A-Z Classes of taxpayers, A-Z
7126.G47 Gärtnerische Productionsgenossenschaft
7126.H65 Homesteaders
7126.I55 Inland shipping on charter lines
7126.I58 Intelligentsia, Self-employed
Kleingärtner see KKA7127.A+

Public finance. Offentliches Finanzrecht
National revenue. Staatseinkommensrecht
Taxation. steurern und Abgaben
Taxation and tax exemption as a measure of social or economic policy. Steuerbefreiung oder Steuervergünstigung als sozial- oder wirtschaftspolitische Massnahme
Classes of taxpayers, A-Z
7126.L35 Landwirtschaftliche Produktionsgenossenschaft
7126.R48 Retail trade, Private
7126.S55 Slaughterhouses
7126.V45 Verkaufsgenossenschaft bildender Künstler
7126.W67 Workers' gardens. Kleingärtner
7127.A-Z By product, A-Z
Tax administration. Abgabenverwaltung
7130 General (Table K11)
Ministerium der Finanzen see KKA7058
Zentrale Finanzdirecktionen see KKA7058
7132 Local tax administration of the national government
Including Abteilungen Abgaben of the Kreisräte und Bezirksräte
7133 Functionaries. Brigaden. Komplex-Brigaden
Including salaries, incentive awards (Leistungsprämien), etc.
7134 Administrative rules, guidelines, etc.
7135 Jurisdiction for tax allocation
Collection and enforcement
7136 General (Table K11)
Administrative acts. Steuerverwaltungsakte
7143 General (Table K11)
7143.2 Discretion
7144 Assessment. Steuerermittlung, Steuerfestsetzung und Steuerveranlagung
Administrative remedies see KKA7445+
7153 Default. Steuersäumnis
Including penalties
7156 Execution. Steuer Einziehungsverfahren
7161.A-Z Classes of taxpayers or lines of business, A-Z
7161.A37 Agricultural and horticultural cooperatives
7161.A78 Artisans' cooperatives
7161.C66 Commission merchants
7161.C73 Credit cooperatives
7161.F58 Fishery cooperatives
Horticultural cooperatives see KKA7161.A37
7161.I58 Intelligentsia
7161.I59 Inter-cooperative organizations
7161.J62 Jockeys

Public finance. Offentliches Finanzrecht
National revenue. Staatseinkommensrecht
Taxation. Steurern und Abgaben
Classes of taxpayers or lines of business, A-Z -- Continued

7161.S25 Salaried employees and wage earners
7161.S45 Self-employed persons
7161.T62 Tobacco wholesale and retail trade
Wage earners see KKA7161.S25

Income tax. Einkommensteuer
7163 General (Table K11)
7167 Assessment. Veranlagung
7169 Taxable income. Exemptions. Einkommen und Freibeträge
7174 Deductions
Salaries and wages. Lohnsteuer
7184 General (Table K11)
7186.A-Z Classes of taxpayers, A-Z
7190 Pensions and annuities. Renten
7191.A-Z Other sources of income, A-Z
7193 Payroll deduction. Withholding tax. Lohnsteuerabzug
7196.A-Z Classes of taxpayers or lines of business, A-Z

Corporation tax. Körperschaftssteuer
7198 General (Table K11)
Cooperatives
7207 General (Table K11)
7208.A-Z Special topics, A-Z
7235 Anwaltskollegien
7258 Foreign corporations and stockholders
7259 Multi-national corporations

Business tax. Gewerbesteuer
7260 General (Table K11)
7261 Assessment. Veranlagung. Hebesätze
7262.A-Z Classes of taxpayers or lines of business, A-Z
7263 Taxation of artisans. Handwerkssteuer

Property tax. Taxation of capital. Vermögensteuer
Including natural and juristic persons, and business enterprises
For real property tax see KKA7400+
7264 General (Table K11)
7264.3 Tax valuation. Bewertung
7264.5 Assessment. Veranlagung
7265 Estate, inheritance, and gift taxes. Erbschaft- und Schenkungsteuern (Table K11)
7266 Church tax. Kirchensteuer (Table K11)
7268 Surtaxes. Zuschlagsteuern. Zuschläge. Haushaltsaufschläge (Table K11)

Public finance. Offentliches Finanzrecht
National revenue. Staatseinkommensrecht
Taxation. Steurern und Abgaben -- Continued
Reichsfluchsteuer see KK7269
Industriebelastungsgesetz und Aufbringungsumlage see KK7270
Aufbringungsumlage see KK7272
Reichsnotopfer see KK7273
Wehrbeitrag see KK7275
Lastenausgleich see KK7277+
Excise taxes. Taxes on transactions. Verbrauchs- und Verkehrssteuern
7284 General (Table K11)
Sales tax
7285 General (Table K11)
7287 Assessment. Veranlagung
7290 Turnover tax. Umsatzsteuer (Table K11)
Including value-added tax
7304 Beförderungssteuer (Table K11)
7306.A-Z Commodities, services, and transactions, A-Z
7307.A-Z Other taxes, A-Z
Kulturabgabe see KKA7424.K85
Customs. Tariff. Zölle. Zolltarife
For trade and tariff agreements not limited to a region, see K4600+
For regional trade and tariff agreements, see the appropriate region
For trade and tariff agreements with the United States, see KF6668
For foreign trade regulations see KKA6792+
7312 General (Table K11)
Trade agreements. Wirtschafts- und Industriekooperationsverträge
Including deposit and registration
7315 General (Table K11)
7315.5.A-Z By region or country, A-Z
Mininsterium für Aussenhandel see KKA6791.5
Subordinate agencies and courts
7319 Amt für Zoll und Kontrolle des Warenverkehrs
Including international and interzonal trade and traffic
7320 Bezirkszollämter
7321 Binnenzollämter
7321.5 Grenzzollämter
Including Eisenbahn-, Wasser- und Luftzollämter
Practice and procedure. Zollüberwachung und Zollverfahren
Including remedies and enforcement

Public finance. Offentliches Finanzrecht
National revenue. Staatseinkommensrecht
Customs. Tariff. Zölle. Zolltarife
Practice and procedure. Zollüberwachung und Zollverfahren -- Continued
7328 General (Table K11)
7329 Procedures concerning West Germany and West Berlin
7345.A-Z Commodities and services, A-Z
Criminal provisions see KKA7475+
Local finance. Gemeindesteuern und Abgaben
Finance reform see KKA7050
7385 General (Table K11)
7387 Budget. Expenditure control
Including accounting and auditing
Intergovernmental fiscal relations see KKA7088
7393 Fees. Fines. Gebühren. Beiträge. Ordnungsstrafen
Including license fees
Taxation
For local ordinances or works on the taxation of a particular locality or municipality, see the locality or municipality
7395 General (Table K11)
Tax administration see KKA7130+
Estate, inheritance, and gift taxes see KKA7265
Real property tax
Including Grunderwerbsteuer
7400 General (Table K11)
7404 Valuation of real property. Assessment. Bodenschätzung. Einheitswertfeststellung
7410.A-Z Types of properties, A-Z
7423 Taxation of motor vehicles. Kraftfahrzeugsteuer (Table K11)
7424.A-Z Other taxes, A-Z
7424.A48 Amusement taxes. Vergnügungssteuer
7424.D64 Dog licenses. Hundesteuer
Kinosteuer see KKA7424.M69
7424.K85 Kulturabgabe
7424.M69 Motion picture theater taxes. Kinosteuer
Tax and customs procedure. Nachprüfungsverfahren
7445 General (Table K11)
7446 Einspruchsverfahren (Tax protest)
7447 Beschwerde (Administrative appeal)
7448 Berufung zum Finanzministerium (Appeal)
7462 Procedures for government business enterprises
7472 Costs
Tax and customs crimes and delinquency. Steuer- und Zollstrafrecht
7475 General (Table K11)

Public finance. Offentliches Finanzrecht
Tax and customs crimes and delinquency. Steuer- und Zollstrafrecht -- Continued
7489 Withdrawal and regret
Individual offenses
7495 Tax evasion and avoidance
Including Steuerhinterziehung, Steuerunterschlagung und Steuerumgehnung
7512 Tax and customs crimes and delinquency. Ordungswidrigkeiten (Table K11)
Government measures in time of war, national emergency, or economic crisis. Emergency and wartime legislation. Notstands- und Kriegsnotrecht. Wirtschaftskrisenrecht
7520 General works
By period
For periods before 1945 see KK7521+
7591-7610 1945- (Table KK-KKC9)
7612 Legislation for liberation from National Socialism and militarism. Denazification. Entnazifizierungsrecht
Legislation for economic and social recovery
7631 General (Table K11)
7638 Reconstruction. Wiederaufbau
For housing see KKA1796+
Finance reform and policies see KKA7058
Land reform and agrarian land policy legislation see KKA6593+
Industrial reform
7674 General (Table K11)
Expropriation and nationalization of business enterprises. Verstaatlichung. Umwandlung in Volkseigene Betriebe
Including business associations
7676 General (Table K11)
7677 Constitutional aspects
Organization and procedure
Including local, provincial, and central; Sequestrierkommissionen
7678 General (Table K11)
7680.A-Z Industries or properties, A-Z
7683.A-Z Special topics, A-Z
National defense. Military law. Wehrverfassungs- und Verwaltungsrecht
For emergency and wartime legislation see KKA7520+
7690 General (Table K11)
Constitution and the military establishment. Control of the Volkskammer
7694 General (Table K11)

National defense. Military law. Wehrverfassungs- und Verwaltungsrecht
Constitution and the military establishment. Control of the Volkskammer -- Continued
7695 Ständiger Ausschuss für Nationale Verteidigung
Organization and administration
7700 General (Table K11)
7701 Nationaler Verteidigungsrat
7702 Ministerium für nationale Verteidigung (National department of defense)
7704 Subordinate agencies. Wehrverwaltung
The armed forces. Nationale Volksarmee
7708 General (Table K11)
Compulsory service. Allgemeine Wehrpflicht
Including the draft (Musterung und Einberufung)
7710 General (Table K11)
7716.A-Z Particular groups, A-Z
7724 Education and training. Career. Dienstlaufbahn
7730 Pay, allowances, and benefits
7741 Uniform regulations. Decorations and medals
Including all branches of service
Personnel
7742 General works
7744 Reserves. Reservisten
Flags. Flaggen und Fahnen
7747 General (Table K11)
7748.A-Z Particular branches of service, A-Z
7748.N39 Navy
7800 Civil status and rights of members of the armed forces
Including civil law relating to military personnel
7806 Civil defense. Zivilverteidigung
East German participation in Warsaw pact
For Warsaw Pact (General) see KZ5965+
7816 General (Table K11)
7818 Military expenditures and contributions of East Germany
7821 Foreign armed forces in East Germany. Stationierung
Including damages (Stationierungsschäden), and Russian battleships in East German coastal and inland waters
Military criminal law and procedure. Wehrstrafrecht. Kriegsstrafrecht
7830 General (Table K11)
Individual offenses
7861 Absence without leave. Unerlaubte Entfernung
7862 Draft evasion. Wehrdienstverweigerung
7863 Cowardice in battle. Feigheit vor dem Feind
7864 Offenses in safeguarding the national borders. Grenzsicherungsdelikte

National defense. Military law. Wehrverfassungs- und Verwaltungsrecht
Military criminal law and procedure. Wehrstrafrecht. Kriegsstrafrecht
Individual offenses -- Continued
7868 Insubordination. Befehlsverweigerung und Nichtausführung eines Befehls
7874 Disclosure of military secrets. Verrat militärischer Geheimnisse
7875 Sabotaging weapons, equipment, or means of defense. Beeinträchtigung und Verlust der Kampftechnik
Including malfunction and loss
7876 Unauthorized use of military equipment. Unberechtigte Benutzung militärischer Geräte
7877 Crimes committed by prisoners of war
7878 Constraint, looting, etc., in wartime. Gewaltanwendung und Plünderung
7879 Theft from the fallen, wounded, or sick
7880 Use of internationally prohibited warfare materials. Anwendung verbotener Kampfmittel
Including equipment, chemicals, etc.
7881 Violation of the rights of prisoners of war. Verletzung der Rechte der Kriegsgefangenen
7882 Neglecting the sign or the rights of the Red Cross
7883 Violation of legal status of members of parliament
Including members of foreign parliaments
7893.A-Z Other offenses, A-Z
7893.G82 Guard duty offenses. Wachdienst-, Streifendienst- und Tagesdienstverfehlungen
7893.R46 Report duty offenses. Meldepflichtverletzungen
7893.S23 Safety regulation violations
Including radio operation, air and water pilotage and navigation, etc.
Courts and procedure. Kriegsgerichte
7900 General (Table K11)
7913 Punishment. Execution. Strafe und Strafvollzug (Table K11)
Military discipline. Law enforcement. Disziplinarrecht
Including all branches of the armed forces
7925 General (Table K11)
7928 Superior orders. Enforcement of orders
7930 Procedure (Table K11)
7935.A-Z Other topics, A-Z
7935.S83 Sperrgebiete
Criminal law. Strafrecht

KKA

Criminal law. Strafrecht -- Continued

7967 Reform of criminal law, procedure, and execution

Including reform of criminal justice administration (Strafjustizreform)

For works limited to a particular subject, see the subject. For works pertaining exclusively to the codes, see the codes

Administration of criminal justice see KKA9430+

7971-7987 General (Table K9a modified)

National legislation

Statutes. Strafrechtsgesetze

Particular acts

Codes. Gesetzbücher

7975.5<date> Individual codes

Arrange chronologically by appending the date of original enactment or revision of the code to KKA7975.5 and deleting any trailing zeros

Each code subarranged by Table K16

Code of 1870 see KK7975.5187

Code of 1871 see KK7975.51871

7975.51968 Code of 1968 (Table K16)

Philosophy of criminal law. Strafrechtsphilosophie

7994 General (Table K11)

Theories of punishment and particular schools of thought see KKA8233+

7996 Socialist theory of criminal law

8020.A-Z Terms and phrases, A-Z

Concepts and principles. Allgemeiner Teil

Applicability and validity of the law. Anwendbarkeit und Geltung des Gesetzes

8024 General works

Territorial applicability. Räumliche Geltung

8034 General works

Conflict of laws

8042 General (Table K11)

8043 Interzonal law. Interzonales Recht

Criminal offense. Verbrechenslehre

8054 General works

8056 Felony, misdemeanor, and transgression. Verbrechen, Vergehen und Verfehlungen

For Ordungswidrigkeiten see KKA5991+

Criminal act. Handlung

8066 General works

Corpus delicti. Fact-pattern conformity. Tatbestand und Tatbestandsmässigkeit

8067 General works

8068 Elements. Objekte und objektive Seite der Straftat

Criminal law. Strafrecht
Concepts and principles. Allgemeiner Teil
Criminal offense. Verbrechenslehre -- Continued
Illegality. Justification of otherwise illegal acts. Rechtswidrigkeit und Rechtfertigung
8086 General (Table K11)
8090 Self-defense or defense of another. Notwehr (Table K11)
8106 Consent of the injured party. Einwilligung
8114 Calculated production risk. Research and development risks. Wirtschaftsrisiko. Forschungs- und Entwicklungsrisiko
8115.A-Z Other grounds for justification, A-Z
8115.S86 Superior orders. Handeln auf Befehl
Criminal intent. Mens rea. Vorsatz
8118 General (Table K11)
8123 Dolus eventualis. Bedingter Vorsatz
Criminal liability. Guilt. Schuld
8130 General (Table K11)
Capacity. Zurechnungsfähigkeit
8132 General (Table K11)
Incapacity and limited capacity. Unzurechnungsfähigkeit und verminderte Zurechnungsfähigkeit
8134 General (Table K11)
8144.A-Z Special topics, A-Z
Punishment
8230 General (Table K11)
Theory and policy of punishment. Strafzweck
For klassische and moderne Strafrechtsschulen see KK8233+
8233 General works
8240 Education of perpetrator. Erziehung des Täters
8242 Schutz- und Unterdrückungszweck (Safeguarding the social and political system)
Criminal anthropology see HV6035+
Measures of criminal responsibility. System der Massnahmen strafrechtlicher Verantwortlichkeit (Einspurigkeit)
For juveniles and young adults see KKA9662+
For execution of sentence see KKA9759.2+
8250 General (Table K11)
8252 Educational measures of the Gesellschaftliche Gerichte. Erziehungsmassnahmen
Cf. KKA3015 Labor law
Cf. KKA3694+ Courts
Imprisonment. Freiheitsstrafen

Criminal law. Strafrecht
Punishment
Measures of criminal responsibility. System der Massnahmen strafrechtlicher Verantwortlichkeit (Einspurigkeit)
Imprisonment. Freiheitsstrafen -- Continued

8253 General (Table K11)
8256 Wiedereingliederung (Measures of rehabilitation and resocialization)
8260 Short-term sentence. Strafhaft

Punishment without imprisonment. Strafen ohne Freiheitsentzug

8261 General (Table K11)
8262 Verurteilung auf Bewährung (Sentencing to probation)
Including terms of probation and duties of enterprises, state organs, cooperatives, and labor collectives
8263 Reprimand. Offentlicher Tadel
8264 Fines. Geldstrafen

Collateral punishment. Zusatzstrafen

8269 General works
8271.A-Z Particular measures, A-Z
8271.D74 Driver's license revocation
8271.P76 Prohibition against practicing a profession. Berufsverbot
8271.P763 Property confiscation. Vermögenseinzug
8278 Commitment to medical or psychiatric treatment or institutions
8301 Expulsion from East Germany. Ausweisung
8302 Capital punishment. Todesstrafe

Sentencing and determining the measure of punishment. Strafzumessungsgrundsätze

8304 General (Table K11)
8307 Absehen von Strafe

Circumstances influencing measures of penalty

8310 General (Table K11)

Aggravating and extenuating circumstances. Strafschärfungs- und Strafmilderungsgründe

8311 General works
8312 Recidivism. Rückfall

Causes barring prosecution or execution of sentence

8322 General (Table K11)

Limitation of actions. Verjährung

8338 General (Table K11)
8338.4.A-Z Crimes exempt from limitation of actions, A-Z
8338.4.C74 Crimes against humanity and human rights
8338.4.T73 Treasonable endangering of the peace
8338.4.W37 War crimes

Criminal law. Strafrecht
Punishment -- Continued
Criminal registers see KKA9796
Criminal statistics see KKA62
Individual offenses. Einzelne Straftaten
Offenses against the sovereignty of East Germany, the peace, humanity, and human rights
Including discrimination against, and prosecution, expatriation, or elimination (genocide) of national, ethnic, racial, or religious minorities

8339 General (Table K11)

8340 Superior orders excluded from justification. Ausschluss des befehlsnotstandes

8340.5 Extension of jurisdiction of the Deutsche Demokratische Republik in prosecuting political crimes committed against other socialist states

8341 Planning, preparing, or participating in an aggressive war. Aggressionskrieg
Including state, party, and economic functionaries, or military officers

8342 Preparation of aggressive acts against the territorial integrity and sovereignty of the Deutsche Demokratische Republik

8343 Recruiting for imperialist military service. Anwerbung für imperialistische Kriegsdienste

8343.5 Participation in imperialist military actions. Teilnahme an Unterdruckungshandlungen

8344 Propaganda endangering the peace. Kreigshetze und Propaganda

8344.5 Prosecution of East German citizens under false jurisdiction claims of West Germany. Völkerrechtswidrige Verfolgung

8345 Fascist propaganda. Faschistische Propaganda, Völker- und Rassenhetze

8345.5 War crimes. Kriegsverbrechen
Including use of internationally prohibited warfare materials, looting, inhuman acts against the population, prisoners of war, neglecting the sign or the rights of the Red Cross, etc.

Offenses against the person
Including aggravating circumstances
Homicide. Crimes against physical inviolability. Straftaten gegen Leben und Gesundheit des Menschen

8356 General (Table K11)

8357 Murder. Mord (Table K11)

8360 Manslaughter. Totschlag

Criminal law. Strafrecht
Individual offenses. Einzelne Straftaten
Offenses against the person
Homicide. Crimes against physical inviolability. Straftaten gegen Leben und Gesundheit des Menschen -- Continued

8372 Negligent homicide. Fahrlässige Tötung
8374 Desertion. Exposing persons to mortal danger. Verletzung der Obhutspflicht
Illegal abortion see KKA8523
8386 Battery. Körperverletzung
8388 Dangerous battery. Gefährliche Körperverletzung
8390 Battery with fatal consequences. Körperverletzung mit Todesfolge
8399 Negligent physical harm. Fahrlässige Körperverletzung
8401 Failure to render assistance. Unterlassene Hilfeleistung

Crimes against personal freedom and dignity. Straftaten gegen Freiheit und Würde des Menschen

8435 General (Table K11)
8436 Rape. Vergewaltigung (Table K11)
8438 Compelling lewd acts. Nötigung und Missbrauch zu sexuellen Handlungen
Including lewd acts with persons incapable of resistance, or committed by persons taking advantage of official or professional position
8440 Pandering and pimping. Kuppelei. Ausnützung und Förderung der Prostitution
8441 Creating a public nuisance. Sexuelle Handlungen in der Offentlichkeit
8450 Obscenity
Including production, exhibition, performance, advertising, etc.
8453 Threats of felonious injury. Bedrohung
8455 Constraint. Nötigung
8457 Unlawful entry. Hausfriedensbruch
8459 Robbery. Raub
8462 Extortion. Erpressung
8463 White slave traffic. Menschenhandel

Libel. Slander. Defamation

8465 General (Table K11)
8467 Insult. Beleidigung
8472 Calumny. Verleumdung
8476 Discrimination
Including national and racial minorities
8494 Violation of confidential disclosures by professional persons. Verletzung des Berufsgeheimnisses

Criminal law. Strafrecht
Individual offenses. Einzelne Straftaten
Offenses against the person
Crimes against personal freedom and dignity. Straftaten gegen Freiheit und Würde des Menschen -- Continued

8496 Opening of letters. Verletzung des Briefgeheimnisses

Crimes against freedom of religion and conscience. Straftaten gegen die Glaubens- und Gewissensfreiheit

8505 General (Table K11)

8507 Blasphemy. Gotteslästerung

8510 Disturbing a religious observance. Störung des Gottesdienstes

Offenses against children and family

Including aggravating circumstances

8516 General (Table K11)

Lewd acts with children or charges. Sexueller Missbrauch von Kindern und Abhängigen

8518 General (Table K11)

8520 Lewd acts with a youth

8521 Homosexual acts with a youth

8523 Illegal abortion. Unzulässig Schwangerschaftsunterbrechung

8526 Incest. Geschlechtsverkehr zwischen Verwandten

8530 Bigamy. Doppelehe

8532 Abduction of a minor from legal custodian. Kindesentführung

Including aggravation by abducting across the borders of East Germany

8535 Abandonment, neglect, or abuse of a child. Verletzung von Erziehungspflichten

Including exposure to an asocial life and prevention of the state's educational measures (Erziehungsmassnahmen)

8536 Exposure to alcoholism. Verleitung zum Alkoholmissbrauch

Including selling of alcoholic beverages to children

8537 Exposure to discriminatory or obscene materials. Verbreitung von Schund- und Schmutzerzeugnissen

Including production, exhibition, performance, advertising, etc.

For obscenity in general see KKA8450

8538 Breach of duty of support. Verletzung der Unterhaltspflicht

Criminal law. Strafrecht
Individual offenses. Einzelne Straftaten -- Continued
Offenses against socialist property and national economy. Straftaten gegen das sozialistische Eigentum und die Volkswirtschaft
8617 General (Table K11)
8618 Property and damages. Sozialistisches Eigentum und Schaden
Including transaction (Verfügung)
8619 Appropriation. Zueignung
8620 Theft of socialist property
Including aggravating and extenuating circumstances
8621 Destruction of socialist property. Beschädigung sozialistischen Eigentums
8622 Fraud. Betrug zum Nachteil sozialistischen Eigentums
8623 Breach of trust. Untreue zum Nachteil sozialistischen Eigentums
8624 Abuse of power. Missbrauch von Verfügungs- und Entscheidungsbefugnissen
8625 Conversion of capital goods. Entzug von Produktionsmitteln
8626 Damage to livestock. Schädigung des Tierbestandes
Wirtschafts- und Entwicklungsrisiko see KKA8114
8628 Violation of price regulations. Verletzung der Preisbestimmungen
Including overselling or underselling prices established by government
8630 False statements in economic reports or in applications to state organs. Falschmeldung und Vorteilserschleichung
8632 Unauthorized possession or disclosure of economic secrets. Unbefugte Erlangung und Offenbarung wirtschaftlicher Geheimnisse
Including technical processes, research results, etc.
8634 Speculative inventory hoarding. Spekulative Warenhortung
Counterfeiting money and stamps. Geld- und Wertzeichenfälschung
Including postage stamps (Postwertzeichen)
8636 General (Table K11)
8637 Passing counterfeit money
8638 Providing material and equipment for counterfeiting. Bereitstellung von Fälschungsmitteln
8640 False assessment of taxes, social insurance dues, etc.
Offenses against private property. Straftaten gegen das persönliche und private Eigentum
Including aggravating circumstances

Criminal law. Strafrecht
Individual offenses. Einzelne Straftaten
Offenses against private property. Straftaten gegen das persönliche und private Eigentum -- Continued
Larceny and embezzlement
8648 General (Table K11)
8652 Theft by gangs. Organisierter Diebstahl. Gruppendiebstahl
Robbery see KKA8459
8680 Destruction of property. Sachbeschädigung
8690 Fraud. Betrug
Extortion see KKA8462
8722 Breach of trust. Untreue
Receiving stolen goods see KKA9243
Assisting the securing of benefits see KKA9244
Criminal societies see KKA9204
Breach of public peace see KKA9202
Threatening the community see KKA9203
Misuse of titles, uniforms, and insignia see KKA9213
Forgery see KKA9276+
Counterfeiting money see KKA8636+
Crimes involving danger to the community. Straftaten gegen die allgemeine Sicherheit
8880 Common danger. Gemeingefahr
8885 Arson
8900 Releasing natural forces. Verursachen einer Katastrophengefahr
Including damaging or destroying dams and other installations
8902 Impairing warning systems or rescue equipment, etc. Beeinträchtigung der Brand- oder Katastrophenbekämpfung
8903 Felonious pollution or contamination of the environment. Verursachung einer Umweltgefahr
Including poisons, parasites, bacteria, morbific agents, etc.
Violating industrial hygiene and safety regulations. Straftaten gegen den Gesundheits- und Arbeitsschutz
8912 General (Table K11)
8914 Product safety. Produzentenhaftung. Gebrauchssicherheit
8920 Causing danger in construction. Gefährdung der Bausicherheit
Crimes affecting traffic. Straftaten gegen die Sicherheit im Verkehr
8930 Dangerous interference with rail, ship, or air traffic
Dangerous interference with street traffic
8940 General (Table K11)

Criminal law. Strafrecht
Individual offenses. Einzelne Straftaten
Crimes involving danger to the community. Straftaten gegen die allgemeine Sicherheit
Crimes affecting traffic. Straftaten gegen die Sicherheit im Verkehr
Dangerous interference with street traffic -- Continued
8944 Driving while intoxicated. Trunkenheitsfahrt
8961 Crimes affecting communication. Straftaten gegen den Nachrichtenverkehr
8965 Abuse of weapons and explosives. Missbrauch von Waffen und Sprengmitteln
Offenses against the government. Political offenses
Including aggravating circumstances
9015 General (Table K11)
High treason and treasonable activities. Hochverrat
9020 General (Table K11)
9032 Undermining the political and social order of the state or preparing to overthrow the government
9033 Gebietseinverleibung (Annexation)
9034 Assault on a prominent government official
9035 Constraining constitutional organs or their members. Nötigung eines führenden Represanten der Deutschen Demokratischen Republik
Disparagement of the state and its symbols see KKA9205
Treason. Landesverrat
9080 General (Table K11)
9084 Treasonable espionage
Subversive activities. Aiding imperialist organizations. Landesverräterischer Treuebruch. Staatsfeindliche Verbindungen
9085 General works
Prying into state secrets see KKA9318
9094 Intelligence activities. Nachrichtendienst
9095 Propaganda endangering the state. Staatsfeindliche Hetze
9096 Treasonable terrorist activities
9097 Sabotage endangering the state or its economy
9099 Treasonable political abduction. Politische Entführung
9100 Treasonable groups or parties
9102 Treasonable endangering of international relations
Treasonable endangering of the peace see KKA8344
Recruiting for foreign military service see KKA8343
Offenses against public order and convenience. Straftaten gegen die staatliche Ordnung
Including aggravating circumstances

Criminal law. Strafrecht
Individual offenses. Einzelne Straftaten
Offenses against public order and convenience. Straftaten gegen die staatliche Ordnung -- Continued
Constraining constitutional organs or their members see KKA9205
Crimes in connection with election and voting. Straftaten gegen Durchführung von Wahlen
9145 General (Table K11)
9162 Falsifying votes and voting results. Wahlfälschung
9170 Obstructing voting. Wahlbehinderung
9192 Opposition to power of the state. Widerstand gegen staatliche Massnahmen
9193 Illegal crossing of the East German borders. Ungesetzlicher Grenzübertritt
9194 Constraining official action. Beeinträchtigung staatlicher oder gesellschaftlicher Tätigkeit
9201 Vandalism. Rowdyism
9202 Breach of public peace. Zusammenrottung
9203 Threatening the community. Androhung von Gewaltakten
9204 Criminal societies. Vereinsbildung zur Verfolgung gesetzwidriger Ziele
9205 Disparagement of the state and its symbols. Herabwürdigung des Staates und der staatlichen oder gesellschaftlichen Symbole
9205.5 Disparagement of foreign dignitaries. Herabwürdigung auslandischer Persönlichkeiten
Prison escape. Mutiny see KKA9254
9213 Usurpation of office. Amtsanmassung
Including misuse of titles, uniforms, insignia, etc.
Tampering with official seals and pawned articles see KKA9262
9215 Damaging official announcements. Beschädigung öffentlicher Bekanntmachungen
Endangering the administration of justice. Straftaten gegen die Rechtspflege
Including aggravating circumstances
False testimony. Falsche Aussage
Including court procedures, notary procedures, patent office procedures, etc.
9220 General (Table K11)
9239 False affirmation. Falsche Versicherung zum Zweck des Beweises
9243 Receiving stolen goods. Hehlerei
9244 Assisting the securing of benefits. Begünstigung
9245 False accusation. Falsche Anschuldigung

Criminal law. Strafrecht
Individual offenses. Einzelne Straftaten
Offenses against public order and convenience. Straftaten gegen die staatliche Ordnung
Endangering the administration of justice. Straftaten gegen die Rechtspflege -- Continued

9247 Bringing false complaint. Vortäuschung einer Straftat

9253 Failure to report felony. Misprision. Unterlassene Verbrechensanzeige

9254 Prison escape. Mutiny. Freeing prisoners. Gefangenenmeuterei. Gefangenenbefreiung

9260 Coercion of testimony. Aussagenerpressung

9262 Tampering with official seals and pawned articles. Interfering with official custody. Gewahrsamsbruch

9263 Intentional misconstruction by law officers. Rechtsbeugung

Forgery and suppression of documents. Urkundenfälschung und Urkundenunterdrückung

9276 General (Table K11)

9277 Damaging or destroying documents. Urkundenvernichtung

9278 False certification. Falschbeurkundung

Crimes against public duty. Straftaten unter Verletzung dienstlicher Pflichten

Corruption. Bestechung

9285 General (Table K11)

9288 Corrupt acts by officials and functionaries. Accepting benefits. Bestechlichkeit, Vorteilsforderung und Vorteilsannahme

9292 Bribery. Granting benefits to officials and functionaries. Bestechung durch Vorteilsanbietung

Usurpation of office see KKA9213

Violating official secrecy. Verletzung der Geheimhaltepflicht

9311 General (Table K11)

9316 Disclosing official secrets. Geheimnisverrat

9318 Prying into state secrets. Eindringen in Staatsgeheimnisse

9336.A-Z Other offenses against the public order, A-Z

9336.A85 Asocial behavior

9336.T67 Torturing animals

Crimes against humanity see KKA8345

Tax and custom crimes see KKA7475+

Military criminal law see KKA7830+

Criminal courts and procedure. Strafgerichtsbarkeit
For works on both criminal law and criminal procedure see KKA7967+
Criticism and reform see KKA7967
9401-9417 General (Table K9a)
Administration of criminal justice. Strafrechtspflege
9430 General (Table K11)
Ministerium der Justiz see KKA3665
Judicial assistance. Rechtshilfe
9432 General (Table K11)
9434 International judicial assistance
9436 Interzonal judicial assistance
Court organization. Gerichtsverfassung
9440 General (Table K11)
9445 Kreisgerichte (Local courts)
9450 Bezirksgerichte (District courts)
9455 Courts of assizes
Including lay judges (Schöffen)
Oberstes Gericht (National supreme court) see KKA3686+
Courts of special jurisdiction. Special tribunals
Gesellschaftliche Gerichte
9471 General (Table K11)
9472 Konfliktskommissionen (Dispute commissions)
9473 Schiedskommissionen (Municipal arbitral boards)
9480 Sühnestelle mit Schiedsmann (Justice of the peace)
Jurisdiction see KKA9576+
Procedural principles. Grundsatzbestimmungen
9485 Due process of law. Rechtschutz für die sozialistische Staats- und Gesellschaftsordnung und für die Bürger. Gesetzlicher Richter. Rechtliches Gehör
Principles of evidence see KKA9599
9504 Publicity and oral procedure. Grundsatz der Offentlichkeit und Mündlichkeit
Double jeopardy and ne bis in idem see KKA9699
9505 Principle of collegiality. Kollegialitätsprinzip
9509 Participation of citizens in criminal procedures. Unmittelbare Mitwirkung der Bürger am Strafverfahren
Including Schöffen (assizes), Vertreter der Kollektive, Gesellschaftlicher Ankläger, and Gesellschaftlicher Verteidiger
Parties to action
9510 General (Table K11)
9512 Person charged. Defendant. Beschuldigter. Angeklagter

Criminal courts and procedure. Strafgerichtsbarkeit
Parties to action -- Continued
9515 State prosecutor. Staatsanwalt
Class here works on the legal status of the prosecutor in criminal procedure
For general works on the office of the public prosecutor see KKA3728+
9517 Gesellschaftlicher Ankläger
9518 Defense attorney
9519 Gesellschaftlicher Verteidiger
9520 Victim. Geschädigter
9522 Judge and assizes
9523 Konflikt- und Schiedskommissionen
Investigation. Ermittlungsverfahren
9529 General works
Techniques of criminal investigation see HV8073+
Public organs for investigation. Staatliche Untersuchungsorgane
Including Untersuchungsorgane des Ministerium des Innern, Ministerium für Staatssicherheit und der Zollverwaltung
9530 General works
9531 Supervision by public prosecutor
Including decision over recourse (Beschwerde) of parties against the organs for investigation
Compulsory measures against suspect or person charged. Securing evidence
9550 General (Table K11)
Search and seizure. Arrest
9553 General (Table K11)
9553.5 Search and seizure prohibited at night
9554 Witnesses
9558 Seized property, real estate, rights, choses in action, etc.
Including sale
9559 Provisional apprehension. Vorläufige Festnahme
Procedure at first instance. Hauptverfahren erster Instanz
9574 General (Table K11)
Jurisdiction
Including competence in subject matter and venue (sachliche und örtliche Zuständigkeit)
9576 General (Table K11)
9577 Venue for crimes committed aboard ships or aircraft
9579 Zusammenhängende Strafsachen
Trial. Hauptverhandlung
9595 General (Table K11)
Evidence. Beweisverfahren
9597 General (Table K11)
9599 Principles of evidence. Beweisgrundsätze (Table K11)

Criminal courts and procedure. Strafgerichtsbarkeit
Procedure at first instance. Hauptverfahren erster Instanz
Trial. Hauptverhandlung -- Continued
Particular proceedings. Besonderheiten des ordentlichen Verfahrens
Gerichtlicher Strafbefehl see KKA9715
Gerichtliche Entscheidung uber polizeiliche Strafverfügung see KKA9715
9647 Proceedings against fugitives and absentees. Verfahren gegen Flüchtige und Abwesende
9647.5 Recourse against decisions of the Gesellschaftliche Gerichte
Procedure in confiscation see KKA9723
Procedure for juvenile delinquency. Strafverfahren gegen Jugendliche
9651 General (Table K11)
9653 Participation of the Jugendhilfe
Punishment. Correctional or disciplinary measures. Massnahmen der Strafrechtlichen Verantwortlichkeit Jugendlicher
9662 General (Table K11)
9665 Judicial orders. Auferlegung besonderer Pflichten durch das Gericht
9666 Punishment without imprisonment. Strafen ohne Freiheitsentzug
9667 Detention
Including Jugendarrest and Freiheitsstrafe (Jugendhaus)
Execution of service see KKA9759.2+
Judicial decisions
Res judicata. Rechtskraft
9698 General (Table K11)
9699 Ne bis in idem. Double jeopardy
Special procedures. Besondere Verfahrensarten
9715 Procedure in case of penal order and penal mandates. Strafbefehls- und Strafverfügungsverfahren
9723 Procedure in confiscation. Verfahren bei selbständiger Einziehung
Remedies. Rechtsmittel
9728 General works
9736 Beschwerde
Appellate procedure
9739 General works
9740 Berufung
9742 Protest of the public prosecutor. Protest des Staatsanwalts
9743 Kassation

Criminal courts and procedure. Strafgerichtsbarkeit -- Continued
Post-conviction remedies
9756 General works
9757 Reopening a case. New trial. Wiederaufnahme des Verfahrens
Execution of sentence. Verwirklichung der Massnahmen der Strafrechtlichen Verantwortlichkeit
Including execution of sentence in juvenile delinquency
Criticism and reform see KKA7967
9760 General (Table K11)
9762 Execution of death penalty by firing squad
Imprisonment. Vollzug der Strafen mit Freiheitsentzug
9769 General (Table K11)
9772 Administration of prisons
Including discipline, hygiene, etc.
9779 Education of prisoners through labor
Wiedereingliederung see KKA8256
9789 Juvenile detention homes. Jugendhäuser
Punishment without imprisonment
9789.2 General works
9789.3 Verurteilung auf Bewährung (Sentencing to probation)
Confiscation or expropriation of private property see KKA5778.6
9791 Absehen von der Verwirklichung der Massnahmen
9796 Criminal registers. Strafregister (Table K11)
Compensation for judicial error and detention pending investigation see KKA5790
Judicial assistance in criminal matters see KKA9432+

German states and provinces (A-Pr)
Including extinct and mediated states, and states in East Germany up to 1952

	Alsace see KJW211+
101-119	Alsace-Lorraine (Table KK-KKC2)
141-159	Altenburg (Table KK-KKC2)
181-199	Andechs (Table KK-KKC2)
241-259	Anhalt (Table KK-KKC2)
261-279	Anhalt-Bernburg (Table KK-KKC2)
281-299	Anhalt-Cöthen (Table KK-KKC2)
301-319	Anhalt-Dessau (Table KK-KKC2)
381-399	Ansbach (Table KK-KKC2)
441-459	Arenberg (Table KK-KKC2)
481-499	Arenberg-Meppen (Table KK-KKC2)
501-999	Baden (Table KK-KKC1)
1001-1019	Baden-Baden (Table KK-KKC2)
1021-1039	Baden-Durlach (Table KK-KKC2)
1041-1539	Baden-Württemberg (State) (Table KK-KKC1)
	Baiern see KKB1601+
1581-1599	Bamberg (Table KK-KKC2)
1601-2099	Bavaria (State) (Table KK-KKC1)
2101-2119	Bayreuth (Table KK-KKC2)
2161-2179	Berg (Table KK-KKC2)
2201-2699	Berlin (State) (Table KK-KKC1)
2701-2719	Birkenfeld (Table KK-KKC2)
2781-2799	Brandenburg (State, 1990-) (Table KK-KKC2)
2801-2819	Brandenburg (Table KK-KKC2)
2821-2839	Brandenburg (Prussian Province) (Table KK-KKC2)
2841-2859	Brandenburg-Ansbach (Table KK-KKC2)
2861-2879	Brandenburg-Kulmbach (Table KK-KKC2)
	Braunschweig see KKB3561+
3001-3499	Bremen (State) (Table KK-KKC1)
3561-3579	Brunswick (Table KK-KKC2)
3581-3599	Brunswick-Lüneburg (Table KK-KKC2)
3601-3619	Brunswick-Wolfenbüttel (Table KK-KKC2)
3621-3639	Cleve (Table KK-KKC2)
3641-3659	Cleve-Berg (Table KK-KKC2)
3681-3699	Coburg (Table KK-KKC2)
3701-3719	Corvey (Table KK-KKC2)
(3741-3759)	Danzig see KKP2935.G35
3781-3799	Detmold (Table KK-KKC2)
	Deutschritterorden see KKC2441+
3821-3839	East Prussia (Prussian Province) (Table KK-KKC2)
3861-3879	Eichsfeld (Table KK-KKC2)
	Elsass see KJW211+
	Elsass-Lothringen see KKB101+

3901-3919 Franconia (Table KK-KKC2)
3921-3939 Frankfurt (Table KK-KKC2)
3961-3979 Friesland (Table KK-KKC2)
3981-3999 Fulda (Table KK-KKC2)
4021-4039 Gotha (Table KK-KKC2)
Greater Hesse see KKB4801+
Gross Hessen see KKB4801+
4081-4099 Halle-Merseburg (Prussian Province) (Table KK-KKC2)
4101-4599 Hamburg (State) (Table KK-KKC1)
4601-4619 Hanau-Lichtenberg (Table KK-KKC2)
4621-4639 Hanau-Münzenberg (Table KK-KKC2)
4661-4679 Hanover (Table KK-KKC2)
4701-4719 Hanover (Prussian Province) (Table KK-KKC2)
4741-4759 Henneberg (Table KK-KKC2)
4781-4799 Hesse (Landgraviate) (Table KK-KKC2)
4801-5299 Hesse (State) (Table KK-KKC1)
Hesse-Darmstadt see KKB4801+
Hesse-Hanau see KKB4621+
5321-5339 Hesse-Homburg (Table KK-KKC2)
5341-5359 Hesse-Kassel (Table KK-KKC2)
5361-5379 Hesse-Nassau (Prussian Province) (Table KK-KKC2)
5401-5419 Hildesheim (Table KK-KKC2)
5441-5459 Hirschberg (Table KK-KKC2)
5501-5519 Hohenlohe (Table KK-KKC2)
5561-5579 Hohenzollern (Prussian Province) (Table KK-KKC2)
5601-5619 Hohenzollern-Hechingen (Table KK-KKC2)
5641-5659 Hohenzollern-Sigmaringen (Table KK-KKC2)
5681-5699 Holstein (Table KK-KKC2)
5721-5739 Hoya (Table KK-KKC2)
5821-5839 Jever (Table KK-KKC2)
5861-5879 Jülich (Table KK-KKC2)
5881-5899 Jülich-Berg (Table KK-KKC2)
5901-5919 Katzenelnbogen (Table KK-KKC2)
5961-5979 Kempten (Table KK-KKC2)
6061-6079 Kniphausen (Table KK-KKC2)
6141-6159 Kurhessen (Prussian Province) (Table KK-KKC2)
6201-6219 Lauenburg (Table KK-KKC2)
6261-6279 Lichtenberg (Table KK-KKC2)
Liechtenstein see KKJ1+
6341-6359 Lippe-Detmold (Table KK-KKC2)
Lorraine see KJW2611+
Lothringen see KJW2611+
6401-6899 Lower Saxony (State) (Table KK-KKC1)
6921-6939 Lübeck (Table KK-KKC2)
6961-6979 Magdeburg (Table KK-KKC2)
6981-6999 Magdeburg (Prussian Province) (Table KK-KKC2)
7021-7039 Mainz (Table KK-KKC2)

7061-7079 Mark (Table KK-KKC2)
7101-7119 Mecklenburg (Table KK-KKC2)
7121-7139 Mecklenburg-Schwerin (Table KK-KKC2)
7141-7159 Mecklenburg-Strelitz (Table KK-KKC2)
7161-7179 Mecklenburg (State, 1990-) (Table KK-KKC2)
7181-7199 Münster (Table KK-KKC2)
7241-7259 Nassau (Table KK-KKC2)
7281-7299 Nassau (Prussian Province) (Table KK-KKC2)
7321-7399 Neuenburg (Table KK-KKC2)
7361-7379 Niederrhein (Table KK-KKC2)
Niedersachsen see KKB6401+
Nordrhein-Westphalen see KKB7401+
7401-7899 North Rhine-Westphalia (State) (Table KK-KKC1)
7921-7939 Oldenburg (Table KK-KKC2)
7961-7979 Osnabrück (Table KK-KKC2)
8001-8019 Ostfalen (Table KK-KKC2)
8041-8059 Paderborn (Table KK-KKC2)
8101-8599 Palatinate (Table KK-KKC1)
Pfalz see KKB8101+
8641-8659 Pfalz-Zweibrüken (Table KK-KKC2)
8761-8679 Pomerania (Prussian Province) (Table KK-KKC2)
Pommern see KKB8761+
8801-8819 Posen (Prussian Province) (Table KK-KKC2)
8841-8859 Posen-Westpreussen (Prussian Province) (Table KK-KKC2)
Preussen see KKB8901+
8901-9399 Prussia (Table KK-KKC1)
For individual Prussian provinces, see the province in its alphabetical position
For Prussia after 1949, see KKC

German states and provinces (Ps-Z)
Including extinct and mediated states, and states in East Germany up to 1952

101-119 Pyrmont (Table KK-KKC2)
141-159 Ravensberg (Table KK-KKC2)
201-219 Reuss (Ältere Linie) (Table KK-KKC2)
221-239 Reuss (Jüngere Linie) (Table KK-KKC2)
261-279 Rhade op de Volme (Table KK-KKC2)
Rheinland-Pfalz see KKC301+
281-289 Rhine Province (Prussian Province) (Table KK-KKC2)
301-799 Rhineland-Palatinate (State) (Table KK-KKC1)
861-879 Rottenburg (Table KK-KKC2)
901-919 Rügen (Table KK-KKC2)
921-939 Saarbrücken (Table KK-KKC2)
941-959 Saarland (State) (Table KK-KKC2)
Saarpfalz see KKC941+
Sachsen see KKC1101+
1001-1019 Saxe-Altenburg (Table KK-KKC2)
1021-1039 Saxe-Coburg-Gotha (Table KK-KKC2)
1041-1059 Saxe-Meiningen (Table KK-KKC2)
1061-1079 Saxe-Weimar-Eisenach (Table KK-KKC2)
1081-1099 Saxony (State, 1990-) (Table KK-KKC2)
1101-1599 Saxony (Table KK-KKC1)
1601-1619 Saxony (Prussian Province) (Table KK-KKC2)
1621-1639 Saxony-Anhalt (State, 1990-) (Table KK-KKC2)
1641-1659 Schaumburg (Table KK-KKC2)
Including Schaumburg-Lippe
1661-1679 Schleswig-Holstein (Table KK-KKC2)
1681-1689 Schleswig-Holstein (Prussian Province) (Table KK-KKC2)
1701-2199 Schleswig-Holstein (State) (Table KK-KKC1)
2201-2239 Schönburg (Table KK-KKC2)
2241-2259 Schönfels (Table KK-KKC2)
2301-2319 Schwaben (Table KK-KKC2)
2321-2339 Schwarzburg-Rudolstadt (Table KK-KKC2)
2341-2359 Schwarzburg-Sonderhausen (Table KK-KKC2)
2381-2399 Silesia (Prussian Province) (Table KK-KKC2)
Including Upper and Lower Silesia
2401-2419 Solms (Table KK-KKC2)
2441-2459 Teutonic Knights (Table KK-KKC2)
Thüringen see KKC2481+
2461-2479 Thuringia (State, 1990-) (Table KK-KKC2)
2481-2499 Thuringia (Table KK-KKC2)
2501-2519 Trier (Table KK-KKC2)
2561-2579 Waldeck (Table KK-KKC2)
2581-2599 Weimar (Table KK-KKC2)
2601-2619 West Prussia (Prussian Province) (Table KK-KKC2)
2621-2639 Westphalia (Table KK-KKC2)

2641-2659	Westphalia (Prussian Province) (Table KK-KKC2)
2681-2699	Wied-Neuwied (Table KK-KKC2)
2701-2719	Winhoring (Table KK-KKC2)
2721-2739	Wittgenstein (Table KK-KKC2)
2801-3299	Württemberg (Table KK-KKC1)
3301-3799	Württemberg-Baden (Table KK-KKC1)
3801-4299	Württemberg-Hohenzollern (Table KK-KKC1)
4301-4319	Würzburg (Table KK-KKC2)

German cities

For former German cities now located in another jurisdiction, see the jurisdiction

5100 Aachen (Aix-la-Chapelle) (Table KK-KKC4)
5120 Ahrweiler (Table KK-KKC4)
5138 Alsfeld (Table KK-KKC4)
5140 Altenburg (Table KK-KKC4)
5160 Altona (Table KK-KKC4)
5170 Ansbach (Mittelfranken) (Table KK-KKC4)
5180 Arnsberg (Table KK-KKC4)
5221-5240 Augsburg (Table KK-KKC3)
5244 Babenhausen (Table KK-KKC4)
5247 Bad Mergentheim (Table KK-KKC4)
5250 Baden-Baden (Table KK-KKC4)
5270 Bamberg (Table KK-KKC4)
5290 Barmen (Table KK-KKC4)
5310 Bayreuth (Table KK-KKC4)
5330 Berchtesgaden (Table KK-KKC4)
5350 Bergedorf (Table KK-KKC4)
5401-5420 Berlin (Table KK-KKC3)
For Berlin (State) see KKB2201+
5441-5460 Berlin, East (Table KK-KKC3)
Berlin, West see KKB2201+
5480 Bielefeld (Table KK-KKC4)
5500 Bingen (Table KK-KKC4)
5540 Bochum (Table KK-KKC4)
5661-5680 Bonn (Table KK-KKC3)
5720 Bramstedt (Table KK-KKC4)
5750 Brandenburg (Table KK-KKC4)
Braunschweig see KKC5960
5881-5900 Bremen (Table KK-KKC3)
For Bremen (State) see KKB3001+
5920 Bremerhaven (Table KK-KKC4)
5940 Breslau (Table KK-KKC4)
5960 Brunswick (Table KK-KKC4)
5980 Celle (Table KK-KKC4)
6000 Chemnitz (Table KK-KKC4)
6020 Coburg (Table KK-KKC4)
Colmar
see KJW
6061-6080 Cologne (Table KK-KKC3)
6100 Constance (Table KK-KKC4)
6120 Crefeld (Table KK-KKC4)
Danzig see KKP2935.G35
6180 Darmstadt (Table KK-KKC4)
6200 Detmold (Table KK-KKC4)
6220 Dinkelsbühl (Table KK-KKC4)

6241-6260 Dortmund (Table KK-KKC3)
6281-6300 Dresden (Table KK-KKC3)
6310 Duisburg (Table KK-KKC4)
6321-6340 Düsseldorf (Table KK-KKC3)
6360 Dusslingen (Table KK-KKC4)
East Berlin see KKC5441+
6400 Eichstatt (Table KK-KKC4)
6430 Elberfeld (Table KK-KKC4)
Elbing see KKP2935.E42
6490 Emden (Table KK-KKC4)
6520 Erfurt (Table KK-KKC4)
6540 Erlangen (Table KK-KKC4)
6570 Essen (Table KK-KKC4)
6600 Flensburg (Table KK-KKC4)
6701-6720 Frankfurt/Main (Table KK-KKC3)
6730 Frankfurt/Oder (Table KK-KKC4)
6750 Freiberg (Table KK-KKC4)
6754 Freiberg im Breisgau (Table KK-KKC4)
6770 Friedberg (Table KK-KKC4)
6800 Friedrichstadt (Table KK-KKC4)
6820 Fürth (Table KK-KKC4)
6850 Fulda (Table KK-KKC4)
6870 Gauting (Table KK-KKC4)
6900 Gelsenkirchen (Table KK-KKC4)
6930 Gera (Table KK-KKC4)
7001-7020 Göttingen (Table KK-KKC3)
7200 Goslar (Table KK-KKC4)
7240 Gottorp (Table KK-KKC4)
7280 Greifswald (Table KK-KKC4)
7350 Hadeln (Table KK-KKC4)
7431-7450 Hagen (Table KK-KKC3)
7480 Halberstadt (Table KK-KKC4)
7510 Halle (Table KK-KKC4)
7551-7570 Hamburg (Table KK-KKC3)
For Hamburg (State) see KKB4101+
7590 Hameln (Table KK-KKC4)
7620 Hamm (Table KK-KKC4)
7671-7690 Hanover (Table KK-KKC3)
7721-7740 Heidelberg (Table KK-KKC3)
7761-7780 Heilbronn (Table KK-KKC3)
7790 Heiligenstadt (Thuringia) (Table KK-KKC4)
7800 Heilsbronn (Bavaria) (Table KK-KKC4)
7820 Helmstadt (Table KK-KKC4)
7830 Herford (Table KK-KKC4)
7840 Hildesheim (Table KK-KKC4)
7860 Hof (Table KK-KKC4)
7870 Horb am Neckar (Table KK-KKC4)

7880	Ingelheim (Table KK-KKC4)
7900	Ingolstadt (Table KK-KKC4)
7940	Jena (Table KK-KKC4)
7990	Kaiserslautern (Table KK-KKC4)
8001-8020	Karlsruhe (Table KK-KKC3)
8041-8060	Kassel (Table KK-KKC3)
8080	Kiel (Table KK-KKC4)
8100	Kissingen (Table KK-KKC4)
8110	Kleve (Table KK-KKC4)
8120	Koblenz (Table KK-KKC4)
	Köln see KKC6061+
	Königsberg see KLB5210
	Konstanz see KKC6100
	Krefeld see KKC6120
8230	Landshut (Table KK-KKC4)
8260	Lauf (Table KK-KKC4)
8301-8320	Leipzig (Table KK-KKC3)
	Liegnitz see KKP2935.L43
8380	Limburg/Lahn (Table KK-KKC4)
8410	Lingen (Table KK-KKC4)
8441-8460	Lübeck (Table KK-KKC3)
8480	Lüneburg (Table KK-KKC4)
8511-8530	Magdeburg (Table KK-KKC3)
8571-8590	Mainz (Table KK-KKC3)
8611-8630	Mannheim (Table KK-KKC3)
8650	Marburg (Table KK-KKC4)
8710	Meissen (Table KK-KKC4)
	Metz see KJW7871+
8720	Minden (Table KK-KKC4)
8740	Moosburg an der Isar (Table KK-KKC4)
8750	Mühlhausen (Table KK-KKC4)
8760	Mülheim/Ruhr (Table KK-KKC4)
	München see KKC8801+
8780	Münster (Table KK-KKC4)
8801-8820	Munich (Table KK-KKC3)
8840	Mussbach (Table KK-KKC4)
8860	Nauheim (Table KK-KKC4)
8870	Naumburg (Table KK-KKC4)
8890	Neuburg an der Donau (Table KK-KKC4)
8910	Neukölln (Table KK-KKC4)
8920	Neuwied (Table KK-KKC4)
8940	Nördlingen (Table KK-KKC4)
	Nürnberg see KKC8961+
8961-8980	Nuremberg (Table KK-KKC3)
9000	Oberammergau (Table KK-KKC4)
9010	Odenthal (Table KK-KKC4)
9020	Offenbach (Table KK-KKC4)

9040	Oldenburg (Table KK-KKC4)
9060	Osnabrück (Table KK-KKC4)
9080	Paderborn (Table KK-KKC4)
9100	Pforzheim (Table KK-KKC4)
9140	Pössneck (Table KK-KKC4)
	Posen see KKP4986
9160	Potsdam (Table KK-KKC4)
9180	Ratisbon (Table KK-KKC4)
9200	Ravensberg (Table KK-KKC4)
	Regensburg see KKC9180
9240	Rostock (Table KK-KKC4)
9260	Rothenburg ob der Tauber (Table KK-KKC4)
9280	Rottweil (Table KK-KKC4)
9300	Saarbrücken (Table KK-KKC4)
9320	Säckingen (Table KK-KKC4)
9330	Sankt Augustin (Table KK-KKC4)
9340	Scheyern (Table KK-KKC4)
9360	Schleswig (Table KK-KKC4)
9370	Schrobenhausen (Table KK-KKC4)
9390	Schwäbisch Gmünd (Table KK-KKC4)
9400	Schwäbisch Hall (Table KK-KKC4)
9410	Schweinfurt (Table KK-KKC4)
9417	Schwerte (Table KK-KKC4)
9420	Segnitz (Table KK-KKC4)
9430	Siegen (Table KK-KKC4)
9450	Soest (Table KK-KKC4)
	Speyer see KKC9470
9470	Spires (Table KK-KKC4)
9490	Steglitz (Table KK-KKC4)
9500	Stendal (Table KK-KKC4)
	Stettin see KKP4987
9520	Stolberg (Table KK-KKC4)
9530	Stralsund (Table KK-KKC4)
	Strassburg see KJW9201+
9571-9590	Stuttgart (Table KK-KKC3)
9630	Treves (Table KK-KKC4)
	Trier see KKC9630
9650	Tübingen (Table KK-KKC4)
9670	Uelzen (Table KK-KKC4)
9680	Ulm (Table KK-KKC4)
9700	Villich (Table KK-KKC4)
9710	Villingen (Table KK-KKC4)
9720	Volkach (Table KK-KKC4)
9725	Warendorf (Table KK-KKC4)
9730	Weimar (Table KK-KKC4)
9750	Wernigerode (Table KK-KKC4)
	West Berlin see KKB2201+

9760	Wetzler (Table KK-KKC4)
9780	Wiedenbrück (Table KK-KKC4)
9791-9810	Wiesbaden (Table KK-KKC3)
9830	Wismar (Table KK-KKC4)
9850	Witzenhausen (Table KK-KKC4)
9870	Worms (Table KK-KKC4)
9890	Würzburg (Table KK-KKC4)
9910	Wunstorf (Table KK-KKC4)
9930	Xanten (Table KK-KKC4)
9970	Zittau (Table KK-KKC4)
9990	Zwickau (Table KK-KKC4)

To determine a subject class number for a given state or province, add the number or numbers in the table for the subject to the basic number for the state or province. For the list of states and provinces and numbers assigned to them, see KKB+

1 Bibliography

<4> Periodicals

For periodicals consisting predominantly of legal articles, regardless of subject matter and jurisdiction, see K1+

For periodicals consisting primarily of informative material (newsletters, bulletins, etc.) relating to a particular subject, see the subject and form division for periodicals

For law reports, official bulletins or circulars, and official gazettes intended chiefly for the publication of laws and regulations, see the appropriate entries in the text or form division tables

7 Monographic series

Official gazettes

Departmental gazettes

see the issuing department or agency

City gazettes

see the issuing city

Military government gazettes

see KK9.73

8 Indexes (General)

10 Regierungsblätter, Gesetzblätter, Verordnungsblätter, Amtsblätter, etc.

(12) Indexes

see KK-KKC1 8

<16-23> Legislative and executive papers

see J351+ ; JS5301+

<16> Indexes (General). Guides

<17> Early and/or discontinued collections

<18> Collections. Selections. Materialien

<19> Order of business

<20> Proceedings. Debates. Votes

<21> Indexes

<22> Bills

<22.5> Indexes. By editor

<23> Other. Miscellaneous

25 Other works relating to legislative history

Legislation

26 Indexes and tables

29 Abridgements and digests

Early territorial laws and legislation

Class here early sources not provided for in KK195+ or by subject

30 Custumals. Private Rechtsaufzeichnungen. By date

32 Landfriedensgesetze. By date

33 Landesfreiheiten. By date

Legislation
Early territorial laws and legislation -- Continued
Landrechte und Landesordnugen see KK-KKC1 43
34 Privileges
e.g. Judenprivileg
Edicts. Mandates
35 Collections. Compilations
Individual
see the subject
Statutes
Including statutory orders and regulations
For statutes, statutory orders, and regulations on a particular subject, see the subject
36.A-Z Early and/or discontinued collections, compilations, and selections. By editor, compiler, or title, A-Z
Including official and private editions
Current and/or continuing collections and compilations
Including official and private editions
39 Comprehensive. By editor or compiler
40 Annotated. By editor
41 Selective. By editor or compiler
Codifications and related material
Class here collections of codes and codifications not limited to subject
Including early codifications
For codes on a subject, see the subject
42 General
43 Landrechte. Landesordnungen. By date
44 Enactments. By date
For enactments of a particular code, see the code
Treaties
General
see KZ
Concordats
see the subject
Court decisions and related material
Including historical sources and authorized and private editions
For court decisions on a particular subject, see the subject
45 Indexes. Digests. Abridgements
For indexes relating to a particular publication, see the publication
46 Several courts
Class here decisions of courts of several jurisdictions
Particular courts and tribunals
48.A-Z State supreme courts (Oberlandesgerichte, Oberste Landesgerichte). By place or name, A-Z
49.A-Z State district courts (Landgerichte). By place or name, A-Z

Court decisions and related material
Particular courts and tribunals -- Continued
52.A-Z Other courts. By place or name, A-Z
Including historical courts and tribunals not provided for by subject
Administrative decisions on a particular subject
see the subject
(53) Encyclopedias
see KK-KKC1 54
54 Encyclopedias. Law dictionaries
For law dictionaries on a particular subject, see the subject
55 Form books
Including graphic materials, blanks, atlases, etc.
For form books on a particular subject, see the subject
56 Yearbooks
Class here publications issued annually, containing information, statistics, etc. about the year just past
For other publications appearing yearly, see K1+
Judicial statistics
57 General
58 Criminal statistics
Including juvenile delinquency
59.A-Z Other. By subject, A-Z
Directories
see KK64+
Trials
see KK65+
Legal research
see KK76+
Legal education
General
see KK89+
Post-law school education see KK-KKC1 255+
The legal profession see KK-KKC1 254+
Legal aid
see KK3792
Rechtsanwaltskammern
see KK122+
Law societies and associations
see KK132.A+

TABLES

67 History of law
For particular sources, see KK195+ or the subject
For the history of a particular subject (including historical sources), see the subject
For auxiliary sciences, see KK175+
For biography, see KK183+
For collections and compilations of sources see KK-KKC1 30+
70 War and emegency legislation
72 Law reform. Criticism
Including reform of general administration of justice
73 Collected works (nonserial)
For monographic series see KK-KKC1 7
74 General works
75 Compends, outlines, etc.
76 Examination aids
77 Popular works
77.5 Civics
78 Addresses, essays, lectures
79.A-Z Manuals and works for particular groups of users. By user, A-Z
Works on diverse aspects of a particular subject and falling within several branches of the law
see KK164
Concepts applying to several branches of the law
see KK945.A+
Private law
80 General (Table K11)
Private international law. Conflict of laws
For works on conflict rules of other branches of law (e.g. criminal law), see the subject
82 General (Table K11)
Interlocal (interstate) and interzonal law
see KK66
84.A-Z Particular branches and subjects of the law, A-Z
85 Intertemporal law. Retroactive law
Including conflict of laws
Civil law
91-95.8 General (Table K10)
Persons
96 General works
Natural persons
97 General (Table K11)
Personality and capacity
Including incapacity
98 General (Table K11)
98.3 Absence and presumption of death
98.4 Insane persons. People with mental disabilities

Civil law
Persons
Natural persons
Personality and capacity -- Continued
Civil registers see KK-KKC1 266.8.R44
98.5 Citizenship
98.7 Personality rights
For protection of personality rights see KK-KKC1 178.3.P76
Juristic persons of private law
100 General (Table K11)
102 Personality and capacity
Including personality rights
For protection of personality rights see KK-KKC1 178.3.P76
103 Associations
Including unincorporated and incorporated societies
104 Foundations. Charitable trusts and uses (Table K11)
Things
106 General (Table K11)
107.A-Z Special topics, A-Z
108 Rights
Including immaterial rights
Legal transactions
109 General works
110.A-Z Special topics, A-Z
Authentication see KK-KKC1 110.S43
Seal see KK-KKC1 110.S43
110.S43 Signature. Seal. Authentication
110.T78 Trusts and trustees
Domestic relations. Family law
112 General (Table K11)
113 Marriage
Including matrimonial actions and dissolution of marriage
114 Matrimonial property and regime (Table K11)
Consanguinity and affinity
Including parent and child
115 General (Table K11)
116 Parental power
117 Stepchildren
118 Adoption (Table K11)
119 Illegitimate children (Table K11)
120 Affiliation. Paternity
122 Guardianship. Curatorship (Table K11)
For guardianship courts see KK-KKC1 266.8.G82
Property
124 General (Table K11)

Civil law
Property -- Continued
125 Possession and violation of possession
126 Ownership. Acquisition and loss
Including ownership (Bruchteilseigentum and Gesamthandseigentum)
Real property
128 General (Table K11)
Land registration law see KK-KKC1 148+
Public and private restraint on real property
129 General works
Zoning laws see KK-KKC1 364
130 Homestead law (Table K11)
Entail see KK-KKC1 407
Entailed estates of the greater nobility see KK-KKC1 400+
132 Ownership. Acquisition and loss
Including contractual acquisition and loss by judicial decree
Rights incident to ownership of land
133 General (Table K11)
134 Law of adjoining landowners (Table K11)
134.3.A-Z Special topics, A-Z
134.3.A57 Air and space above ground
134.3.B68 Boundaries
134.3.R56 Riparian rights. Water rights
Space above ground see KK-KKC1 134.3.A57
Water rights see KK-KKC1 134.3.R56
136 Superfices
Rights as to the use and profits of another's land
137 General works
138 Emphyteusis
139.A-Z Servitudes (real and personal), A-Z
139.C65 Conveyance and life annuities
Life annuities see KK-KKC1 139.C65
139.R45 Rentenreallast
Tithes see KK-KKC1 139.R45
140 Right of preemption
142.A-Z Types of real property, A-Z
Rentengüter see KK-KKC1 399.8.R45
Hypothecation
143 General (Table K11)
144 Mortgage. Hypotheca
145 Land charge
146 Rent charge
147 Pledges (Table K11)
Land register and registration
148 General (Table K11)

Civil law
Property
Land register and registration -- Continued
149 Cadastral surveys. Cadasters
Inheritance. Succession upon death
150 General (Table K11)
Intestate and testamentary succession
Including wills
152 General (Table K11)
153 Executors and administrators
154.A-Z Other special topics, A-Z
155 Contract of inheritance
156 Unworthiness of heirs. Disinheritance
157 Certificate of inheritance. Proof of heirship
Obligations
158 General (Table K11)
159 Extinction of obligation
Nonperformance. Damages
160 General (Table K11)
160.A-Z Special topics, A-Z
Contracts
162 General (Table K11)
Individual contracts and obligations
164 Sale (Table K11)
165 Exchange. Barter
Lease. Landlord and tenant
166 General (Table K11)
167 Termination of lease
168 Protection of the tenant
169 Procedure and execution
Including eviction
Housing. Apartments
170 General (Table K11)
Emergency measures. Disaster relief
172 General (Table K11)
173 Special topics, A-Z
173.R44 Rent control
174 Pacht (Table K11)
Contracts of service and labor
175 General (Table K11)
176 Servants (Table K11)
Employees and labor contract see KK-KKC1 227
177.A-Z Other contracts, A-Z
Delicts. Torts
178 General (Table K11)
178.3.A-Z Special topics, A-Z
178.3.I45 Illegality

Civil law
Obligations
Delicts. Torts
Special topics, A-Z -- Continued
178.3.L52 Liability
178.3.P76 Protected rights
180.A-Z Individual torts, A-Z
Commercial law
181-185.8 General (Table K10)
Commercial courts see KK-KKC1 240
186 Merchant and business enterprise (Table K11)
Including firma, good will, accounting, etc.
187 Agency (Table K11)
Including commercial agents
188 Commercial registers
Commercial transactions
189 General (Table K11)
190 Sale (Table K11)
192 Consignment (Table K11)
193 Warehousing
Freight forwarders and carriers see KK-KKC1 208
Negotiable instruments. Titles of credit
Including Rekta-, Order-, Inhaber-, Legitimations- and Traditionspapiere
194 General (Table K11)
Bills of exchange
195 General (Table K11)
195.3.A-Z Special topics, A-Z
Checks
196 General (Table K11)
196.3.A-Z Special topics, A-Z
Stock certificates and bonds see KK-KKC1 216.5.S86
196.5.A-Z Other special, A-Z
197 Criminal provisions
Banking. Stock exchange
198 General (Table K11)
199 State supervision
200.A-Z Types of banks and credit institutions, A-Z
200.B35 Banks of issue
200.B84 Building and loan associations
200.M67 Mortgage banks
200.S29 Savings banks
Banking transactions
202 General (Table K11)
202.3 Loans. Credit
202.4 Deposit banking
202.6 Consortium

Commercial law
Commercial transactions
Banking. Stock exchange
Banking transactions -- Continued
202.8 Account current
203.A-Z Other special, A-Z
Investments
204 General (Table K11)
205.A-Z Special topics, A-Z
Carriers. Carriage of goods and passengers
For regulatory aspects of transportation see KK-KKC1 431+
206 General (Table K11)
207 Coastwise and inland shipping
Including passengers and goods
Bus lines see KK-KKC1 431.9.B88
Railroads see KK-KKC1 432+
Airlines
see KK6920+
208 Freight forwarders and carriers
208.3.A-Z Other special topics, A-Z
Insurance
209 General (Table K11)
210.A-Z Branches of insurance, A-Z
210.A22 Accident insurance (Table K11)
Guaranty see KK-KKC1 210.T58
210.H42 Health. Life (Table K12)
210.L52 Liability (Table K12)
Life see KK-KKC1 210.H42
210.L58 Litigation (Table K12)
210.P76 Property (Table K12)
210.T58 Title insurance. Guaranty (Table K11)
210.5.A-Z Individual risks and damages, A-Z
Business associations
212 General (Table K11)
Personal companies (Unincorporated business associations)
213 General (Table K11)
214.A-Z Special types of companies, A-Z
Stock companies (Incorporated business associations)
215 General (Table K11)
Stock corporations
216 General (Table K11)
216.5.A-Z Special topics, A-Z
Bonds see KK-KKC1 216.5.S86
216.5.S86 Stock certificates. Bonds
217.A-Z Other types of companies, A-Z
218 Cooperative societies (Table K11)

Commercial law
Business associations -- Continued
219 Combinations. Industrial trusts
Including business concerns, consortia, etc.
Intellectual and industrial property
Including copyright, patents, trademarks, unfair competition, etc.
220 General (Table K11)
222.A-Z Special topics, A-Z
Labor law
Including works on both labor law and social insurance and private labor law as it applies to the labor contract and to the labor-management relationship
Criticism and reform see KK-KKC1 241
224 General (Table K11)
225 Ministerium für Arbeit und soziale Fürsorge (Department of labor and social affairs)
Including subordinate agencies
226 Labor contract and employment (Table K11)
227 Labor-management relations (Table K11)
Collective bargaining and labor agreements
229 General (Table K11)
230.A-Z By industry, occupation, or group of employees, A-Z
Collective labor disputes
Including strikes
232 General (Table K11)
233.A-Z By industry, occupation, or group of employees, A-Z
234 Labor unions
235 Employers' associations
Protection of labor
237 General (Table K11)
238.A-Z Special topics, A-Z
238.D44 Child labor
Holidays see KK-KKC1 238.V32
238.H65 Home labor
238.H68 Hours of labor
238.L32 Labor hygiene and safety
Leave of absence see KK-KKC1 238.V32
Safety equipment see KK-KKC1 238.L32
Sick leave see KK-KKC1 238.V32
238.V32 Vacations. Holidays
Including leave of absence and sick leave
238.W35 Women's labor
238.5.A-Z By industry, occupation, or group of employees, A-Z
239 Labor supply. Manpower control (Table K11)
Including employment agencies
Labor courts and procedure
240 General (Table K11)

Labor law
Labor courts and procedure -- Continued
240.3 Several courts
240.5.A-Z Particular labor courts, A-Z
240.7.A-Z Special topics, A-Z
Social legislation
241 Social reform and policies
Including all branches of social legislation
241.5 General (Table K11)
241.7 Organization and administration
For department of labor and social affairs see KK-KKC1 225
Social insurance
242 General (Table K11)
242.3.A-Z Branches of social insurance, A-Z
242.3.H42 Health insurance
242.3.S62 Social security
242.3.U53 Unemployment insurance
242.3.W67 Workers' compensation
242.5.A-Z By industry, occupation, or group of employees, A-Z
Social services. Public welfare
244 General (Table K11)
245.A-Z Services or benefits, A-Z
245.E38 Educational assistance
Infant welfare see KK-KKC1 245.M38
245.I58 Institutional care
245.M38 Maternal or infant welfare
245.N87 Nursing aid
245.R45 Rent subsidies
245.3.A-Z Beneficiary groups, A-Z
245.3.A88 Asocial types
245.3.C44 Children
245.3.D58 Disabled
245.3.E43 Elderly
245.3.E92 Evacuated and homeless
245.3.F35 Families
Homeless see KK-KKC1 245.3.E92
Juveniles see KK-KKC1 245.3.C44
245.3.P45 Pensioners
245.3.P66 Poor
245.3.P74 Prisoners of war
245.3.R43 Refugees
245.3.W37 War victims and invalids
245.5.A-Z Special topics, A-Z
246 Disaster relief
Social courts and procedure
247 General (Table K11)

TABLES

Social legislation
Social courts and procedure -- Continued
247.3 Several courts
247.5.A-Z Particular social courts, A-Z
247.7.A-Z Special topics, A-Z
Competence conflicts between administrative, labor, and social courts see KK-KKC1 324.5
248 Competence conflicts between social and labor courts
Courts and procedure
The administration of justice. The organization of the judiciary
Administration of criminal justice see KK-KKC1 475.92+
Criticism and reform see KK-KKC1 72
249 General
249.5 Justizministerium (Department of justice)
Including subordinate agencies
Judicial statistics see KK-KKC1 57+
Courts
250 History
Class here works on defunct historic courts
250.A-Z Particular courts, A-Z
250.5.F48 Feudal and servitary courts
250.5.L35 Landgerichte, Older
Manorial courts see KK-KKC1 250.5.P38
250.5.P38 Patrimonial and manorial courts
Servitary courts see KK-KKC1 250.5.F48
252 General (Table K11)
Particular courts and tribunals
252.5 Amtsgerichte (Magistrate courts)
252.6 Landgerichte (State district courts)
252.7 Oberlandesgerichte (State supreme courts)
252.8 Military government courts
252.9.A-Z Other, A-Z
253.A-Z Courts of special jurisdiction, A-Z
For courts of special jurisdiction not listed below, see the subject, e.g. KK-KKC1 240+ Labor courts; KK-KKC1 247+ Social courts; etc.
253.C65 Competence conflict courts
253.C68 Courts of honor
253.J88 Justices of the peace
The legal profession
Including judicial officers and personnel
254 General (Table K11)
Law school education
see KK89+
Post-law school education
Including examinations, Vorbereitungsdienst, admission to the bar, etc.

Courts and procedure
The legal profession
Post-law school education -- Continued
255 General
255.3 Boards and commissions
255.5 Judicial personnel other than lawyers
Judges
256 General (Table K11)
256.3.A-Z Special topics, A-Z
Staatsanwaltschaft (Office of the public prosecutor)
257 General (Table K11)
257.2.A-Z Particular agencies, A-Z
Notaries see KK-KKC1 266.8.N68
258 Practice of law
Including attorneys and legal consultants
Judicial assistance
259 General (Table K11)
259.3 International judicial assistance
Interzonal judicial assistance
see KK3799
259.5 Foreign judgments (Conflict of laws)
Judicial review see KK-KKC1 260.5.A+
Procedure in general
Including all branches of law
260 General (Table K11)
260.5.A-Z Special topics, A-Z
Civil procedure
261-265.8 General (Table K10)
266.A-Z Special procedures, A-Z
266.S94 Summary proceedings. Summarishes Verfahren
266.2 Remedies
266.4 Arbitration
Including commercial arbitration
266.5 Costs (Table K11)
Noncontentious jurisdiction
266.7 General (Table K11)
266.8.A-Z Branches of noncontentious jurisdiction, A-Z
Children (General) see KK-KKC1 266.8.D65
Civil registers see KK-KKC1 266.8.R44
266.8.D65 Domestic relations
Including children (General)
266.8.G82 Guardianship court (Table K12)
266.8.I54 Inheritance (Probate) court (Table K12)
Matrimonial property registers see KK-KKC1 266.8.R44
266.8.N68 Notaries (Table K12)
Probate court see KK-KKC1 266.8.I54
Recording see KK-KKC1 266.8.R44

TABLES

Courts and procedure
Noncontentious jurisdiction
Branches of noncontentious jurisdiction, A-Z -- Continued
266.8.R44 Registration. Recording
Including civil registers, registers of matrimonial property, etc.
Insolvency
267 General (Table K11)
267.5 Execution
Including procedures
Bankruptcy
268 General (Table K11)
268.5.A-Z Special topics, A-Z
269 Debtors' relief
269.3 Costs
270 Public law (Table K11)
Constitutional law
History
271 General works
Estates. Classes
271.2 General (Table K11)
271.3 Nobility
For dynastic rules, see KK295+
273 Volksklassen
Peasantry see KK-KKC1 396+
275 Landstände. Provinzialstände. Landschaft
275.5.A-Z Other special topics, A-Z
275.5.J87 Juristic personality of dynasty
Legal status of dynasty see KK-KKC1 275.5.J87
275.5.P73 Prerogatives. Privileges
Privileges see KK-KKC1 275.5.P73
Feudal law
277 General (Table K11)
277.5.A-Z Special topics, A-Z
Military government (1945-1955)
see KK4964+
279 Constitutional reform. Criticism
281 Bibliography
Sources
Including historical sources and related material
282.3 Collections. Compilations
Constitutions
Including oktroyierte Verfassungen
Collections see KK-KKC1 282.3
282.4 Individual constitutions. By date of constitution
Subarrange each by Table K17
282.7 Individual sources other than constitutions
e.g. Organisation edits of Baden (Grand duchy)

Constitutional law -- Continued
Court decisions
284 Indexes and tables. Digests
284.3 Serials
284.5 Monographs. By date
285.78 Conferences. Symposia
285.8 General works. Treatises
Intergovernmental relations and relations to empire and church
see KK4481 ; KK4574+ ; KK4723+ ; KK5075+
286.A-Z Constitutional principles, A-Z
286.R85 Rule of law
286.S46 Separation of power
286.5 Sources and relationships of the law
287 Territory (Table K11)
287.5 Foreign relations
Individual and state
288 General (Table K11)
288.5 Nationality and citizenship
289.A-Z Particular groups, A-Z
Fundamental rights and constitutional guaranties
290 General (Table K11)
Equality before the law. Antidiscrimination in general
290.2 General (Table K11)
290.3.A-Z Groups discriminated against, A-Z
290.3.W66 Women
290.5.A-Z Individual rights or guaranties, A-Z
290.5.A78 Right of asylum
290.5.P48 Right to petition
290.6 Civic duties
292 Political parties
292.3.A-Z Other special topics, A-Z
Election law see KK-KKC1 294+
292.5 Internal security
Organs of government
292.7 General works
The people
293 General works
Election law
294 General (Table K11)
294.5.A-Z Special topics, A-Z
294.5.A44 Alien suffrage
294.5.D73 Dreiklassenwahlsysem
The legislature. Legislative power
294.7 History
Including Hoftage, Provinziallandtage, Kammern, Herrenhaus, Abgeordnetenhaus, etc.
295 General works

TABLES

Constitutional law
Organs of government
The legislature. Legislative power -- Continued
Landtag
295.3 General (Table K11)
295.5.A-Z Special topics, A-Z
295.5.I58 Investigative power
Including committees (Untersuchungsausschüsse)
The head of state
History
296 General works
Kings. Princes and rulers
296.3 General works
296.5.A-Z Special topics, A-Z
296.5.B57 Birth rights
296.5.C35 Capacity and disability
Disability see KK-KKC1 296.5.C35
296.5.E43 Election
Emergency powers see KK-KKC1 296.5.W37
296.5.L44 Legislative power
296.5.S92 Succession
296.5.T73 Treatymaking power
296.5.W37 War and emergency powers
Military governors
see KK4967+
296.7 General works
296.9 Ministerpräsident
The central government. Kanzlei. Kabinett und Ministerien
History
298 General (Table K11)
298.5.A-Z Special topics, A-Z
298.5.C36 Capella. Hofkapelle
298.5.C42 Chancellery. Hofkanzlei. Staatskanzlei
298.5.C68 Councils. Hofräte
298.5.P74 Privy council. Geheime Rat
299 General (Table K11)
299.5.A-Z Particular departments, A-Z
Class here departments not provided for by subject
The judiciary see KK-KKC1 248.2+
Constitutional courts (tribunals) and procedure
300 History
301 General (Table K11)
302.A-Z Special topics, A-Z
302.C67 Constitutional torts. Verfassungsbeschwerde (Table K11)
Secular ecclesiastical law
History
306 General (Table K11)

Secular ecclesiastical law
History -- Continued
Church finance and state
see KK386+
Secularization
see KK314.3
306.5.A-Z Special topics, A-Z
306.5.C48 Church property
Treaties between church and state
Including concordats (Catholic Church) and contracts (Protestant church)
For treaties on a particular subject, see the subject
For treaties in general, see KZ
307 Collections. Compilations
308 Individual concordats and contracts. By date
309 General works
310 General (Table K11)
312 Constitutional guaranties
313 System of church-and-state relationship
314 Religious corporations and societies
315 Church autonomy and state supervision
Administrative law
316 General (Table K11)
317 Sources of administrative law
Administrative process
318 General (Table K11)
319 Administrative acts and enforcement (Table K11)
320 Legal transactions and public contracts
Administrative courts and procedure
322 General (Table K11)
323 Several courts
324.A-Z Particular courts, A-Z
324.5 Competence conflicts between administrative, labor, and social courts
Indemnification for acts performed by government
325 General (Table K11)
325.2 Eminent domain (Table K11)
325.5 Government liability (Table K11)
326.A-Z Other special topics, A-Z
Administrative organization
327 General (Table K11)
328 Körperschaften des öffentlichen Rechts (Corporations)
329 Anstalten des öffentlichen Rechts (Institutions)
330 Stiftungen des öffentlichen Rechts (Endowments and foundations)
332 Business enterprises owned or controlled by government
Administrative divisions and departments of the state

TABLES

Administrative law
Administrative organization
Administrative divisions and departments of the state -- Continued
333 General (Table K11)
334 Central government. Oberste Landesbehörde
Including department of the interior and subordinate agencies
District government. Provincial government. Mittelbehörden
Including Regierungsbezirke (Bezirksverbände), Provinzialverbände, etc.
335 General (Table K11)
335.2.A-Z Districts, A-Z
Local government other than municipal. Gemeindeverbände
Including Kreistag, Kreisausschuss, Landrat, Oberkreisdirektor, Kreisrat, etc.
335.3 General (Table K11)
335.4.A-Z Kreise, A-Z
335.5.A-Z Amter, A-Z
335.6.A-Z Landschaftsverbände, A-Z
Other supramunicipal corporations or cooperatives
336 Municipal services and powers beyond corporate limits. Übergemeindliche Zusammenarbeit
336.5.A-Z Gemeindezwëckverbände (Special districts), A-Z
Gemeindespitzenverbände
see KK5928+
Municipal government
337 General (Table K11)
338 Autonomy and self-government. State supervision (Table K11)
339 Municipal territory. Boundaries
340 Names. Flags. Insignia. Seals
341 Citizens and residents
342 Constitution and organization of municipal government (Table K11)
Including city mayor, city director, councils, civic associations, elected and honorary officers, etc.
For works on municipal civil service, see KK5968+
For works on officers and employees of an individual municipality, see the municipality
343 Municipal finance and economy (Table K11)
Including municipal property
343.5 Municipal public services (Table K11)
Including public utilities
344 Civil service (Table K11)
Police and public safety

Police and public safety -- Continued
345 General (Table K11)
Police magistrates
346 General (Table K11)
346.5.A-Z Special topics, A-Z
347 Police measures
348 Police force (Table K11)
Public safety
349 General (Table K11)
350.A-Z Hazards and preventive measures, A-Z
350.F57 Fire prevention and control
350.N82 Nuclear power. Reactions. Radiation
Radiation see KK-KKC1 350.N82
Reactors see KK-KKC1 350.N82
Control of individuals
352 General (Table K11)
353 Identification and registration (Table K11)
354 Immigration and naturalization
354.3.A-Z Particular groups, A-Z
354.3.A45 Aliens
354.5.A-Z Special topics, A-Z
Control of social activities
355 General (Table K11)
355.3.A-Z Special activities, A-Z
355.3.G35 Gambling. Glücksspiel
355.5 Disaster control. Disaster relief
Public property. Public restraint on private property
356 General (Table K11)
Government property. Powers and control
356.2 General (Table K11)
356.3 Records management. Access to public records (Table K11)
Including data bases and data protection
For violation of privacy see KK-KKC1 180.A+
357 Roads and highways (Table K11)
Water resources
Including rivers, lakes, water courses, etc.
358 General (Table K11)
359 Registers
359.3.A-Z Particular bodies and districts, A-Z
State preserves. Forests
360 General (Table K11)
Wilderness preservation see KK-KKC1 376
360.3 Forest and rural police
Architectural and historic monuments see KK-KKC1 389
Public land law
361 Land reform and land policy legislation
For agricultural land law see KK-KKC1 402+

Public property. Public restraint on private property
Public land law -- Continued
362 General (Table K11)
Regional planning
For jurisdiction and organization, see KK6137
363 General (Table K11)
364 City planning and redevelopment. Zoning
365 Building laws (Table K11)
Homestead law see KK-KKC1 130
Entail see KK-KKC1 407
Fideicommissum see KK-KKC1 400+
Public health
366 General (Table K11)
367.A-Z Special topics, A-Z
367.B87 Burial and cemetery laws
Cemetery laws see KK-KKC1 367.B87
367.C65 Contagious and infectious diseases
367.D74 Drinking water standards
367.D78 Drug laws
Including pharmacists and pharmacies
Infectious diseases see KK-KKC1 367.C65
Pharmacists and pharmacies see KK-KKC1 367.D78
367.R44 Refuse disposal
367.S77 Street cleaning
Medical legislation
368 General (Table K11)
369.A-Z The health professions, A-Z
369.3.A-Z Auxiliary (paramedical) professions, A-Z
370 Hospitals and other medical institutions (Table K11)
370.3.A-Z Other health organizations, institutions, or services, A-Z
Ambulance service see KK-KKC1 370.3.E44
370.3.E44 Emergency medical services. Ambulance service
370.5.A-Z Special topics, A-Z
Eugenics
see KK6230+
372 Veterinary medicine and hygiene. Veterinary public health (Table K11)
372.2 Animal protection. Animal welfare. Animal rights (Table K11)
Including prevention of cruelty to animals
For animal rights as a social issue see HV4701+
Environmental law
373 General (Table K11)
374 Environmental planning and conservation of resources
Environmental pollution
375 General (Table K11)
375.5.A-Z Pollutants, A-Z

Environmental law -- Continued
376 Wilderness preservation (Table K11)
Including plant and wildlife conservation
Cultural affairs
377 General (Table K11)
377.5 Kultusministerium (Department of cultural affairs)
Including subordinate agencies, commissions, councils, boards, etc.
Education
378 General (Table K11)
378.4 Students. Schüler
378.5 Teachers
379 Elementary and secondary education
379.2 Education of children with disabilities (Table K11)
379.5 Vocational education (Table K11)
380 Higher education (Table K11)
381 Private schools (Table K11)
382 Adult education. Continuing education
382.5.A-Z Special topics, A-Z
382.5.B62 Boards. Commissions. Conferences
Commissions see KK-KKC1 382.5.B62
Conferences see KK-KKC1 382.5.B62
382.5.P37 Participation in school government
382.5.T48 Textbooks
382.7 Physical education. Athletics
Science and the arts
383 General (Table K11)
384.A-Z Special topics, A-Z
Academies see KK-KKC1 384.P82
384.P82 Public institutions. Academies
384.S72 Statistical services
Public collections
385 General (Table K11)
386 Archives
387 Libraries
388 Museums and galleries
389 Historic buildings and monuments
Economic law. Regulation of industry, trade, and commerce
390 General (Table K11)
391 Economic constitution (Table K11)
392 Wirtschaftesministerium (Department of commerce)
Including subordinate agencies and courts
Economic control and policy
see KK6428+
393 Corporate representation of industry, trade, and commerce
Standards and norms
see KK6554+

TABLES

Economic law. Regulation of industry, trade, and commerce -- Continued
Labeling
see KK6564
394 Licensing. State supervision
Advertising
see KK6580
Agriculture
History
395 General works
Rural (peasant) land tenure and peasantry
396 General works
397 Mark communities. Village communities
Manorial estates. Seigniories
398 General works
399.A-Z Special topics, A-Z
399.M35 Manorial serfdom
399.S47 Serfs
Leasehold for years and inheritance
399.5 General works
399.8.A-Z Special topics, A-Z
399.8.E72 Erbzingsgüter
399.8.I58 Interim farm and interim
399.8.R45 Rentengüter
Entailed estates of the greater nobility. Fideicommissum
400 General (Table K11)
400.2 Inheritance and succession
400.7 Courts and procedure
Land reform and agrarian land policy
402 General (Table K11)
403 Restraint on alienation of agricultural land
404 Consolidation of land holdings. Commasation
Homestead law see KK-KKC1 130
405 General (Table K11)
406 Ministerium für Ernährung, Landwirtschaft, Weinbau und Forsten (Department of agriculture, viticulture, and forestry)
Including subordinate agencies and boards
407 Entail (Table K11)
408.A-Z Agricultural industries and trades, A-Z
408.A54 Animal industry
409.A-Z Agricultural products, A-Z
410 Corporate representation. Agricultural societies
411 Agricultural courts
412 Viticulture (Table K11)
413 Apiculture. Beekeeping
413.5 Horticulture

Economic law. Regulation of industry, trade, and commerce
Agriculture -- Continued
414 Forestry (Table K11)
Including timber and game laws
414.5.A-Z Special topics, A-Z
415 Fishery
Mining and quarrying
416 General (Table K11)
417.A-Z By resource, A-Z
417.C6 Coal
417.5.A-Z Special topics, A-Z
Manufacturing industries
418 General (Table K11)
418.5.A-Z Types of manufactures, A-Z
418.7.A-Z Special topics, A-Z
Food processing industries
419 General (Table K11)
419.5.A-Z By industry, A-Z
419.5.C47 Cereal products
419.7.A-Z Special topics, A-Z
420 Construction and building industry (Table K11)
422 International trade (Table K11)
Domestic trade
423 General (Table K11)
424 Wholesale trade
425 Retail trade
425.3.A-Z Modes of trading, A-Z
425.5.A-Z Products, A-Z
426 Second-hand trade
Including auction houses, pawnbrokers, etc.
426.5.A-Z Service trades, A-Z
Artisans
427 General (Table K11)
427.2 Corporate representation. Associations
Including guilds, brotherhoods, etc.
427.3.A-Z Crafts, A-Z
427.3.G64 Goldwork. Silverwork
Including regulation of fineness and hallmarks
Silverwork see KK-KKC1 427.3.G64
427.5.A-Z Special topics, A-Z
Public utilities. Power supplies
428 General (Table K11)
428.3.A-Z By utility, A-Z
428.5.A-Z Special topics, A-Z
429 Industrial arbitral courts and procedure
429.5 Business ethics. Courts of honor
430 Criminal provisions

Transportation
431 General (Table K11)
Road traffic
431.3 General (Table K11)
431.5 Traffic regulations and enforcement (Table K11)
431.7 Carriage of passengers and goods
431.9.A-Z Special topics, A-Z
431.9.B88 Bus lines
Railroads
Including carriage of passengers and goods
432 General (Table K11)
432.3.A-Z Special topics, A-Z
Pipelines
see KK6919
Aviation
see KK6920
Water transportation. Domestic shipping
Including carriage of passengers and goods
433 General (Table K11)
433.5.A-Z Special topics, A-Z
433.5.H37 Harbors and ports of entry
Communication. Mass media
434 General (Table K11)
435 Postal services (Table K11)
436 Telecommunication
437 Radio and television communications (Table K11)
438 Press law
438.3.A-Z Special topics, A-Z
438.3.C65 Constitutional aspects. Freedom of communication
Freedom of communication see KK-KKC1 438.3.C65
Professions
439 General (Table K11)
440.A-Z Individual professions, A-Z
440.5 Professional ethics. Courts of honor
For a particular court of honor, see the profession
Public finance
442 General (Table K11)
443 Organization and administration
444 Budget. Accounting and auditing
Including Kassen and Rechnungshöfe
445 Public debts. Loans
445.5 Money. Coinage (Table K11)
Including mint regulations
State revenue
446 General (Table K11)
446.5 Fees. Fines

Public finance
State revenue -- Continued
Taxation
Including taxes shared by the state and municipality
For local ordinances and works on the taxation of a particular locality or municipality, see the locality or municipality
447 General (Table K11)
Income tax
see KK7163+
Sales tax
see KK7285+
448 Estate, inheritance, and gift taxes (Table K11)
Property tax. Taxation of capital
449 General (Table K11)
449.5.A-Z Special topics, A-Z
450 Taxation of motor vehicles
450.3 Beer tax
450.5 Taxes from gambling tables. Casinos
Customs. Tariff
452 General (Table K11)
452.3.A-Z Special topics, A-Z
452.5 Local finance. Local taxation (Table K11)
Tax and customs courts and procedure
453 General (Table K11)
453.3 Several courts
453.5.A-Z Particular courts, A-Z
454.A-Z Special topics, A-Z
Tax and customs crimes and delinquency
see KK7475+
Government measures in time of war, national emergency, or economic crisis
455 General (Table K11)
456.A-Z Particular measures or claims, A-Z
456.I53 Industrial priorities and allocations
456.I58 Insolvent debtors. Wartime and crisis relief
Manpower control see KK-KKC1 456.U53
456.M55 Military requisitions from civilians
Price control see KK-KKC1 456.R38
456.R38 Rationing. Price control
456.U53 Unemployment and manpower control
Wartime and crisis relief see KK-KKC1 456.I58
Legislation for liberation from National Socialism and militarism
Legislation for economic and social recovery and restitution
457 General (Table K11)
457.3.A-Z Groups of victims or types of damage, A-Z
457.5.A-Z Special topics, A-Z
Military law

Military law -- Continued
458 General (Table K11)
459 Compulsory service (Table K11)
460.A-Z Individual branches of service, A-Z
460.2 Civil defense
Military criminal law and procedure
460.3 General (Table K11)
460.4.A-Z Individual offenses, A-Z
460.5.A-Z Special topics, A-Z
Criminal law
460.6 Reform of criminal law, procedure, and execution
461-465.8 General (Table K10)
Philosophy of criminal law
see KK7994+
Concepts and principles
466 General works
467.A-Z Special topics, A-Z
Punishment
468 General (Table K11)
469.A-Z Special topics, A-Z
Criminal registers
see KK9796+
470.A-Z Individual offenses, A-Z
470.B42 Blasphemy
470.D74 Driving while intoxicated
470.I56 Intoxication
Criminal courts and procedure
Criticism and reform see KK-KKC1 460.6
471-475.8 General (Table K10)
Administration of criminal justice
Criticism and reform see KK-KKC1 460.6
476 General (Table K11)
Justizministerium see KK-KKC1 249.5
Judicial statistics see KK-KKC1 58
Judicial assistance
477 General works
478 International judicial assistance
Interzonal judicial assistance
see KK9436
479 Foreign judgments (Conflict of laws)
Court organization
480 General (Table K11)
480.5 Several courts
481.A-Z Particular courts, A-Z
482 Procedural principles
483 Pretrial procedures (Table K11)
484 Procedure at first instance (Table K11)

Criminal law
Criminal courts and procedure
Administration of criminal justice -- Continued
485 Judicial decisions and remedies (Table K11)
Execution of sentence
Criticism and reform see KK-KKC1 460.6
486 General (Table K11)
Imprisonment
487 General (Table K11)
488.A-Z Penal institutions, A-Z
490.A-Z Other special, A-Z
490.C36 Capital punishment

TABLES

To determine a subject class number for a given state or province, add the number or numbers in the table for the subject to the basic number for the state or province. For the list of states and provinces and numbers assigned to them, see KKB+

1.A12	Bibliography
<1.A13>	Periodicals
	For periodicals consisting predominantly of legal articles, regardless of subject matter and jurisdiction, see K1+
	For periodicals consisting primarily of informative material (newsletters, bulletins, etc.) relating to a particular subject, see the subject and form division for periodicals
	For law reports, official bulletins or circulars, and official gazettes intended chiefly for the publication of laws and regulations, see the appropriate entries in the text or form division tables
1.A14	Monographic series
	Official gazettes
	Departmental gazettes
	see the issuing department or agency
	City gazettes
	see the issuing city
	Military government gazettes
	see KK9.73
1.A15	Indexes (General)
1.A155	Regierungsblätter, Gesetzblätter, Verordnungsblätter, Amtsblätter, etc.
(1.A158)	Indexes
	see KK-KKC2 .A15
<1.A16-.A23>	Legislative and executive papers
	see J352+ ; JS5301+
<1.A16>	Indexes (General). Guides
<1.A17>	Early and/or discontinued collections
<1.A18>	Collections. Selections. Materialien
<1.A19>	Order of business
<1.A20>	Proceedings. Debates. Votes
<1.A215>	Indexes
<1.A22>	Bills
<1.A225>	Indexes. By editor
<1.A23>	Other. Miscellaneous
1.A25	Other works relating to legislative history
	Legislation
1.A26	Indexes and tables
1.A29	Abridgements and digests
	Early territorial laws and legislation
	Class here early sources not provided for in KK195+ or by subject
1.A3	Custumals. Private Rechtsaufzeichnungen. By date
1.A32	Landfriedensgesetze. By date
1.A33	Landesfreiheiten. By date

Subdivisions under states (500 nos.)
Legislation
Landrechte und Landesordnugen see KK-KKC2 1.A43
1.A34 Privileges
e.g. Judenprivileg
Edicts. Mandates
1.A35 Collections. Compilations
Individual
see the subject
Statutes
Including statutory orders and regulations
For statutes, statutory orders, and regulations on a particular subject, see the subject
1.A36A-.A36Z Early and/or discontinued collections, compilations, and selections. By editor, compiler, or title, A-Z
Including official and private editions
Current and/or continuing collections and compilations
Including official and private editions
1.A39A-.A39Z Comprehensive. By editor or compiler and date
1.A4A-.A4Z Annotated. By editor and date
1.A415A-.A415Z Selective. By editor or compiler and date
Codifications and related material
Class here collections of codes and codifications not limited to subject
Including early codifications
For codes on a subject, see the subject
1.A42 General
1.A43 Landrechte. Landesordnungen. By date
1.A44 Enactments. By date
For enactments of a particular code, see the code
General
see KZ
Concordats
see the subject
Court decisions and related material
Including historical sources and authorized and private editions
For court decisions on a particular subject, see the subject
1.A45 Indexes. Digests. Abridgements
For indexes relating to a particular publication, see the publication
1.A46 Several courts
Class here decisions of courts of several jurisdictions
Particular courts and tribunals
1.A48A-.A48Z State supreme courts (Oberlandesgerichte, Oberste Landesgerichte). By place or name, A-Z, and date
1.A49A-.A49Z State district courts (Landgerichte). By place or name, A-Z, and date

Court decisions and related material
Particular courts and tribunals -- Continued
1.A52A-.A52Z Other courts. By place or name, A-Z, and date
Including historical courts and tribunals not provided for by subject
Administrative decisions on a particular subject
see the subject
(1.A53) Encyclopedias
see KK-KKC2 1.A54
1.A54 Encyclopedias. Law dictionaries
For law dictionaries on a particular subject, see the subject
1.A55 Form books
Including graphic materials, blanks, atlases, etc.
For form books on a particular subject, see the subject
1.A56 Yearbooks
Class here publications issued annually, containing information, statistics, etc. about the year just past
For other publications appearing yearly, see K1+
Judicial statistics
1.A57 General
1.A58 Criminal statistics
Including juvenile delinquency
1.A59A-.A59Z Other. By subject, A-Z
Directories
see KK64+
Trials
see KK65+
Legal research
see KK76+
Legal education
General
see KK89+
Post-law school education see KK-KKC2 7.92
The legal profession see KK-KKC2 7.9+
Legal aid
see KK3792
Rechtsanwaltskammern
see KK122+
Law societies and associations
see KK132.A+

1.A67 History of law
For particular sources, see KK195+ or the subject
For the history of a particular subject (including historical sources), see the subject
For auxiliary sciences, see KK175+
For biography, see KK183+
For collections and compilations of sources see KK-KKC2 1.A3+

1.A73 Collected works (nonserial)
For monographic series see KK-KKC2 1.A14

1.A74 General works

1.A75 Compends, outlines, etc.

1.A76 Examination aids

1.A77 Popular works

Works on diverse aspects of a particular subject and falling within several branches of the law
see KK164.A+

Concepts applying to several branches of the law
see KK945.A+

Private law

1.8 General

Private international law. Conflict of laws
For works on conflict rules of other branches of law e.g. criminal law), see the subject

1.82 General

Interlocal (interstate) and interzonal law
see KK66

1.85 Intertemporal law. Retroactive law
Including conflict of laws

Civil law

2 General

Persons

2.2 General works

2.3.A-Z Special topics, A-Z

2.4 Things

Domestic relations. Family law

2.6 General

2.62 Marriage
Including matrimonial actions and dissolution of marriage

2.63 Matrimonial property and regime

2.64 Consanguinity and affinity
Including parent and child

Property

2.8 General

2.82 Real property

2.9.A-Z Other special topics, A-Z

3 Inheritance. Succession upon death

TABLES

Civil law -- Continued
Obligations
3.22 General
Contracts
3.24 General
Individual contracts and obligations
Lease. Landlord and tenant
3.3 General
Housing. Apartments
3.34 General
3.4 Emergency measures. Disaster relief
3.5 Pacht
Contracts of service and labor
3.6 General
3.7 Servants
3.8.A-Z Other contracts, A-Z
3.9 Delicts. Torts
Commercial law
4 General
4.2 Commercial registers
Commercial transactions
4.22 General
4.3 Negotiable instruments. Titles of credit
Including Rekta-, Order-, Inhaber-, Legitimations- and Traditionspapiere
Banking. Stock exchange
5 General
5.3.A-Z Types of banks and credit institutions, A-Z
5.3.B35 Banks of issue
5.3.B84 Building and loan associations
5.3.M67 Mortgage banks
5.3.S29 Savings banks
5.4 Banking transactions
5.45 Investments
Carriers. Carriage of goods and passengers
For regulatory aspects of transportation see KK-KKC2 16.4+
5.5 General
5.53.A-Z Special topics, A-Z
5.6 Insurance
Business associations
5.7 General
5.8 Stock companies (Incorporated business associations)
6 Intellectual and industrial property
Including copyright, patents, trademarks, unfair competition, etc.

Labor law
Including works on both labor law and social insurance and private labor law as it applies to the labor contract and to the labor-management relationship
6.3 General
6.4 Labor-management relations
6.6 Collective labor disputes
6.7 Labor courts and procedure
Social legislation
6.8 General
Social insurance
7 General
7.2.A-Z Branches of social insurance, A-Z
7.2.H42 Health insurance
7.2.S62 Social security
7.2.U53 Unemployment insurance
7.2.W67 Workers' compensation
Social services. Public welfare
7.4 General
7.5.A-Z Services or benefits, A-Z
7.5.E38 Educational assistance
Infant welfare see KK-KKC2 7.5.M38
7.5.I58 Institutional care
7.5.M38 Maternal or infant welfare
7.5.N87 Nursing aid
7.5.R45 Rent subsidies
7.52.A-Z Beneficiary groups, A-Z
7.52.A88 Asocial types
7.52.C44 Children
7.52.D58 Disabled
7.52.E43 Elderly
7.52.E92 Evacuated and homeless
7.52.F35 Families
Homeless see KK-KKC2 7.52.E92
Juveniles see KK-KKC2 7.52.C44
7.52.P45 Pensioners
7.52.P66 Poor
7.52.P74 Prisoners of war
7.52.R43 Refugees
7.52.W37 War victims and invalids
7.6 Social courts and procedure
Courts and procedure
7.7 The administration of justice. The organization of the judiciary
Courts
7.73 History
Class here works on defunct historic courts
7.75.A-Z Particular courts, A-Z

Courts and procedure
Courts
History
Particular courts, A-Z -- Continued
7.75.F48 Feudal and servitary courts
7.75.L35 Landgerichte, Older
Manorial courts see KK-KKC2 7.75.P38
7.75.P38 Patrimonial and manorial courts
Servitary courts see KK-KKC2 7.75.F48
7.8 General
The legal profession
Including judicial officers and personnel
7.9 General
7.92 Post-law school education
Including examinations, Vorbereitungsdienst, admission to the bar, etc.
7.93 Judges
7.94 Staatsanwaltschaft (Office of the public prosecutor)
7.96 Practice of law
Including attorneys and legal consultants
7.98 Procedure in general
Including all branches of law
7.99 Civil procedure
Noncontentious jurisdiction
8 General
8.2.A-Z Branches of noncontentious jurisdiction, A-Z
Children see KK-KKC2 8.2.D65
Civil registers see KK-KKC2 8.2.R44
8.2.D65 Domestic relations
Including children (General)
8.2.G82 Guardianship court
8.2.I54 Inheritance (Probate)
Matrimonial property registers see KK-KKC2 8.2.R44
8.2.N68 Inheritance (Probate)
Probate court see KK-KKC2 8.2.I54
Recording see KK-KKC2 8.2.R44
8.2.R44 Registration. Recording
Including civil registers, registers of matrimonial property, etc.
Insolvency
8.25 General
8.27 Execution
Including procedures
8.3 Bankruptcy
8.4 Debtors' relief
8.5 Costs
8.6 Public law
Constitutional law

Constitutional law -- Continued
History
8.62 General works
Estates. Classes
8.7 General
8.8 Landstände. Provinzialstände. Landschaft
8.82 Feudal law
Sources
Constitutions
8.83<date> Individual constitutions. By date of constitution
Subarrange by main entry
Individual and state
8.84 General
8.85 Nationality and citizenship
8.87.A-Z Particular groups, A-Z
Fundamental rights and constitutional guaranties
9 General
9.2.A-Z Individual rights or guaranties, A-Z
9.2.A78 Right of asylum
9.2.P48 Right to petition
Election law see KK-KKC2 9.5
Organs of government
9.3 General works
The people
9.5 Election law
9.6 The legislature. Legislative power
The head of state
History
9.62 General works
9.625 Kings. Princes and rulers
9.63 General works
9.64 Ministerpräsident
The central government. Kanzlei. Kabinett und Ministerien
9.7 History
9.8 General
Constitutional courts (tribunals) and procedure
9.82 History
9.85 General
Secular ecclesiastical law
10 History
Treaties between church and state
Including concordats (Catholic Church) and contracts (Protestant church)
For treaties on a particular subject, see the subject
For treaties in general, see KZ
10.2 Collections. Compilations
10.3 General works

TABLES

Secular ecclesiastical law -- Continued
10.4 System of church-and-state relationship
10.42 Religious corporations and societies
Administrative law
10.5 General
Administrative process
10.52 General
10.53 Administrative acts and enforcement
10.6 Administrative courts and procedure
10.7 Indemnification for acts performed by government
Administrative organization
10.78 General
10.8 Körperschaften des öffentlichen Rechts (Corporations)
10.82 Anstalten des öffentlichen Rechts (Institutions)
10.84 Stiftungen des öffentlichen Rechts (Endowments and foundations)
10.86 Business enterprises owned or controlled by government
Administrative divisions and departments of the state
10.88 General
10.9 Central government. Oberste Landesbehörde
Including department of the interior and subordinate agencies
10.92 District government. Provincial government. Mittelbehörden
Including Regierungsbezirke (Bezirksverbände), Provinzialverbände, etc.
10.95 Local government other than municipal. Gemeindeverbände
Including Kreistag, Kreisausschuss, Landrat, Oberkreisdirektor, Kreisrat, etc.
10.97 Municipal government
11 Civil service
Police and public safety
11.2 General
11.22 Police magistrates
11.3 Police force
11.4 Public safety
11.45 Control of individuals
11.5 Control of social activities
Public property. Public restraint on private property
11.6 General
11.65 Water resources
Including rivers, lakes, water courses, etc.
11.68 State preserves. Forests
Public land law
11.7 General
11.73 Regional planning
11.76 Public health

	Medical legislation
11.78	General
11.8	Veterinary medicine
	Environmental law
12	General
12.3	Environmental pollution
12.4	Wilderness preservation Including plant and wildlife conservation
	Cultural affairs
12.6	General
	Education
12.62	General
12.625	Teachers
12.63	Elementary and secondary education
12.65	Vocational education
12.68	Higher education
12.69	Adult education. Continuing education
	Science and the arts
12.7	General
	Public collections
13	General
13.3	Archives
13.4	Museums and galleries
13.6	Historic buildings and monuments
	Economic law. Regulation of industry, trade, and commerce
14	General
	Economic control and policy see KK6428+
14.2	Corporate representation of industry, trade, and commerce
	Standards and norms see KK6554+
	Labeling see KK6564
14.3	Licensing. State supervision
	Advertising see KK6580
	Agriculture
	History
	Rural (peasant) land tenure and peasantry
14.4	General works
14.45	Mark communities. Village communities
14.48	Leasehold for years and inheritance
14.5	Entailed estates of the greater nobility. Fideicommissum
	Land reform and agrarian land policy
14.6	General
14.62	Restraint on alienation of agricultural land
14.65	Consolidation of land holdings. Commasation

Economic law. Regulation of industry, trade, and commerce
Agriculture -- Continued
14.67 General
14.69 Entail
14.72.A-Z Agricultural industries and trades, A-Z
14.72.A54 Animal industry
14.76.A-Z Agricultural products, A-Z
14.78 Agricultural courts
15 Viticulture
15.2 Apiculture. Beekeeping
15.3 Horticulture
15.5 Forestry
Including timber and game laws
15.6 Fishery
15.65 Mining and quarrying
15.67 Manufacturing industries
15.69 Food processing industries
15.7 Construction and building industry
15.8 International trade
Domestic trade
15.9 General
15.92 Wholesale trade
15.93 Retail trade
Artisans
15.96 General
15.97.A-Z Corporate representation. Associations. By craft, A-Z
Including guilds, brotherhoods, etc.
15.97.G64 Goldwork. Silverwork
Including regulation of fineness and hallmarks
Silverwork see KK-KKC2 15.97.G64
Public utilities. Power supplies
16 General
16.3.A-Z By utility, A-Z
16.35 Criminal provisions
Transportation
16.4 General
Road traffic
16.42 General
16.44 Traffic regulations and enforcement
16.46 Railroads
Including carriage of passengers and goods
16.6 Water transportation. Domestic shipping
Including carriage of passengers and goods
Communication. Mass media
16.7 General
16.73 Postal services
16.74 Telecommunication

	Communication. Mass media -- Continued
16.8	Radio and television communications
16.83	Press law
16.9	Professions
	Public finance
17	General
	State revenue
17.2	General
17.25	Fees. Fines
	Taxation
	Including taxes shared by the state and municipality
	For local ordinances and works on the taxation of a particular locality or municipality, see the locality or municipality
17.3	General
	Income tax
	see KK7163+
	Sales tax
	see KK7285+
17.4	Estate, inheritance, and gift taxes
17.5	Property tax. Taxation of capital
17.6	Taxation of motor vehicles
17.63	Beer tax
17.68	Taxes from gambling tables. Casinos
17.7	Customs. Tariff
17.72	Tax and customs courts and procedure
	Tax and customs crimes and delinquency
	see KK7475+
	Government measures in time of war, national emergency, or economic crisis
17.8	General
17.82	Legislation for economic and social recovery and restitution
	Military law
17.85	General
18	Civil defense
18.2	Military criminal law and procedure
	Criminal law
18.3	General
18.4	Punishment
18.5.A-Z	Individual offenses, A-Z
18.5.B42	Blasphemy
18.5.D74	Driving while intoxicated
18.5.I56	Intoxication
	Criminal courts and procedure
18.6	General
	Administration of criminal justice
18.7	General
	Judicial statistics see KK-KKC2 1.A58

TABLES

Criminal law
Criminal courts and procedure
Administration of criminal justice -- Continued
Judicial assistance
18.8 General works
18.9 International judicial assistance
Interzonal judicial assistance
see KK9436
18.92 Foreign judgments (Conflict of laws)
Court organization
18.93 General
19.A-Z Particular courts, A-Z
19.2 Procedure at first instance
Execution of sentence
19.4 General
Imprisonment
19.5 General
19.6.A-Z Penal institutions, A-Z
19.7.A-Z Other special, A-Z
19.7.C36 Capital punishment

1.A1	Bibliography
<1.A15>	Periodicals
	For periodicals consisting predominantly of legal articles, regardless of subject matter and jurisdiction, see K1+
	For periodicals consisting primarily of informative material (newsletters, bulletins, etc.) relating to a particular subject, see the subject and form division for periodicals
	For law reports, official bulletins or circulars, and official gazettes intended chiefly for the publication of laws and regulations, see the appropriate entries in the text or form division tables
1.A17	Official gazettes
	Including historical sources
	Legislative documents
	Including historical sources
	Cf. JS5301+ Municipal documents of local governments
1.A2	Serials
1.A25	Monographs. By date
1.A3	Statutes (federal and/or state) affecting cities, etc. By date of publication
	Including historical sources
	Charters (Privileges), ordinances, and local laws
	Including historical sources
1.A4	Serials
1.A45A-.A45Z	Collections. By editor or compiler, A-Z
1.A5	Individual charters or acts of incorporation. By date of publication
	Collections of decisions and rulings
	Including historical sources
1.A6	Serials
1.A65	Monographs
	Yearbooks. Judicial statistics. Surveys of local administration of justice
1.A7	Serials
1.A75	Monographs
1.A8A-.A8Z	Special agencies, courts, or topics, A-Z, and date
	Directories
	see KK64.5
	Legal profession
	see KK3704+
	Legal aid
	see KK3792
	History
	For biography, see KK183+
	For the history of a particular subject, see the subject
1.A85	Sources
	Class here sources not falling under one of the categories above
1.A9-Z	General works

Particular subjects
Private law
Including civil and commercial law
2 General (Table KK-KKC11)
Domestic relations. Marriage. Parent and child
2.2 General (Table KK-KKC11)
2.3.A-Z Special topics, A-Z
Property. Law of things. Real property
3 General (Table KK-KKC11)
3.2 Servitudes (Table KK-KKC11)
3.3 Hypotheca. Land charge. Rent charge. Pledges (Table KK-KKC11)
3.4 Land register (Table KK-KKC11)
3.5.A-Z Special topics, A-Z
Inheritance. Succession upon death
4 General (Table KK-KKC11)
4.2 Intestate and testamentary succession (Table KK-KKC11)
4.3.A-Z Special topics, A-Z
Obligations
5 General (Table KK-KKC11)
5.3.A-Z Special topics, A-Z
5.3.S34 Sales. Kauf
5.3.S94 Suretyship. Bürgschaft
6 Merchant and business enterprise (Table KK-KKC11)
6.2 Commercial registers (Table KK-KKC11)
6.3 Banking. Negotiable instruments (Table KK-KKC11)
6.35 Maritime law (Table KK-KKC11)
6.4 Insurance (Table KK-KKC11)
6.5 Business associations (Table KK-KKC11)
Labor law. Social insurance. Public welfare
7 General (Table KK-KKC11)
7.3.A-Z Particular groups, A-Z
7.4.A-Z Particular agencies, institutions, or courts, A-Z
Courts and procedure see KK-KKC3 8.4+
City constitution and government
8 General (Table KK-KKC11)
8.2 Legislative functions. City council, etc. (Table KK-KKC11)
Including elections
8.3 Executive functions. Mayor and administrative departments. Municipal civil service (Table KK-KKC11)
Including elections
Judicial functions. City courts and procedure
8.4 General (Table KK-KKC11)
8.5.A-Z Particular courts, A-Z
8.5.F74 Friedensgerichte
8.5.G45 Gemeindegerichte
8.7.A-Z Special topics, A-Z

Particular subjects
City constitution and government
Special topics, A-Z -- Continued
8.7.M85 Municipal territory. Gemeindegebiet
Including boundaries (Gemeindegrenzen) and corporation (Eingemeindung)
8.8 Secular ecclesiastical law (Table KK-KKC11)
Municipal civil service see KK-KKC3 8.3
Police and public safety. Police force
Including control of individuals
9 General (Table KK-KKC11)
9.3.A-Z Particular groups or activities, A-Z
9.3.M54 Minorities (ethnic, religious, racial)
9.5.A-Z Particular safety hazards or preventive measures, A-Z
9.5.F57 Fire
9.6.A-Z Particular transgressions, A-Z
9.8.A-Z Special topics, A-Z
9.8.S95 Sumptuary laws
Public property. Public restraint on private property
10 General (Table KK-KKC11)
10.3 Eminent domain. Expropriation (Table KK-KKC11)
10.5 Roads. Water resources. Parks (Table KK-KKC11)
Public land law. City planning. Zoning. Building
11 General (Table KK-KKC11)
11.5.A-Z Special topics, A-Z
Public health. Medical legislation
12 General (Table KK-KKC11)
12.2 Burial and cemetery laws (Table KK-KKC11)
12.3 Contagious and infectious diseases (Table KK-KKC11)
12.5 Health professions and hospitals (Table KK-KKC11)
12.7.A-Z Special topics, A-Z
12.7.D74 Drinking water
12.8 Environmental laws (Table KK-KKC11)
Cultural affairs
13 General (Table KK-KKC11)
13.2 Education. Schools. Institutions (Table KK-KKC11)
13.3 Theater. Orchestra (Table KK-KKC11)
13.4 Public collections (Table KK-KKC11)
13.5.A-Z Historic buildings and monuments, A-Z
Industry, trade, and commerce
14 General (Table KK-KKC11)
14.2 Trade. Conditions and modes of trading (Table KK-KKC11)
14.3.A-Z Particular industries, trades, and services, A-Z
14.3.A35 Agriculture
14.3.B73 Brewing
14.3.F78 Fruits and vegetables
14.3.H68 Hotels, taverns, restaurants

Particular subjects
Industry, trade, and commerce
Particular industries, trades, and services, A-Z -- Continued
Restaurants see KK-KKC3 14.3.H68
Taverns see KK-KKC3 14.3.H68
Vegetables see KK-KKC3 14.3.F78

14.4.A-Z Artisans, A-Z
14.5.A-Z Professions, A-Z
Health professions see KK-KKC3 12.5
15.A-Z Corporate representation, A-Z
15.B62 Boards of trade
15.C42 Chambers of commerce
15.G55 Guilds
15.T72 Trade associations
Public utilities
16 General (Table KK-KKC11)
16.5.A-Z Special topics, A-Z
Public finance
17 General (Table KK-KKC11)
17.3.A-Z Local agencies, A-Z
17.5.A-Z Sources of revenue. Taxes, fees, and fines, A-Z
17.5.C45 Church taxes
17.7 Offenses (Violation of ordinances) and administration of criminal justice. Correctional institutions (Table KK-KKC11)
18.A-Z Other subjects, A-Z
Supramunicipal corporations and organizations
see the appropriate state, using subdivision 336 from Table KK-KKC1

.A1 Bibliography

<.A15> Periodicals

For periodicals consisting predominantly of legal articles, regardless of subject matter and jurisdiction, see K1+

For periodicals consisting primarily of informative material (newsletters, bulletins, etc.) relating to a particular subject, see the subject and form division for periodicals

For law reports, official bulletins or circulars, and official gazettes intended chiefly for the publication of laws and regulations, see the appropriate entries in the text or form division tables

.A17 Official gazettes

Including historical sources

Legislative documents

Including historical sources

Cf. JS5301+ Municipal documents of local governments

.A2 Serials

.A25 Monographs. By date

.A3 Statutes (federal and/or state) affecting cities, etc. By date of publication

Including historical sources

Charters (Privileges), ordinances, and local laws

Including historical sources

.A4 Serials

.A45A-.A45Z Collections. By editor or compiler, A-Z

.A5 Individual charters or acts of incorporation. By date of publication

Collections of decisions and rulings

Including historical sources

.A6 Serials

.A65 Monographs

Yearbooks. Judicial statistics. Surveys of local administration of justice

.A7 Serials

.A75 Monographs

.A8A-.A8Z Special agencies, courts, or topics, A-Z, and date

Directories

see KK64.5.A+

Legal profession

see KK3704+

Legal aid

see KK3792

History

.A85 Sources

Class here sources not falling under one of the categories above

.A9-.Z General works

Particular subjects

Particular subjects -- Continued

Private law

Including civil and commercial law

.13 General (Table KK-KKC11)

Domestic relations. Marriage. Parent and child

.15 General (Table KK-KKC11)

.16.A-Z Special topics, A-Z

Property. Law of things. Real property

.18 General (Table KK-KKC11)

.2.A-Z Special topics, A-Z

Inheritance. Succession upon death

.22 General (Table KK-KKC11)

.23.A-Z Special topics, A-Z

Obligations

.25 General (Table KK-KKC11)

.26.A-Z Special topics, A-Z

.26.S34 Sales. Kauf

.26.S94 Suretyship. Bürgschaft

.27 Merchant and business enterprise (Table KK-KKC11)

.28 Banking. Negotiable instruments (Table KK-KKC11)

.3 Labor law. Social insurance. Public welfare (Table KK-KKC11)

City constitution and government

.32 General (Table KK-KKC11)

.33.A-Z Special topics, A-Z

.33.M85 Municipal territory. Gemeindegebiet

Including boundaries (Gemeindegrenzen) and corporation (Eingemeindung)

.335 Secular ecclesiastical law (Table KK-KKC11)

Police and public safety. Police force

.34 General (Table KK-KKC11)

.35.A-Z Particular groups or activities, A-Z

.35.M54 Minorities (ethnic, religious, racial)

.36.A-Z Particular safety hazards or preventive measures, A-Z

.36.F57 Fire

.37.A-Z Particular transgressions, A-Z

.38.A-Z Special topics, A-Z

.38.S95 Sumptuary laws

Public property. Public restraint on private property

.39 General (Table KK-KKC11)

Public land law. City planning. Zoning. Building

.4 General (Table KK-KKC11)

.42.A-Z Special topics, A-Z

Public health. Medical legislation

.44 General (Table KK-KKC11)

.46.A-Z Special topics, A-Z

.46.D74 Drinking water

Particular subjects -- Continued

.48 Environmental laws (Table KK-KKC11)

Cultural affairs

.5 General (Table KK-KKC11)

.52.A-Z Special topics, A-Z

Industry, trade, and commerce

.55 General (Table KK-KKC11)

.57.A-Z Particular industries, trades, and services, A-Z

.57.A35 Agriculture

.57.B73 Brewing

.57.F78 Fruits and vegetables

.57.H68 Hotels, taverns, restaurants

Restaurants see KK-KKC4 .57.H68

Taverns see KK-KKC4 .57.H68

Vegetables see KK-KKC4 .57.F78

.6.A-Z Artisans, A-Z

.62.A-Z Professions, A-Z

.63.A-Z Corporate representation, A-Z

.63.B62 Boards of trade

.63.C42 Chambers of commerce

.63.G55 Guilds

.63.T72 Trade associations

Public utilities

.7 General (Table KK-KKC11)

.73.A-Z Special topics, A-Z

Public finance

.75 General (Table KK-KKC11)

.77.A-Z Sources of revenue. Taxes, fees, and fines, A-Z

.77.C45 Church taxes

.8 Offenses (Violation of ordinances) and administration of criminal justice. Correctional institutions (Table KK-KKC11)

.83.A-Z Other subjects, A-Z

Supramunicipal corporations and organizations see KK-KKC1 336

TABLES

Indexes. Registers
For indexes relating to a particular collection, see the publication
0.2 General and comprehensive indexes. Nachschlagewerke. By date of publication
0.3 Indexes to decision published in law journals. By date of publication
0.4 General collections. By initial date of period covered
0.5.A-Z Selections. By editor, compiler, or title, A-Z
0.6.A-Z Collections of key holdings (Leitsätze). By editor or compiler, A-Z
0.7 Summaries of judgments

.x2 Indexes. Registers. By date of publication
For indexes relating to a particular collection, see the publication
.x4 General collections. By initial date of period covered
.x5 Selections. By editor, compiler, or title
.x7 Summaries of judgments

.xA3 Autobiography. Reminiscences. By date

.xA4 Letters. Correspondence. By date

Including individual letters, general collections, and collections of letters to particular individuals

Class correspondence on a particular subject with the subject

Reminiscences see KK-KKC7 .xA3

Knowledge. Concept of law see KK-KKC7 .xA7+

.xA7-.xZ Biography and criticism

0	General (Table K11)
	Authorship
	Including multiple authorship and author cooperatives
0.2	General works
0.22	Anonyms and pseudonyms
0.23	Intangible property. Immaterialgüterrecht
0.3	Plagiarism
0.4	Formalities
	Including registration of claim, transfer, licenses, deposit, and notice
0.5	Protected works
	Including original works, subsequent rights, idea and title
	Scope of protection
0.6	General works
0.62	Personality rights. Urheberpersönlichkeitsrecht
	Mechanical reproduction
0.63	General works
0.64	Documentation and dissemination
	Including fair use
0.65	Exhibition. Ausstellungsrechte
	Performing rights. Aufführungsrechte
	Cf. KK2700 Quasi copyright
0.7	General works
0.72	Societies and industrial trusts. Verwertungsgesellschaften
0.73	Broadcasting rights. Senderechte
0.75	Recording devices. Schallplatten- und Tonbandrechte
	Including phonographs, magnetic recorders, and jukeboxes
0.76	Filming and photographing
0.78	Translation. Übersetzungsrechte
0.8	Employees' copyright. Unselbständiger Urheber (Arbeitsverhaltnis)
0.82	Duration and renewal
0.85	Delicts. Torts
0.9	Criminal provisions. Urheberstrafrecht

TABLES

1 General (Table K11)

2 Military requisitions from civilians. Requisitioned land

Including contracts for work and labor

For damages and compensation see KK-KKC9 16+

3 Control of property. Confiscations. Sperre und Einzug von Vermögen

Including enemy and alien property

For damages and compensation see KK-KKC9 16+

4 Control of unemployment. Arbeitslosigkeitskontrolle

Control of manpower. Arbeitseinsatz

5 General

6 Prisoners of war. Einsatz von Kriegsgefangenen

Compulsory and forced labor

see KK7586

7 Insolvent debtors. Wartime and crisis relief. Zwangsvollstreckungsnotrecht (Table K11)

For moratorium, see KK4384

For composition and deferment of execution, see KK4357+

For agricultural credits, see KK6639+

8 Finances

For special levies, war taxes, etc., see KK7270+

For procurement and defense contracts see KK-KKC9 20+

Industrial priorities and allocations. Economic recovery measures. Wirtschaftsaufbaugesetze

9 General (Table K11)

10.A-Z By industry or commodity, A-Z

Subarrange each by Table K12

Strategic material. Stockpiling. Vorratswirtschaft

11 General (Table K11)

12.A-Z By commodity, A-Z

12.F66 Food (Table K12)

Rationing. Price control

13 General (Table K11)

14.A-Z By commodity, A-Z

Rent control

see KK1816

15 Criminal provisions

War damage compensation. Kriegsschäden- und Kriegsfolgeschädenrecht

Including foreign claims settlement

Cf. KK3503+ , Social services

16 General (Table K11)

17 Administration and procedure

18.A-Z Particular claims, A-Z

Confiscations see KK-KKC9 18.R47

Military occupation damages see KK-KKC9 18.R47

War damage compensation. Kriegsschäden- und Kriegsfolgeschädenrecht
Particular claims, A-Z -- Continued
18.P47 Personal damages. Property loss or damages (Table K12)
Property loss or damages see KK-KKC9 18.P47
18.R46 Reparations. Demontage (Table K12)
18.R47 Requisitions. Confiscations. Military occupation damages (Table K12)
19.A-Z Particular victims, A-Z
Subarrange each by Table K12
Military occupation. Procurement. Besatzungs- und Besatzungskostenrecht
20 General (Table K11)
Administration, jurisdiction, and courts see KK4872.R443
Military occupation damages see KK-KKC9 18.R47

TABLES

0 General (Table K11)

Contract. Articles of partnership

Including liberty of contract

0.13 General works

0.14 Void and voidable contracts. Partnership de facto. Fehlerhafte Gesellschaft

0.2 Registration

Partners

0.3 General works

0.32 Minors as partners

0.33 Unfair competition and restraint of trade

Management. Geschäftsführung

0.35 General works

0.36 Control of partners

0.37 Voting

Including resolutions and objections

0.38 Entering, leaving, and exclusion of partners

0.39 Partnership as partner

0.4 Capital and profits

0.5 Accounting. Financial statements. Auditing

Agency and prokura

see KK2078+

0.6 Liability

Including debtor and creditor and limitation of actions

Termination. Beendigung

0.65 General works

0.7 Dissolution and separation. Vormögensauseinandersetzung. Teilung

0.9 Inheritance and succession

Including executors and administrators

.A2	Local laws. Ordinances. By date of publication
.A3A-.A3Z	Decisions. Rulings. By name of court, agency, etc., A-Z, and date
.A5	Miscellaneous documents
.A7	History
.A8-.Z	General works. Treatises

INDEX

INDEX

INDEX

INDEX

INDEX

C

INDEX

INDEX

INDEX

INDEX

D

INDEX

INDEX

E

INDEX

INDEX

INDEX

I

INDEX

INDEX

L

O

P

INDEX

INDEX

INDEX

V

W

GPO U.S. GOVERNMENT PRINTING OFFICE: 2008–330–111/60013